Microsoft®

Commerce Server 2000

Pocket Consultant

Brad Wist

PUBLISHED BY
Microsoft Press
A Division of Microsoft Corporation
One Microsoft Way
Redmond, Washington 98052-6399

Library of Congress Cataloging-in-Publication Data
Wist, Brad.
Microsoft Commerce Server 2000 Pocket Consultant / Bradley M. Wist.
p. cm.
Includes index.
ISBN 0-7356-1416-4
1. Microsoft Commerce server. 2. Electronic commerce. I. Title.

HF5548.32 .W575 2001
005.7'13769--dc21 2001044949

Printed and bound in the United States of America.

1 2 3 4 5 6 7 8 9 QWE 6 5 4 3 2

Distributed in Canada by Penguin Books Canada Limited.

A CIP catalogue record for this book is available from the British Library.

Microsoft Press books are available through booksellers and distributors worldwide. For further information about international editions, contact your local Microsoft Corporation office or contact Microsoft Press International directly at fax (425) 936-7329. Visit our Web site at www.microsoft.com/mspress. Send comments to *mspinput@microsoft.com*.

Acquisitions Editor: Juliana Aldous Atkinson
Project Editor: Jean Trenary

Body Part No. X08-04521

Contents at a Glance

Part VI
Transactions and Processing

Part VII
Content Selection Framework

Table of Contents

Acknowledgments

I would like to thank you, the reader, for choosing this book. I hope that you find this book useful and worthwhile.

I must thank my family, Colleen and Braeden, for their love, patience, and support. And my thanks, too, for the times when they pulled me away from the computer for a few minutes or hours. That time helped as well.

I'd also like to extend my thanks to all of my family and friends for their understanding, patience, and years of putting up with me and my eccentricities. Sorry; I can't promise any changes there.

I also want to thank my agent, Neil Salkind, and all of Studio-B staff for their help and guidance. They've been invaluable.

Finally, I must thank my editors at Microsoft Press, Juliana Aldous Atkinson and Jean Trenary, and the crew at nSight who have contributed to this book, including Sarah Hains, Bob Dean, and Teresa Horton. The many suggestions, corrections, clarifications, and questions that they offered have helped make this a much better book.

Introduction

In late 2000, Microsoft introduced its latest version of e-commerce software, taking a large step toward building more scalable and more powerful Web sites. Microsoft Commerce Server 2000 is part of the first generation of the Windows .NET Server family that Microsoft is introducing.

The world of e-commerce is growing daily. As the days and months go by, it becomes more clear that companies need to provide a presence on the Internet. More and more shoppers are expecting to find products available on the Internet, and the number of buyers and puchases being made on the Internet continues to grow. The goal of Commerce Server 2000 is to enable companies to quickly and easily build and deploy e-commerce sites.

However, Commerce Server 2000 is not solely aimed at business-to-consumer (B2C) e-commerce sites. Commerce Server 2000 is designed to support business-to-business (B2B) sites as well. Whether the site is designed to be a part of the supply chain or target corporate customers, Commerce Server 2000 provides the tools to make it happen. B2B communications can even be improved by integrating the site with other business customers or supplies using Microsoft BizTalk Server.

This book has been written to provide a single resource that you can turn to whenever you need to accomplish a task using Commerce Server 2000. The focus of the book is to provide information on how to accomplish the tasks that you will most likely need to undertake. Whether you want to be able to work with user profiles, authenticate users against a database or Active Directory service, search a catalog, or select content targeted for the current user, this book will guide you. In it, you'll find sample code that is used to demonstrate various techniques in implementing the desired functionality. Wherever possible, the code is written to be completely self-contained and includes notes on how you might extend the code to fit into an overall Web site.

What's New in Commerce Server 2000

Microsoft has made another significant upgrade to its e-commerce software by introducing Commerce Server 2000. The core components have been rewritten to take advantage of COM+ technology. This means that you can expect performance to increase for these components, even beyond the additional code and component redesigns.

In building Commerce Server 2000, Microsoft sought to accomplish several goals. The first was to provide functionality in critical areas of creating and running a business on the Internet, including the following:

- **Business processing pipelines** Used to run information through a set of standard, defined processes to complete purchases, identify ads, select content, and perform other common tasks.
- **Profiling system** Used to maintain user data and other information, cached locally on the Web server for efficiency
- **Targeting system** Used to select content and other information that can be targeted to users based on a number of different criteria
- **Product catalog system** Used to manage products in a catalog for selection and searching
- **Business Analytics system** Used to analyze users, products, purchases, advertisements, and site performance so that improvements can be made to the site on a continuing basis

A second goal is to improve site management capabilities from earlier versions. Commerce Server 2000's Business Desk provides this functionality for each e-commerce site. The Business Desk is a Dynamic HTML (DHTML) Web site designed for use with Microsoft Internet Explorer 5.5. It includes a number of Web components that provide the tools to dynamically manage the site. In addition, system management tools are provided as a Microsoft Management Console (MMC) snap-in called the Commerce Server Manager.

Another goal is to provide the ability to rapidly build and deploy an e-commerce site into production. Microsoft has developed several Solution Sites that are designed to provide examples of how to develop sites and to serve as a starting point in building and deploying sites. In addition, Commerce Server 2000 provides new capabilities to package and deploy a Web site from the development environment into production using the Site Packager tools.

Who This Book Is For

This book covers planning, building, and maintaining e-commerce Web sites using Microsoft Commerce Server 2000. It's designed for the following audience:

- Web developers (programmers, engineers, and QA personnel)
- Web site system administrators
- Web site managers
- E-commerce system integrators

In the book, I make the assumption that you are familiar with Active Server Pages (ASP) and Web development on the Microsoft platform. I also assume that you are familiar with Microsoft Internet Information Services (IIS).

How This Book Is Organized

In this book, we'll look at how you can use the tools and functionality provided by Commerce Server 2000 to build an e-commerce site. This book is intended to serve as a reference, so you can look into individual sections and chapters to get the information you need about any task you might have to accomplish. To help you with this, the book is organized into sections that logically group related tasks and features.

Part I of this book, "Getting Started with Microsoft Commerce Server 2000," provides an introduction and overview of Commerce Server 2000. Chapter 1 covers installing and configuring the Commerce Server 2000 application. Chapter 2 introduces the Solutions Sites and Sitelets that are available for use in developing Commerce Server 2000 sites.

Part II of this book, "Management Services and Tools," covers the management services and tools that are used in a Commerce Server 2000 site. Chapter 3 examines the Commerce Server Manager, an MMC snap-in that is used to administer the back-end systems that support the site. Chapter 4 dives into the Business Desk, which is provided for business users to manage individual e-commerce sites. Chapter 5 takes an in-depth look at Business Analytics and the Commerce Server 2000 tools that are used to analyze site usage and performance. Chapter 6 covers the Commerce Server Site Packager that is used to pack and unpack sites and site resources for deployment to other machines.

Part III of this book, "Site Architecture and Basics," covers some of the basics that you'll use throughout the design and development of your Commerce Server 2000 site. Chapter 7 covers those first steps you'll need to take in building your site, including setting up the site and providing the basic framework of resources and application configuration settings. Chapter 8 continues by introducing a number of common Commerce Server 2000 components that you'll use throughout your site.

Part IV of this book, "User Management," covers user management and profiles on the site. Chapter 9 examines the tasks you need to accomplish to provide user authentication and security for your site, including authenticating users and maintaining user accounts. Chapter 10 provides an in-depth discussion of how Commerce Server 2000 profiles are used to provide access to user, organization, address, and other information.

Part V of this book, "The Catalog System," covers the Catalog Management System, introducing the concepts, tools, and components you'll need to design, implement, and use various catalogs on your site. Chapter 11 provides a discussion of the topics you'll need to know to design a Commerce Server 2000 catalog, including how the catalogs are organized and managed on the site. Chapter 12 covers the Commerce Server 2000 components that are used to manage and retrieve catalog information. Chapter 13, "Catalog Searching," demonstrates the variety of ways that you can search the catalogs for information.

Part VI of this book, "Transactions and Processing," covers transactions and order processing on your site, from utilizing the basket to completing an order. Chapter 14 provides an introduction to the the OrderGroup and OrderForm objects that are used to maintain the basket and orders for the site, as well as the components that are used to work with those items. Chapter 15 demonstrates in detail the many tasks involved in processing orders on your Commerce Server 2000 site, from placing items in the basket to completing and processing the purchase. Chapter 16 introduces the Commerce Server 2000 pipelines that are used to process orders and other information in an efficient and scalable manner. Chapter 17 demonstrates how to build your own custom pipeline components and functionality to use in your pipelines.

Part VII of this book, "Content Selection Framework," covers the content selection framework in Commerce Server 2000 that is used to select and target content for individual users based on a variety of criteria. Chapter 18 provides detailed coverage of the use and management of campaigns—advertising, discount, and direct mail—on your site. Chapter 19 dives into the process for selecting content for an individual user based on selection criteria that you define. Chapter 20 covers the use of the Predictor Service to make predictions and suggestions for users and to predict information about users based on data that you've collected on your site.

Throughout the book, you'll see numerous examples of code that demonstrate the techniques and components discussed in each chapter. You'll get practical advice on building the site and designing your code to achieve the goals outlined in the book.

Conventions Used in This Book

In this book, I make use of several conventions to help keep the text clear. Code listings and terms are maintained in `monospace type`. New terms are shown in *italics*.

Other conventions include:

Note To provide details on a point that needs emphasis

Tip To offer helpful hints or additional information

Caution To warn you when there are potential problems you should look out for

Real World To provide real-world advice when discussing advanced topics.

Support

Every effort has been made to ensure the accuracy of this book. Microsoft Press provides corrections for books through the World Wide Web (WWW) at the following address:

http://mspress.microsoft.com/support

If you have comments, questions, or ideas regarding this book, please send them to Microsoft Press using either of the following methods:

Postal Mail:

Microsoft Press
Attn: *Microsoft Commerce Server 2000 Pocket Consultant* Editor
One Microsoft Way
Redmond, WA 98052-6399

E-mail:

MSPINPUT@MICROSOFT.COM

Please note that product support is not offered through this e-mail address. For support information, visit Microsoft's Web site at *http://support.microsoft.com/directory*.

Part I

Getting Started with Microsoft Commerce Server 2000

Part I of this book provides an introduction and overview of Microsoft Commerce Server 2000. Chapter 1 covers installation and configuration of the Commerce Server 2000 application. Chapter 2 introduces the Solution Sites and Sitelets that are available for use in developing Commerce Server 2000 sites.

Chapter 1

Installing and Configuring Commerce Server 2000

You've taken a good first step as you prepare to build your e-commerce sites with Microsoft Commerce Server 2000 by purchasing this book. The next step you'll need to address is installing and configuring Commerce Server 2000.

In this chapter, we'll take a look at what it will take to install and configure Commerce Server 2000. What will the machines look like where the software will be installed? In what environment will the Web sites be built? How will the software be distributed on your site?

System Requirements

Before you begin to install Commerce Server 2000, be sure that your servers will support the application.

Note You can get the most up-to-date hardware and software minimum requirements from *http://www.microsoft.com/commerceserver/evaluation/default.asp.*

Hardware

As you set up your environment, you'll find that hardware requirements depend on the purpose of the installation. For instance, in building a production server, you should expect to meet greater requirements. This allows you to support the additional functionality and greater usage that you'll need in production. At the same time, your development systems need less in the way of resources, as they won't see nearly the same level of usage.

You should also plan on setting up a test environment, sometimes called a *staging environment,* for your site. Once you develop or make changes to your site, you can roll those changes out to the test or staging servers. There, you can test the new pages or new Web site to ensure that everything is working properly. Once you've taken the pages through a complete test process, you'll be ready to move them out to production. In this way, you can continue to modify and test your site without impacting the current production site.

The staging environment that you set up should be an exact duplicate of the production environment, at least for identical types of servers (Web, application, database). You won't necessarily need the same number of servers. For instance, if your production site includes five Web servers connected and managed with App Server and two clustered SQL servers, your staging environment might include only two Web servers with App Server and two clustered databases.

This setup provides you with machines that are available to move into production on short notice in the event that you need to replace faulty hardware or you have a sudden surge in site usage.

System Requirements for the Production and Staging Environments

The production and staging environments will include both Web servers, which run the commerce sites, and related database servers. As a reference, the following are recommendations for the minimum requirements for a Web server running Commerce Server 2000:

- **Central processing unit (CPU)** 600 megahertz (MHz) or faster
- **Memory** 512 megabytes (MB) random access memory (RAM)
- **Disk** 100 MB of free disk space
- **Network interface card (NIC)** 100 megabits per second (Mbps)

You'll also need to provide a database server. In a production environment, you should always maintain database servers separate from the Web servers. You'll want to use the following as minimum guidelines for your database server:

- **CPU** 2 × 600 MHz or faster
- **Memory** 512 MB RAM
- **Disk** 100 MB of free disk space
- **NIC** 100 Mbps

System Requirements for the Development Environment

In the development environment, you can use scaled-down servers that provide enough power for you to develop and test the sites. You won't need as much horsepower because you won't need to support the same usage level. Development servers should meet the following minimum requirements:

- **CPU** 400 MHz or faster
- **Memory** 256 MB RAM
- **Disk** 100 MB of free disk space
- **NIC** 100 Mbps

The database server in the development environment should meet these minimum requirements:

- **CPU** 400 MHz or faster
- **Memory** 256 MB RAM
- **Disk** 100 MB of free disk space
- **NIC** 100 Mbps

Software

To install Commerce Server 2000, you'll need to start by properly configuring the software on the server. You should have Microsoft Windows 2000 or Microsoft Windows 2000 Advanced Server and the latest service pack installed. If you're not going to install Microsoft SQL Server 2000 on this server, then you'll need to install Microsoft Data Access Components 2.6 (or later). Next, install any necessary hot fixes for the Windows operating system.

On the database server, make sure you have installed either SQL Server 2000 or Microsoft SQL Server 7, with Service Pack 2. Ensure also that you have the Full Text Search feature installed and enabled on the database because without it, you'll be unable to create catalogs, as the catalog creation process will fail when the full text index is being configured. SQL Server 7 does not install this feature automatically, but it is installed by default with SQL Server 2000.

Commerce Server 2000 Components

Commerce Server 2000 includes several sets of components that are grouped into various sets of features that can be installed on the various servers on your sites, as listed in Table 1-1. Depending on how you want to structure your e-commerce site, you might choose to install some or all of these components.

Table 1-1. Commerce Server 2000 Installation Features and Components

Features	Description
Runtime Objects	Installs the core Commerce Server 2000 run-time components, including the following: • Catalog components • Profile system components
Predictor	Installs the Predictor Service components, which are used to compare and make predictions about products and users based on other parameters and data.
Direct Mailer	Sends personalized or nonpersonalized mail to large groups of recipients.
Analysis and Data Warehouse	Installs the Analysis and Data Warehouse components, used to import and manage Web site data from Web log files, Commerce Server databases, and other data sources.
Software Development Kit (SDK)	Installs the SDK files and documentation, including code samples, tools, sitelets, and more.
Administration Tools	Installs the Commerce Server Manager snap-in, which is a Microsoft Management Console (MMC) tool. It also installs the Data Warehouse, Predictor, and Profile Management snap-ins. Other tools, such as the Pipeline Editor, are also installed.
Online Documentation	Installs the online help documentation.

Installation Process

Installing Commerce Server 2000 is fairly simple and painless. First, prepare the servers as already discussed. You should also be familiar with the complete installation process.

Note You can get the most up-to-date installation procedures from the Microsoft Web site at *http://support.microsoft.com/support/commerceserver/2000/install/default.asp.*

You can run the installation by executing SETUP.EXE, which then takes you through the Commerce Server 2000 Setup Wizard. The following sections focus on each page in the setup wizard.

Welcome To Commerce Server 2000 Setup Wizard

When you run the setup wizard, the first thing you'll see is the Welcome To Commerce Server 2000 Setup Wizard page. From here, you'll proceed through the installation steps.

Prerequisites

The Prerequisites page, shown in Figure 1-1, gives you the opportunity to review the prerequisites for Commerce Server 2000 before you proceed with the installation. Clicking View The Commerce Server 2000 Installation Guide links you to the installation guide on the Microsoft Web site. You can use this information to ensure you have the latest installation procedures.

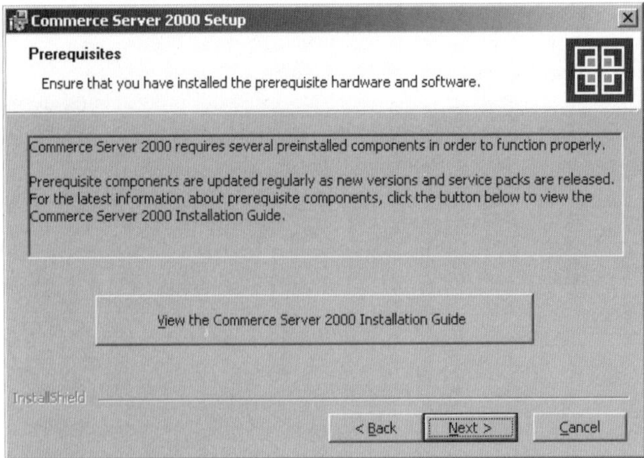

Figure 1-1. *The Prerequisites page provides a link with information about the prerequisites for installing Commerce Server 2000.*

License Agreement

Of course, you'll want to review the License Agreement wizard page for the software. You will need to accept the agreement before proceeding with the installation.

Customer Information

On the Customer Information wizard page, you can provide customer information that identifies the customer and company that has purchased the software.

Destination Folder

You specify the folder where the Commerce Server 2000 software should be installed in the Destination Folder wizard page. By default, the software is installed in the \Program Files\Microsoft Commerce Server directory. You can choose a different installation path by clicking Change and typing in a new path.

Setup Type

You'll need to decide what type of installation you want to perform. The Setup Type wizard page, shown in Figure 1-2, provides three options, listed below.

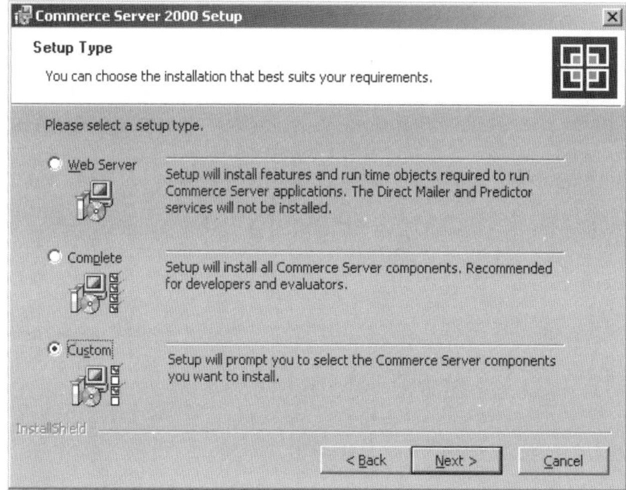

Figure 1-2. *You select the type of setup you'll be performing in the Setup Type wizard page.*

- **Web Server** The Web Server option automatically installs all of the Commerce Server 2000 components, with the exception of the Predictor, Direct Mailer components, and SDK.

- **Complete** The Complete option installs all of the Commerce Server 2000 components, including the SDK.
- **Custom** The Custom option allows you to choose the Commerce Server 2000 components that you want to install. You'll be able to select any combination of the features in the next step in the Setup wizard, the Custom Setup page (see Figure 1-3).

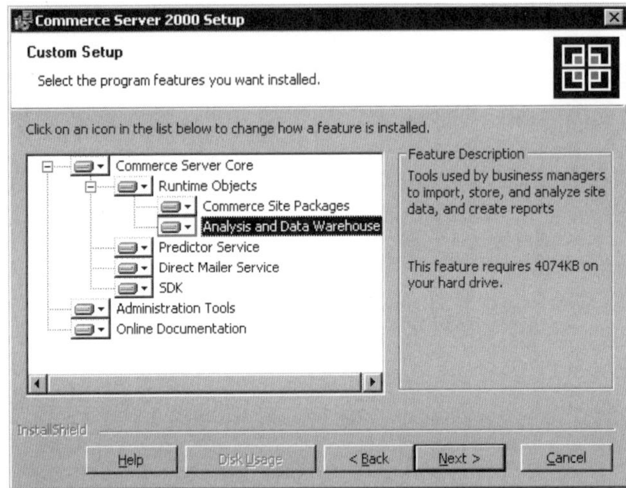

Figure 1-3. *Using the Custom Setup wizard page, you can select which features to install.*

Administration Database Configuration

To install Commerce Server 2000, you'll need to provide the name of the database server that will house the MSCS_Admin administrative database in the Administration Database Configuration wizard page. If you're installing onto SQL Server 2000, you can specify any instance of SQL Server on the server. Additionally, you'll specify the user ID and password for the account that will be used to create and maintain the administrative database.

Direct Mailer Database Configuration

If you're installing the Direct Mailer Service, you'll need to specify the server and database instance for SQL Server 2000, if appropriate, of the DirectMailer database, which will hold the Direct Mail data. In the Direct Mailer Database Configuration wizard page, you'll also provide the user ID and password for the account that will be used to create and maintain this database.

Ready To Install

In the Ready To Install wizard page, click Install to confirm that you're ready to proceed with the installation. The installation itself will take several minutes, depending on the server.

Installing Commerce Server 2000

As the installation proceeds, you'll see the Installing Commerce Server 2000 wizard page, which keeps you informed of the progress of the installation (see Figure 1-4).

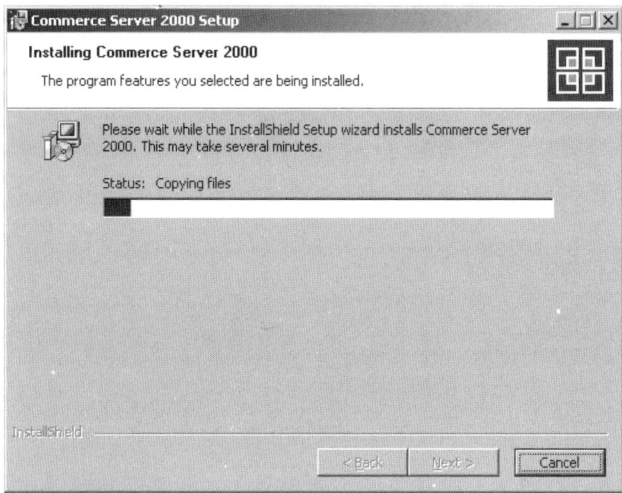

Figure 1-4. *The Installing Commerce Server 2000 wizard page tracks the progress of the installation.*

Completing The Commerce Server 2000 Setup Wizard

Finally, you'll be presented with a message in the Completing The Commerce Server 2000 Wizard page indicating that you have successfully completed the installation of Commerce Server 2000. Click Finish to complete the process. You are now ready to begin building your sites.

Performing a Silent Installation

There might be times when you want to perform an automated installation of Commerce Server 2000, which allows you to install the application silently, without stepping through each page of the Setup Wizard. You can do so by providing all of the detail required to perform the installation on the command line of the setup application.

This is possible because the installation package is built as a Microsoft Installer package. The installation is performed by the MSIEXEC.EXE application, which installs the MSI file, in this case COMMERCE SERVER 2000.MSI. To run the installation, issue the command

```
msiexec <options> "<drive letter>:\Commerce Server 2000.msi"
```

where you'll provide a list of options, including the option that identifies the MSI file to be installed and other parameters that define how the installation should be performed. These command-line option switches are listed in Table 1-2. Some of these options are general options that apply to the MSIEXEC.EXE application itself.

Note The COMMERCE SERVER 2000.MS1 file is at the root of the specified drive.

Table 1-2. MSIEXEC Application Command-Line Option Switches

Switch	Parameter	Description
/I	*.msi	Installs the installation package MSI file.
/Q	{N,B,R,F}	Specifies the level of the user interface that will be displayed: **N (None)** No user interface (UI) is displayed. This is silent mode. **B (Basic)** The standard installation UI. **R (Reduced)** Displays the dialog box at the completion of the installation. **F (Full)** Displays verbose installation information and a dialog box at the completion of the installation. Only one of these options may be specified.
/L	[i][w][e][a][r] [u][c][m][p] [v] [*]	Specifies the type of logging to be used by the installation package by identifying the type of information logged and the location of the log file. These options log the following information: **i** Status messages. **w** Nonfatal warning messages. **e** All error messages. **a** Action startups (when an action is started). **r** Action-specific reports (status of individual actions). **u** User requests. **c** Initial user interface parameters. **m** Out of memory reports. **p** Terminal properties. **v** Verbose output. * All of the above. Any or all of these switches can be applied.

In addition to the command-line options that apply to the MSIEXEC.EXE application, you can provide options specific to the Commerce Server 2000 installation package. These options, listed in Table 1-3, enable you to specify all of the information required to automate the installation.

Table 1-3. Commerce Server 2000 General Installation Command-Line Parameters

Parameter	Possible Values	Description
INSTALLLEVEL	{100,200}	Specifies the type of installation: **100** Web Server **200** Complete
CS_ADMIN_SERVER	<computername>	Name of the server that will hold the MSCS_Admin database
CS_ADMIN_UID	<user id>	SQL Server User ID that will be used to access (and create) the MSCS_Admin database
CS_ADMIN_PASSWORD	<password>	Password for the SQL Server User ID that will be used to access (and create) the MSCS_Admin database
CS_DML_UID	<user id>	SQL Server User ID that will be used to access (and create) the Direct Mailer database
CS_DML_PASSWORD	<password>	Password for the SQL Server User ID that will be used to access (and create) the Direct Mailer database

In addition, you can identify services to add or delete using similar options, as listed in Table 1-4.

Table 1-4. Installation Command-Line Parameters to Add or Remove Commerce Server 2000 Features

Parameter	Possible Values	Description
ADD_CORE DEL_CORE	1	Adds/Removes the Core Commerce Server 2000 components
ADD_ADMIN DEL_ADMIN	1	Adds/Removes the Commerce Server Manager and other administrative tools
ADD_RUNTIME_OBJECTS DEL_RUNTIME_OBJECTS	1	Adds/Removes the Commerce Server 2000 run-time objects
ADD_SITE_PACKAGES DEL_SITE_PACKAGES	1	Adds/Removes the Blank Site package
ADD_ANALYSIS_DW DEL_ANALYSIS_DW	1	Adds/Removes the Analysis and Data Warehouse components

(continued)

Table 1-4. *(continued)*

Parameter	Possible Values	Description
ADD_PREDICTOR DEL_PREDICTOR	1	Adds/Removes the Predictor Service
ADD_DIRECT_MAILER DEL_DIRECT_MAILER	1	Adds/Removes the Direct Mailer Service
ADD_DEBUG DEL_DEBUG	1	Adds/Removes debugging files
ADD_SDK DEL_SDK	1	Adds/Removes the Commerce Server 2000 SDK
ADD_SDK_SAMPLES DEL_SDK_SAMPLES	1	Adds/Removes the SDK Sample files
ADD_DOCS DEL_DOCS	1	Adds/Removes online documentation

When you install the Commerce Server 2000 components, you'll also need to identify the user accounts under which several of the components and services run, as listed in Table 1-5. You can specify that the components all run under the same user account information or define information for each individual component.

Table 1-5. Installation Command-Line Parameters That Identify the User Account Information Under Which the Commerce Server 2000 Components and Services Run

Parameter	Possible Values	Description
ALL_SERVICE_UID	<user id>	User ID under which the Direct Mailer Service, Predictor Service, List Manager Service, and Event Log COM+ component will run
ALL_SERVICE_PWD	<password>	Password for the user ID under which the Direct Mailer Service, Predictor Service, List Manager Service, and Event Log COM+ component will run
ALL_SERVICE_DOM	<domain>	Domain for the user ID under which the Direct Mailer Service, Predictor Service, List Manager Service, and Event Log COM+ component will run
DML_SERVICE_UID	<user id>	User ID under which the Direct Mailer Service will run
DML_SERVICE_PWD	<password>	Password for the user ID under which the Direct Mailer Service will run
DML_SERVICE_DOM	<domain>	Domain for the user ID under which the Direct Mailer Service will run

(continued)

Table 1-5. *(continued)*

Parameter	Possible Values	Description
PRED_SERVICE_UID	<user id>	User ID under which the Predictor Service will run
PRED_SERVICE_PWD	<password>	Password for the user ID under which the Predictor Service will run
PRED_SERVICE_DOM	<domain>	Domain for the user ID under which the Predictor Service will run
LM_SERVICE_UID	<user id>	User ID under which the List Manager Service will run
LM_SERVICE_PWD	<password>	Password for the user ID under which the List Manager Service will run
LM_SERVICE_DOM	<domain>	Domain for the user ID under which the List Manager Service will run
EVLOG_SERVICE_UID	<user id>	User ID under which the Event Log COM+ component will run
EVLOG_SERVICE_PWD	<password>	Password for the user ID under which the Event Log COM+ component will run
EVLOG_SERVICE_DOM	<domain>	Domain for the user ID under which the Event Log COM+ component will run

Using all of these command-line parameters, we can build automated installation commands to perform several tasks. For instance, to perform a complete installation, you might use a command line similar to the one shown in the following code:

```
msiexec /I "commerce server 2000.msi" /L* c:\csinstall.log /Qn _
 INSTALLLEVEL=200 ALL_SERVICE_UID=CSAccount _
 ALL_SERVICE_PWD=CSPassword ALL_SERVICE_DOM=CSDomain _
 CS_ADMIN_SERVER=%COMPUTERNAME% _
 CS_DML_SERVER=%COMPUTERNAME% CS_ADMIN_UID=sqlUserID _
 CS_ADMIN_PASSWORD=sqlUserPassword CS_DML_UID=sqlUserID _
 CS_DML_PASSWORD=sqlUserPassword
```

In this case, the installation will silently install all components. In addition, the service and COM+ components will be configured to run under the user account CSDomain\CSAccount. Database access will be performed using the sqlUserID account.

Another variation might include the following code, which is used to perform a Web Server installation:

```
msiexec /I "commerce server 2000.msi" /L* c:\csinstall.log /Qn _
  INSTALLLEVEL=100 ALL_SERVICE_UID=CSAccount _
  LL_SERVICE_PWD=CSPassword _
  ALL_SERVICE_DOM=CSDomain CS_ADMIN_SERVER=%COMPUTERNAME% _
  CS_ADMIN_UID=sqlUserID CS_ADMIN_PASSWORD=sqlUserPassword
```

In this case, the installation will be performed as a Web install. The Commerce Server 2000 services and COM+ components will be configured to run under the user account CSDomain\CSAccount and Database access will be performed using the sqlUserID account.

Migrating from Site Server 3 Commerce Edition

So you've already got an e-commerce site in production using Microsoft Site Server 3 Commerce Edition, but now you want to upgrade to Commerce Server 2000. What does this mean for you and your site? Well, the good news is that you will be provided with tools that will give you many more features and capabilities and that will be much more powerful and scalable. The migration is not a simple update task, but you can get there from here.

The first step in performing this migration is to carefully identify the features of Site Server 3 Commerce Edition that you're using on your site. Then, you'll have to identify how and where those features are implemented in Commerce Server 2000. Table 1-6 provides a summary of Site Server 3 Commerce Edition features and their Commerce Server 2000 counterparts.

Table 1-6. Site Server 3 Commerce Edition and Commerce Server 2000 Corresponding Features

Site Server 3 Commerce Edition	Commerce Server 2000
Ad Server	Campaigns
Analysis	Data Warehouse Business Analytics
Catalog	Product Catalog System

(continued)

Table 1-6. *(continued)*

Site Server 3 Commerce Edition	Commerce Server 2000
Commerce Interchange Pipeline	Microsoft BizTalk Server 2000
Content Replication	Application Center
Cross-Sell	Product Catalog System Campaigns
Direct Mail	Direct Mailer
Knowledge Manager	Microsoft Content Manager Server
Order Processing Pipeline	Order Processing Pipelines
Membership (LDAP)	User Profile, Profiling System Active Directory and/or SQL Server
Personalization	Content Selection Framework
Posting Acceptor	Windows 2000 Web Distributed Authoring and Versioning (WebDAV)
Predictor	Predictor Service
Search	Product Catalog System Microsoft Windows 2000 Index Server
Site Vocabulary	Site Terms

Unfortunately, for the majority of these features, there is no direct migration path. To take advantage of the new features and capabilities offered by Commerce Server 2000 and Windows 2000, you'll need to rewrite much of your e-commerce site code. Most of the Commerce Server 2000 components have been modified or have evolved.

In some cases, there might be tools that can assist in the migration of data from Site Server 3 Commerce Edition to Commerce Server 2000 (such as the Membership Migration Tool in the Commerce Server 2000 SDK) that can be used to migrate user data from the Membership Directory to Active Directory in Windows 2000. In addition, transaction data can be migrated using the Transaction Migration tool in the Commerce Server 2000 Resource Kit. Pipelines written in Site Server 3 Commerce Edition will probably function in Commerce Server 2000; however, the components that they use will not take advantage of the new pipeline objects and capabilities.

Finally, before you start planning this migration, you'll want to read the white paper, "Migrating from Site Server to Commerce Server 2000," which provides more detailed information on planning and performing the migration. It can be found on Microsoft's Commerce Server 2000 site at *http://www.microsoft.com/commerceserver/techinfo/deployment/2000/wp_sscemigration.asp/*.

Uninstalling Commerce Server 2000

To uninstall Commerce Server 2000, go to the Windows Control Panel and open Add/Remove Programs. Select Commerce Server 2000 from the Currently Installed Programs list and click Remove, as shown in Figure 1-5. This uninstalls the application software.

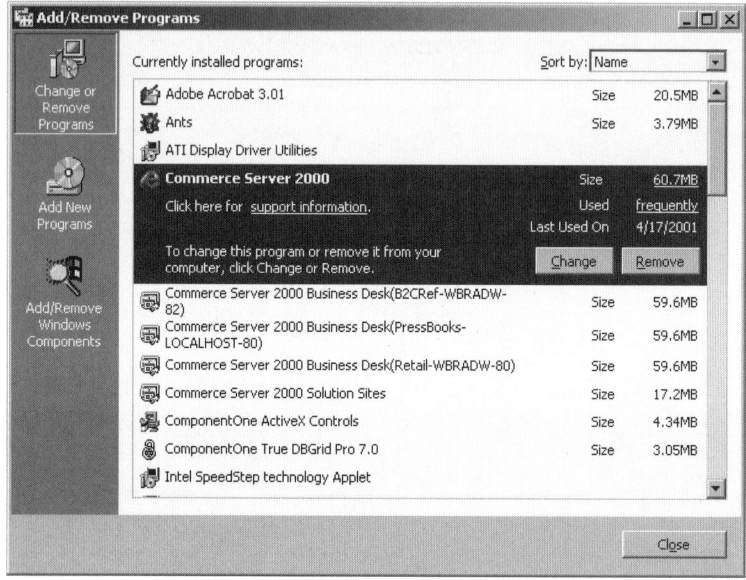

Figure 1-5. *You can uninstall Commerce Server 2000 using the Add/Remove Programs tool in Control Panel.*

Once the application is removed, you'll need to clean up the data files and any other unnecessary files that might remain on the system. You can delete any of the files that remain in the installation folder, which is \Program Files\Microsoft Commerce Server by default.

You'll then need to delete any databases that have been established for the application and related sites. To open SQL Server Enterprise Manager, select Programs from the Start menu, select Microsoft SQL Server, and then click Enterprise Manager. From within Enterprise Manager, open the Microsoft SQL Servers container and the SQL Server Group in which you've registered this server. Open the desired SQL Server container and then select the Databases folder and delete the MSCS_Admin and DirectMailer databases, as well as databases for any sites that you have created.

If, during a custom installation, you opted to install Data Warehouse, you should be sure to delete any Data Warehouse databases. In SQL Server 2000, use the Analysis Manager (see Figure 1-6) to select and delete the databases. In SQL Server 7, you should use the Online Analytical Processing (OLAP) Service Manager to do the same.

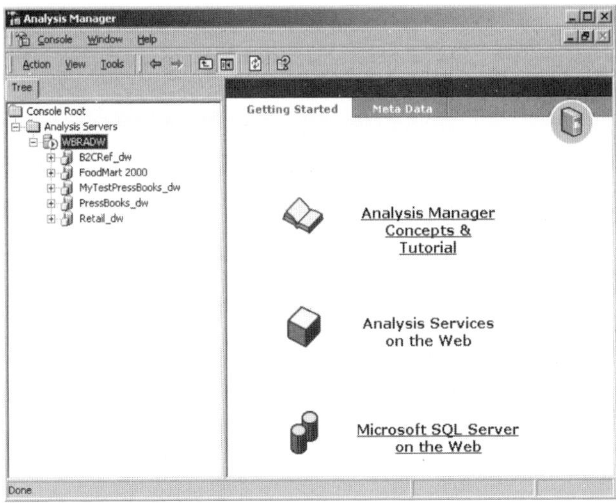

Figure 1-6. *In SQL Server 2000, use Analysis Manager to uninstall any Data Warehouse databases that you've created.*

Chapter 2

Solution Sites, Sitelets, and Samples

As you prepare to build your sites with Microsoft Commerce Server 2000, you need to get the initial site established and configured. You can do so manually, which requires these basic steps:

- Create the required databases and tables.
- Make the proper entries in the MSCS_Admin database to denote the Commerce Server 2000 site, so that it can be managed from the Commerce Server Manager.
- Create and configure necessary areas of Microsoft Active Directory service if you expect to use it.
- Create and configure the required virtual directories and/or Web sites in Microsoft Internet Information Services (IIS).
- Create and configure the public Web site pages.
- Create and configure the basic Business Desk site, providing functionality to manage the public site.
- Build interactivity between the Business Desk site and the public site.
- Create and configure the supporting files, such as pipeline files, GLOBAL.ASA, and others.

Fortunately, Commerce Server 2000 provides a way to perform some of these steps automatically. When you create your site with one of the Solution Sites available from Microsoft, some or all of these steps are taken care of for you. In this chapter, we'll take a brief look at what each of the available Solution Sites offer you in building your site. In addition, we'll take a look at the sitelets that get installed as part of the Commerce Server 2000 Software Development Kit (SDK). These provide examples of how to perform particular tasks or implement a particular functionality in your site.

Sample Catalogs

Before you build your sites, you might want to identify catalog data that you can use in the site. In the end, you'll want to provide a catalog that represents the products you'll be selling. However, you can start off by providing some sample data to test your site. Fortunately, Microsoft has provided two sample catalogs that you can use for just this purpose. To find the BOOKSFULL.XML and HARDWAREFULL.XML catalogs, go to *http://www.microsoft.com/commerceserver/downloads*, and click the Commerce Server 2000 Trial Software—Tutorial Files link. These catalogs are stored in Extensible Markup Language (XML) format and can be imported directly to your site using the import methods in the Business Desk.

Installing Solution Sites

Once the Commerce Server 2000 software is installed, you might want to install the available Solution Sites that we'll be covering in this chapter. You can use these sites as a starting point in building your commerce sites or as examples of how to implement various features in Commerce Server 2000.

Commerce Server 2000 installs one Solution Site, the Blank Site, with the basic installation. However, two other sites—Retail and Supplier Active Directory—are available for download from the Microsoft Web site at *http://www.microsoft.com/commerceserve/downloads/solutionsites.asp*. The package is available in English, French, German, and Japanese. You can download and install the sites directly from that location. Once installed, the packages will appear in the Commerce Server 2000 Solution Sites folder. These sites demonstrate possible business-to-consumer (B2C) and business-to-business (B2B) implementations, respectively.

More Info Other Commerce Server 2000 Sample Sites

In addition to the basic Microsoft Solution Sites, as of this writing, there are several other sample sites that Microsoft has provided on the Web. These sites, Sweet Forgiveness and Microsoft Reference Architecture for Commerce: Business to Consumer, are designed to show different implementations of a Commerce Server 2000 Web site.

To find the Sweet Forgiveness site, go to *http://www.microsoft.com/commerceserver/downloads*, and click the Commerce Server 2000 Sample Site: Sweet Forgiveness link. The site is a multinational, multicurrency B2C e-commerce store. Microsoft developed this site to demonstrate some of the ways you can implement a localized, multinational site.

The Microsoft Reference Architecture for Commerce: Business to Consumer site was developed to demonstrate how you can implement a Commerce Server 2000 site using XML and Extensible Stylesheet Language (XSL). To find this sample site, go to *http://msdn.microsoft.com/code*, expand the Sample Applications and Reference Architectures node, and then click the Reference Architecture for Commerce: B2C node.

Once the Solution Site packages have been downloaded and installed on your system, you're ready to create the sites themselves. The result of the download will be two .pup files that will be created and placed in the Solution Sites folder. You can create one or more sites based on each file. You can double-click the .pup file and unpack the Solution Site. Detailed directions on creating a site based on any .pup file are provided in Chapter 6, "Site Packager."

The Blank Site Solution Site

The Blank Site Solution Site is installed automatically with Commerce Server 2000. It provides a basic structure that you can use to build your site, but it leaves the actual building of the site for you to handle. As Table 2-1 shows, most of the tasks you'll need to perform when you first build your site are taken care of for you. The databases and Web sites are created for you so you don't have to create and configure them manually. In addition, a standard Business Desk site is created (assuming you chose to have it created when installing the site) to provide a starting point for you.

Table 2-1. Tasks Performed Automatically by the Blank Site Solution Site

Task	Performed
Create entries in MSCS_Admin database	Yes
Create and configure database and tables	Yes
Create and configure Active Directory entries	No
Create and configure IIS Web sites	Yes
Create and configure public site pages	No
Create and configure Business Desk site pages	Yes
Provide interactivity between Business Desk and public site	Yes
Create and configure supporting files	Partially

As you can see, there are several tasks that are not done for you. No changes are made to the Active Directory, so if you want to integrate with Active Directory, you'll have to do so yourself. Additionally, only the following very basic pages are provided in the public site:

- **CSAPP.INI** This file provides the initial configuration information about the site. It's data is used by Commerce Server 2000 components to access the site databases.
- **DEFAULT.ASP** This page is simply a space holder and is essentially blank.
- **GLOBAL.ASA** This page provides a starting point for building your initialization code. It includes some very basic functionality you'll need, but you'll still have to provide the most important code.

Finally, there are two pages that are automatically installed that enable interactivity between the Business Desk and the public site. These pages, BDREFRESH.ASP and REFRESHAPP.ASP, allow the Business Desk to issue catalogs and profile changes and refresh cache data on the public site.

As you can see, when starting with the Blank Site, you will still have to provide the core set of functionality, designing and building your Web site on your own. This might seem like the harder approach because it forces you to spend time building in the functionality that you want on your site, but it is the recommended approach. Using this method, you can build exactly the features you want in just the way that you want. You'll be able to target your code to specifically meet your requirements. In most cases, this means that you'll end up with more efficient code. If you are diligent in design and construction of the site, your code should be much easier to maintain, as well.

The Retail Site Solution Site

The Retail Site Solution Site provides an out-of-the-box solution for getting a B2C site up and running in a very short time. When you unpack the site, it creates everything you'll need to open up your site (see Table 2-2). You simply need to provide a catalog of products and tax and shipping configuration information, so that the purchase process can be completed.

Table 2-2. Tasks Performed Automatically by the Retail Site Solution Site

Task	Performed
Create entries in MSCS_Admin database	Yes
Create and configure database and tables	Yes
Create and configure Active Directory entries	No
Create and configure IIS Web sites	Yes
Create and configure public site pages	Yes
Create and configure Business Desk site pages	Yes
Provide interactivity between Business Desk and public site	Yes
Create and configure supporting files	Yes

The Retail Site provides very flexible code that allows you to change functionality simply by modifying several values in the site's configuration data using the Commerce Server Manager. For instance, by adjusting the Form Login Options setting in the site's App Default Config object (see Figure 2-1), you can specify whether or not you will force users to log in to the site and when they must do so.

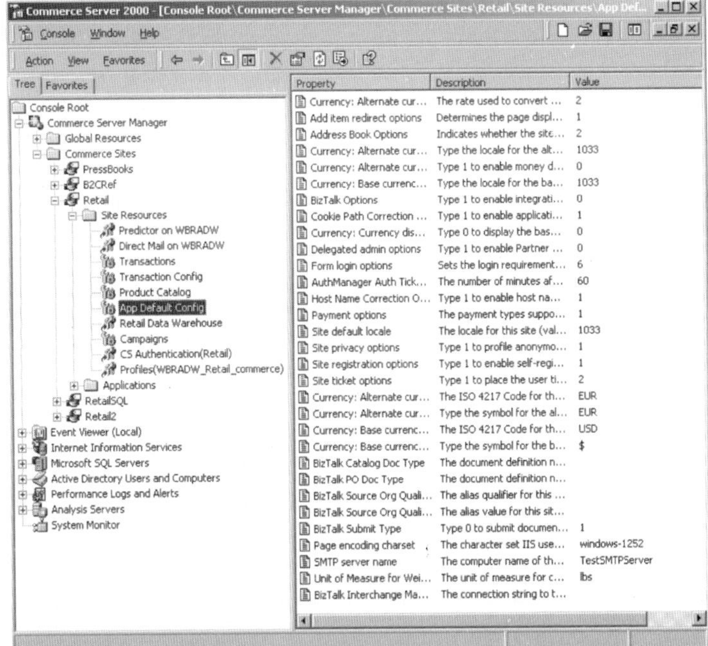

Figure 2-1. *By modifying the App Default Config parameters in the Retail Site, you can change the way the site behaves.*

The Retail Site provides the ability for both registered and anonymous users to enter the site, browse or search for products, and purchase items. In addition, registered users can save profile information about themselves, maintain an address book to store their shipping and billing addresses, and examine their purchase history. Users can search for products using both a free-text keyword search and a scroll-down approach. User profile data is maintained within the SQL Server database.

The disadvantage to using the Retail Site is that it is not focused on providing a targeted solution. Rather, the code in the site is designed to handle any possible functionality. Table 2-3 shows the number of lines of code needed to implement several of the pages in the Retail Site. For instance, if you know that your site will require users to log in, you don't need to always check the configuration settings to determine if the user can be anonymous and then provide code to handle anonymous usage. You can thus reduce the amount of code you'll have to run to provide the functionality you need.

Table 2-3. Lines of Code Used to Implement Some Base Pages

Base Page Name	Lines of Code
DEFAULT.ASP	4302
PRODUCT.ASP	5257
BASKET.ASP	5557

In addition, until you become familiar with the structure of the Retail Site code, you'll likely find it difficult to make substantive changes to the site. Many users have found it to be more difficult to maintain the Retail Site code than it is to maintain their own code. Of course, your experience might be different.

The Supplier Active Directory Site

The Supplier Active Directory site is similar to the Retail Site (see Table 2-4). It provides all the same basic functionality, but it also provides some additional functionality. The first obvious difference is that user profile data, as well as data for organizations, is maintained in Active Directory. The site supports the use of organizations to which users can belong. You can create organizations and assign user accounts with administrative rights to the organization. Those users have access to a Partner Desk area of the e-commerce site, where they can create and manage user accounts within the organization.

Table 2-4. Tasks Performed Automatically by the Supplier Active Directory Site Solution Site

Task	Performed
Create entries in MSCS_Admin database	Yes
Create and configure database and tables	Yes
Create and configure Active Directory entries	Yes
Create and configure IIS Web sites	Yes
Create and configure public site pages	Yes
Create and configure Business Desk site pages	Yes
Provide interactivity between Business Desk and public site	Yes
Create and configure supporting files	Yes

You'll find that the code base for this site is identical to that of the Retail Site. The Partner Desk and Active Directory portions of the code are used in this site, based on the configuration settings that are made. This means that the same advantages and disadvantages apply when you use this as a basis for your own site.

Sitelets

The Commerce Server 2000 SDK includes a set of sitelets. These sitelets are simply self-contained subsections of a Web site that are used to demonstrate the implementation of one particular area of a potential e-commerce site. You can use them as examples of how to build particular features. If you're not sure how to accomplish a particular task, you can consult these sitelets for guidance, presented in a more condensed format than it is in the Solution Sites. The SDK contains sitelets for the feature areas covered in the following sections.

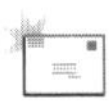

Note The Commerce Server 2000 SDK is installed by the Commerce Server 2000 setup package. It is not installed if you select Web Server as the installation method. It will be installed if you select Complete, and it is available for installation if you select Custom. See Chapter 1, "Installing and Configuring Commerce Server 2000," for more details.

Ad

The Ad sitelet demonstrates how you can use the Profiling system in conjunction with the Targeting system to display targeted advertisements on your e-commerce site. It shows how you can set up the context used in selecting ad content to display to your users in the GLOBAL.ASA's InitCSF() method. It also includes sample code that selects the ad that will be displayed in the GetAdContent() function in the ADVERTLIB.ASP file.

Auction

The Auction sitelet demonstrates how you can implement auction features on your site. You can specify that particular products from your catalogs are available for auction. The InitAuctions() method in the AUCTIONLIB.ASP file initializes the Auction component, which is used to manage the auctions on your site. The GetActiveAuctionList() method is used to list those auctions. With the Auction component, you can retrieve lists of products that are available for auction. In addition, you can enter and evaluate bids.

The Auction sitelet includes additional pages for the Business Desk that can be used to manage and monitor the ongoing progress of auctions from the Business Desk.

Catalog

The Catalog sitelet includes code that allows users to browse and search for products in the catalog. It also includes pages that are used to display individual products from the catalog.

Discount

The Discount sitelet includes code that applies discounts to products in your catalog. As users add products to their baskets, discounts are displayed, and the discounts are applied as the purchases are completed.

Order

The Order sitelet contains the pages necessary to complete a purchase, including gathering shipment and billing information and calculating totals, tax, and other charges. Other pages are provided to display an order summary and confirmation, receipt, and history.

Passport

The Passport sitelet includes code that shows how you can integrate your site with Microsoft Passport. Your users can use their passport IDs to log in to your site and provide billing and shipping information automatically from the data stored in their Passport accounts.

Profile

The Profile sitelet includes files that demonstrate how to have users create and manage their own profiles. In addition, the sitelet includes pages that allow a user to log in to the site and authenticate their login based on the parameters they've supplied.

Samples

The Commerce Server 2000 SDK provides sample code that covers a number of tasks or techniques that you might find useful in developing or managing your site. The samples are organized into different functional areas, each of which are introduced in the following sections. The samples are located in the C:\Program Files\Microsoft Commerce Server\SDK\Samples folder by default.

Business Analytics

This folder contains a number of Business Analytics code samples and scripts, organized into two subfolders.

Schema Tool

The Schema Tool folder contains Microsoft Visual Basic code that allows you to browse the Commerce Server 2000 Data Warehouse schema.

Scripts

The Scripts folder contains the following useful VBScripts and SQL scripts that can be used to work with Business Analytics data:

- **ANALYSIS–NEW DYNAMIC OLAP REPORT SCRIPT.SQL** This script creates a new dynamic Online Analytical Processing (OLAP) report in the Business Analytics system.
- **ANALYSIS–NEW DYNAMIC SQL REPORT SCRIPT.SQL** This script creates a new dynamic SQL report in the Business Analytics system.

- **ANALYSIS–NEW STATIC OLAP REPORT SCRIPT.SQL** This script creates a new static OLAP report in the Business Analytics system.
- **ANALYSIS–NEW STATIC SQL REPORT SCRIPT.SQL** This script creates a new static SQL report in the Business Analytics system.
- **CREATESCHEMAOBJECT.VBS** This script modifies the existing Business Analytics logical schema by adding a new class and its members.

Management

The Management folder contains sample pages and code that can be used in various site management tasks. These code sets are organized into the groups detailed in the following sections.

BizDesk

This folder contains files that can be used as a starting point for developing custom Business Desk modules.

BizDesk Installer

This folder contains Microsoft Visual C++ code that adds configuration information for a new Business Desk module to an existing Business Desk.

PuP Resource

This folder contains Visual Basic code that implements the Commerce Server Site Packager (IpuP) interface and is used to package a specific set of database tables from an SQL Server database.

ResourceConfig

This folder contains Visual Basic code that is used to add configuration information for a custom resource to the Commerce Server Administration database.

Site Status

This folder contains a sample Microsoft Management Console (MMC) snap-in that is used to open and close Commerce Server sites. The code is written in Visual C++.

Widgets

This folder contains Active Server Page (ASP) pages that demonstrate the use of the various HTML components used in the Business Desk.

Marketing

This folder contains several sample code sets related to marketing functions in Commerce Server 2000, grouped into three areas, as covered in the following sections.

DBScripts

The DBScripts folder contains several database scripts that are used to delete marketing-related tables and data from the database.

Debug

The Debug folder contains ASP code examples that can be used to dump and trace Content Selection scoring. This information can be useful in debugging problems on the site.

Headlines

The Headlines folder shows how the Content Selection framework can be extended with custom components developed in Visual Basic and Visual C++ components.

Order Processing

The Order Processing folder contains a sample implementation of a pipeline component written in both Visual Basic and Visual C++ using Active Template Library (ATL). In addition, there is a sample Business Desk module that can be used to manage the MinMaxShip pipeline component.

Privacy

The Privacy folder contains two VBScript files that can be used to delete or unlink data in the Data Warehouse from a user. This helps ensure that the information about the user remains private and cannot be traced back to that user. The two files are as follows:

- **DELETEDETAILEDDATA.VBS** This file deletes data about a given user from the Data Warehouse.
- **DISCONNECTDETAILEDDATA.VBS** The file removes the information relating data to a given user from the Data Warehouse.

Sitelets

This folder contains the sitelets discussed earlier in this chapter.

Solution Sites

This folder holds a single .idl file that provides a list of constants and their values that are used in the Solution Sites. This file makes an excellent reference.

Part II

Management Services and Tools

Part II of this book covers the management services and tools that are used in a Commerce Server 2000 site. Chapter 3 examines the Commerce Server Manager, a Microsoft Management Console (MMC) snap-in that is used to administer the back-end systems that support the site. Chapter 4 covers the Business Desk, which is provided for business users to manage their individual e-commerce sites and its contents. Chapter 5 takes an in-depth look at Business Analytics and the Commerce Server 2000 tools that are used to analyze site usage and performance. Chapter 6 covers the Commerce Server Site Packager that is used to pack and unpack sites and site resources for deployment to other machines.

Chapter 3

Commerce Server Manager

The primary means of administering Microsoft Commerce Server 2000 is the Commerce Server Manager (CSM), shown in Figure 3-1. The CSM is a Microsoft Management Console (MMC) snap-in that provides the ability to manage the resources and configuration settings that are available to your sites. These resources are used in the various Commerce Server 2000 applications in your site, which may be located on multiple Web servers.

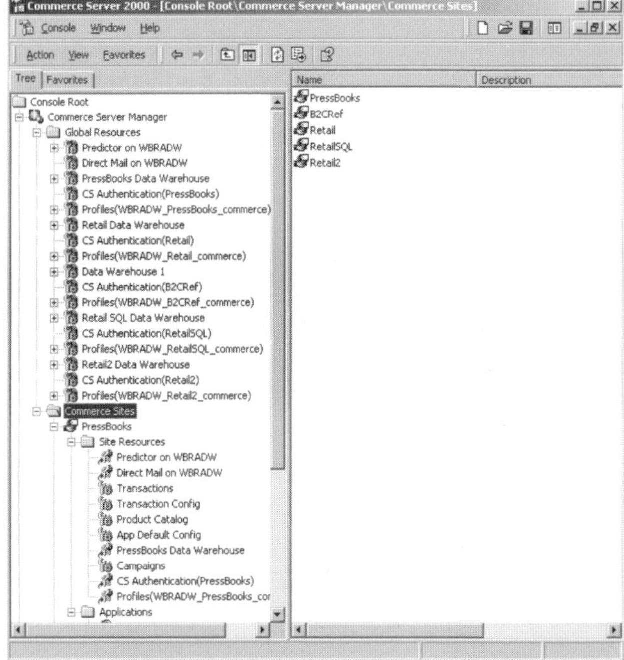

Figure 3-1. *The Commerce Server Manager is an MMC snap-in, used for managing and configuring Commerce Server resources.*

Commerce Server 2000 resources can be generally grouped into global resources, which are available to all of the Commerce Server 2000 applications on your site, and site resources, which are defined for each Commerce Server 2000 site. You find this same division within CSM, where there are separate folders for global resources and commerce sites. The Commerce Sites folder contains a list of sites, and beneath each site can be found its site resources.

Global Resources

You should be aware that two of the global resources—Predictor and Direct Mailer Service resources—are truly global, in that they are used by all of the sites. There are also three separate resources that are created for each site that are also listed in the Global Resources folder: the Data Warehouse, Commerce Server (CS) Authentication, and Profiles resources.

We cover each of these resources in depth in the appropriate chapters of this book. For now, however, let's take a look at the properties that are defined for each of these resources and the effects they have on your sites.

Predictor

The Predictor resource is used to analyze patterns of data, particularly pertaining to users, their profiles, and their buying patterns, and to build predictions about those users. The prediction might simply be a recommendation for a product based on what other similar users have purchased, or it might be a guess concerning some fact about the user based on his or her behavior or attributes and similar behaviors of other users. This is covered in greater detail in Chapter 19, "Content Selection."

Direct Mailer

The Direct Mailer resource is used to manage the sending of e-mails from your Commerce Server 2000 sites. The resource contains properties, shown in Figure 3-2 and listed in Table 3-1, that define how the Direct Mailer feature runs.

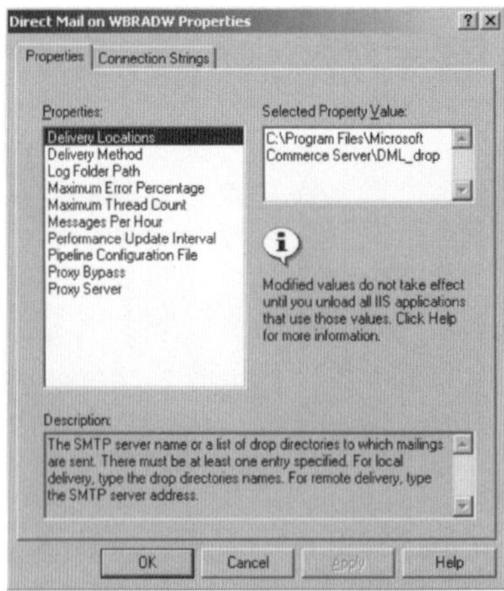

Figure 3-2. *Modify properties to configure how the Direct Mailer resource functions.*

Table 3-1. Direct Mailer Resource Properties

Property	Description
Delivery Locations	Location where the e-mails will be sent. This is either a drop directory or a Simple Mail Transfer Protocol (SMTP) server, depending on the Delivery Method setting.
Delivery Method	Identifies the method of delivery of the e-mails, as follows: SMTP server e-mails are sent to the SMTP server specified in Delivery Locations. Drop Directory locally e-mails are placed in the drop directory specified in Delivery Locations.
Log Folder Path	Location of the Direct Mailer Service operational log file.
Maximum Error Percentage	Percentage of nonfatal errors per job (based on the number of errors and the total number of e-mails sent) that will cause the Direct Mailer job to be stopped. If the value is 50, when over half of the e-mails sent result in errors, the job is halted. If the value is 100, the job is halted if all of the e-mails report errors.
Maximum Thread Count	Number of system threads that the Direct Mailer resource can use for each job.
Messages Per Hour	Maximum number of e-mails that can be sent each hour. This allows you to throttle the e-mail transmissions. Using 0 allows the system to send the e-mails as quickly as possible.
Performance Update Interval	Number of seconds between each update of the performance statistics that identify how well the Direct Mailer resource is functioning.
Pipeline Configuration File	Location and name of the Direct Mailer pipeline file that controls how the e-mails are processed.
Proxy Bypass	Name of the site that can be used by users directly, without going through the proxy server.
Proxy Server	Name of the proxy server that is used to access the site, if any.
Direct Mailer Database	Holds the connection string to the Direct Mailer database.

Data Warehouse

A Data Warehouse resource is created for each site for which you've chosen to install the Data Warehouse resources. The default name of the resource will be Data Warehouse 1 when you install the resource by unpacking the site (see Chapter 6, "Site Packager," for more details). However, I recommend changing the name to something in the format of <SiteName> Data Warehouse or something else that better identifies the Data Warehouse and the site to which it belongs. Regardless, the name of the resource presented here will reflect the name you've chosen in creating the resource when unpacking the site. The resource contains a set of properties that define how and where the data is tracked (see Figure 3-3).

By examining the properties, you'll find that they hold information about the database and analysis server used to process this data.

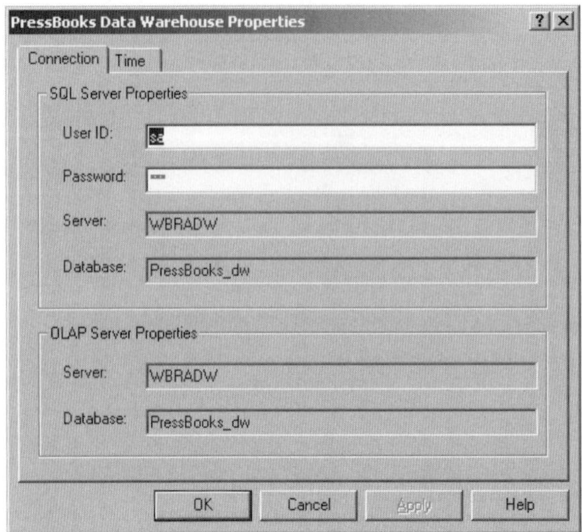

Figure 3-3. *The Data Warehouse resource properties identify the database in which the data is being stored.*

In addition, the Data Warehouse resource includes settings that determine how the time of imported data is normalized. For instance, you can define for analysis and tracking purposes that the week will start on Sunday, Monday, or any other day of the week. You can also define which time zone you'll use as a basis for tracking the times of purchases and other activities (see Figure 3-4). This might be particularly helpful if you're hosting your site at a facility in one location, but your corporate headquarters are located in a separate location and time zone.

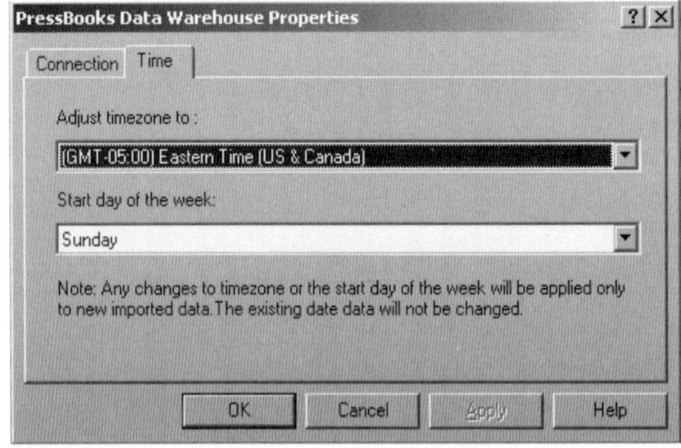

Figure 3-4. *You can adjust the Time properties of the Data Warehouse resource to meet your needs by identifying the starting day of the week and the time zone that you'll use to normalize your tracking data.*

Task History

The Data Warehouse resource also includes a Task History feature that provides a summary of all of the tasks that have been performed by the Data Warehouse.

CS Authentication

The CS Authentication resource is used to define how authentication is enforced (see Figure 3-5). Table 3-2 lists and describes the CS Authentication resource properties.

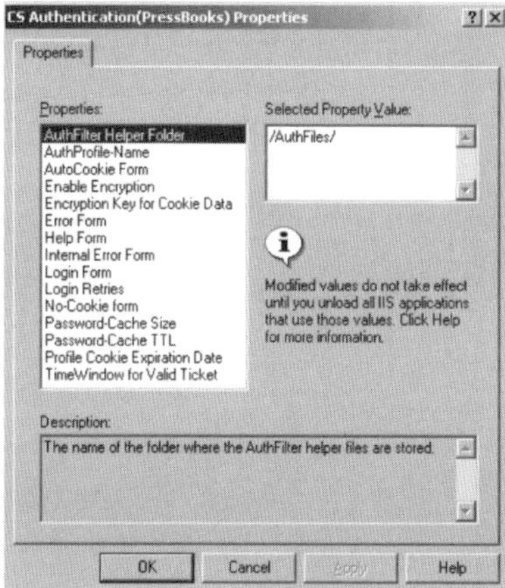

Figure 3-5. *The CS Authentication properties dialog box can be used to administer and configure settings that define how the authentication works on your site.*

Table 3-2. CS Authentication Resource Properties

Property	Description
AuthFilter Help Folder	Web directory (under the site's virtual root) where the AuthFilter helper files are located.
AuthProfile-Name	Name of the profile object to use when the Profiling System data source is partitioned.
AutoCookie Form	Name of the form to display when AutoCookies are enabled.
Enable Encryption	Enables encryption of cookie data.
Encryption Key for Cookie Data	Encryption key used when encrypting or decrypting cookie data.
Error Form	Name of the form to display if an Access Denied error occurs.
Help Form	Name of the form that contains help information for logging in.

(continued)

Table 3-2. *(continued)*

Property	Description
Internal Error Form	Name of the form to display for additional error handling.
Login Form	Name of the form to display when a user attempts to log in to the site.
Login Retries	Number of times a user can attempt to log in to the site before being redirected to another page.
No-Cookie Form	Name of the form to display if the user's browser is not configured to support cookies and the site requires them.
Password-Cache Size	The number of users' credentials that will be cached.
Password-Cache TTL	Time in minutes until a user's credentials will be cached.
Profile Cookie Expiration Date	Date on which the AutoCookie expires.
TimeWindow For Valid Ticket	Time in minutes that a user's credentials will remain valid.

Profiles

The Profiles resource is used to store and manage profile data sources and definitions (see Figure 3-6) such as User, Organizations, and Addresses. These are covered in more detail in Chapter 10, "Profiles." Table 3-3 lists and describes each of the Profiles resource properties.

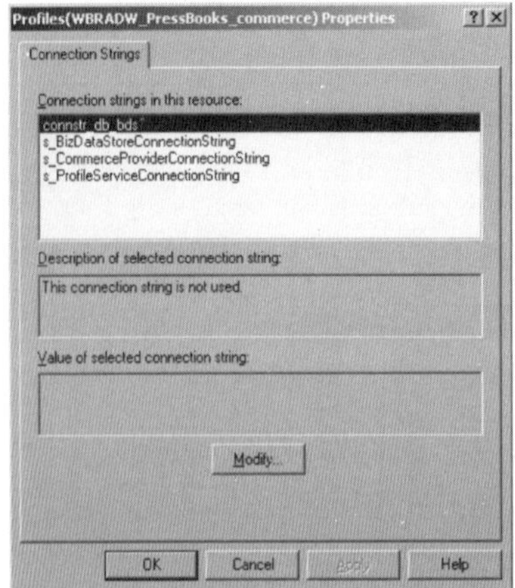

Figure 3-6. *Profiles Resource properties are used to configure and manage the collection of data for your Web site.*

Table 3-3. Profiles Resource Properties

Property	Description
connstr_db_bds	Not used
s_BizDataStoreConnectionString	Connection string to the Profiles database
s_CommerceProviderConnectionString	Connection string that uses the Commerce Server OLE DB provider
s_ProfileServiceConnectionString	Connection string to the Profile Service

Commerce Sites

In addition to the global resources that are available, there are resources and applications that are specific to each individual site. These are contained within the Commerce Sites folder in CSM.

Site Resources

The resources that are available to the site are all defined within the Site Resources area.

Predictor

The Predictor resource includes the single property *s_RefResource*, which points to the Predictor global resource. The Predictor global resource uses the Predictor Service to analyze patterns of data in the Data Warehouse and predict or make recommendations based on that analysis. The Predictor Service is covered in more detail in Chapter 20, "Predictor Service."

Direct Mailer

The Direct Mailer resource includes the single property *s_RefResource*, which points to the Direct Mailer global resource. The Direct Mailer global resource works with the List Manager service and Business Analytics to generate custom e-mails that will be sent to a list of users that you provide. The e-mails can be personalized for each recipient. The Direct Mailer service is covered in more detail in Chapter 18, "Campaign Management."

Transactions

The Transactions resource includes the single property *Transactions Database*. This property is a database connection string to the Transactions database, which is used to store information about the user's basket and orders.

Transactions Config

The Transactions Config resource includes the single property *Transactions Config Database*. This property is a database connection string to the Transactions Configuration database, which is used to store information about the configuration of the transaction system, including data status codes and other lookup information, tax and shipping data, and more.

Product Catalog

The Product Catalog resource includes the single property *Catalog Database*. This property is a database connection string to the Catalog database, which is used to store catalog information and describe the structure of the existing catalogs, including the category, product, and property definitions, as well as the actual products.

App Default Config

The App Default Config resource contains settings, listed in Table 3-4, that define how the site should perform. Some of these will apply more to sites built based on the Solution Sites, and you might not use some of these settings, but they're all available.

Table 3-4. App Default Resource Properties

Property	Description
Add Item Redirect Options	Specifies how the site should act when an item is added to the basket, as follows: 0: Redirect to the basket page. 1: Continue displaying the current page.
Address Books Options	Identifies whether the site provides an address book for the shoppers, as follows: 0: Address book is disabled. 1: Address book is read-only. 2: Address book is read/write.
AuthManager Auth Ticket Timeout	Number of minutes for which an authentication ticket is good before it expires.
BizTalk Catalog Doc Type	Document definition name used by BizTalk Server for catalogs.
BizTalk Options	Identifies if the site is integrated with BizTalk Server, as follows: 0: Integration is disabled. 1: Integration is enabled.
BizTalk PO Doc Type	Document definition name used by BizTalk Server for purchase orders.
BizTalk Source Org Qualifier	Organization qualifier property name passed to BizTalk Server.
BizTalk Source Org Qualifier Value	Organization qualifier property value passed to BizTalk Server.
BizTalk Submit Type	Identifies whether the documents should be submitted to BizTalk Server synchronously or asynchronously, as follows: 0: Synchronously. 1: Asynchronously.

(continued)

Table 3-4. *(continued)*

Property	Description
Cookie Path Correction Options	Specifies the manner of cookie path corrections, as follows: 1: Application-based corrections. 2: Filter-based corrections.
Currency: Alternate Currency Code	ISO 4217 code for the alternate currency.
Currency: Alternate Currency Conversion Rate	Rate used to convert between the base and alternate currency.
Currency: Alternate Currency Locale	Locale ID for the alternate currency, as selected from these options: 1031: German 1033: English 1034: Spanish 1036: French 1041: Japanese
Currency: Alternate Currency Options	Identifies how the alternative currencies are shown, as follows: 0: Display one currency at a time. 1: Display two currencies simultaneously.
Currency: Alternate Currency Symbol	Monetary symbol associated with the alternate currency.
Currency: Base Currency Code	ISO 4217 code for the base currency.
Currency: Base Currency Locale	Locale ID for the base currency as selected from these options: 1031: German 1033: English 1034: Spanish 1036: French 1041: Japanese
Currency: Base Currency Symbol	Monetary symbol for the base currency.
Currency: Currency Display Order Options	Determines how the currencies are displayed, as follows: 0: Base currency is displayed first. 1: Alternate currency is displayed first.
Delegated Admin Options	Identifies whether the site will allow partner or corporate organizations to manage their own user base and accounts through the Partner Desk (or similar functionality), as follows: 0: Disable Partner Services. 1: Enable Partner Services

(continued)

Table 3-4. *(continued)*

Property	Description
Form Login Options	Defines the requirements for shoppers to log in to the site, as follows: 0: Users cannot log in; only Guest shoppers are used. 1: Shopper must log in when entering the site. 2: Login is optional when user enters the site. 5: Login is required at the time of purchase. 6: Login is optional any time. 7: Internet Information Services (IIS) authentication is required.
Host Name Correction Options	Identifies whether host name correction is used in the site, as follows: 0: Host name correction is disabled. 1: Host name correction is enabled.
Page Encoding Charset	The page encoding character set for the site.
Payment Options	Identifies the options supported by the site for payment, as follows: 1: Credit card payments are supported. 4: Shoppers maintain accounts that are billed. 5: Both options are supported.
SMTP Server Name	Name of the SMTP mail server being used with this site.
Site Default Locale	The Locale ID for this site, as selected from these options: 1031: German 1033: English 1034: Spanish 1036: French 1041: Japanese
Site Privacy Options	Defines how anonymous users are tracked; used if developing a site based on one of the Solution Sites, as follows: 1: Anonymous users are profiled. 2: Anonymous users are not profiled and tracked.
Site Registration Options	Identifies whether shoppers can register themselves; used if developing a site based on one of the Solution Sites, as follows: 0: Self-registration is disabled. 1: Self-registration is enabled.

(continued)

Table 3-4. *(continued)*

Property	Description
Site Ticket Options	Identifies where the user's authentication ticket should be placed; used if developing a site based on one of the Solution Sites, as follows: 1: Ticket is in the Uniform Resource Locator (URL). 2: Ticket is in the cookie.
Unit Of Measure For Weight	Unit of measure used to calculate product shipping costs.

Site Data Warehouse

The Site Data Warehouse resource includes the single property *s_RefResource*, which points to the site's Data Warehouse global resource.

Campaigns

The Campaigns resource includes the single property *Campaigns*. This property is a database connection string to the Campaigns database, which is used to store information about advertising campaigns that will be used within the site.

Site CS Authentication

The Site CS Authentication resource includes the single property *s_RefResource*, which points to the site's CS Authentication global resource.

Profiles

The Profiles resource includes the single property *s_RefResource*, which points to the site's Profiles global resource.

Adding Resources

You can add a new resource to your site at any time. There are actually two ways to start this process. One way is from within CSM, and the other way is from the Commerce Server Site Packager tool. You can add a new resource from within CSM by following these steps:

1. Right-click the Site Resources folder.
2. Point to New.
3. Select Add Resource (see Figure 3-7). You are then prompted to select the .pup file that contains the resource you want to add to this site. The unpack process then guides you through adding the resource to the site.

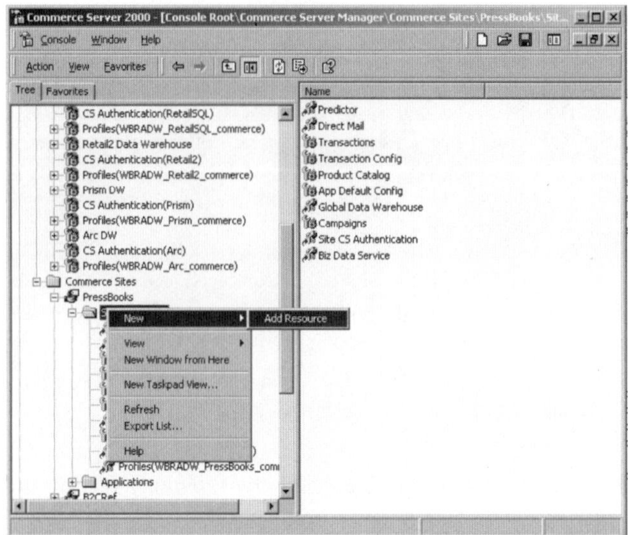

Figure 3-7. *You can add a new resource to the site from within CSM.*

You can add the resource directly from the Commerce Server Site Packager tool by following these steps:

1. Launch the Solution Sites program in the Commerce Server 2000 program group.
2. Open the .pup file to which you would like to add the resource.
3. Select Perform A Custom Unpack using the Commerce Server Site Packager (see Chapter 6, "Site Packager," for more details).
4. Select Add Resources In The Package To An Existing Site.

Delete Resources

You can also delete a resource from the site in the Site Resources folder by right-clicking the name of the resource and selecting Delete from the shortcut menu. This removes the resource from the available resources for the site, but it does not remove any of the files or databases that the resource uses.

Applications

Applications in Commerce Server 2000 represent the Web addresses that are accessed as a part of the site. This might include the actual e-commerce site, the Business Desk, and any other supporting sites that are used in the seamless site. The application can include a number of different servers. When an application is added to Commerce Server, the MSCS_Admin database is updated with the appropriate configuration data, which is then reflected in the properties listed in the following sections. When you add a Web server to the application, the Web pages are installed on the Web server.

Application Properties

The application in Commerce Server 2000 is defined by a number of properties. You can view these properties by right-clicking the desired application in CSM and selecting Properties from the shortcut menu.

General Properties Table 3-5 shows the properties listed in the General tab of the Application Properties dialog box.

Table 3-5. Application General Properties

Property	Description
Display Name	Name of the Commerce Server site as it will be displayed in CSM
Web Servers In This Application Are Running IIS	Read-only property that signifies that the server is running IIS
Nonsecure Host Name	Host name for the site when accessing it in nonsecure mode
IIS Application Path	The application path in IIS for this Commerce Server site
Enable HTTPS	Check box that identifies whether the site will use Secure Sockets Layer (SSL)
Secure Host Name	Host name for the site that is used when accessing the site via SSL
Autocookie	Check box that identifies whether the site will support Autocookie generation for anonymous users
Authentication Filter	Identifies the type of authentication filter that is being used on this site
Set Cookie Path To Application	Indicates whether cookies will be shared among other applications on the site
Number Of Share Domain Levels	Specifies how many domain levels applications need in common to share a cookie

Tip In addition to working with the application properties shown, you can also generate a new encryption key, which is used to encrypt and decrypt cookie data, by clicking Generate New Encryption Key. You are prompted to confirm that you want to replace the key (see Figure 3-8). Replacing the encryption key renders all of the older authentication tickets unusable because the encryption key will change. However, once the encryption key is updated, you can continue using the site as normal.

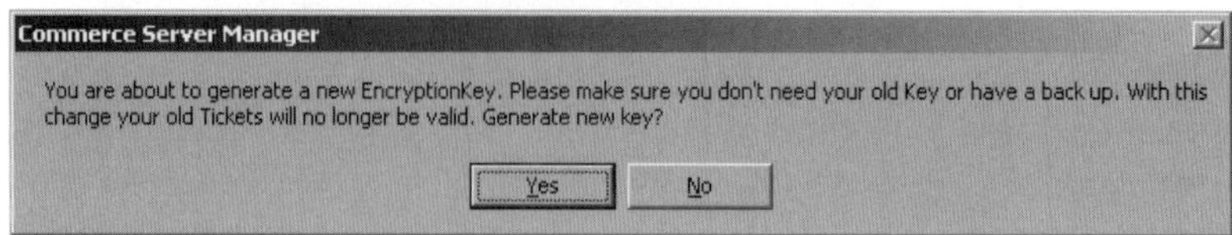
Commerce Server Manager

You are about to generate a new EncryptionKey. Please make sure you don't need your old Key or have a back up. With this change your old Tickets will no longer be valid. Generate new key?

Yes No

Figure 3-8. *You are prompted to confirm the change before generating a new cookie encryption key.*

Application Web Server Properties Table 3-6 shows the properties that are defined in the Web Servers tab of the Application Properties dialog box.

Table 3-6. Application Web Server Properties

Property	Description
IIS Web Site	The IIS Web site where the Commerce Server site is installed
TCP Port	The Transmission Control Protocol (TCP) port that the Commerce Server site will be accessed through (typically port 80)
SSL Port	The TCP port that the Commerce Server site will be accessed through using SSL (typically port 443)
Local Domain	Name of the local domain

Tip If the IIS properties ever change, you should be sure that you have the correct settings on all of your Web servers. You can do this by updating the properties manually in the CSM. Alternatively, in the Web Server Properties dialog box, you can click Synchronize Values. This reads the Web server settings from the first Web server. All Web servers in a Web farm must have the same settings.

Application Server Properties

Each individual server within the Applications folder has a set of configurable properties associated with it. You can view those properties by right-clicking the server name and selecting Properties from the shortcut menu. These properties are listed and described in Table 3-7.

Table 3-7. Application Server Properties

Property	Description
Server Name	Name of the server where the Commerce Server site is installed
IP Address	Internet Protocol (IP) address for the Web server
Log File Path	Location where the IIS Web logs are maintained
Log File Period	How often a new log file is created from this site

Adding an Application

You can add an application to the site at any time by completing the following steps:

1. Right-click the Applications folder in the CSM.
2. Point to New.
3. Select Add Application from the shortcut menu (see Figure 3-9). You are prompted to identify the .pup file that contains the application that is being added to the site.
4. You can then select the application you wish to unpack for your site. For information on how to use Site Packager, see Chapter 6, "Site Packager."

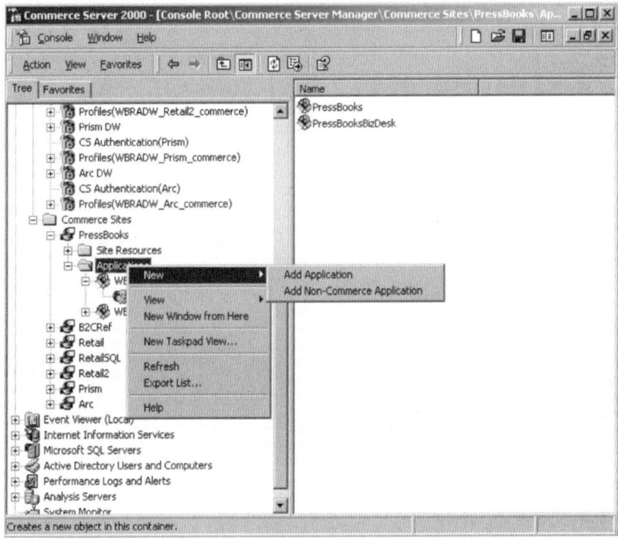

Figure 3-9. *You can add an application to the site by right-clicking the Applications folder, pointing to New, and then selecting Add Application or Add Non-Commerce Application, as appropriate.*

In addition, you can add a new application to your site directly from the Commerce Server Site Packager by completing these steps (more detail can be found in Chapter 6):

1. Launch the Solution Sites from Commerce Server 2000 in the Programs Group of the Start menu.
2. Select the .pup file you wish to install.
3. Select Custom Unpack in the Commerce Server Site Packager Unpack page.
4. Select Add An Application In The Package To An Existing Site.

   From there, you can follow the steps of the Commerce Server Site Packager Wizard to put the application on your site.

Adding a Noncommerce Application

You can add a noncommerce application to your site by completing the following steps:

1. Right-click the Applications folder.
2. Point to New.
3. Select Add Non-Commerce Application from the shortcut menu.

   Including a noncommerce application allows you to easily import the Web server log files into the site's Data Warehouse for analysis.

Deleting an Application

You can delete an application by right-clicking the desired application and selecting Delete from the shortcut menu.

Adding a Web Server

At times, your site may experience heavy traffic, requiring support from more than one Web server. To prepare for these times, put multiple Web servers in place within the Commerce Server site to support the system. To do this, follow these steps (more detail can be found in Chapter 6):

1. Unpack the appropriate .pup file for the site you're building by using the Commerce Server Site Packager's Custom Unpack option.
2. Select Add A Web Server To An Existing Application In An Existing Site.
3. Follow the rest of the steps to complete the installation.

Caution Adding a Web server to the application adds all of its Web pages (Hypertext Markup Language [HTML], Active Server Pages [ASP], and images) to the application. The server must already have IIS 5.0 (or later) and Commerce Server 2000 installed on it. If you attempt to unpack a .pup file that has already been installed, Commerce Server 2000 assumes that you are attempting to add a new server to the application.

Manually Adding and Configuring a Web Server You can add a new Web server without using the Site Packager tool. This can be done manually by properly configuring the target Web server, as discussed in Chapter 1, "Installing and Configuring Commerce Server 2000," in the section on manually installing Commerce Server 2000, and installing all the required Web pages. You can also use Microsoft Application Center 2000 to distribute the Web server content files and components.

Simply configuring the Web server properly, however, does not complete the task, because the MSCS_Admin database is not updated through this process. You must synchronize the values for the application to ensure that the Web server's configuration matches that of the other servers in the Web farm. You can do this as previously discussed in the "Application Properties" section of this chapter, or you can make use of a routine similar to the JoinWebFarm method, which can be found in the GLOBAL_SITECONFIG_LIB.ASP file in the Solution Sites folder. Essentially, this code processes the array of Web servers in the site and ensures that the appropriate values are all synchronized. If your site is a part of a Web farm, you can run code similar to this sample to properly configure the site as a part of the farm. This will help consolidate the data and the Web sites in the Commerce Server Administrative database, site database, and site Data Warehouse.

```
Sub JoinWebFarm(ByRef iWebServerCount)
 Dim mscsSiteCfg, mscsSync
 Dim sWebServerMachine, iCurrWebServer
 Dim arrWebServerMachines, arrWebServerNames, _
  arrWebServerInstances

 Set mscsSiteCfg = GetSiteConfigObject()
 sWebServerMachine = GetComputerName()

 arrWebServerMachines = mscsSiteCfg.MakeArrayFromString( _
  mscsSiteCfg(MSCSCommerceAppName).Value.Fields( _
  WEB_SERVER_MACHINE).Value)

 iWebServerCount = _
  mscsSiteCfg(MSCSCommerceAppName).Value.Fields( _
  WEB_SERVER_COUNT).Value
 ' Is the Web Server machine already in the Web farm?
 If Not IsEntityInArray(sWebServerMachine, _
  arrWebServerMachines) Then
    If iWebServerCount > 0 Then
     iCurrWebServer = _
      mscsSiteCfg(MSCSCommerceAppName).Value.Fields( _
      CURRENT_WEB_SERVER).Value + 1
     arrWebServerNames = mscsSiteCfg.MakeArrayFromString( _
      mscsSiteCfg(MSCSCommerceAppName).Value.Fields( _
      WEB_SERVER_NAME).Value)
     arrWebServerInstances = mscsSiteCfg.MakeArrayFromString( _
      mscsSiteCfg(MSCSCommerceAppName).Value.Fields( _
      WEB_SERVER_INSTANCE).Value)
    Else
     Const L_BAD_NUMBEROFSERVERS_PROPERTYVALUE_ERRORMESSAGE = _
      Found an improper number of servers."
     Err.Raise vbObjectError + 2100, _
      GetErrorSource("JoinWebFarm()"), _
      FormatOutput(L_TermDefinition_Text, _
      Array(L_Bad_NumberOfServers_PropertyValue_ErrorMessage, _
      iWebServerCount))
    End If
```

(continued)

(continued)

```
    ReDim Preserve arrWebServerMachines(iWebServerCount)

    ReDim Preserve arrWebServerNames(iWebServerCount)

    ReDim Preserve arrWebServerInstances(iWebServerCount)

    arrWebServerMachines(iWebServerCount) = sWebServerMachine

    arrWebServerNames(iWebServerCount) = arrWebServerNames(0)

    arrWebServerInstances(iWebServerCount) = _
     arrWebServerInstances(0)

    iWebServerCount = iWebServerCount + 1

    With mscsSiteCfg(MSCSCommerceAppName).Value

    .Fields(WEB_SERVER_MACHINE).Value = _
     mscsSiteCfg.MakeStringFromArray(arrWebServerMachines)

    .Fields(WEB_SERVER_NAME).Value = _
     mscsSiteCfg.MakeStringFromArray(arrWebServerNames)

    .Fields(WEB_SERVER_INSTANCE).Value = _
     mscsSiteCfg.MakeStringFromArray(arrWebServerInstances)

    .Fields(CURRENT_WEB_SERVER).Value = iCurrWebServer

    .Fields(WEB_SERVER_COUNT).Value = iWebServerCount

    End With

' Update Admin Data with information about

' the new webserver added to the WebFarm

    Call mscsSiteCfg.SaveConfig()
```

(continued)

(continued)

```
' Syncs up Datawarehouse related information like _
 ' LogFileDirectory,
' Directory index files and the logfile type etc
' so that the new webserver is in sync with the DataWarehousing
' for the Application.
   Set mscsSync = CreateObject("Commerce.PrivateDWMBToAdmin")
   Call mscsSync.Run(MSCSCommerceSiteName, MSCSCommerceAppName)
 End If
End Sub
```

Deleting a Web Server

You can delete a Web server from the site by right-clicking the desired server and selecting Delete from the shortcut menu.

Chapter 4

Business Desk

The Business Desk application was developed to provide a Web-based method to manage an e-commerce site. With it, a business manager and other privileged users can manage the site, its contents, and shoppers. In addition, Business Desk users can use the business analytics tools to analyze the performance of a site and make improvements. Because the Business Desk is a Web-based application, the business manager does not need physical access to the Web server. Instead, the Business Desk can be accessed remotely.

Business Desk Web Site

If you build a Microsoft Commerce Server 2000 site based on any of the Solution Sites, you can also build the site's supporting Business Desk by adding the Business Desk application in the Select Applications page of the Solution Site installation, as shown in Figure 4-1.

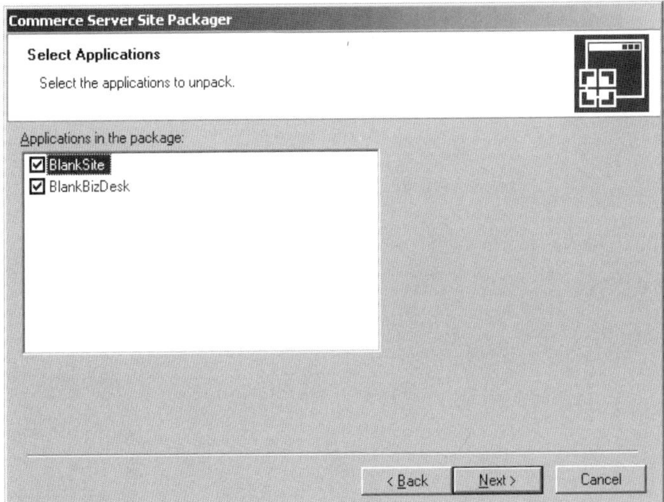

Figure 4-1. *You can create the Business Desk application Web site when you're installing the site from the .pup file.*

Once the Business Desk Web site is created, you can configure it to make it secure against unauthorized users. Out of the box, the site is configured to force users to authenticate in the local domain of the Web server through Integrated Windows Security. This means that the user must have Microsoft Internet Explorer to access the site, and Internet Explorer 5.5 or later is required to run Business Desk.

Installing Business Desk

To install the Business Desk application, the client browser must be configured to allow the installation of Microsoft ActiveX components. In Internet Explorer 5.5, complete the following steps:

1. From the Tools menu, select Internet Options.
2. Click the Security tab and then click Custom Level.
3. In the Security Settings dialog box, you can configure the Download Signed ActiveX Controls security setting (see Figure 4-2) to allow the installation of Signed ActiveX Controls. This allows the creation of the .hta file, and the office Web components are installed on the server.

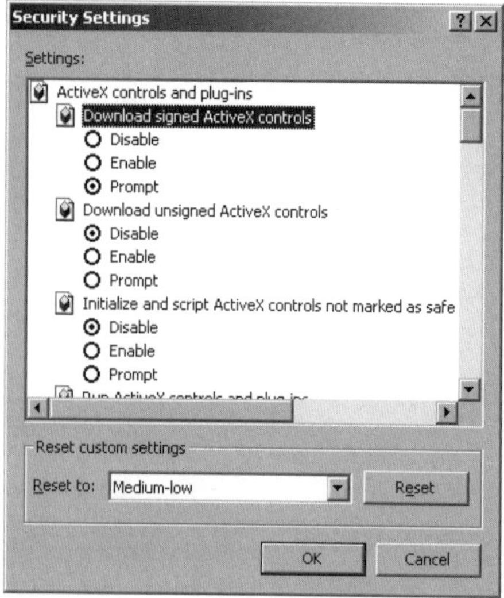

Figure 4-2. *The Internet Explorer Security Settings dialog box allows you to download ActiveX components.*

If the security settings are not properly configured, you get a message like the one shown in Figure 4-3.

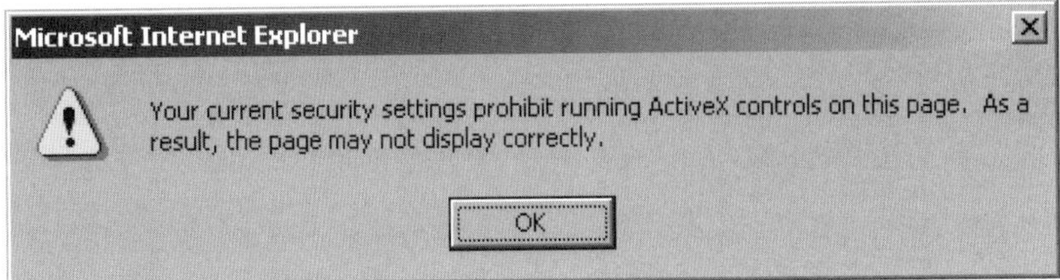

Figure 4-3. *If you're unable to install the Business Desk application, you'll get an error message similar to this one.*

Once the Business Desk Web site is created, you can install the Business Desk application on your machine simply by accessing the Business Desk site, such as *http://www.mysite.com/bizdesk/*. This automatically takes you through the Business Desk installation process, which ensures that the client machine has the required office Web components. If it does not, those components are installed on the client machine. In addition, the Business Desk HTML Application will be installed on the client machine. The default location for this application is the \Program Files\Microsoft Commerce Server directory, but you can choose to install it to another directory (see Figure 4-4).

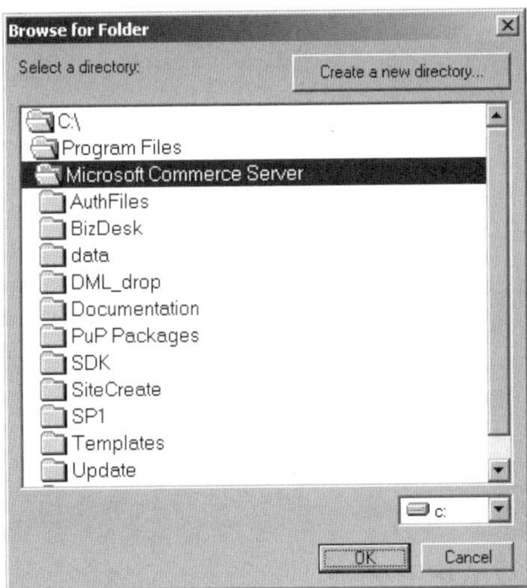

Figure 4-4. *You can define where the HTML Application (.hta) file is installed.*

The end result of the of the Business Desk installation is the creation of the Business Desk HTML Application on the client machine and creation of an .hta file locally on the user's computer. An HTML Application is a file that automatically configures Internet Explorer to load a given URL, and is typically displayed without an address bar, toolbar, and menus. An example of this file is represented in the following code:

```
<HTML>
<HEAD>
 <TITLE>Business Desk: Retail-LOCALHOST:80 -
     Microsoft Commerce Server</TITLE>
 <HTA:APPLICATION ID="Retail_LOCALHOST_80"
 APPLICATIONNAME="Retail_LOCALHOST_80"
 BORDER='thick'
 CAPTION='yes'
 ICON="Retail LOCALHOST 80.ico"
 SHOWINTASKBAR='yes'
 SINGLEINSTANCE='yes'
 SYSMENU='yes'
 WINDOWSTATE='maximize'
 VERSION='1.0'
 >
<SCRIPT LANGUAGE=VBScript>
<!--
'~~~~~~~~~~~~~~~~~~~~~~~~~~~~~~~~~~~~~~~~~~~~~~~~~~~~~~~~~~~~~~~~~~~~~~~~~~~~
'BizDesk Framework: context menu handler to turn off context menus
sub document_onContextMenu()
  ' -- disallow default context menu unless in entry fields
  if not (window.event.srcElement.tagName = "INPUT" or _
   window.event.srcElement.tagName = "TEXTAREA") then
        window.event.returnValue = false
  end if
end sub
'~~~~~~~~~~~~~~~~~~~~~~~~~~~~~~~~~~~~~~~~~~~~~~~~~~~~~~~~~~~~~~~~~~~~~~~~~~~~
```

(continued)

(continued)

```
' BizDesk Framework: key down handler to turn off keys
sub document_onKeyDown()
  window.event.returnValue = false
end sub
'-->
</SCRIPT>
</HEAD>
<FRAMESET>
   <FRAME SRC='http://localhost:80/retailbizdesk/bizdesk.asp'
   SCROLLING='no' APPLICATION='yes'
   STYLE='HEIGHT: 100%; WIDTH: 100%; BORDER: none'
   BORDER='0' FRAMEBORDER='0' FRAMESPACING='0'>
  <H3><FONT color='red'>Business Desk requires _
   Internet Explorer v5.5 or greater with frames enabled.</FONT>
  </H3>
  </FRAME>
</FRAMESET>
</HTML>
```

Business Desk System Requirements

As mentioned previously, to run the Business Desk, the user must be running Internet Explorer 5.5 or later because the Business Desk takes advantage of Dynamic HTML (DHTML) behaviors that were introduced in Internet Explorer 5.5.

Hardware Requirements

A system must meet the following hardware requirements to run Business Desk:

- 266 MHz or faster Pentium-compatible central processing unit (CPU)
- 5 MB of free hard disk space
- CD-ROM or DVD-ROM drive
- VGA or higher resolution monitor set to 800 × 600 pixel resolution or higher
- Microsoft Mouse or compatible pointing device

Uninstalling Business Desk

You can uninstall the Business Desk from your machine at any point by completing the following steps:

1. From the Add/Remove Programs application in Windows, click Start.
2. Select Settings.
3. Select Control Panel to open the Control Panel folder.
4. Double-click the Change or Remove Programs icon to launch the application (see Figure 4-5).
5. Click the Business Desk that you want to uninstall.
6. Click Change/Remove. This immediately uninstalls the Business Desk application (.hta file) and all associated icons from your system.

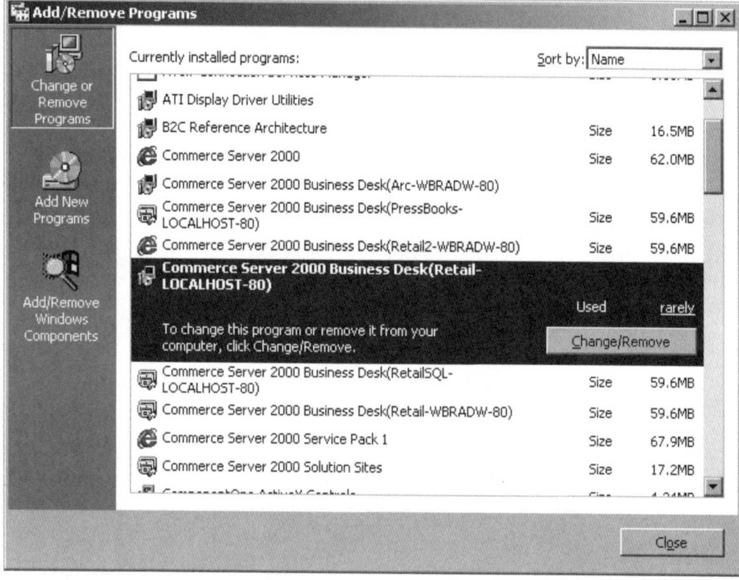

Figure 4-5. *Uninstall the Business Desk application using Add/Remove Programs.*

Business Desk Organization

The Business Desk is composed of a set of modules, made up of both Extensible Markup Language (XML) files and Active Server Pages (ASP). Each module provides organization, dividing the Business Desk functionality into five categories. The modules are described in the following sections.

Analysis

The Analysis module is used to create and view reports about user activity on your site. It includes the following features:

- **Reports** This feature is a list of reports available to be run using the data in the site's data warehouse. These are covered in more detail in Chapter 5, "Business Analytics."
- **Completed Reports** The Completed Reports page enables you to view the results of a report that you have run.
- **Segment Viewer** With the Segment Viewer you can identify usage trends and make marketing decisions based on similarities among users.

Campaigns

The Campaigns module is used to create and manage marketing campaigns, including discount campaigns, advertising campaigns, and direct mail campaigns for the site. It includes the following features:

- **Campaign Manager** In the Campaign Manager you can manage customers, campaigns, and the particular items that make up those campaigns, such as advertising, discount, and direct mail campaigns.
- **List Manager** This feature is used to manage, import, or export lists of users that can be used as a source of recipients for a direct mail campaign. These lists are typically created by running a static report in the Business Analytics section of the Business Desk.
- **Campaign Expressions** You use Campaign Expressions for targeting an ad or discount to groups of users.
- **Target Group** A Target Group is a list of users that have been grouped together based on user activity (for example, items purchased).
- **Reference Tables** You use the Reference Tables module to set the size of the content that is displayed on your site, to manage the names of Page Groups, and to establish industry codes so that you can prevent two ads from the same industry from showing up on the same page at the same time.
- **Publish Campaigns** The Publish Campaigns module lets you immediately update your site with the information that you have just added to your Web site.

Catalog

The Catalogs module is used to manage catalogs in the site. It includes the following features:

- **Catalog Designer** This feature is used to design the catalogs, defining the categories, types of products, and the properties of those products that will be found within the site's catalogs.

- **Catalog Editor** You can use the Catalog Editor module to view, find, and delete existing products, categories, catalogs, and catalog sets. You can also import catalogs from either XML or CSV (comma-separated value) files.
- **Catalog Sets** A catalog set is a group of one or more catalogs that you make available to different users or organizations.

Orders

The Orders module is used to provide support to the order process. Its features include the following:

- **Basket Manager** You can use the Basket Manager to delete baskets that users have abandoned.
- **Data Codes** You use the Data Codes module to add codes that will appear on the Web site and help you track orders placed by users.
- **Order Status** Order Status codes are assigned to orders so that you can find them in the order process. By default, Commerce Server has three codes: 4 (New Order), 2 (Saved Order), and 1 (Basket).
- **Shipping Methods** Used to create and modify shipping methods that are used in the default shipping components that ship with Commerce Server 2000. To create or modify shipping methods, you'll use the following process:

  1. Open Business Desk.
  2. Open the Orders section in the left navigation panel.
  3. Click the Shipping Methods link to load the Shipping Methods summary page (see Figure 4-6).
  4. Click the New Shipping Method toolbar button, and select the new shipping method that you'll be creating from the list of Charge By Weight, Charge By Quantity, or Charge By Subtotal. If you're modifying an existing shipping method, select it in the list and click the Open Shipping Method toolbar button. This loads the Shipping Method editing page (see Figure 4-7). Each page will look a little different, depending on whether you're charging by weight, quantity, or value.
  5. Provide a name for the shipping method.
  6. Specify that the shipping method is enabled so that it will be available for use on the site.
  7. In the Rates section of the page, enter the applicable rates by first clicking New.
  8. In the left text box, provide a number for the weight, quantity, or value that will be used to select this rate.
  9. In the right text box, provide the rate for shipping items up to the specified weight, quantity, or value.
  10. Click Accept to store the shipping rate.

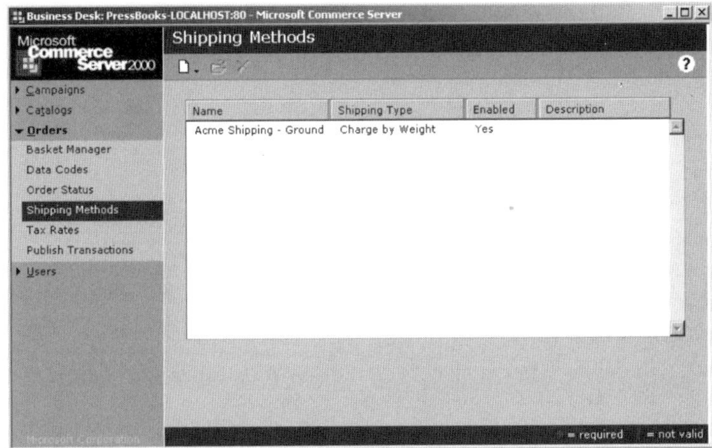

Figure 4-6. *You can access the shipping methods from the Shipping Method summary page. From here, you can create new methods or modify the existing methods.*

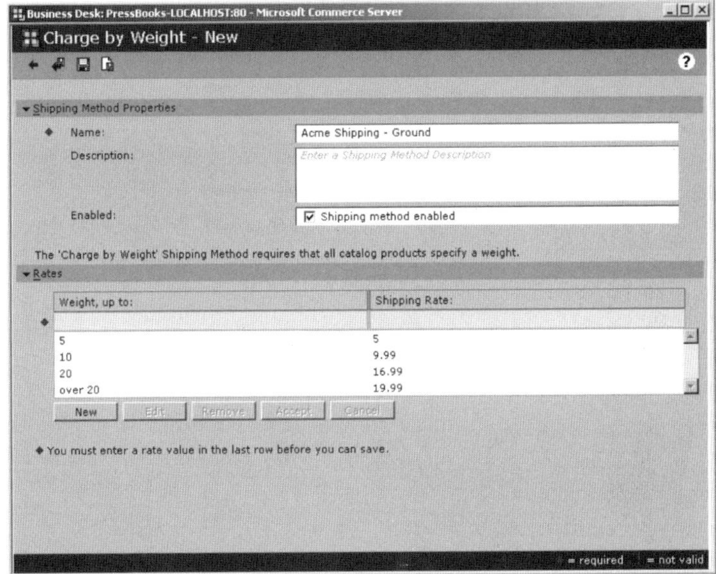

Figure 4-7. *You specify the shipping method information and the rates that will be charged when this method is selected by the shopper.*

11. Add more weight, quantity, or value "up to" entries as needed.
12. When you are finished, ensure that a value is provided for the Over *X* entry, where *X* is the maximum number you've already specified. This entry will hold the shipping rate for any purchases that exceed the weight, quantity, or values that you've already provided.
13. Click Save on the toolbar to save these shipping methods.

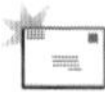

Note Although you can use the default shipping component provided with Commerce Server 2000, you might want to look into purchasing a third-party product to handle these calculations. In addition, you might find that your shipping company of choice provides components that integrate with Commerce Server 2000 automatically and handle many of the tasks that have just been outlined.

- **Tax Rates** The Tax Rates module lets you add tax rates for different countries or regions and states or provinces. This information is used as the basis for determining tax information for the simple tax components shipped with Commerce Server 2000. You enter tax rates into the system using the following process:

1. Open the Business Desk Application.
2. Open the Orders section in the left navigation panel.
3. Click the Taxes link to load the Tax Rate page (see Figure 4-8).

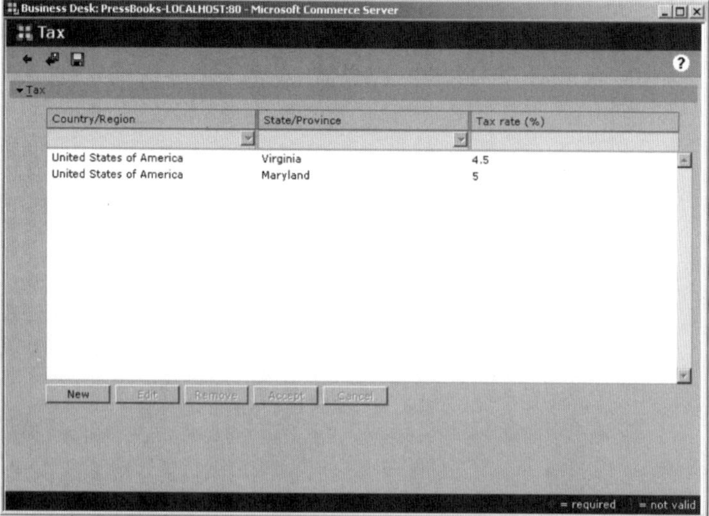

Figure 4-8. *You can enter new or modify existing tax rates for the simple tax component in Commerce Server 2000 through the Business Desk.*

4. Click New to start entering a new tax rate. Select an existing entry and click Edit to modify an existing tax rate.
5. In the Country/Region drop-down menu, select the country or region for this tax rate.
6. In the State/Province drop-down menu, select the state or province for this tax rate.
7. In the Tax Rate (%) text box, enter the tax rate as a percentage. In this case, entering **5** provides a 5 percent tax on sales made to customers in the identified region.
8. Click Accept to accept the tax rate.
9. Click Save on the toolbar to save the tax rates as they appear on this page.

Note The simple tax component that is shipped with Commerce Server 2000 should not be used for your public store. You should purchase a third-party component package to handle your tax calculations.

- **Publish Transactions** The Publish Transactions module lets you immediately update your site with the information that you have just added to your Web site.

Users

The Users module is used to manage the collection of user data on your Web site. You can define what data is collected and what data is exported to the Data Warehouse. You also use the Users module to manage user and organization profiles. Its features include the following:

- **Users** You use the Users module to enter and manage information about guest and registered users who visit your site.
- **Organizations** The Organizations module is used to add organizations to your site and specify information about them. Using this module, you can group your shoppers based on corporate organization membership and then determine what will be displayed to them based on that organization.
- **Profile Designer** The Profile Designer module is used to edit and manage profile definitions. Profiles are used to define how some standard elements, such as users, organizations, and addresses, are defined in the site. A profile lists the types of properties that each of these elements will contain.
- **Site Terms Editor** The Site Terms Editor module is used to edit and manage site terms. These site terms can be used as lookup information for drop-down boxes so that you can ensure that your shoppers will select the proper entries. For instance, you might have a site term for User Sex, where users can identify if they are male or female. If this was left for users to enter on their own, they might enter M, F, Male, Female, or something else entirely

different and inaccurate. Instead, you can define a site term for User Sex that has display text of Male or Female with values of M and F, respectively, to ensure that only those options are provided.

- **Publish Profiles** The Publish Profiles module is used to publish profile definition changes to your Web site before you can add data to new profile properties.

Business Desk Pages

The Business Desk Web site is made up of a combination of XML and ASP pages, as described in the following sections.

XML Pages

The various modules and the available actions within each module are defined within a set of XML documents known as the *master configuration file* and the *module configuration file.*

Master Configuration File

The BIZDESK.XML file is the master Business Desk configuration file. Shown in the following code, it contains the XML tags that define which modules will be available and shown in the Business Desk.

```
<?xml version = '1.0' encoding='windows-1252' ?>
<config xmlns="x-schema:bdconfig-schema.xml">
<categories>
   <category id="analysis">
      <name>Anal&lt;U&gt;y&lt;/U&gt;sis</name>
      <key>y</key>
      <tooltip>Design, Run, and View Analysis Reports</tooltip>
   </category>
   <category id="campaigns">
      <name>&lt;U&gt;C&lt;/U&gt;ampaigns</name>
      <key>c</key>
      <tooltip>Manage Campaigns</tooltip>
   </category>
   <category id="catalogs">
      <name>Ca&lt;U&gt;t&lt;/U&gt;alogs</name>
      <key>t</key>
```

(continued)

(continued)

```
      <tooltip>Design and Edit Your Catalogs</tooltip>
   </category>
   <category id="orders">
      <name>&lt;U&gt;O&lt;/U&gt;rders</name>
      <key>o</key>
      <tooltip>Manage Orders</tooltip>
   </category>
   <category id="users">
      <name>&lt;U&gt;U&lt;/U&gt;sers</name>
      <key>u</key>
      <tooltip>Manage Users and Organizations</tooltip>
   </category>
   <category id="framework">
      <name>do not delete</name>
      <key>|</key>
      <tooltip>do not delete - used by framework</tooltip>
   </category>
</categories>
<moduleconfigs>
   <moduleconfig id="analysis.xml" category="analysis"/>
   <moduleconfig id="marketing_cmanager.xml _
    category="campaigns"/>
   <moduleconfig id="catalogs_designer.xml"category="catalogs"/>
   <moduleconfig id="catalogs_editor.xml" category="catalogs"/>
   <moduleconfig id="catalog_sets.xml" category="catalogs"/>
   <moduleconfig id="basketcare.xml" category="orders"/>
   <moduleconfig id="baskets.xml" category="orders"/>
   <moduleconfig id="application.xml" category="orders"/>
   <moduleconfig id="orders.xml" category="orders"/>
   <moduleconfig id="shipping_methods.xml" category="orders"/>
   <moduleconfig id="tax.xml" category="orders"/>
```

(continued)

(continued)

```
    <moduleconfig id="refreshcache.xml" category="orders"/>
    <moduleconfig id="users.xml" category="users"/>
    <moduleconfig id="organizations.xml" category="users"/>
    <moduleconfig id="profiles.xml" category="users"/>
    <moduleconfig id="bdmaster.xml" category="framework"/>
</moduleconfigs>
</config>
```

Master Configuration File Tags

The master configuration file tags are described as follows:

- **Config** The root of the master module configuration file.
- **Categories** Contains all of the category tags within the master module configuration file.
- **Category** Contains the information that describes each Business Desk module. These modules, by default, are Analysis, Campaigns, Catalogs, Orders, and Users. Each of these modules contains the tags shown in Table 4-1, which define each submodule.

Table 4-1. Child Elements of the Category Tag

Tag	Description
Name	The name of the module, as it will appear in the left-hand navigation bar of the Business Desk
Key	The key used for accessibility in the Business Desk
Tooltip	A description used to provide help to users of the Business Desk

- **Moduleconfigs** Contains the moduleconfig tags that define each of the modules that are a part of the Business Desk.
- **Moduleconfig** Specifies each module XML file that is a part of the Business Desk. The moduleconfig tag contains the attributes listed in Table 4-2.

Table 4-2. Moduleconfig Attributes

Attribute	Description
Id	The name of the XML file that contains the module configuration data
Category	The category under which this module should appear in the navigation panel

Module Configuration File

The Business Desk includes a number of module configuration files, as shown in the following code:

```
<?xml version = '1.0' encoding='windows-1252' ?>

<config xmlns="x-schema:bdmodule-schema.xml">

<actions>
   <action id='orders/orderstatus_list.asp'

       helptopic='cs_ft_orders_EXTN.htm'>

       <name>Order Status</name>

       <tooltip>View Order Status</tooltip>

       <tasks>

       <task icon='taskopen.gif' id='open'>

          <postto action='orders/orderstatus_view.asp'

          formname='selectform' />

          <name>&lt;U&gt;O&lt;/U&gt;pen</name>

          <key>o</key>

          <tooltip>Open Order</tooltip>

       </task>

       <task icon='taskdelete.gif' id='delete'>

          <postto action='orders/orderstatus_list.asp'

          formname='delform' />

          <name>&lt;U&gt;d&lt;/U&gt;elete</name>

          <key>d</key>

          <tooltip>Delete Order</tooltip>

       </task>

       <task icon='taskfind.gif' id='find'>

          <goto action='orders/orderstatus_list.asp'/>

          <name>&lt;U&gt;F&lt;/U&gt;ind</name>

          <key>f</key>

          <tooltip>Find Orders</tooltip>

       </task>

       </tasks>

   </action>
```

(continued)

(continued)

```
    <action id='orders/orderstatus_view.asp'
        helptopic='cs_ft_orders_EXTN.htm'>
        <name>Order Properties</name>
        <tooltip>View Order Properties</tooltip>
        <tasks>
        <task icon='taskback.gif' id='back'>
            <goto action='orders/orderstatus_list.asp' />
            <name>&lt;U&gt;B&lt;/U&gt;ack</name>
            <key>b</key>
            <tooltip>Back to Order Status List</tooltip>
        </task>
        </tasks>
    </action>
</actions>
<modules>
    <module id='orders/orderstatus_list.asp'>
        <name>Order Status</name>
        <tooltip>View Order Status</tooltip>
    </module>
</modules>
</config>
```

Module Configuration File Tags

The module configuration files tags used in the previous code are described as follows:

- **Config** The root of the module configuration XML document
- **Actions** Contains all of the action elements that define the actions available to this module
- **Action** Contains data that defines how the available actions will function in the module's pages, as listed in Tables 4-3 and 4-4

Table 4-3. Action Tag Attributes

Attribute	Description
Helptopic	Name of the help file that corresponds to this action
Id	The relative Uniform Resource Locator (URL) for the page where this action takes place

Table 4-4. Child Elements in the Action Tag

Tag	Description
Name	Name of the action that will be taken
Tooltip	Description of the action that will be taken
Tasks	Contains the task elements that define the tasks for this action

- **Tasks** Contains all of the existing task elements in this action
- **Task** Contains information about the tasks that will be contained in the toolbar of each page in the module, as shown in Tables 4-5 and 4-6

Table 4-5. Task Tag Attributes

Attribute	Description
Icon	The relative path to the icon that will be displayed on the toolbar.
Id	Identifies the task. Using certain IDs results in special actions in the Business Desk, such as: • **Back** Automatically reenabled when a task is executed • **Find** Toggles the display of the Find pane on the page • **Save, Saveback, Savenew** Enabled or disabled automatically by the Business Desk if the appropriate event handlers are configured properly on the sheet

Table 4-6. Task Tags

Tag	Description
Goto	Contains the URL of the page to which users are sent when they click on this toolbar button. The URL is specified in the action attribute of this element.
Postto	Contains the URL of the page to which users are sent when they click on this toolbar button. It also specifies the form that is submitted to that URL. The URL is specified in the action attribute. The form name is specified in the formname attribute.
Name	The name of this task.
Key	The key used for accessibility in the Business Desk.
Tooltip	A description used to provide help to users for this task.

- **Modules** Contains a list of module elements
- **Module** Contains information about each module that appears in each category of the Business Desk, as listed in Tables 4-7 and 4-8.

Table 4-7. Module Tag Attribute

Attribute	Description
Id	The name and relative path to the ASP page that contains the code for this module

Table 4-8. Child Elements of the Module Tags

Tag	Description
Name	The name of this module, as it should appear in the navigation panel of the Business Desk
Tooltip	The tooltip description that appears over the navigation link

ASP Pages

There are a number of ASP pages that provide the basic framework of the Business Desk Web site. In the following sections, we examine a few of the more prominent pages.

GLOBAL.ASA

The GLOBAL.ASA file is used to initialize a number of variables and objects that are used throughout the Business Desk. Some of the more interesting variables are those that are used to set the mode in which the Business Desk is running. Some of these are covered in more detail in the section entitled "Debugging the Business Desk," later in this chapter.

DEFAULT.ASP

The DEFAULT.ASP page is used to initialize and install the Business Desk components and application on the client machine.

BIZDESK.ASP

The BIZDESK.ASP page provides the basic framework of the Business Desk. It sets the frames that are used for the various portions of the application. In addition, it includes the VBScript routines that provide the functionality for many of the pages and the toolbars on each page.

Tip If you are working with the Business Desk in development mode, you can open the Business Desk in the browser by navigating to the BIZDESK.ASP page.

Debugging Business Desk Pages

From time to time, you may need to debug the activities in the Business Desk. By default, the Business Desk is set up to trap all errors and only show basic error messages. Unfortunately, this can make identifying the cause of an error difficult. You can run the Business Desk in *development mode* to perform more extensive debugging by setting the MSCSEnv variable in the GLOBAL.ASA file to Development, rather than Production. This variable is used throughout the Business Desk code to detemerine actions that should be taken. It also affects how a set of variables that define the behavior of the Business Desk are set. These variables include the following:

- **Verbose_Output** Specifies that verbose output will be provided when loading Business Desk objects.

- **Show_Object_Errors** Any errors that occur while loading Business Desk objects will be shown in a separate window. This is extremely useful when attempting to determine what objects are not being properly initialized.
- **Auto_Redirect_Enabled** Forces all pages to be run within the Business Desk.
- **Force_HTA_Only** Raises an error if the Business Desk is not run from the .hta file.
- **Allow_Context_Menus** Allows right-click shortcut menus in the site.
- **Show_Debug_Text** Shows debug text in the status bar of the browser.

Setting the MSCSEnv value to Development will have an impact on how error handling is handled on each page. Typically, a page might include the following code:

```
If Application("MSCSEnv") = 1 Then

        On Error Resume Next

End If
```

When the Business Desk is in *production mode*, errors are trapped and do not cause the Business Desk to break. When in development mode, errors are not trapped. Instead, processing ends when the error occurs, and you are better able to debug the problems.

Tip You'll find that not all On Error Resume Next statements are surrounded by a check of the MSCSEnv variable. When you're debugging a problem but don't see the error being raised through the browser, you might want to check each ASP page you're working with to ensure that the On Error Resume Next statements are not being called.

Event Log

Whenever you're attempting to debug a problem in the Business Desk, you should also be sure to check the application event log on the system. A number of errors generated by the various Commerce Server 2000 objects are reported in the event log, and this information can help you to narrow down the possibilities for the cause of the problem.

Securing the Business Desk

When you set up the Business Desk, you should ensure that the site is secure and cannot be accessed by unauthorized users. The first step in doing this is to ensure that anonymous access is disabled and that only Integrated Windows Authentication is allowed to the Business Desk Web site. You do this through Internet Information Services (IIS) Manager by selecting the site and directory and modifying the Directory Security settings, as shown in Figure 4-9.

You'll then need to define the user accounts that are authorized to access the Business Desk. You should make sure the Internet Guest account does not have access to the site. By default, users in the local Administrators group have full access. Users in the Everyone group also have access to the site, but you should remove these users and specifically define the users that are granted access.

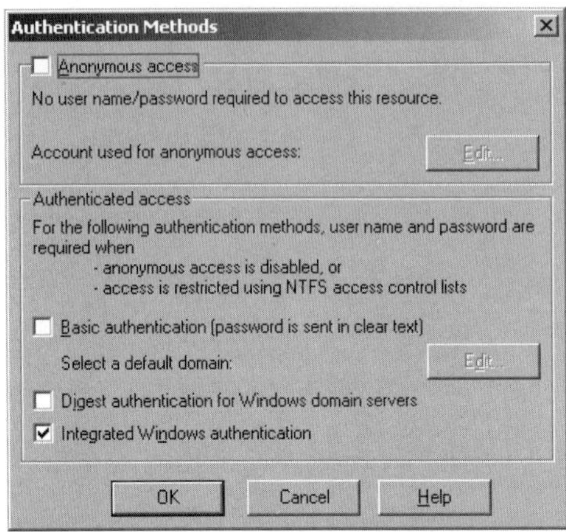

Figure 4-9. *You can secure the Business Desk by ensuring that the site requires Integrated Windows Authentication in the Authentication Methods dialog box.*

BizDesk Security Object

In addition to securing the Business Desk through file permissions on the pages, you can also control whether the current user has access rights to any given page.

Tip This is particularly useful when displaying menu selections on a page. You don't want to show menu selections for pages that a user doesn't have access to.

Commerce Server 2000 provides the BizDeskSecurity object that identifies whether the user can access a page. The object is declared as a global object in GLOBAL.ASA, with the following code:

```
<OBJECT RUNAT=Server SCOPE=Application
ID=g_MSCSBizDeskBizDeskSecurity
PROGID="Commerce.BizDeskBizDeskSecurity">
</OBJECT>
```

The object has a single method, CanUserAccess(). By providing a page to the method, the method returns a Boolean response that identifies whether the user can access the identified page, as shown in this example:

```
If g_MSCSBizDeskBizDeskSecurity.CanUserAccess( _
 "CatalogEditor.asp") Then

   'display the link

End If
```

Chapter 5

Business Analytics

Microsoft Commerce Server 2000 provides a set of tools that allow business and site managers to analyze the performance of a site. Using business analytics, you can identify usage patterns on the site, sales on the site, and more. With this information, you can determine which areas of your site are the most popular and most accessed, and you can determine those areas that need the greatest improvement. When you are running an e-commerce site, you should make the purchase process as simple and usable as possible. The business analytics tools are extremely helpful in this regard.

Using Business Analytics

The bulk of the business analytics functions are accessible via the Business Desk, within the Analysis section. You can use the Reports module to view dynamically generated reports generated in real time, so that each view you have is based on the most recent data. You can also generate new static reports. These reports are built, maintained, and available for viewing at any time. Each view includes the data as of when the last report was generated. Finally, you can also view data segments to perform data mining and better analyze the patterns in the site's data.

Note Prior to generating any of the Analysis reports, you must first import the required data into the site's Data Warehouse.

Data Warehouse

If you have installed the Data Warehouse resource for your site, a database is created with your site's name and suffixed with a _dw. This serves as the physical store of data in your Data Warehouse. In addition, an Online Analytical Processing (OLAP) database will be created to store the cubes that can be used for analysis of the data.

Data Warehouse Classes

When the data is imported from the commerce database to the Data Warehouse, it is organized into a logical schema. This represents the data in a more understandable manner, so that developers can query the data without understanding the intricacies of the underlying physical structure.

Campaign Classes

The campaign classes are designed to maintain information about the campaigns that are used within the Commerce Server 2000 application. Using these classes, listed in Table 5-1, you can report on how campaigns are being utilized and performing.

Table 5-1. Campaign Classes

Class	Description
AdItem	Data about scheduled advertising on the site
Campaign	Data about the various campaigns on the site
CampaignEvent	Stores event information for marketing campaigns
CampaignItem	Data describing each item in the campaign
CampaignItemTypes	Data representing categories for custom Web page content associated with campaigns
Creative	Data describing how the campaign content is to be displayed
CreativeSize	Data representing size of custom content on the Web page
CreativeType	Data that is used to categorize type of content for the Web
CreativeTypeXRef	Data that relates custom content as a part of a campaign with the type of of content
Customer	Data that represents the customer who is using or viewing the campaign
DMItem	Data about Direct Mail campaign items
EventType	Data used to categorize campaign-related events
IndustryCode	Data that categorizes the industry of a customer or campaign item
OrderDiscount	Data about discount campaigns
PageGroup	Data representing groups of custom content used on Web pages in a campaign
PageGroupXRef	Data linking custom content with the page group that can contain the content
Target	Data about target users who should receive custom content or campaigns
TargetGroup	Data defining groups of targets that should receive custom content or campaigns
TargetGroupXRef	Data that links a target group and the related custom content

Catalog Classes

The catalog classes, described in Table 5-2, are used to organize catalog information for analysis in the Data Warehouse. By including this data in the Data Warehouse, you can perform more explicit analyses based on the properties and products within the catalog.

Table 5-2. Catalog Classes

Class	Description
CatalogGlobal	Data that contains all catalogs on the site
Category	Data that describes the categories within a catalog
CatHierarchy	Data that describes the level of hierarchy in the catalog
Products	Data that contains all of the products from the catalog

Profile Management Classes

The profile management classes, listed in Table 5-3, are used to maintain user information to be analyzed.

Table 5-3. Profile Management Classes

Class	Description
Address	User and organization address data
RegisteredUser	Data on both anonymous and registered users on the site

Transaction Classes

The transaction classes, described in Table 5-4, hold the data that represent an online transaction on the site. These include purchases being made through the use of the shopping baskets, as users add and remove items from the basket or through a purchase order.

Table 5-4. Transaction Classes

Class	Description
Basket	Data about products that are added and removed from a user's basket
Order	Data about orders that are submitted or saved in the system
OrderFormHeader	Data from the OrderForm header for each order
OrderFormLineItems	Data from the OrderForm line items for each order
OrderGroup	Data that describes purchase order information
OrderGroupAddresses	Mailing and shipping address data for purchase orders

Web Log Classes

The Web log classes, listed in Table 5-5, are used to organize the data imported from the Web Server logs.

Table 5-5. Web Log Classes

Class	Description
HitsInfo	Data about the hits your site receives
HostnameRef	Data relating a host name with an Internet Protocol (IP) address
HTTPStatus	Hypertext Transfer Protocol (HTTP) status codes
ImportOptions	Options that define how the Web log import is performed
IPRef	Data concerning IP references and lookups
LevelNDir	Hierarchy of directories in the site. *N* can be a value from 1 to 6.
LogUser	Data about how the user accesses and uses the site
OpenUserVisit	Data about user visits that were open when the data was imported
Referrer	Data containing Uniform Resource Locators (URLs) that referred users to this site
ReferrerDomain	Data containing the domain of a referrer
Request	Data about requests that are made to the site
TaskHistory	Data tracking the history of Data Transformation Service (DTS) tasks on the site
URI	Contains Uniform Resource Identifiers (URIs) to identify URLs and queries
URIQuery	Data containing a URI query that is associated with a transaction request
UserAgent	Data about a user's browser and operating system
Visit	Data detailing a user's visit to the site
VisitInfo	Data describing a completed visit to the site
Win32Status	Win32 status codes

Web Topology Classes

The Web topology classes, described in Table 5-6, contain information about the organization and layout of your Web site.

Table 5-6. Web Topology Classes

Class	Description
Crawler	Data about a Web crawler on the site
MVQStringName	Data containing names for custom multivalue query strings
ServerBinding	Data linking the virtual server and its server
ServerGroup	Data representing server groups

(continued)

Table 5-6. *(continued)*

Class	Description
Site	Data detailing the Commerce Server 2000 site
SiteSummary	Data summarizing the site
SiteURL	Data containing the URL-based connections between the site and the virtual servers
SVQStringName	Data containing names for custom single-value query strings
VirtualServer	Data about virtual servers on the site

Other Classes

There are additional classes that are not detailed as a part of the previous categories, as listed in Table 5-7. These are sometimes used in multiple categories, in supporting tasks and calculations in the Data Warehouse, or as summaries of other data.

Table 5-7. Other Classes

Class	Description
CampaignEventsByDateAndUser	Data summarizing event data, grouped by date and user
CommerceEvent	Data linking commerce events and Data Warehouse classes that use the events
Date	Data representing dates and times
FirstURIByDate	Data summarizing the first URI in each visit, grouped by date
HitsByHour	Data summarizing hit information, grouped by hour
LastURIByDate	Data summarizing the last URI in each visit, grouped by date
LinkMVQStringName	Data linking a SiteURL to an MVQStringName
LinkSVQStringName	Data linking a SiteURL to an SVQStringName
RequestByDateByURIByQueryString	Data summarizing request information, grouped by date, URI, and query string
UniqueUserKeyByDate	Data summarizing user information, grouped by date

OLAP Cubes

To support data analysis, Commerce Server 2000 creates OLAP cubes within SQL Analysis Services. These cubes can be accessed directly to retrieve the data and perform queries and analysis. Each cube is defined by a set of dimensions and measures. The dimensions are the attributes that describe the data being collected and put into the cube. The measures are the values being reported on, whether a total, average, or some other calculated value. Each cube is built based on a number of source tables, and the resulting cube data is stored in the identified fact table. The cubes that are built by Commerce Server 2000 are listed in the following sections.

Bandwidth Cube

Table 5-8 displays the attributes of the Bandwidth cube.

Table 5-8. Bandwidth Cube Attributes

Cube Attribute	Values
Dimensions	DateHour Day of Week Hour of Day Site SiteUnfiltered
Measures	Hits Count Total Bytes Received Total Bytes Sent
Calculated measures	Bandwidth
Source tables	DateDimensionView Site SiteDimensionView
Fact table	HitsByHour

Basket Events Cube

Table 5-9 lists the attributes of the Basket Events cube.

Table 5-9. Basket Events Cube Attributes

Cube Attribute	Values
Dimensions	DateHour Events Products Site SiteUnfiltered UserType RegisteredUser
Measures	Events
Calculated measures	None
Source tables	DateDimensionView EventsDimensionView Products RegisteredUserDimensionView Site SiteDimensionView UserType
Fact table	Basket

Buyer Visits Cube

The attributes of the Buyer Visits cube are displayed in Table 5-10.

Table 5-10. Buyer Visits Cube Attributes

Cube Attribute	Values
Dimensions	BuyerType Site SiteUnfiltered UserType
Measures	Count Sales Total Sales User Count Visit Count
Calculated measures	Avg Visits Pct Users Visits Per Buy
Source tables	Site SiteDimensionsView
Fact table	UserBrowsingtoPurchaseFactView

Campaign Cube

The attributes of the Campaign cube are listed in Table 5-11.

Table 5-11. Campaign Cube Attributes

Cube Attribute	Values
Dimensions	Advertiser DateHour Events Page Group Site UserType URI Campaign
Measures	Count Events
Calculated measures	None
Source tables	Campaign CampaignItemDimensionView Customer DateDimensionView EventsDimensionView SiteDimensionsView PageGroupDimensionView RequestsByURI UserType
Fact table	CampaignEvent

Entry Pages Cube

The Entry Pages cube attributes are displayed in Table 5-12.

Table 5-12. Entry Pages Cube Attributes

Cube Attribute	Values
Dimensions	Date Site URI
Measures	Visit Count
Calculated measures	Pct Visits
Source tables	DateDimensionView RequestsByURI SiteDimensionView
Fact table	FirstURIByDate

Exit Pages Cube

Table 5-13 describes the attributes of the Exit Pages cube.

Table 5-13. Exit Pages Cube Attributes

Cube Attribute	Values
Dimensions	Date Site URI
Measures	Visit Count
Calculated measures	Pct Visits
Source tables	DateDimensionView RequestsByURI Site SiteDimensionView
Fact table	LastURIByDate

OrderEvents Cube

The attributes of the OrderEvents cube are given in Table 5-14.

Table 5-14. OrderEvents Cube Attributes

Cube Attribute	Values
Dimensions	DateHour Day of Week Events Hour of Day Site SiteUnfiltered UserType Week of Year

(continued)

Table 5-14. *(continued)*

Cube Attribute	Values
Measures	Count Events
Calculated measures	None
Source tables	DateDimensionView EventsDimensionView Site SiteDimensionView UserType
Fact table	Order

Page Usage Cube

Table 5-15 lists the attributes of the Page Usage cube.

Table 5-15. Page Usage Cube Attributes

Cube Attribute	Values
Dimensions	Date HTTP Status Is Request Level Directory Site URI Win32Status
Measures	Hits Count
Calculated measures	None
Source tables	DateDimensionView HTTPStatus Level1Dir Level2Dir Level3Dir Level4Dir Level5Dir Level6Dir RequestsByURI SiteDimensionView Win32Status
Fact table	HitsInfo

Sales Cube

The attributes of the Sales cube are described in Table 5-16.

Table 5-16. Sales Cube Attributes

Cube Attribute	Values
Dimensions	Date Products Site Customer Orders UserType
Measures	Quantity Revenue
Calculated measures	None
Source tables	DateDimensionView OrderFormLineItems OrderGroup Products RegisteredUserDimensionView Site SiteDimensionView
Fact table	BasketItemOrderView

Users Cube

The Users cube attributes are described in Table 5-17.

Table 5-17. Users Cube Attributes

Cube Attribute	Values
Dimensions	Date Site SiteUnfiltered UserType
Measures	Requests Users Visits
Calculated measures	None
Source tables	DateDimensionView UserStatusView Site SiteDimensionsView
Fact table	UniqueUserKeyByDate

Web Usage Cube

Table 5-18 lists the attributes of the Web Usage cube.

Table 5-18. Web Usage Cube Attributes

Cube Attribute	Values
Dimensions	Date DateHour Day of Week Hour of Day Referrer RegisteredUser Site UserType SiteUnFiltered Week of Year
Measures	Duration Requests Visits
Calculated measures	Avg Requests Per Week of Year Avg Visits Per Week of Year Avg Requests Per Hour of Day Avg Visits Per Hour of Day Avg Requests Per Day of Week Avg Visits Per Day of Week Avg Requests Avg Duration
Source tables	DateDimensionView LogUser ReferrerDomain RegisteredUserDimensionView Site SiteDimensionView UserType
Fact table	VisitInfo

Weekly User Trends Cube

The Weekly User Trends cube attributes are given in Table 5-19.

Table 5-19. Weekly User Trends Cube Attributes

Cube Attribute	Values
Dimensions	Date Site SiteUnfiltered Week of Year

(continued)

Table 5-19. *(continued)*

Cube Attribute	Values
Measures	Num of Users Num of New Users Repeat Users
Calculated measures	Repeat User Pct
Source tables	DateDimensionsView Site SiteDimensionsView
Fact table	UserTrendsByDateView

Commerce Server Reports

Commerce Server 2000 ships with a number of built-in reports, both dynamic and static, that are ready for you to use. In addition, each of the reports is categorized into one of the following categories based on its purpose:

- **Advertising** These reports are used to analyze the use of advertisements on the Web site. The following advertising reports are provided for your use:
  - Ad Placement
  - Ad Reach and Frequency Per Campaign
  - Ad Reach and Frequency Per Campaign Item
  - Ad Reach and Frequency Per Day
  - Campaign Event Summary
  - Campaign Item Summary
- **Diagnostic** These reports are used to diagnose problems and performance issues on the site. The following diagnostic reports are provided to analyze site usage:
  - Bandwidth Summary
  - Bandwidth Trends
  - Hits by HTTP Status
  - Hits by Win32 Status
- **Query string** These reports are used to analyze the way in which data is passed in query strings. The following reports are designed to identify how data is passed from page to page via query strings:
  - Query Strings (multivalue)
  - Query Strings (single value)
- **Sales** These reports are used to analyze the sale of products on the site. The following reports are built to analyze the sales performance of the site:
  - Customer Sales
  - Order Events

  - Product Sales
  - Shopping Basket Events
- **User** These reports are used to analyze data about the users who visit your site. The following reports are provided to analyze user characteristics and behaviors:
  - Distinct Users and Visits by Week
  - Distinct Users by Day
  - New Registered Users
  - Registered User Properties
  - Registered Users by Date Registered
  - User Days to Register
  - User Registration Rate
  - User Trends
- **Visit** These reports are used to analyze data about the visitation habits of users to the site. The following reports are generated to analyze how the site is accessed and utilized:
  - Entry Pages
  - Exit Pages
  - General Activity Statistics
  - User Visit Trends
- **Web usage** These reports are used to analyze site usage by visitors. The following reports are built to analyze how the Web servers are being used:
  - Directories
  - Entry Path Analysis
  - Top Referring Domains by Requests
  - Top Requested Pages
  - Usage Summary by Day of Week
  - Usage Summary by Hour of Day
  - Usage Summary by Week of Year
  - Usage Trends
  - Visits by Browser, Version, and OS

Importing Data Using DTS

All of the reports depend on the data that is placed in the Data Warehouse. Before you can run the reports, you first must get the data into the Data Warehouse. To do this, you'll need to run a number of SQL Server DTS tasks that Commerce Server 2000 provides. These tasks, covered in the following sections, are designed to import the data from the Commerce Server 2000 database into the associated Data Warehouse.

Creating the DTS Package

To create a typical SQL Server DTS task that you'll use to import the site data into the Data Warehouse, complete the following steps:

1. From the Start Menu, select Programs and Microsoft SQL Server.
2. Open Microsoft SQL Server Enterprise Manager.
3. Open the Microsoft SQL Server Container.
4. Open the SQL Server Group where your database is registered.
5. Open your site database.
6. Open the Data Transformation Services folder.
7. Right-click Local Packages.
8. Select New Package from the shortcut menu. This loads the DTS package editor.
9. From the Task menu, select the task that you want executed. For instance, you might select Web Server Log Import (Commerce Server). This places the task icon in the DTS package area. You can also add tasks from the toolbox on the left side of the window.
10. The properties dialog box for the task should be loaded. If it is not, right-click the icon you just added and select Properties. Configure the task as appropriate (see the following sections for more details) and click OK.
11. Add as many tasks as needed in the package, following steps 9 and 10 for each.
12. If you provide more than one task, define the order in which they will be processed. Select the first task and then, while pressing CTRL, select the second task. From the Workflow menu, select On Completion. This adds a line between the two icons in the work area, showing the workflow between the two tasks.
13. Repeat step 12 to provide workflow for each of the tasks.
14. If you did not add the Report Preparation (Commerce Server) task, do so.
15. Ensure that Report Preparation (Commerce Server) is the last task in the workflow. This task must be completed before the data imported is ready to be used in Business Analytics.
16. Save the DTS package by clicking Save on the toolbar.

Note The last task of your data import process should be report preparation to prepare the data for use in the reports by building OLAP cubes with the imported data.

Campaign Data Import

This task is used to import the campaign data, which is used to analyze how the campaigns are being used (see Figure 5-1). The data imported covers the display of advertisements and discounts that are displayed and used throughout the site. With this data, you can determine how often these elements are being displayed and how often shoppers are clicking them.

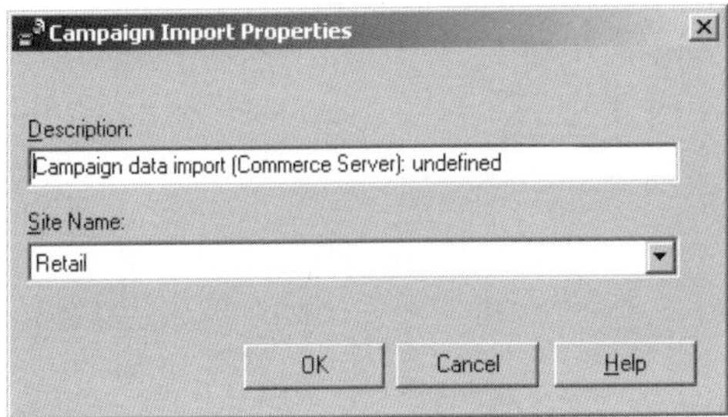

Figure 5-1. *The Campaign Import DTS task is managed through its Properties dialog box.*

You can use this information to generate reports for advertisers on your site or to determine which discounts are the most popular or least popular on your site.

Configuration Synchronization

This task is used to synchronize the Data Warehouse with the site (see Figure 5-2). It should be run whenever the site configuration changes to be sure that those changes are reflected in the Data Warehouse.

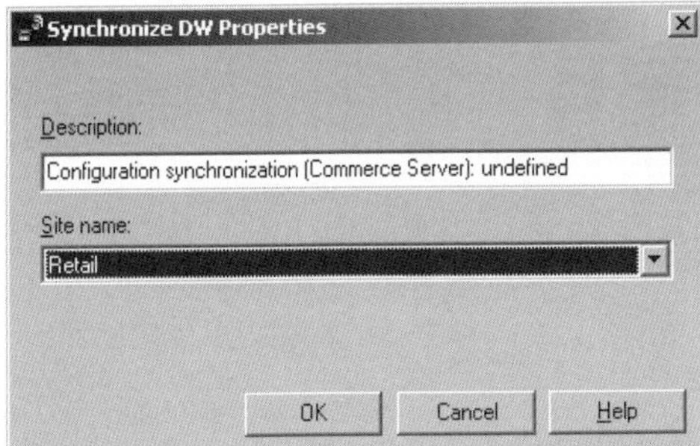

Figure 5-2. *The Synchronize Data Warehouse DTS task is managed through its Properties dialog box.*

Data Deletion

This task deletes data from the Data Warehouse (see Figure 5-3). You can use it to delete Web log data to reduce the size of the Data Warehouse. You can also use the task to empty the Data Warehouse to clear out test data.

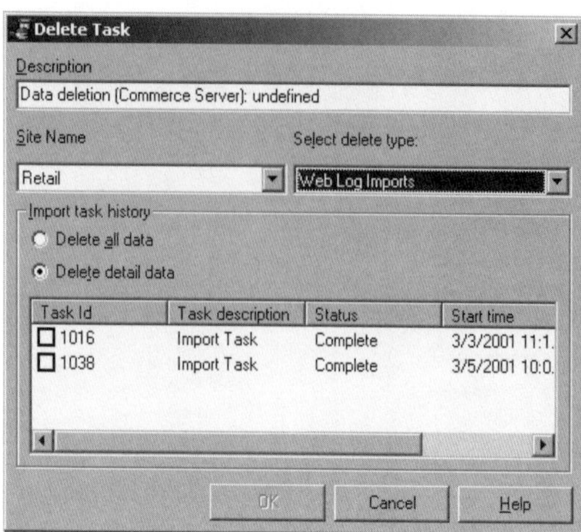

Figure 5-3. *The Data Deletion DTS task is managed through its Properties dialog box.*

IP Resolution

This task is used to resolve IP addresses to actual names (see Figure 5-4).

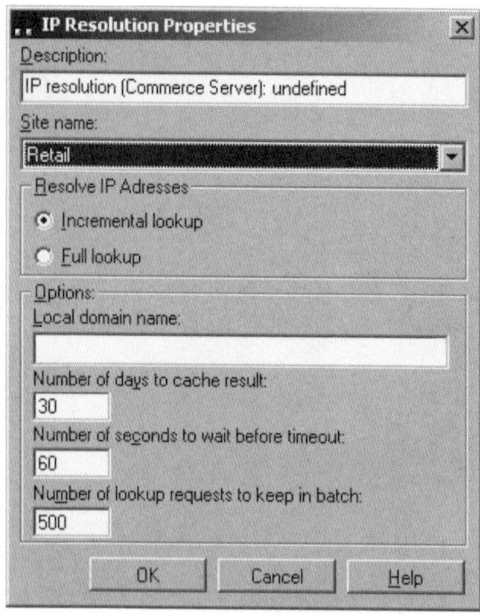

Figure 5-4. *The IP Resolution DTS task is managed through its Properties dialog box.*

Note This is not necessary for any of the prebuilt analysis reports, as none of those reports are dependent on IP addresses.

Product Catalog Import

This task is used to import product catalog data into the warehouse so that you can include the descriptive product data from the catalog in your analysis (see Figure 5-5).

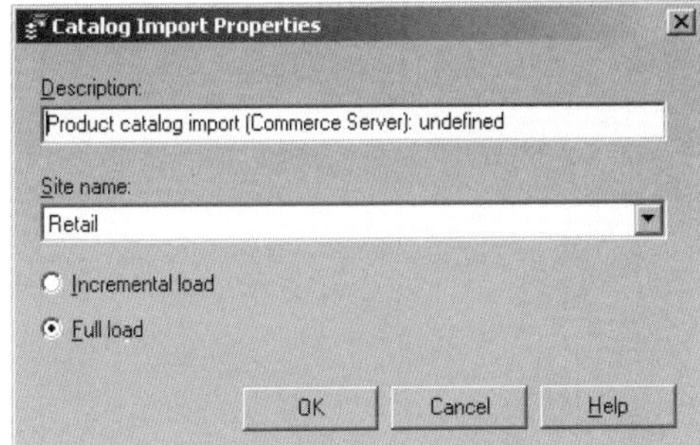

Figure 5-5. *The Product Catalog DTS task is managed through its Properties dialog box.*

Report Preparation

This task is used to build the OLAP cubes that are used to perform the analyses (see Figure 5-6).

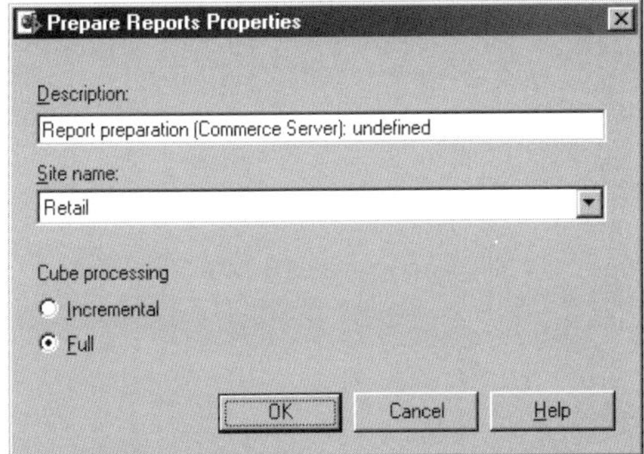

Figure 5-6. *The Report Preparation DTS task is managed through its Properties dialog box.*

Note This task must be run after data imports or deletion before any reports or analyses can be performed.

Transaction Data Import

This task is used to import transaction-related data, which includes data about the purchases or shopping activities of users, such as when a user adds or removes items from his or her basket (see Figure 5-7).

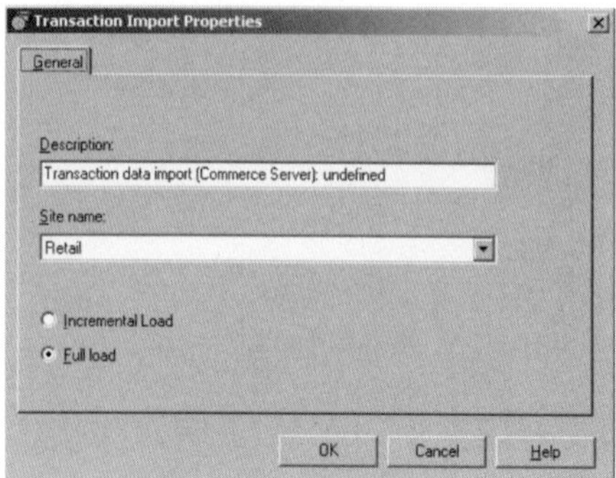

Figure 5-7. *The Transaction Data DTS task is managed through its Properties dialog box.*

User Profile Data Import

This task is used to import user profile data for registered and guest users of the site (see Figure 5-8). The data includes information that the users provide and data about their behavior.

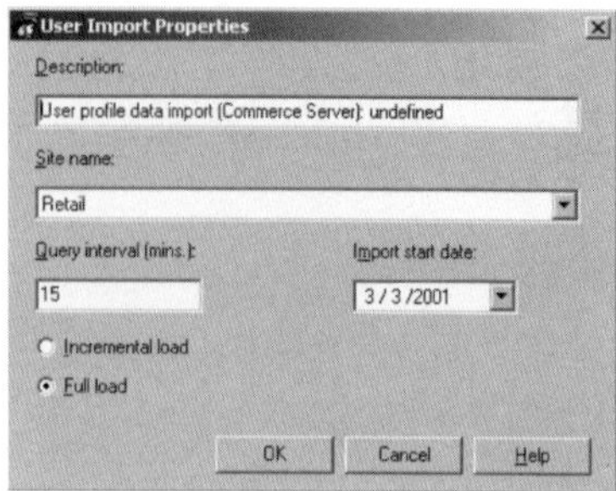

Figure 5-8. *The User Profile DTS task is managed through its Properties dialog box.*

Web Server Log Import

This task is used to import Web server logs into the Data Warehouse (see Figure 5-9). These logs are used to track how users access and utilize the site.

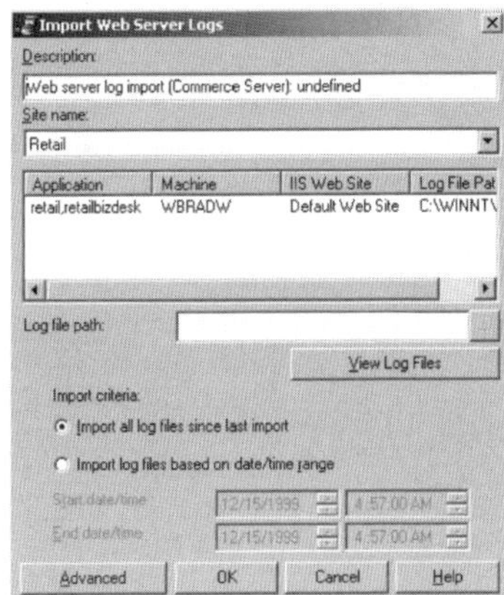

Figure 5-9. *The Import Web Server Logs DTS task is managed through its Properties dialog box.*

Generating a Report

When it's time to generate the report, you'll do so from the Business Desk's Analysis section (see Figure 5-10). You can select the report you want to build and click Run on the toolbar.

Note Before you can generate a report, the DTS Report Preparation task must be run.

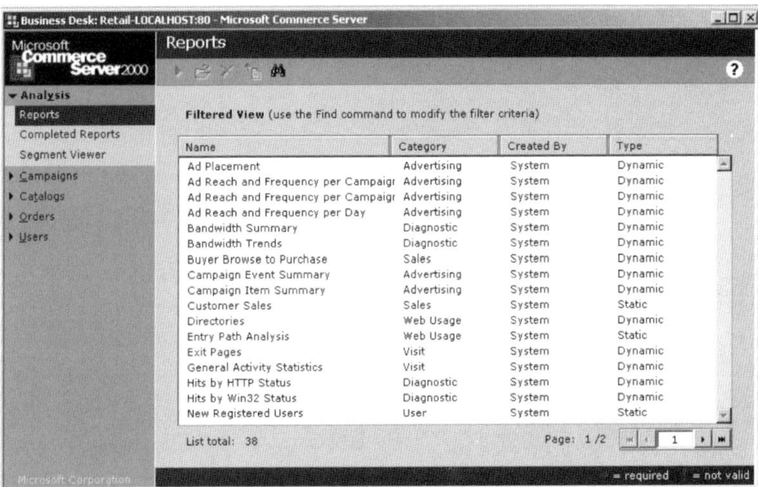

Figure 5-10. *Available reports are listed in the Business Desk Analysis section.*

Building a Static Report

Building a static report creates and stores the report, with its data, as a snapshot of the data at the time when the report is generated. The report is not re-created each time it's viewed. Static reports are typically used to generate lists that can be put to other uses, such as generating mailing lists.

When you create the report, you may need to provide information that will be used to define the report. You can define what data you want returned or what data you want included in the report (see Figure 5-11). Each report might allow you to specify different parameters.

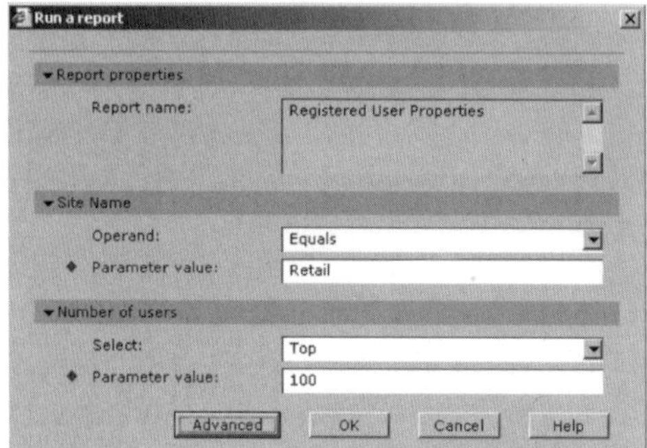

Figure 5-11. *Running a report might require you to complete a dialog box that defines how data will be selected for the report.*

When you build a static report, it is displayed in the Completed Reports section of the Business Desk. From that list, you can open and display any of the completed reports (see Figure 5-12).

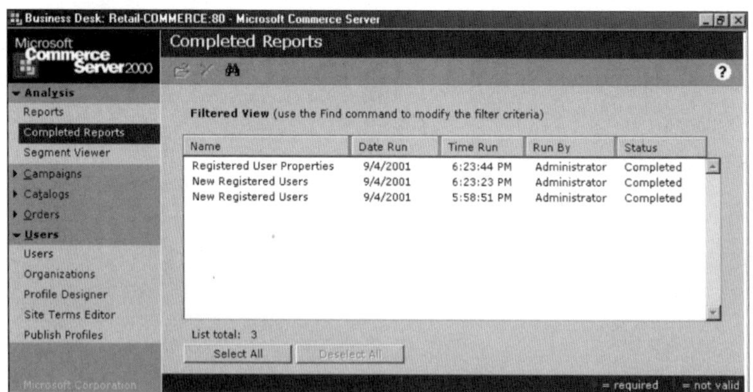

Figure 5-12. *When a static report is built, it appears in the Completed Reports page in the Business Desk.*

Building a Dynamic Report

If you want to build a dynamic report, simply select it from the list and click the Run button on the toolbar. The report is generated and displayed in a separate instance of the browser and built in a pivot table that can be further used to analyze the data.

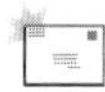

Note The reports make use of the Microsoft Office Web Controls to build and manage the pivot table and data.

Custom Reports

Of course, you are not limited to those reports provided with Commerce Server 2000. You can build your own static or dynamic custom reports to meet the needs of your site. Each type is defined differently.

Building a Static Report

To build a static report, you need to decide how you'll define the data source for the report. You can do so with a standard SQL query into the database or by creating a multidimensional expression (MDX) query to the OLAP cubes directly.

Using SQL to Build a Static Report

To perform a SQL query, you create the query and define parameters that will be used to set the scope of the query. You then add the report definition and its elements to the report database. In this example, assume that you will be querying the database to retrieve users based on their sex and those that have provided e-mail addresses.

In this example, before you can begin building the static report, you must first add a property named "sex" to the user's profile and mark it as exported. You can do this from the Commerce Server Manager by taking the following steps:

1. Open Commerce Server Manager.
2. Open the Global Resources folder.
3. Open the Profiles resource for the site you're working with.
4. Open the Profile Catalog.
5. Open the Profile Definitions.
6. Select the User Object. This will load the Profile Editor in the right pane.
7. Select the General Information section.
8. Press Add and select Add A New Property.
9. Provide the name "sex" and display name of "Sex".
10. In the Advanced Attributes section, click on the ellipses button in the Map To Data line.
11. In the dialog box that is shown, click on the ProfileService_SQLSource data source and the User object under that source.

12. Select the available field for the Sex to be stored in. Fields that are available are shown as normal text, while fields that are not available are grayed out. You can select the Custom Property 1 (STRING) field or any other appropriate field. Click OK when you've selected the field.
13. Select the check box on the Exported line.
14. Click Apply.
15. Save the profile definition by clicking Save in the CSM toolbar.

Note The steps outlined above provide a simple approach to provide the Sex property. It does not demonstrate the addition of fields to the data source to specifically store sex data, nor does it outline the ability to link the field to Site Terms to limit what the user might enter. The process of managing profiles is covered in much greater detail in Chapter 9, "User Authentication."

Now that you've added the Sex property to the user profile, you can begin building your static report using SQL.

Step 1: Defining the Query The first step is to define the SQL query that you'll use to retrieve the information you want in a sample query, such as this:

```
SELECT
    TOP 25 UserID rcp_guid, Email rcp_email, FirstName,
    LastName, sex
FROM
    RegisteredUser
WHERE
    sex = 'M'
AND
    Email IS NOT NULL
ORDER BY
    rcp_email ASC
```

You could run this query in SQL Server Query Analyzer, against the site's Data Warehouse database, such as retail_dw. The purpose is to test this query, which will serve as the basis of your report, to ensure it returns the data you're expecting.

Note You can create the queries in this and the following steps in Query Analyzer or your favorite editor. The end product of these steps will be a series of SQL statements that you'll execute to insert the report definitions into the database for later use.

Step 2: Defining the Query Parameters You can then take the sample query and insert the parameters you want to use to customize the results. In this case, the person creating the report might want more than the top 25 users, so you can define a parameter called TopCount. In addition, you can define parameters that will allow the user to specify whether the sex should be male or female and whether the e-mail should or should not exist, as follows:

```
SELECT
    [$TopCount] UserID rcp_guid, Email rcp_email,
    FirstName, LastName, Sex
INTO
    [$ResultTable]
FROM
    RegisteredUser
WHERE
    [$Sex]
AND
    [$HasEmail]
ORDER BY
    rcp_email ASC
```

The parameter that identifies the resulting table created with the results is a special parameter, ResultTable. The system automatically provides the value for this parameter and uses the value to create the table where this data will be stored.

Step 3: Creating the Report Definition Next, you need to create and insert the report definition into the Data Warehouse Report table, as shown in the following example. This allows the report to show up in the list of reports in the Business Desk.

Note The sample SQL statements shown in the next few sections should all be put together as one script and run.

```
set nocount on

DECLARE @Static_SQL tinyint
DECLARE @ReportID int
DECLARE @ReportStatusID int
SET @Static_SQL = 2
```

(continued)

(continued)

```
INSERT INTO Report
   (DisplayName, Description, ReportType, Category, Query,
   DMExport, UPMExport, CreatedBy, Protected)
VALUES
   ('Users By Sex', 'Select User by their Sex', @STATIC_SQL,
   'Users',
   'SELECT
   [$TopCount] UserID rcp_guid, Email rcp_email,
   FirstName, LastName, Sex
   INTO
   [$ResultTable]
   FROM
   RegisteredUser
   WHERE
   [$Sex]
   AND
   [$HasEmail]
   ORDER BY
   rcp_email ASC',
   1, 1, 'brad', 0)
```

At the same time, you should retrieve the report ID from the table for the newly inserted report. This is used in the following steps as you associate your parameters and other report information with this report. You can get this information using the following statement within the same SQL process as the previous statements:

```
SELECT @ReportID = @@IDENTITY
```

Step 4: Creating the Report Dimensions With the report created, you need to insert the dimensions into the ReportDimensions table of the Data Warehouse, as follows:

```
INSERT INTO ReportDimension
   (ReportID, DimensionType, DisplayName, FieldName, Ordinal)
VALUES
   (@ReportID, 0, "Email", "rcp_email", 1)
INSERT INTO ReportDimension
   (ReportID, DimensionType, DisplayName, FieldName, Ordinal)
```

(continued)

(continued)

```
VALUES
   (@ReportID, 0, "UserID", "rcp_guid", 2)
INSERT INTO ReportDimension
   (ReportID, DimensionType, DisplayName, FieldName, Ordinal)
VALUES
   (@ReportID, 0, "First Name", "First Name", 3)
INSERT INTO ReportDimension
   (ReportID, DimensionType, DisplayName, FieldName, Ordinal)
VALUES
   (@ReportID, 0, "Last Name", "LastName", 4)
INSERT INTO ReportDimension
   (ReportID, DimensionType, DisplayName, FieldName, Ordinal)
VALUES
   (@ReportID, 0, "Sex", "Sex", 5)
```

Step 5: Creating the Report Parameters You then need to insert the parameters for the report into the ReportParameters table of the Data Warehouse. You need to insert each of the parameters you've defined for the query, as follows:

```
Declare @ParamType_SingleValue tinyint
Declare @ParamType_Expression tinyint
Declare @ParamType_SelectOrder tinyint
Select @ParamType_SingleValue = 0
Select @ParamType_Expression = 1
Select @ParamType_SelectOrder = 2

Declare @DataType_integer tinyint
Declare @DataType_text tinyint
Select @DataType_integer = 2
Select @DataType_text = 5

Declare @ExpOpnd_GreaterThanOrEquals tinyint
Declare @ExpOpnd_Equals tinyint
Select @ExpOpnd_GreaterThanOrEquals = 8
Select @ExpOpnd_Equals = 1
```

(continued)

(continued)

```
Declare @SelectOrderOpnd_Top tinyint

Select @SelectOrderOpnd_Top = 2
```

For parameters that appear in the Select portion of the statement, you define the ParamType as @ParamType_SelectOrder. For the first parameter, you're selecting the Top N values, so you should use the @SelectOrderOpnd_Top constant for the Opnd1 field, as shown here:

```
INSERT INTO ReportParam

   (ReportID, ParamName, ParamDescription, ParamType, DataType,
   Opnd1, Val1, Opnd2, Val2, FieldName, Ordinal)

VALUES

   (@ReportID, '[$TopCount]', Number of Users',
   @ParamType_SelectOrder, @DataType_integer,
   @SelectOrderOpnd_Top, '25', 0, '0', '', 1)
```

The next parameter is used to define part of the Where clause, in this case matching the sex of the user, so you specify the ParamType field as @ParamType_Expression. Because you want to match the value provided, you specify the @ExpOpnd_Equals constant as the Opnd1 field, as follows:

```
INSERT INTO ReportParam

   (ReportID, ParamName, ParamDescription, ParamType, DataType,
   Opnd1, Val1, Opnd2, Val2, FieldName, Ordinal)

   VALUES

   (@ReportID, '[$Sex]', 'Sex of Users', @ParamType_Expression,
   @DataType_Text, @ExpOpnd_Equals, 'M', 0, '0', 'Sex', 2)
```

Finally, you also must make sure that you don't return any users who do not have an e-mail address, so check to make sure that the e-mail address is not null. The easiest way to do this is to directly write the statement out by specifying the ParamType as @ParamType_SingleValue, and passing it the value "Email IS NOT NULL." This replaces the [$HasEmail] parameter with that string in the following example:

```
INSERT INTO ReportParam

   (ReportID, ParamName, ParamDescription, ParamType, DataType,
   Opnd1, Val1, Opnd2, Val2, FieldName, Ordinal)

VALUES

   (@ReportID, [$HasEmail]','Email Qualifier', @ParamType_Single
   Value, @DataType_text, 0, ' Email I
```

With the SQL script written and put together, you can run the script to create the report definition and store it in the Data Warehouse.

Using MDX to Build a Static Report

You can also develop a report based on an MDX query of data in the OLAP cubes. In this case, let's use a typical example where you would like to select your top customers, perhaps so that you can offer them special discounts or other offers.

Step 1: Defining the Query As with the SQL query, you can start by writing a sample MDX query to retrieve the data you'll want, as in this example:

```
SELECT
   {Measures.Quantity, Measures.Revenue}
ON COLUMNS,

    TopCount({RegisteredUserDimensionView.RegisteredUserID.members},
    25, Measures.Revenue)

ON ROWS
FROM
    Sales
WHERE
    (PressBooks)
```

Step 2: Defining the Parameters Next, you'll add the parameters to the query, as follows:

```
SELECT
   {Measures.Quantity, Measures.Revenue}
ON COLUMNS,
    [$TopCount]({RegisteredUserDimensionView.RegisteredUserID.
    members}, [$TOPCOUNT], Measures.Revenue)
ON ROWS
FROM
    Sales
WHERE
    ([$SiteName])
```

Step 3: Creating the Report Definition Once you have the query defined, you can create the report definition and insert the definition into the Report table of the Data Warehouse, as shown in the following example. This ensures that the report appears in the reports list in the Business Desk.

```
Declare @Static_MDX tinyint

Declare @ReportID int

Select @Static_MDX = 3

SET NOCOUNT ON

INSERT INTO Report

   (DisplayName, Description, ReportType, Category, Query,
   CreatedBy, Protected)

   VALUES

   ('Top Buying Customers', 'Customers who bought the most',
   @Static_MDX, 'Sales',

   'SELECT

   {Measures.Quantity, Measures.Revenue}

ON COLUMNS,

   [$TopCount](
   {RegisteredUserDimensionView.RegisteredUserID.members},
   [$TOPCOUNT], Measures.Revenue)

ON ROWS

FROM

   Sales

WHERE

   ([$SiteName])',

'MyUserAccount', 0)
```

You need the report ID that is created when you insert the report definition into the database, so you retrieve it using the following SQL statement as a part of the previous command:

```
Select @ReportID = @@IDENTITY
```

Step 4: Creating the Report Parameters Finally, you'll need to insert the parameters for the MDX query into the ReportParam table in the Data Warehouse. These parameters are used to define what selections appear in the dialog box to filter the data in the report, as shown here:

```
Declare @ParamType_SelectOrder tinyint
Declare @ParamType_SiteName tinyint
Select @ParamType_SelectOrder = 2
Select @ParamType_SiteName = 4

Declare @DataType_integer tinyint
Declare @DataType_text tinyint
Select @DataType_integer = 2
Select @DataType_text = 5

Declare @SelectOrderOpnd_Top tinyint
Select @SelectOrderOpnd_Top = 2

Declare @SiteNameOpnd_Equals tinyint
Select @SiteNameOpnd_Equals = 1

INSERT INTO ReportParam
   (ReportID, ParamName, ParamDescription, ParamType, DataType,
   Opnd1, Val1, Ordinal)
VALUES
   (@ReportID, '[$TopCount]', 'Number of Customers',
   @ParamType_SelectOrder, @DataType_integer,
   @SelectOrderOpnd_Top, 25, 1)
INSERT INTO ReportParam
   (ReportID, ParamName, ParamDescription, ParamType, DataType,
   Opnd1, Val1, Ordinal)
VALUES
   (@ReportID, '[$SiteName]', 'Site Name', @ParamType_SiteName,
   @DataType_Text, @SiteNameOpnd_Equals, 'Retail', 2)
```

With the script provided in the last two sections, you can build the report definition and insert it into the Data Warehouse and it will be ready to be used.

Building a Dynamic Report

When you build a dynamic report, you decide whether you will query the data using SQL or through the OLAP cubes. Then, you define an Extensible Markup Language (XML) document that serves as the framework for the data. This document holds the definition of the report that will be created, its source, and its layout.

Using SQL to Build a Dynamic Report

As an example, let's assume that you want to query the database to retrieve a list of users who are male.

Step 1: Defining the Query The first step in building the report is defining the query that will retrieve the desired information. You write a query that will retrieve information from the Registered User class in the Data Warehouse. In this example, the query might look like the following:

```
SELECT
    FirstName, LastName, Email rcp_email, UserID rcp_guid, sex
FROM
    RegisteredUser
WHERE
    Sex = 'M'
```

Step 2: Building the XML Framework Document The XML document contains the definition of the report, including the SQL query you just created. The ConnectionString tag includes the database connection string. However, the Initial Catalog and Data Source entries do not include values. These are automatically retrieved from the MSCS_Admin database when the report is created. The CommandText tag holds the SQL query that will define the data that is retrieved, as follows:

```
<xml xmlns:x='urn:schemas-microsoft-com:office:excel'>
<x:PivotTable>
    <x:OWCVersion>9.0.0.3821</x:OWCVersion>
    <x:DisplayFieldList/>
    <x:FieldListTop>300</x:FieldListTop>
    <x:FieldListLeft>800</x:FieldListLeft>
    <x:FieldListBottom>700</x:FieldListBottom>
    <x:FieldListRight>1000</x:FieldListRight>
    <x:CacheDetails/>
```

(continued)

(continued)

```
    <x:ConnectionString>Provider=SQLOLEDB;Integrated
    Security=SSPI;

    Initial Catalog=;Data Source=

    </x:ConnectionString>

    <x:CommandText>

    SELECT

             FirstName, LastName, Email rcp_email, UserID
             rcp_guid, sex

    FROM

             RegisteredUser

    WHERE

             Sex = 'M'

    </x:CommandText>

</x:PivotTable>

</xml>
```

Step 3: Creating the Report Definition Finally, you need to insert the report definition into the Data Warehouse database and provide the title description, XML definition, and more information about the report. This information, shown in the following example, is used to list the report in the Business Desk and to generate the report for display to the user.

```
Declare @Dynamic_SQL tinyint

Select @Dynamic_SQL = 0

INSERT INTO Report

   (DisplayName, Description, ReportType, Category, CreatedBy,
   Protected, ShowPivot, ShowChart, XMLData, Definition)

VALUES

   ('Registered Male Users', 'Registered Male Users',
   @Dynamic_SQL, 'User', brad', 0, 1, 0,

   <xml  xmlns:x="urn:schemas-microsoft-com:office:excel">

   <x:PivotTable>

   <x:OWCVersion>9.0.0.3821</x:OWCVersion>

   <x:DisplayFieldList/>

       <x:FieldListTop>300</x:FieldListTop>
```

(continued)

(continued)

```
        <x:FieldListLeft>800</x:FieldListLeft>

        <x:FieldListBottom>700</x:FieldListBottom>

        <x:FieldListRight>1000</x:FieldListRight>

    <x:CacheDetails/>

    <x:ConnectionString>Provider=SQLOLEDB;Integrated
    Security=SSPI;

        Initial Catalog=;Data Source=

    </x:ConnectionString>

    <x:CommandText>

        SELECT

                    FirstName, LastName, Email rcp_email,
                    UserID rcp_guid, sex

        FROM

                    RegisteredUser

        WHERE

                    Sex = "M"

    </x:CommandText>

</x:PivotTable>

</xml>',

'Retrieve a list of male users registered on the site')
```

Note Specifying a value of 0 for the ReportType field indicates the report is based on a SQL query. A value of 1 indicates that the report is generated from an OLAP cube.

Using Cubes to Build a Dynamic Report

You can also create a dynamic report that queries the OLAP cubes directly. In this way, you can simply specify the OLAP cube that you will load. Of course, we assume here that you've already created the appropriate OLAP cube.

Step 1: Building the XML Document The XML Framework document in this case is used to define the source of the data, including the name of the OLAP cube that will be loaded for the report. The OLAP cube's name is specified in the DataMember tag. The ConnectionString tag includes the database connection string. However, the Initial Catalog and Data Source entries do not include values. These are automatically retrieved from the MSCS_Admin database when the report is created, as follows:

```
<xml  xmlns:x='urn:schemas-microsoft-com:office:excel'>
<x:PivotTable>
   <x:OWCVersion>9.0.0.3821</x:OWCVersion>
   <x:DisplayFieldList/>
   <x:FieldListTop>300</x:FieldListTop>
   <x:FieldListLeft>800</x:FieldListLeft>
   <x:FieldListBottom>700</x:FieldListBottom>
   <x:FieldListRight>1000</x:FieldListRight>
   <x:CacheDetails/>
   <x:ConnectionString>Provider=MSOLAP;Initial  Catalog=;Data
   Source=;Client Cache Size=25;Auto Synch Period=10000
   </x:ConnectionString>
   <x:DataMember>Users</x:CommandText>
</x:PivotTable>
</xml>
```

Step 2: Creating the Report Definition You next need to insert the report definition, including the XML Framework document, into the Report table in the Data Warehouse, as follows:

```
Declare @Dynamic_MDX tinyint
Select @Dynamic_MDX = 1
INSERT INTO Report
   (DisplayName, Description, ReportType, Category, CreatedBy,
   Protected, ShowPivot, ShowChart, XMLData, Definition)
VALUES
   ('Site Users', 'Users of the Site', @Dynamic_MDX, 'User',
   'brad', 0, 1, 0,
   <xml  xmlns:x="urn:schemas-microsoft-com:office:excel">
   <x:PivotTable>
   <x:OWCVersion>9.0.0.3821</x:OWCVersion>
```

(continued)

(continued)

```
   <x:DisplayFieldList/>

       <x:FieldListTop>300</x:FieldListTop>

       <x:FieldListLeft>800</x:FieldListLeft>

       <x:FieldListBottom>700</x:FieldListBottom>

       <x:FieldListRight>1000</x:FieldListRight>

   <x:CacheDetails/>

   <x:ConnectionString>Provider=MSOLAP;Initial  Catalog=;
   Data Source=;Client Cache Size=25;Auto Synch
   Period=10000

   </x:ConnectionString>

   <x:DataMember>Users</x:CommandText>

</x:PivotTable>

</xml>',

'A report from an OLAP cube that retrieves a list of Male
Registered Users')
```

Note Specifying a value of 0 for the ReportType field indicates the report is based on a SQL query. A value of 1 indicates that the report is generated from an OLAP cube.

Chapter 6

Site Packager

Once you have developed your site, you will need to deploy it into the staging, test, and production environments. This used to be a challenging task, to ensure that you were able to correctly move all of the files, resources, and configuration settings from the development environment and install the site on another server. Fortunately, Microsoft Commerce Server 2000 includes the Commerce Site Packager application, which is used to package an e-commerce site from one server and deploy it to other servers. The resulting package has a .pup extension.

Deploying a Site Using Site Packager

A Commerce Server site consists of a number of elements, including the Web site and its virtual directories, the Web files, databases, and other resources. Each of these elements can be included within the site package. From within the package, you can select those resources you wish to unpack when deploying the site. Table 6-1 identifies the data, settings, and other elements that are included by each resource in the .pup file.

Table 6-1. Resources Included in the Package File

Resource	Data
App Default Config	All property values
Campaigns	Ad_item Campaign Campaign_item Campaign_item_types Creative Creative_property Creative_property_value Creative_size Creative_type Creative_type_xref Customer Dm_item Event_type Industry_code

(continued)

Table 6-1. *(continued)*

Resource	Data
Campaigns *(continued)*	Order_discount Order_discount_expression Order_discount_misc Page_group Page_group_xref Target Target_group Target_group_xref
CS Authentication	Settings in AUTHSETUP.INI
Data Warehouse	None
Direct Mailer	None
Predictor	None
Product Catalog	CatalogAttributes CatalogCustomCatalogs CatalogCustomPrices CatalogDefinitions CatalogDefinitionProperties CatalogEnumValues CatalogGlobal CatalogSet_Info CatalogSet_Catalogs CatalogStatus CatalogToVendorAssociation CatalogUsedDefinitions *x*_Hierarchy *x*_ProductsComplete *x*_Relationships
Profiles	Schema script and data script
Transactions	TransCategory TransDimension
TransactionsConfig	Decode Region RegionalTax ShippingConfig TableShippingRates

Creating a Site Package

Once you've developed the site and have determined that you're ready to deploy it, you can go ahead and create the site package. The process requires several steps, enumerated in the following sections.

Step 1: Generate Profile Schema Structured Query Language Script if Necessary

If you have made any changes, additions, or customizations to any profile schemas, you'll need to generate a Structured Query Language (SQL) script that will build the appropriate schema in the system. You can do this from within Microsoft SQL Server Enterprise Manager by selecting each of the tables that is a part of the profile, right-clicking, and selecting Generate SQL Script from the Tasks menu. By default, the tables that are a part of the profile schema include the Addresses, OrganizationObject, and UserObject tables.

If you add additional profile stores in the profile system, you'll need to provide a separate SQL script for each.

Note If you have not made any changes to the profile schemas, you do not need to provide a schema script.

Step 2: Build a Profile Data Population Script if Necessary

If you want to prepopulate the profile system with data, such as general or administrative user accounts, basic organization groups, or other data, you can build a SQL script that inserts the desired data into the appropriate tables. The file will include a basic INSERT SQL statement to insert the appropriate data into the profile object data table, such as the following:

```
Insert INTO [UserObject]

   ( [g_user_id],[u_user_title], [u_first_name], [u_last_name],
   [u_user_security_password], [g_org_id],
   [i_account_status], [u_logon_name], [d_date_last_changed],
   [d_date_created], [u_user_security_password], [g_org_id],
   [i_account_status], [i_partner_desk_role] )

VALUES

   (N'{590858DB-08A7-11D3-B8C4-00104B95EEEE}', N'', N'Joe',
   N'User', N'joeuser@somewhere.com', getdate(),
   getdate(),'password',
   N'{590858E1-08A7-11D3-B8C4-00104B95AE0E}', 1, 1 )

GO
```

Note If you don't want to prepopulate the profile with any data, you don't need to provide this script.

Step 3: Launch Site Packager

Once the two script files are created, if they are needed, you can begin building the actual .pup file using the Commerce Server Site Packager application. You launch the Site Packager from the Start menu by pointing to Programs, then Microsoft Commerce Server 2000, and then selecting Commerce Site Packager.

Step 4: Select the Package An Existing Site Option

To create the .pup file, select the Package An Existing Site option from the choices presented in the Welcome To The Commerce Server Site Packager page.

Step 5: Identify Site and Package File

You'll then have to select the site that you'll be packaging. The sites that are listed in the Admin database are displayed in the Site To Package drop-down list box. Your server must be a part of the Web application that you're packaging. You'll also have to provide the name and path of the .pup file that you are creating (see Figure 6-1).

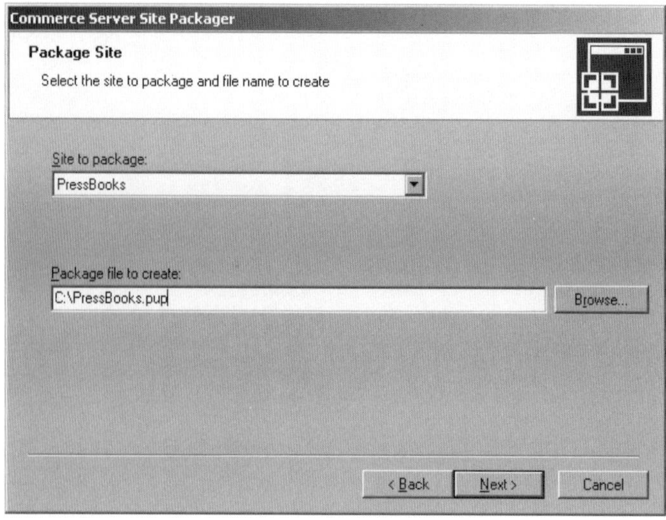

Figure 6-1. *When you create a .pup file, you'll need to specify the name and location where the file should be created.*

Step 6: Specify Profile Schema Script and Data Population Script

Once the site is identified, the packaging of the site begins. After the available resources are included in the .pup file, you are prompted to identify the profile schema script and profile prepopulation script that should also be included in the .pup file (see Figure 6-2). If you are going to use the default profile schema, you must specify the default SQL schema, as found in the Commerce Server directory, such as C:\Program Files\Microsoft Commerce Server\PROFILESQL.SQL.

If you don't want to prepopulate the profile objects with data, you don't need to specify a prepopulation script.

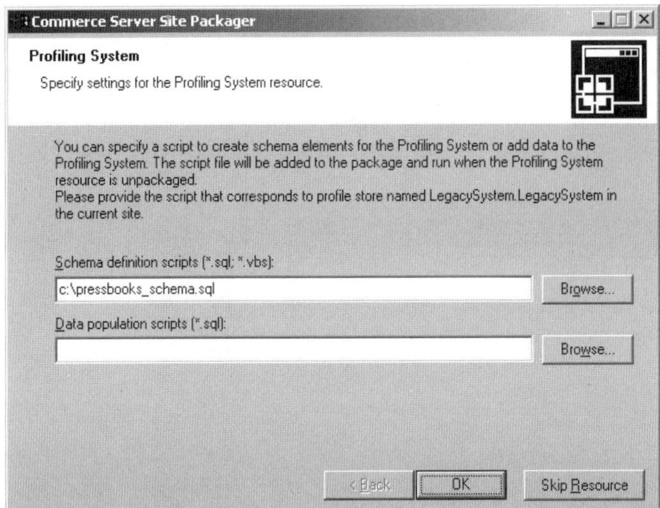

Figure 6-2. *In creating the .pup file, you'll need to identify the SQL script that defines the profile objects in the database.*

Once the profile scripts are specified, the site's .pup file is created, and the site is then ready to be deployed, as indicated in the Packaging Is Complete page. You can use the .pup file to deploy it as a new site or as an additional Web server in your server farm for an existing e-commerce application.

Unpacking and Deploying a Site

You can use the .pup file in several different ways when deploying your site. The first is to deploy the entire site, creating a new e-commerce application. The second is to add another application to the site. For instance, the retail .pup file contains two separate applications: the Retail Commerce Store and the Business Desk. The third is to create and add an additional Web server to the Web application, creating what can be used as a Web farm, all of which are a part of the same e-commerce site. Finally, you can use the .pup file to add new or updated resources to a site or to deploy various resources onto separate servers in the site.

The process of unpackaging a site is basically the same regardless of how the .pup file will be used.

Step 1: Run Commerce Site Packager

To launch the Commerce Site Packager, click Start, point to Programs, point to Microsoft Commerce Server 2000, and then select Commerce Site Packager in the Welcome To The Commerce Server Site Packager page. You can then specify that you will be unpacking an existing .pup file.

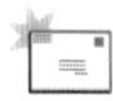

Note If you double-click a .pup file from Windows Explorer, you skip the Welcome To The Commerce Server Site Packager page; you are taken immediately to the next page.

Step 2: Select Custom Unpack

Next, specify the name and path of the .pup file (see Figure 6-3) in the Unpack page. You can also decide to use the quick or custom unpack method. The custom method is recommended, as it gives you more control over what is being installed on your system.

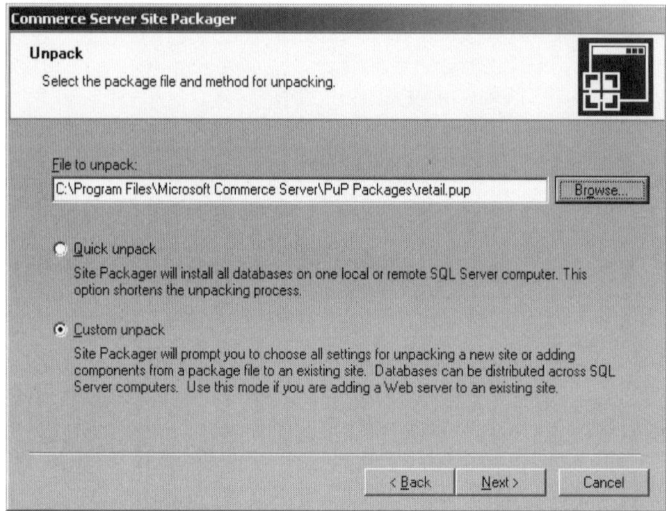

Figure 6-3. *You must identify the .pup file that you are unpacking. In addition, you should identify how you will be unpacking the site. A custom unpack of the site is recommended.*

Step 3: Select Unpack Method

At this point, you need to specify whether you are creating a new site or adding resources, an application, or a Web server to an existing site using the Unpack Method page, shown in Figure 6-4. In our example, we demonstrate creating a new site. The process is the same for each method, although you can skip steps as appropriate.

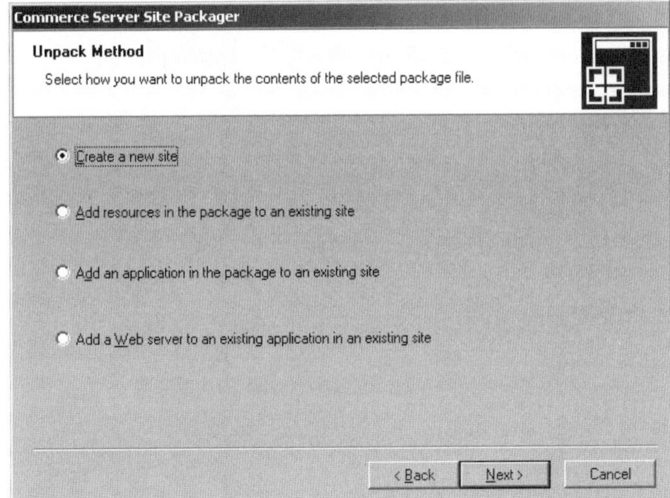

Figure 6-4. *You'll need to identify what you're doing in unpacking this .pup file: Are you creating a new site, or adding a resource, application, or Web server to an existing site?*

Step 4: Specify Site

You'll then have to specify the site to which this site is being unpacked in the Site Name page. In this case, you'll provide the name of a new site, which must not match any of the existing sites already created.

Step 5: Select Resources

Next, you'll need to specify the resources that you want to install on this server in the Select Resources page (see Figure 6-5). You can select any combination of available resources. For instance, on your base Web servers, you might not want to install the Data Warehouse and Direct Mail resources. If you're not planning on using the Predictor service, you might not want to install that resource. You can also install all of the resources.

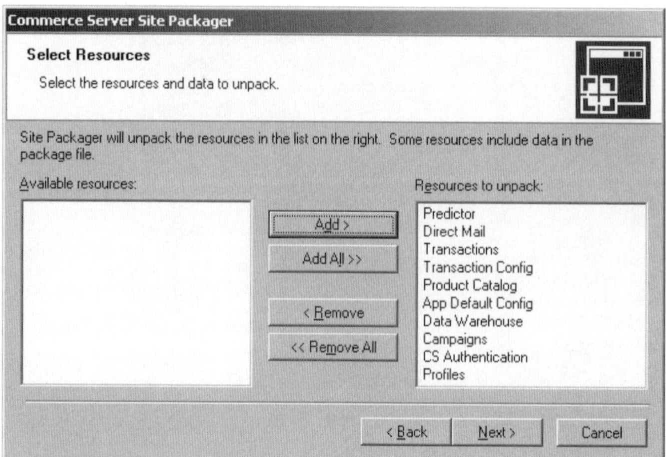

Figure 6-5. *You can select those resources that you want to unpack to this site.*

Step 6: Specify Global Resource Pointers

If you're installing any global resources, you'll need to identify the resources to which they will point in the Global Resource Pointers page, shown in Figure 6-6. For instance, the Predictor and Direct Mail resources should point to a single global resource, so you can select the existing one (assuming that one already exists). Typically, the other resources are created for this site.

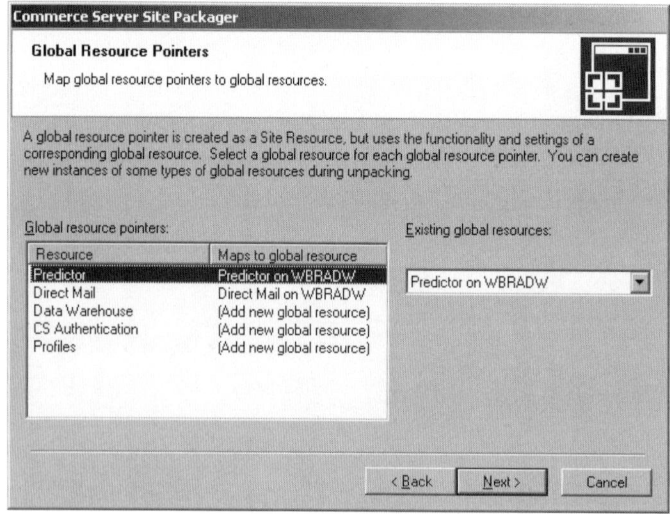

Figure 6-6. *When you are unpacking global resources, you have to define whether the resource will use a new resource or an existing one.*

Step 7: Identify Databases

The next step is identifying the databases in which each of the resources will be installed in the Database Connection Strings page (see Figure 6-7). You can specify a single database for all of the resources, a different database for each, or any combination of the two. If the database does not exist, it will be created.

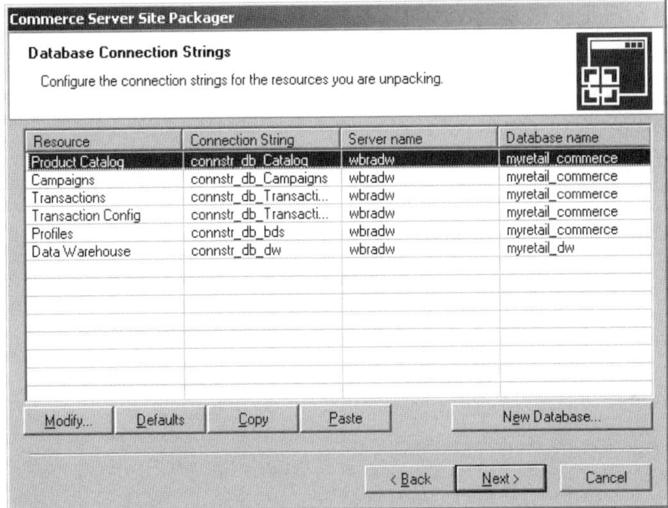

Figure 6-7. *You must define which databases will be used to store site information.*

Step 8: Provide Database Connection User Name and Password

For each of the databases you specify in the preceding step, you need to provide a user name and password that will be used to connect to the database (see Figure 6-8).

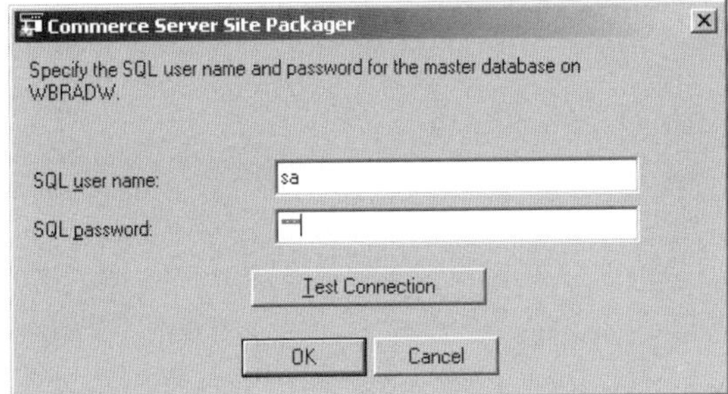

Figure 6-8. *Of course, you'll have to tell the resources how they can connect to those databases.*

Step 9: Select Applications

Now, you'll need to identify the applications that you want to install on this server in the Select Applications page. Note that all of the applications in the .pup file are selected by default.

Step 10: Specify Internet Information Services Web and Virtual Directories

Finally, you'll need to specify the Internet Information Services (IIS) Web and Virtual Directory for each of the applications that you are installing in the Select IIS Web Sites And Virtual Directories page, shown in Figure 6-9. By default, these will be the same as the source of the .pup file. Therefore, for the Blank site, the virtual directory will always be Blank and Blankbizdesk. If you're using the Blank site as a starting point for your site, you'll want to change the virtual directory to be one named for your site.

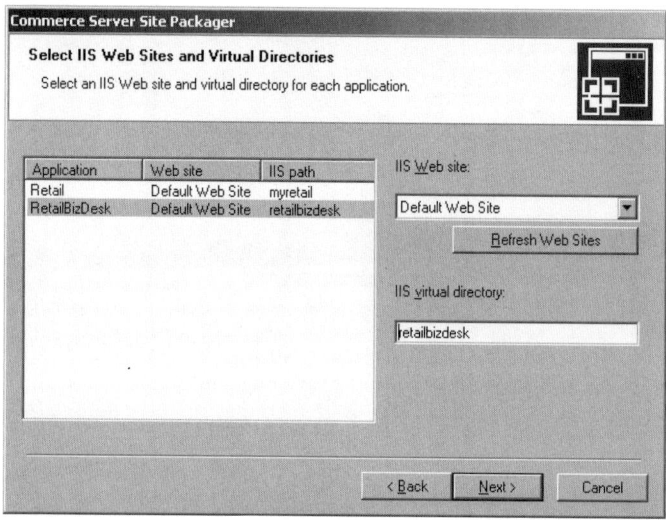

Figure 6-9. *You'll need to identify the Web site and virtual directories that will hold the applications that you're installing.*

Once this information is provided, the installation of the site begins in earnest.

Step 11: Provide Data Warehouse Connection Information

If you've selected the Data Warehouse resource to be installed, you'll be prompted in the Data Warehouse page to provide connection information to the Data Warehouse.

Step 12: Provide Profile Schema and Population Scripts

If you've selected to install the Profile Service resource, you'll need to specify the schemas that are used to define and construct the profile system. You'll do so in two pages. The first Profiling System page is used to specify the profile schema, site terms, and expressions that are used in the profile service (see Figure 6-10). These scripts define how the profile objects are stored within the system.

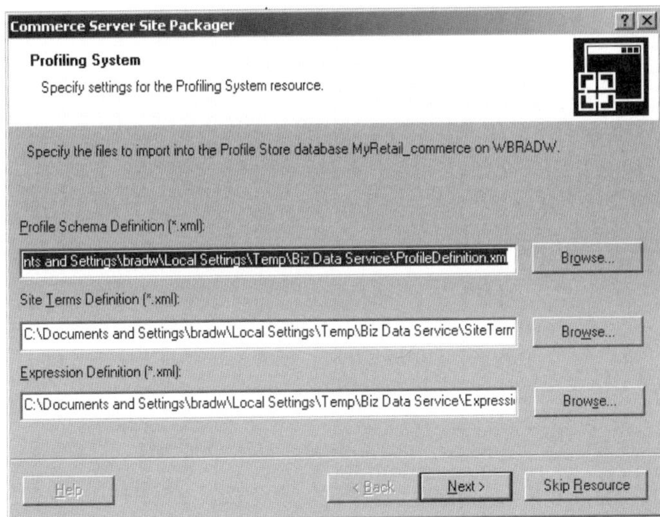

Figure 6-10. *If you're installing the Profile resource, you'll need to provide information about the schema definitions.*

The second Profiling System page, shown in Figure 6-11, is used to identify the schema definition script that is used to build the SQL Server tables that will hold each of the profile objects. This is the same SQL script that is generated to document the tables in the database. In addition, you can provide the data population SQL script to prepopulate the tables with data, if desired.

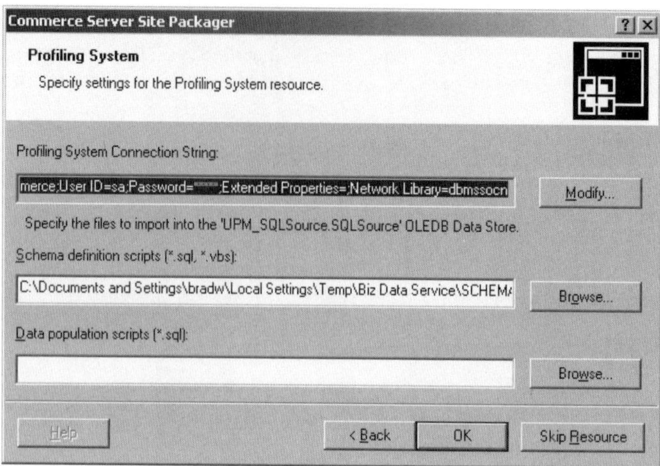

Figure 6-11. *You must identify the SQL script that will create the database tables that will hold the profile objects.*

Step 13: Finish Site Packager

Finally, the Site Packager completes its process, displaying the Unpacking Is Complete page (see Figure 6-12), which announces the completion of the unpackaging process. It also notifies you if any errors were encountered. In the event of errors, you can view the PUP.LOG file to determine what the errors were and which corrective actions to take.

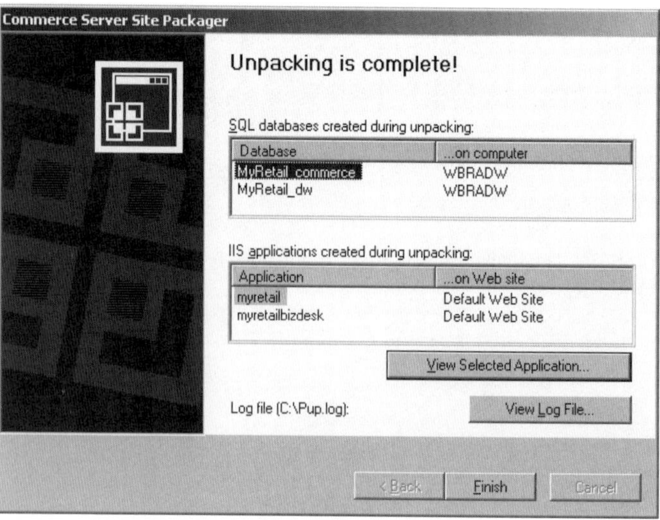

Figure 6-12. *You'll be informed when the site is finished unpacking.*

Step 14: Data Transformation Services Additional or Other Support Tables and Data

Once you have completed unpacking the site from the .pup file, you might find it necessary to copy other tables from the database to provide additional lookup data, reference information, or some other support role. However, if they're not a part of the basic commerce site, they are not automatically installed. You will need to copy them over, and if necessary, populate them with data. SQL Server Data Transformation Services (DTS) tasks are a prime candidate to accomplish this. You can use DTS tasks to move both the tables and any data that is necessary.

Step 15: Transfer and Register Components

Finally, you'll need to be sure that you transfer any components that will be used by your site. This applies to both COM+ components and pipeline components that will be used within your site. You'll want to be sure that the components are properly registered. In the event of pipeline components, you'll also want to ensure that they are registered as such. You can find more information on building pipeline components in Chapter 17, "Building Custom Pipeline Components."

One way to register the components is to manually use the RegSvr32 tool to register the component and then the Pipeline Registration Wizard to register the pipeline component. You can also build a .reg file that will create the appropriate entries in the server's Registry to account for all of this information. Doing this requires several steps that can easily be performed on your development machine, as follows:

1. **Use binary compatibility** Although this is not absolutely necessary, it will save you a lot of grief down the road. Whenever building components, you should also set the binary compatibility as soon as possible. With pipeline components, the interfaces should not change, so you can set this immediately.
2. **Create the pipeline component** Compile the component as you normally would.
3. **Register the pipeline component** On your development machine, register the component as usual.
4. **Register with the Pipeline Registration Wizard** Use the Pipeline Registration Wizard to register the component for use in the pipeline. See Chapter 17 for more information on this tool.
5. **Export the component key from the Registry** Using RegEdit, open the Registry and find the entry for your component. If the component is named MyComponent.MyPipe, then look for the corresponding entry in the HKEY_CLASSES_ROOT hive of the Registry, as shown in the following code:

   ```
   Windows Registry Editor Version 5.00

   [HKEY_CLASSES_ROOT\MyComponent.MyPipe]
   @="Pricing.CPricing"

   [HKEY_CLASSES_ROOT\MyComponent.MyPipe\Clsid]
   @="{41AAD88A-DD6B-4ED0-A9AB-9E1A63479745}"
   ```

   Export that entry by highlighting it and selecting Export Registry File from the Registry menu. Save the settings to a file.

6. **Export the Class Identifiers (CLSID) component key from the Registry** From the component key, look up the CLSID value, which will be a globally unique identifier (GUID), such as {41AAD88A-DD6B-4ED0-A9AB-9E1A63479745}. Find that value under the HKEY_CLASSES_ROOT\CLSID hive, as shown in the following code:

```
[HKEY_CLASSES_ROOT\CLSID\{41AAD88A-DD6B-4ED0-A9AB-
9E1A63479745}]
@="MyComponent.MyPipe"
"AppID"="{41AAD88A-DD6B-4ED0-A9AB-9E1A63479745}"

[HKEY_CLASSES_ROOT\CLSID\{41AAD88A-DD6B-4ED0-A9AB-
9E1A63479745}\Implemented Categories]

[HKEY_CLASSES_ROOT\CLSID\{41AAD88A-DD6B-4ED0-A9AB-
9E1A63479745}\Implemented Categories\{0DE86A53-2BAA-11CF-
A229-00AA003D7352}]

[HKEY_CLASSES_ROOT\CLSID\{41AAD88A-DD6B-4ED0-A9AB-
9E1A63479745}\Implemented Categories\{0DE86A57-2BAA-11CF-
A229-00AA003D7352}]

[HKEY_CLASSES_ROOT\CLSID\{41AAD88A-DD6B-4ED0-A9AB-
9E1A63479745}\Implemented Categories\{40FC6ED5-2438-11CF-
A3DB-080036F12502}]

[HKEY_CLASSES_ROOT\CLSID\{41AAD88A-DD6B-4ED0-A9AB-
9E1A63479745}\Implemented Categories\{CF7536D0-43C5-11D0-
B85D-00C04FD7A0FA}]

[HKEY_CLASSES_ROOT\CLSID\{41AAD88A-DD6B-4ED0-A9AB-
9E1A63479745}\Implemented Categories\{D2ACD8E0-43C5-11D0-
B85D-00C04fD7A0fA}]

[HKEY_CLASSES_ROOT\CLSID\{41AAD88A-DD6B-4ED0-A9AB-
9E1A63479745}\InprocServer32]
@="C:\\Components\\MyComp.dll"
"ThreadingModel"="Apartment"

[HKEY_CLASSES_ROOT\CLSID\{41AAD88A-DD6B-4ED0-A9AB-
9E1A63479745}\ProgID]
@="MyComponent.MyPipe"

[HKEY_CLASSES_ROOT\CLSID\{41AAD88A-DD6B-4ED0-A9AB-
9E1A63479745}\Programmable]

[HKEY_CLASSES_ROOT\CLSID\{41AAD88A-DD6B-4ED0-A9AB-
9E1A63479745}\TypeLib]
@="{842D21C3-77E6-4A20-8B96-1235C12C8F47}"

[HKEY_CLASSES_ROOT\CLSID\{41AAD88A-DD6B-4ED0-A9AB-
9E1A63479745}\VERSION]
@="8.0"
```

Highlight the CLSID value and choose Export Registry File from the Registry menu. Save the settings to a file.

7. **Export the TypeLib component key from the Registry. Find the TypeLib entry in the CLSID component key** It will be a GUID, such as {842D21C3-77E6-4A20-8B96-1235C12C8F47}. Find this value in the HKEY_CLASSES_ROOT\TypeLib hive, as shown here, and export it as previously outlined:

```
[HKEY_CLASSES_ROOT\TypeLib\{842D21C3-77E6-4A20-8B96-
1235C12C8F47}]

[HKEY_CLASSES_ROOT\TypeLib\{842D21C3-77E6-4A20-8B96-
1235C12C8F47}\8.0]
@="MyComponent"

[HKEY_CLASSES_ROOT\TypeLib\{842D21C3-77E6-4A20-8B96-
1235C12C8F47}\8.0\0]

[HKEY_CLASSES_ROOT\TypeLib\{842D21C3-77E6-4A20-8B96-
1235C12C8F47}\8.0\0\win32]
@="C:\\Components\\MyComp.dll"

[HKEY_CLASSES_ROOT\TypeLib\{842D21C3-77E6-4A20-8B96-
1235C12C8F47}\8.0\FLAGS]
@="0"

[HKEY_CLASSES_ROOT\TypeLib\{842D21C3-77E6-4A20-8B96-
1235C12C8F47}\8.0\HELPDIR]
@="C:\\Components"
```

8. **Merge the three saved Registry export files into one file that can be distributed with the components** When you double-click the file, the Registry entries in the .reg file are merged into the Registry. This registers the component and sets it up to work with the pipeline.

Running Scripts with the PUP

At times, you might find it necessary to execute scripts before, after, or during the unpacking of a site to set or modify some configuration settings or take some other actions. The Site Packager automatically executes specially named scripts at the appropriate time in the process.

Prepackaging Scripts

The prepackaging script is used to identify a script that should be run as soon as the unpackaging process is started. This can be used to alter configuration settings or prepare the server for the site that is about to be unpacked. The script file is automatically run if it exists within the .pup file and is named PRE<*SITENAME*>.VBS where *SITENAME* is the name of the site. For the Retail site, for instance, the prepackaging script would be named PRERETAIL.VBS. A prepackaging script is provided with one parameter, mode (/s), which indicates whether the Site Packager is running in silent mode or normal installation mode.

Postpackaging Scripts

The postpackaging script is executed when the site unpacking process is completed. It can be used to modify site settings or perform some cleanup after the unpacking is completed. The Site Packager automatically executes this script if it is in the .pup file and is named POST<*SITENAME*>.VBS, where *SITENAME* is the name of the site. For instance, if this is the Retail site, the postpackaging script would be named POSTRETAIL.VBS. A postpackage script is provided with two parameters: Sitename in quotation marks ("MySite") indicating which site the script should make its changes to, and Mode (/s:), which indicates the installation mode.

Application Scripts

You can also provide a script that will be executed immediately after each application in the .pup file is installed. For instance, you can provide a script that will execute as soon as the Business Desk application is installed. This allows you to build a script that takes specific actions on a particular application in the site. Application scripts must be named UNPACK.VBS and be located in the root directory of each application. If the file is present, it is automatically executed by the Site Packager using the Windows cscript command.

The command line that executes the script can contain six switches, described in Table 6-2, that provide parameters for the script. These parameters can be used to take specific actions or fill in needed information about the site. They are accessed from within the script by using the symbols %1, %2, %3, %4, and %5.

Table 6-2. Application Script Parameters

Parameter Name	Parameter Switch	Description
Site Name	/n:"*SITENAME*"	This switch specifies the name of the site.
Application Name	/r:"*APPNAME*"	This switch specifies the name of the application.
Server Instance	/I:*N*	This switch provides the number of the Web server instance.
Virtual Directory	/v:"*PATH*"	This switch identifies the virtual directory for the site.
Application Path	/d:"*PATH*"	This switch identifies the location or path of the application on the server.
Mode	/s	If this switch is specified, the script runs in silent mode and does not display message boxes or other feedback.

Because the application scripts are simply files that are placed in the root of the directory for a particular application, those files remain in place once the site is deployed. Be sure to either remove that file or secure it so that it cannot be accessed by anyone who is accessing the site itself.

Tip If you install the Retail Solution Site, you can look at a sample application script in the RetailBizDesk site. The file is located in the virtual root and is named UNPACK.VBS.

Running the Site Packager from the Command Line

Up until this point, the discussion of the Site Packager has revolved around the manual execution of the application, whether packing or unpacking a site. However, you can automate this process to a great extent and minimize the amount of interaction you must have with a server to get your site deployed. This capability can be invaluable when you need to deploy the site onto numerous servers in your Web farm.

The Site Packager application can be executed from the command line by using the run-time file PUP.EXE with a set of switches, listed in Table 6-3, that define how the tool will function.

Table 6-3. Site Packager Application Switches

Switch	Mode	Description
/p	Pack	This switch instructs Site Packager to pack the site.
/u	Unpack	This switch instructs the Site Packager to unpack the site.
/r	Both	This switch instructs the Site Packager to display the Select Resources dialog box.
/s:"*SITENAME*"	Both	This switch indicates the name of the site to package.
/a:"*APPNAME*"	Both	This switch indicates the name of the application.
/w:"*WEBNAME*"	Unpack	This switch indicates the name of the Web server.
/f:"*PUPFILE*"	Both	This switch gives the name and path of the resulting .pup file.
/I:"*INIFILE*"	Both	This switch provides the name and path of the .ini file that guides the execution of the Site Packager.

Issuing the command-line command to pack a site might look like the following:

```
C:\Program Files\Microsoft Commerce Server\PUP.EXE /p /s:Retail
/f:"C:\Commerce Server\PUP\Retail.PUP"
/i:"C:\Commerce Server\PUP\packRetail.INI"
```

The command-line command to unpack a site might look like this:

```
C:\Program Files\Microsoft Commerce Server\PUP.EXE /u /s:Retail
/f:"C:\Commerce Server\PUP\Retail.PUP"
/i:"C:\Commerce Server\PUP\packRetail.INI"
```

Note Commerce Server 2000 doesn't provide a completely silent mode when packing a site. The Commerce Server Site Packager Profiling System dialog box is displayed so you can select the profile schema SQL scripts. You must click Next to proceed with the packing process.

To guide the execution of both the packing and unpacking of a site from the command line, an .ini file that holds a list of the activities that should be completed when the site is being packed or unpacked is created. You can find sample .ini files in the \Program Files\Microsoft Commerce Server\SiteCreate directory. The .ini file is separated into several sections:

- General
- ConnStrs
- Resource Entries
- Application Entries

The General section of the .ini file is used to provide general information about the site, including its name and description and the resources and the applications that are included in the .pup file, as shown here:

```
[General]
SiteName=Retail
Description=Retail site
NumOfResources= 11
NumOfApplications= 2
Resource0=App Default Config
Resource1=Product Catalog
Resource2=Campaigns
Resource3=Site Data Warehouse
Resource4=Transactions
Resource5=Transaction Config
Resource6=Direct Mail
Resource7=Predictor
Resource8=Biz Data Service
Resource9=Global Data Warehouse
Resource10=Site CS Authentication
Application0=Retail
Application1=RetailBizDesk
NumOfConnStrs= 6
```

When packing the site, all resources are included, so the NumOfResources entry is ignored. If you are unpackaging a site, the resource list is used to display information about the number of resources in the site.

Based on the NumOfConnStrs in the General section of the .ini file, the Site Packager uses the connection strings specified in the ConnStrs section to establish the connection string values to access the database. A set of connection string properties and values are supplied for each resource that needs one, as shown here:

```
[ConnStrs]

ConnStrResourceName0=Product Catalog

ConnStrPropertyName0=connstr_db_Catalog

ConnStrValue0=Provider=SQLOLEDB;Persist Security Info=False;User
ID=;Password=;Initial Catalog=Retail_commerce;Data
Source=SERVERNAME;

ConnStrResourceName1=Campaigns

ConnStrPropertyName1=connstr_db_Campaigns

ConnStrValue1=Provider=SQLOLEDB;Persist Security Info=False;User
ID=;Password=;Initial Catalog=Retail_commerce;Data
Source=SERVERNAME;

ConnStrResourceName2=Transactions

ConnStrPropertyName2=connstr_db_Transactions

ConnStrValue2=Provider=SQLOLEDB;Persist Security Info=False;User
ID=;Password=;Initial Catalog=Retail_commerce;Data
Source=SERVERNAME;

ConnStrResourceName3=Transaction Config

ConnStrPropertyName3=connstr_db_TransactionConfig

ConnStrValue3=Provider=SQLOLEDB;Persist Security Info=False;User
ID=;Password=;Initial Catalog=Retail_commerce;Data
Source=SERVERNAME;

ConnStrResourceName4=Biz Data Service

ConnStrPropertyName4=connstr_db_bds

ConnStrValue4=Provider=SQLOLEDB;Persist Security Info=False;User
ID=;Password=;Initial Catalog=Retail_commerce;Data
Source=SERVERNAME;

ConnStrResourceName5=Global Data Warehouse

ConnStrPropertyName5=connstr_db_dw

ConnStrValue5=Provider=SQLOLEDB;Persist Security Info=False;User
ID=;Password=;Initial Catalog=Retail_dw;Data Source=SERVERNAME;
```

For each of the resources listed in the General section, settings can be supplied here to impact how those resources are configured in the site, as follows:

```
[App Default Config]
[Product Catalog]
UseData = 1
[Campaigns]
UseData = 1
[Site Data Warehouse]
[Transactions]
UseData = 1
[Transaction Config]
UseData = 1
[Direct Mail]
GlobalResourceName=Direct Mail on SERVERNAME
[Predictor]
GlobalResourceName=Predictor on SERVERNAME
[Biz Data Service]
UseData = 1
GlobalResourceName= (Add new global resource)
[Global Data Warehouse]
UseData = 1
GlobalResourceName= (Add new global resource)
[Site CS Authentication]
GlobalResourceName= (Add new global resource)
```

Finally, for each of the applications specified in the General section, settings are provided that define configuration settings for each application in the site, as shown here:

```
[Retail]

ASPDir=

VRoot=

Website=

UseData = 1

[RetailBizDesk]

ASPDir=

VRoot=

Website=

UseData = 1
```

Part III

Site Architecture and Basics

Part III of this book covers some of the basics that you'll use throughout the design and development of your Commerce Server 2000 site. Chapter 7 covers those first steps you'll need to take in building your site, including setting up the site and providing the basic framework of resources and application configuration settings. Chapter 8 continues by introducing a number of common Commerce Server 2000 components that you'll be using throughout your site.

Chapter 7

Building the Site

Creating your site and bringing it to completion involves a number of steps. The rest of the chapters in this book cover each of the steps and tasks that you'll need to complete to implement each functionality. The first step, however, is to actually build the site. This involves creating the site's virtual directory in Internet Information Services (IIS), establishing the databases that will be used to store information for the site, creating the resources that will be used throughout the site, and otherwise preparing the site for use.

Using the Blank Site

Of course, you can create all of the elements of the Microsoft Commerce Server 2000 site manually, establishing the databases, resources, and virtual directories. However, I recommend starting with the Blank Site Solution Site, which creates the basic site infrastructure that Commerce Server requires. This allows you to develop the site itself and its content to meet your needs.

Note You could also use the other Solution Sites—Retail, Supplier, or others that might be introduced in the future—but they provide a basic site with a lot of extra code that is difficult to maintain and customize.

To build a site based on the Blank Site, click Start and point to Programs, point to Microsoft Commerce Server 2000, and then select Solution Sites. This opens a folder on your machine where the Solution Sites have been created, typically \Program Files\Microsoft Commerce Server\PuP Packages (see Figure 7-1). If you haven't installed the Solution Sites from the Web, then the Blank Site .pup file is the only one in this folder. You can double-click the BLANK.PUP icon to launch the Commerce Site Packager and create the site. This process is described in more detail in Chapter 6, "Site Packager."

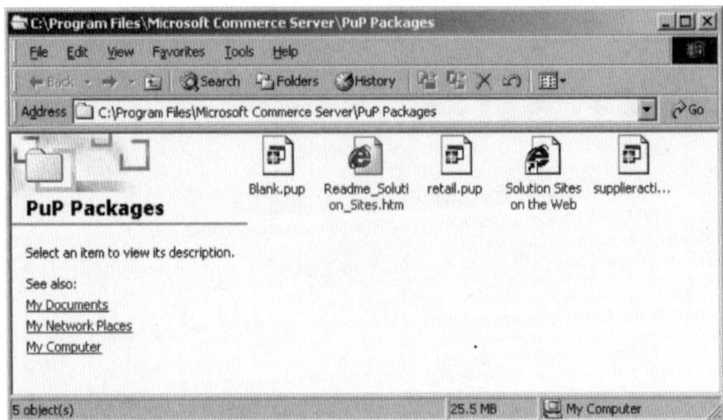

Figure 7-1. *This folder holds the Solution Sites that you've installed in Commerce Server. Typically, these are found in \Program Files\Microsoft Commerce Server\PuP Packages.*

CSAPP.INI

Every Commerce Server 2000 site will contain a file named CSAPP.INI that holds the name of the Commerce Server application that is being used. This name is important because it is used to initialize a number of components that are employed throughout the site. You can find the name in the SiteName key within the file. The contents of CSAPP.INI will look like the following:

```
SiteName=BlankSite

AddressKeyName=blanksite

RelativeURL=blanksite

CreatedBy=Author

CreatedDate=1999.04.02 00:00:00

Version=4.0.0000
```

Typically, you'll retrieve this information and any other necessary data from the CSAPP.INI file when the site first starts by writing code in the GLOBAL.ASA file.

GLOBAL.ASA

The GLOBAL.ASA file is used to store application level code that is called at specific times, such as when an application or a session is starting or ending. Typically, you'll use GLOBAL.ASA to initialize the Commerce Server site by retrieving starting configuration information and initializing select components that will be used throughout the site. In particular, you'll want to provide code in the Application_OnStart event, which fires the first time the application is started.

Using Application Variables

To make the various settings and resources available throughout the site, you'll want to load the required objects or settings into the Application object. Values set in the Application object are available to all users in the site. By using the Application object, you can load and initialize the Commerce Server objects and data once, when the application starts. Then, when the resource is needed, it can be quickly retrieved from the Application object rather than being loaded and initialized on each page.

Real World You'll notice that within the Solution Sites, the Microsoft code tends to follow some particular naming conventions. These are certainly not universally followed. Some developers prefer to simply denote all objects with a prefix of obj or just o. You should consider adopting and documenting some naming convention for your site, whether it is the one followed by Microsoft or your own.

Of particular note, you'll see that all global objects and values that are related to Commerce Server have the prefix MSCS. If the object is a local instance of an object related to Commerce Server, the prefix will be mscs. Thus, you might have an application (MSCSProductCatalog) that holds the global copy of the product catalog object, but the local instance of the object is mscsProductCatalog. You might set the value in a line like this:

```
Set mscsProductCatalog = Application("MSCSProductCatalog")
```

Setting Common Names and Settings

To start the process of initializing the site, you'll want to retrieve common names and values that you'll need throughout the site. This configuration information is used frequently, on almost every page.

SiteName

The first such value will be the name of the site. As previously mentioned, you'll retrieve this from the CSAPP.INI file. This is the only code that is actually built into the GLOBAL.ASA file,and it looks something like the following code sample.

```
<SCRIPT LANGUAGE=VBScript RUNAT=Server>

Const PRODUCTION = 1

Const DEVELOPMENT = 0

Const ENGLISH_UNITED_STATES = &H0409

Sub Application_OnStart()

   Call Main()

End Sub
```

(continued)

(continued)

```
Function GetSiteName()
   Const CONFIG_FILE                = "CSApp.ini"
   Const ForReading                 = 1
   Const TristateUseDefault         = -2

   Dim objPage, objFSO, objConfigFile
   Dim sPath, sLine

   Set objPage = Server.CreateObject("Commerce.Page")
   sPath = Server.MapPath("\" & objPage.VirtualDirectory)
   Set objPage = Nothing

   Rem Open the config file for reading
   Set objFSO = _
    Server.CreateObject("Scripting.FileSystemObject")
   Set objConfigFile = objFSO.OpenTextFile(sPath & "\" & _
    CONFIG_FILE, ForReading, False, TristateUseDefault)
   sLine = objConfigFile.ReadLine
   objConfigFile.Close

   Set objConfigFile = Nothing
   Set objFSO = Nothing

   GetSiteName = GetKeyValue(sLine, "SiteName")
End Function

Rem Returns the value part of a key=value pair
Function GetKeyValue(ByVal sKeyValuePair, ByVal sKey)
   Dim iPos
   Dim s

   Rem Replace tab character with space
   sKeyValuePair  = Trim(Replace(sKeyValuePair, Chr(9), Chr(32)))
   sKey           = Trim(sKey)

   iPos = InStr(1, sKeyValuePair, "=", vbTextCompare)
```

(continued)

(continued)

```
   Rem Return empty string if invalid key=value pair syntax
   If IsNull(iPos) Or iPos = 0 Then
       GetKeyValue = ""
   Else
       Rem Extract the key part from key=value pair
       s = Trim(Left(sKeyValuePair, (iPos - 1)))
       Rem If specified key exists in key=value pair
       If StrComp(sKey, s, vbTextCompare) = 0 Then
              GetKeyValue = Trim(Right(sKeyValuePair, _
               Len(sKeyValuePair) - iPos))
       Else
              Rem Otherwise, return empty string
              GetKeyValue = ""
       End If
   End If
End Function

Sub Main()
   Dim MSCSSiteName
   MSCSSiteName                              = GetSiteName()
   Application("MSCSCommerceSiteName")       = MSCSSiteName
End Sub
</SCRIPT>
```

Notice that the CSAPP.INI file is opened using the FileSystemObject and the SiteName value is retrieved. As an end result, the SiteName is then stored in the Application("MSCSCommerceSiteName") variable. The name is then available throughout the site and can be used to initialize other objects.

Initializing the AppConfig Object

The AppConfig object is used to access the primary site configuration settings from the database. You can initialize it using the following code:

```
set MSCSAppConfig = Server.CreateObject("Commerce.AppConfig")
call _
 MSCSAppConfig.Initialize(Application("MSCSCommerceSiteName"))
set Application("MSCSAppConfig") = MSCSAppConfig
```

Retrieving the Options Dictionary

The Options Dictionary is a dictionary object that holds the site configuration settings. This is retrieved from the AppConfig object as follows:

```
Set MSCSOptionsDictionary = _
 MSCSAppConfig.GetOptionsDictionary("")

Set Application("MSCSOptionsDictionary") = MSCSOptionsDictionary
```

Through the Options Dictionary, you can access the many configuration settings in the various resources on the site. Many of these values can be found in the App Default Config object in the Commerce Server Manager, as listed in Table 7-1.

Table 7-1. App Default Config Configuration Settings

Programmatic Name	App Default Config in the Commerce Server Manager
i_AddItemRedirectOptions	Add item redirect options
i_AddressBookOptions	Address book options
f_AltCurrencyConversionRate	Currency: Alternate currency conversion rate
i_AltCurrencyLocale	Currency: Alternate currency locale
i_AltCurrencyOptions	Currency: Alternate currency options
i_BaseCurrencyLocale	Currency: Base currency locale
i_BillingOptions	Payment options: Billing options
i_BizTalkOptions	BizTalk options
i_CookiePathCorrectionOptions	Cookie path correction options
i_CurrencyDisplayOrderOptions	Currency: Currency display order options
i_DelegatedAdminOptions	Delegated admin options
i_FormLoginOptions	Form login options
i_FormLoginTimeOut	AuthManager Auth ticket timeout
i_HostNameCorrectionOptions	Host name correction options
i_PaymentOptions	Payment options
i_SitePrivacyOptions	Site privacy options
i_SiteRegistrationOptions	Site registration options
i_SiteTicketOptions	Site ticket options
s_AltCurrencySymbol	Currency: Alternate currency symbol
s_BaseCurrencySymbol	Currency: Base currency symbol
s_BizTalkCatalogDocType	BizTalk catalog doc type
s_BizTalkConnString	BizTalk connection string
s_BizTalkOrderDocType	BizTalk PO doc type
s_BizTalkSourceQualifierID	BizTalk source org qualifier
s_BizTalkSourceQualifierValue	BizTalk org qualifier value
s_BizTalkSubmittypeQueue	BizTalk submit type
s_PageEncodingCharset	Page encoding charset
s_SMTPServerName	SMTP server name
s_WeightMeasure	Unit of measure for weight

There are other configuration settings that are accessed in different places within the Commerce Server Manager, as properties of the other site resources. Some are also available from the properties of the application itself within the Commerce Server Manager. A few are not directly available, but must be accessed programmatically using the AppConfig object. These properties are listed in Table 7-2.

Table 7-2. Other Configuration Settings

Programmatic Name	Value/Description
i_IsFullTextSearchInstalled	Indicates whether SQL Server has full-text search enabled.
s_BizDataStoreConnectionString	Profile service: s_BizDataStoreConnectionString
s_CampaignsConnectionString	Campaigns: connstr_db_Campaigns
s_CatalogConnectionString	Product catalog: connstr_db_Catalog
s_CommerceProviderConnectionString	Profile service: s_CommerceProviderConnectionString
s_NonSecureHostname	This value is set in the GLOBAL.ASA file to the nonsecure host name of the application.
s_ProfileServiceConnectionString	Profile service: s_ProfileServiceConnectionString
s_SecureHostname	This value is set in the GLOBAL.ASA file to the secure host name of the application.
s_SiteName	Name of the site.
s_ TransactionConfigConnectionString	Transaction config: connstr_db_TransactionConfig
s_TransactionsConnectionString	Transactions: connstr_db_Transactions

Using the Options Dictionary, you can retrieve any of these values directly, using a statement such as the following:

```
sHostName = MSCSOptionsDictionary.s_NonSecureHostName
```

Storing Common Database Connection Strings

You will likely find it useful to retrieve and store the most commonly used database connection strings directly in the Application object, as shown in the following code sample. In this way, they are readily available when you need them and don't have to be retrieved from the Options Dictionary object.

```
Application("sProfileCS") = _
 Application("MSCSOptionsDictionary").s_ProfileServiceConnectionString

Application("sCatalogCS") = _
  Application("MSCSOptionsDictionary").s_CatalogConnectionString
```

(continued)

(continued)

```
Application("sBizDataCS") = _
 Application("MSCSOptionsDictionary").s_BizDataStoreConnectionString

Application("sTransactionCS") = _
 Application("MSCSOptionsDictionary").s_TransactionsConnectionString
```

Initializing Components

You should also initialize and store any of the Commerce Server components that you are planning to use on the site. For instance, the following code sample loads and initializes several of the key components:

```
'Create a Commerce.AppFramework Object

Set MSCSAppFramework = _
  Server.CreateObject("Commerce.AppFrameWork")

Set Application("MSCSAppFramework") = MSCSAppFramework


'Create a Commerce.ProfileService Object for this app

Set MSCSProfileService = _
  server.CreateObject("Commerce.ProfileService")

Call MSCSProfileService.Initialize(Application("sProfileCS"), _
 SCHEMA_CATALOG)

Set Application("MSCSProfileService") = MSCSProfileService


'Create a Commerce.ProfileService Object for this app

Const ADO_CONNECTION_STRING = True

Set MSCSCatalogManager = _
  server.CreateObject("Commerce.CatalogManager")

Call MSCSCatalogManager.Initialize(Application("sCatalogCS"), _
 ADO_CONNECTION_STRING)

Set Application("MSCSCatalogManager") = MSCSCatalogManager


'Create a Commerce.Datafunctions Object for this app

Set MSCSDataFunctions = _
  Server.CreateObject("Commerce.DataFunctions")

MSCSDataFunctions.Locale = _
 MSCSOptionsDictionary.i_SiteDefaultLocale

MSCSDataFunctions.CurrencySymbol = _
  MSCSOptionsDictionary.s_BaseCurrencySymbol

Set Application("MSCSDataFunctions") = MSCSDataFunctions
```

(continued)

(continued)

```
'Create a Commerce.CacheManager Object for this app

Set MSCSCacheManager = InitCacheManager(MSCSOptionsDictionary)

Set Application("MSCSCacheManager") = MSCSCacheManager

'Create a Commerce.MessageManager Object for the app

Set MSCSMessageManager = InitMessageManager()

Set Application("MSCSMessageManager") = MSCSMessageManager
```

Each of these components is discussed in greater detail in later chapters. However, they're loaded now so that they're available throughout the site. This means that they only have to be loaded and initialized once, which greatly increases the scalability and performance of the site.

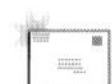

Note The CacheManager and MessageManager components are initialized in subroutines within GLOBAL.ASA. The code isn't shown here, but is detailed in Chapter 8, "Common Components."

Although most of the Commerce Server components should be initialized and stored in the Application object during site startup, the AuthManager object cannot be. This is because it has dependencies on the individual page and looks for each Active Server Page (ASP) page's OnStart and OnEnd events. Therefore, the AuthManager should be created and initialized on each ASP page in which it is used.

Loading Additional Values

The Application object also is useful for storing other information and settings that might be used throughout the site. For instance, you can store the locations and names of the various pipelines that you are going to use in a dictionary in the Application object, as shown in the following code sample. In this way, if you need to change the location or name of a pipeline file, you need to do so in just one place.

```
'load a list of pipelines and their locations

Const WEBSITE_ROOT_DIRECTORY = "\"

set dPipeline = server.CreateObject("Commerce.Dictionary")

sPipelineDir = server.MapPath(WEBSITE_ROOT_DIRECTORY & _
 MSCSAppFramework.VirtualDirectory) & "\pipeline\"

dPipeline.Basket = sPipelineDir & "basket.pcf"

dPipeline.Total = sPipelineDir & "total.pcf"

Set Application("dPipeline") = dPipeline
```

Adding New Resources and Properties

You may find that you want to provide additional configuration settings beyond the ones that are present in the system. As an example, let's assume you want to be able to send an e-mail to your users acknowledging and confirming their orders at your site. You could use Collboration Data Objects (CDO) for Microsoft Windows 2000 to generate and send the e-mail.

Note You'll see this example implemented in Chapter 15, "Order Processing."

Extending the App Default Config Resource Using Structured Query Language Scripts

To provide flexibility, you'll define properties in the App Default Config object to hold the name and e-mail account from which the e-mail will be sent. In this case, you can name the properties EmailName and EmailAddress.

There's no direct way to extend the App Default Config object to include your new properties, but you can create the desired properties within the Structured Query Language (SQL) database tables directly. In this case, the tables you're interested in—Extendedprops and Resourceprops—are located in the MSCS_Admin database. You'll need to insert the property first into the Extendedprops table, and then into the Resourceprops table. The stored procedure shown in the following code sample allows you to do what is necessary to create the new property in the App Default Config resource, based on the parameters that you pass to it:

```
CREATE PROCEDURE dbo.spCreateApp Default ConfigResource

@Property nvarchar(255) ,      -- property name

@Value nvarchar(255) ,         -- property value

@Description nvarchar(255) ,   -- property description

@DisplayName nvarchar(255) ,   -- property display name

@VarType int ,                 -- 8 is string, 3 is integer

@ResourceID int                -- resource ID of the App Default
                               -- Config resource for this site
```

(continued)

(continued)

```
AS

/* First, create the property schema */

insert into extendedprops

   (s_resourcetype, s_propertyname,

   f_isconnstr, f_ishidden, f_issimplelist,

   s_description, i_vartype, s_displayname)

VALUES

   ('AppConfigDefault', @Property,

   0, 0, 0,

   @Description, 8, @DisplayName)

/* Now add the property to the appropriate App */
 /* Default Config resource */

insert into resourceprops

   (i_resourceid, s_propertyname,

   i_vartype, s_value)

VALUES

   (@ResourceID, @Property,

   @VarType, @Value)
```

In this case, by executing the following SQL statement, the property EmailAddress was created in the App Default Config resource for the site. By checking the values in the Site, Resources, and SiteResources tables, you can determine the correct ResourceID to pass (in this case, 172):

```
spcreateApp Default Configresource

   'EmailAddress',

   'YourEmail@yoursite.com',

   'Email Address from which the order confirmation email will
   be sent',

   'Order Email Address', 8, 172
```

By checking the App Default Config object in the Commerce Server Manager, you'll see that the property has now been created in the resource. You might have to refresh the resource by right-clicking it and selecting Refresh before the property appears in the list (see Figure 7-2).

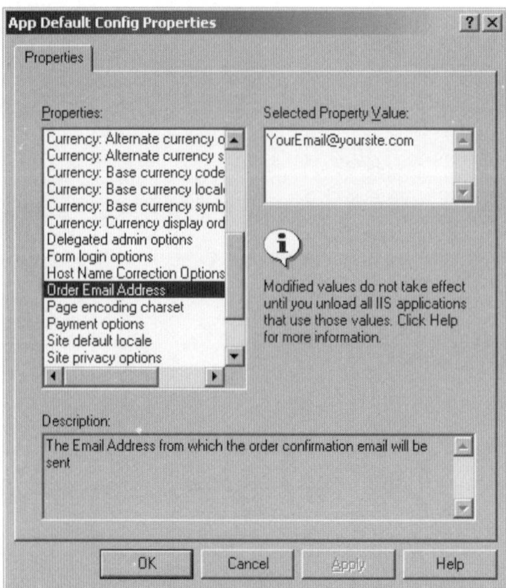

Figure 7-2. *The new property is created by inserting it into the database; it then shows up in the App Default Config resource's Properties list.*

Creating a New Resource

In some cases, you might want to create a new resource to hold these properties. You'll do so using the following steps:

1. Create the Resource Class in Systemprops.
2. Create the Resource Property Schema in Extendedprops.
3. Create the Resource instance.

Note The Commerce Server Software Development Kit includes a tool that assists in performing Steps 1 and 2. This tool can be found in the Samples\Management\ResourceConfig directory within the SDK, or you can follow the simple steps outlined next.

Step 1: Creating the Resource Class

The first step in creating a new resource is to define the Resource Class, used to define the resource that you're creating. The class is defined in the Systemprops database table in the MSCS_Admin database using the following code:

```
insert into SystemProps
   (s_Name, s_ClassName,
   s_ResourceType, f_ResourceFlags,
   f_PupFlags)
```

(continued)

(continued)
```
VALUES
   ('', 'OrderEmailClass',
   'OrderEmail', 2,
   0)
```
Table 7-3 outlines the ResourceFlags that can be set for the resource when it is defined.

Table 7-3. ResourceFlags Values

Value	Description
1	Refers to a global resource
2	Can be displayed in Commerce Server Manager Microsoft Management Console (MMC)
4	Resource has its own MMC snap-in
8	Resource is an application within the site
16	Resource is a physical resource, which requires a global resource
64	Identifies Addresses and AddressItems in resources, which may not be related to Commerce Server
128	Resource uses a nonstandard snap-in extension
256	Resource should never be packaged by Commerce Site Packager

Step 2: Creating the Resource Property Schema

Next, you'll need to create the resource properties that will be stored within the new resource object. In this case, we'll create two properties, s_EmailAddress and s_EmailName, to hold the return e-mail address and sender's name, respectively. We can insert these properties directly into the Extendedprops database table using the following code:

```
insert into ExtendedProps

VALUES
   ('OrderEmail', 's_EmailAddress',
   0, 0, 0,
   'Address from which the Order Confirmation Email is sent',
   8, '', 's_EmailAddress')

insert into ExtendedProps

VALUES
   ('OrderEmail', 's_EmailName',
   0, 0, 0,
   'Name of Account from which Order Confirmation Email is
   Sent',
       8, '', 's_EmailName')
```

Step 3: Creating the Resource Instance

Finally, you create the actual instance of the resource to appear in the application. To do this, you'll make use of the Commerce Server SiteConfig or GlobalConfig object, depending on whether you are creating a site resource or global resource. In this example, you're creating a site resource, so you'll use the SiteConfig object.

Start by loading the SiteConfig object and initializing it, passing it the name of your site ("myblanksite" in this example). You'll then call the CreateComponentConfig method, identifying the Resource Name and the Class Name. The Class Name must match the class you created in Step 1. You then provide the values for the properties you created in Step 2. Once that is done, you use the SaveConfig method to save the changes you made to the site configuration. Follow this code example:

```
sSiteName = "myblanksite"

sResourceName = "Order Confirmation Email"

Set oSiteConfig = CreateObject("Commerce.SiteConfig")

Call oSiteConfig.Initialize(sSiteName)

oSiteConfig.CreateComponentConfig sResourceName,"OrderEmailClass"

oSiteConfig.Fields(sResourceName).Value.Fields( _
 "s_EmailName").Value = "Customer Service"

oSiteConfig.Fields(sResourceName).Value.Fields( _
 "s_EmailAddress").Value = "youremail@yoursite.com"

oSiteConfig.SaveConfig
```

Once these steps have been completed, you will have created a new resource that is available in the Commerce Server Manager MMC (see Figure 7-3).

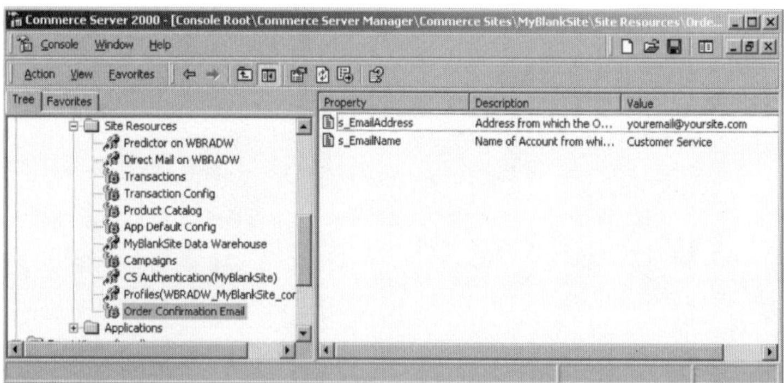

Figure 7-3. *The new resource is created by defining the class and property schemas and then creating an instance of the object in the site.*

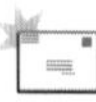

Note If you were creating a Global Config object, you would use the same process, but would create the Commerce.GlobalConfig object and use its CreateServiceConfig method.

Component Reference

The following sections summarize the components that are used in the site configuration system. The corresponding tables provide a quick reference to the properties and methods of each of the components.

AppConfig

The AppConfig object provides access into the primary configuration settings that are used throughout the site (see Table 7-4).

Table 7-4. AppConfig Object Methods

Method	Description
DecodeStatusCode	Gets the status description based on a status code value. These values are stored in the Decode table in the database.
GetCountryCodeFromCountryName	Returns the country abbreviation (code) based on the supplied country name.
GetCountryNameFromCountryCode	Returns the country name based on the supplied country abbreviation (code).
GetCountryNamesList	Returns a list of country names, sorted alphabetically.
GetOptionsDictionary	Returns dictionary of configuration settings.
GetRegionCodeFromCountryCodeAndRegionName	Returns the region abbreviation (code) for the supplied country code and region name.
GetRegionNameFromCountryCodeAndRegionCode	Returns the region name for the supplied country code and region abbreviation (code).
GetRegionNameFromCountryCode	Returns a list of region names for the supplied country code.
Initialize	Initializes the object.
RefreshCache	Refreshes the object's cache.

GlobalConfig

The GlobalConfig object allows you to access and manage global configuration resources within the Commerce Server installation. Its properties and are described in Table 7-5, and its methods are described in Table 7-6.

Table 7-5. GlobalConfig Object Properties

Property Name	Data Type	Description
Fields	Fields object	Returns fields corresponding to the global resources in Commerce Server

Table 7-6. GlobalConfig Object Methods

Method	Description
CreateServiceConfig	Creates a global resource and saves its configuration data
CreateSiteConfig	Creates a site in Commerce Server
DeleteServiceConfig	Deletes a global resource and its configuration data
DeleteSiteConfig	Deletes a site and its associated configuration settings from Commerce Server
GetIfCollection	Converts values in the Fields object into SimpleList or variant arrays
GetResourcePropAttrib	Returns a dictionary of key/value pairs that contain the attributes of a resource property
Initialize	Initializes the GlobalConfig object
MakeArrayFromSimpleList	Converts a SimpleList into an array
MakeArrayFromString	Converts values from the Fields object that are encoded as an array within the string into an array
MakeSimpleListFromArray	Converts an array into a SimpleList
MakeStringFromArray	Converts an array into a string
MakeStringFromSimpleList	Converts a SimpleList into a string
SaveConfig	Saves the GlobalConfig settings
Sites	Returns a list of all the sites in the Commerce Server installation

SiteConfig

The SiteConfig object is provided to allow you to access and manage site resources within a Commerce Server site. Its properties are described in Table 7-7, and its methods are described in Table 7-8.

Table 7-7. SiteConfig Object Properties

Property Name	Data Type	Description
Fields	Fields object	Returns fields corresponding to the site resources in the current site

Table 7-8. SiteConfig Object Methods

Method	Description
AddRefToGroupComponent	Adds a reference to a global resource to the site
CreateComponentConfig	Creates a site resource in the site
DeleteComponentConfig	Deletes a site resource from the site
DeleteSQLScript	Deletes the identified SQL script from the database
ExportResource	Saves the resource definition and data to a file
GetAppsInSite	Returns a list of applications for the site
GetIfCollection	Converts values in the Fields object into SimpleList or variant arrays
GetResourcePropAttrib	Returns a dictionary of key/value pairs that contain the attributes of a resource property
GetSQLScript	Retrieves the identified SQL script from the database
ImportResource	Loads a resource definition and data from a file
Initialize	Initializes the SiteConfig object
MakeArrayFromSimpleList	Converts a SimpleList into an array
MakeArrayFromString	Converts values from the Fields object that are encoded as an array within the string into an array
MakeSimpleListFromArray	Converts an array into a SimpleList
MakeStringFromArray	Converts an array into a string
MakeStringFromSimpleList	Converts a SimpleList into a string
PutSQLScript	Stores the SQL script in the database
SaveConfig	Saves the site configuration settings

SiteConfigReadOnly

The SiteConfigReadOnly object is provided to allow you to access site resources within a Commerce Server site. Table 7-9 describes this object's properties, and Table 7-10 describes its methods.

Table 7-9. SiteConfigReadOnly Object Properties

Property Name	Data Type	Description
Fields	Fields object	Returns fields corresponding to the site resources in the current site

Table 7-10. SiteConfigReadOnly Object Methods

Method	Description
GetAppsInSite	Returns a list of applications for the site
GetIfCollection	Converts values in the Fields object into SimpleList or variant arrays
Initialize	Initializes the SiteConfig object
MakeArrayFromSimpleList	Converts a SimpleList into an array
MakeArrayFromString	Converts values from the Fields object that are encoded as an array within the string into an array
MakeSimpleListFromArray	Converts an array into a SimpleList
MakeStringFromArray	Converts an array into a string
MakeStringFromSimpleList	Converts a SimpleList into a string

Chapter 8

Common Components

There are a number of common components that you will use throughout your Microsoft Commerce Server 2000 site. Some of these are at the core of Commerce Server functionality, and others provide useful assistance in performing various functions. These essential components are introduced in the sections that follow.

SimpleList

The SimpleList object provides a single-element array of variants, which can be any value or object. The array can hold any type of object, including other SimpleList objects, Dictionary objects, or other types of components. The SimpleList is primarily used whenever a list of objects is needed. An example of the SimpleList in action is the Items SimpleList in the OrderForm (see Chapter 14, "Order Basics," for more details).

The SimpleList provides an array of elements, each called Item. The Item property is used to reference each item in the list. You can determine how many items are in the list by checking the list's Count property.

Creating a SimpleList

You can create a SimpleList object directly in Active Server Page (ASP) or any other language by using the PROGID Commerce.SimpleList, shown here:

```
Set sl = server.createobject("Commerce.SimpleList")
```

Adding Items to the SimpleList

You can add a new item to the list using the SimpleList's Add method. Simply pass to it an object or value that you want to add to the list, as shown in this example:

```
sl.Add oSomeObject

sl.Add "Welcome to my site"
```

Counting the Items in the SimpleList

You can determine how many items are in the list by checking the SimpleList's Count property, shown here:

```
lCount = sl.Count
```

Parsing the SimpleList

You can parse through the items in the SimpleList using a For-Next loop, as shown in the following example. This allows you to access each item in the list.

```
For i = 0 to sl.Count - 1

    Set item = sl(i)

    'now item is a reference to the individual element in the
      'SimpleList

Next
```

You can also parse through the SimpleList using a For Each loop, as shown here:

```
For Each item in sl

    'now item is a reference to the individual element in the
      'SimpleList

Next
```

Deleting an Item from the SimpleList

You can delete any item from the SimpleList, given the index of that item. For instance, if you wanted to parse through the list of items to identify an item with the value of Delete Me and delete it, you could do so using the following code:

```
For i = 0 to sl.Count - 1

    Set item = sl(i)

    If item = "Delete Me" Then

        sl.Delete i

    End If

Next
```

Dictionary

The Dictionary object, used throughout Commerce Server components, contains a list of name and value pairs of data. The value is a variant type that holds any data type or object. The Dictionary allows you to dynamically and easily add new keys to the object, simply by assigning a value to the key.

Note The Dictionary object uses a hashing mechanism to provide for fast retrieval of data. However, this means that the keys may not be returned in the same order in which they were entered into the Dictionary.

Creating a Dictionary

You can create a new Dictionary using the PROGID Commerce.Dictionary, shown here:

```
Set d = Server.CreateObject("Commerce.Dictionary")
```

Accessing the Value of a Dictionary Key

There are several different syntaxes that you can use to access the value of a Dictionary key. Each of the following lines of code is identical, in that each retrieves the value of the key MyKeyName from the Dictionary:

```
x = d.Value("MyKeyName")

x = d("MyKeyName")

x = d.MyKeyName
```

Adding a New Key

You can add a new name and value pair to the Dictionary simply by assigning a value to the name, which is also called the key. Notice in this code sample that if you are assigning an object to the dictionary key, you must use the Set statement:

```
Set d.SomeObject = oSomeObject

d.MyNewKey = "MyNewValue"
```

Retrieving the Value from a Key

You can retrieve a value from the Dictionary by using the name of the key to access the value. Notice, as seen in the following example, that if you are retrieving an object from the Dictionary, you must use the Set statement:

```
Set oMyObject = d.SomeObject

sMyValue = d.MyNewKey
```

If the key does not exist when you attempt to retrieve the value, a Null value is returned. You can test for this when retrieving a value from the Dictionary, if necessary, using the code shown here:

```
If Not IsNull(d.MyNewKey) Then

   sMyValue = d.MyNewKey

End if
```

Retrieving the Dictionary Keys

You can retrieve the list of the Keys in a Dictionary using a For Each loop, as shown in this example:

```
For Each key In d

    'key now holds the name of a key in the dictionary

Next
```

Parsing the Dictionary

You can use a For Each loop, as shown in the following code sample, to retrieve the name and value of each key in the Dictionary as well:

```
For Each key In d

    'Write Each Key name/value pair to the web page

    Response.Write key & " = " & d(key)

Next
```

AppFramework

The AppFramework object is provided for working with Web pages. It is used to perform a number of functions, some of which are outlined in the sections that follow.

Creating the AppFramework Object

You can create the AppFramework object using the PROGID Commerce.AppFramework.

Getting the Virtual Directory

The most common use of the component will likely be to identify the virtual directory of the site. When you need to build a link dynamically on the site, you'll need the name of the virtual directory. The AppFramework object's VirtualDirectory method, shown here, returns this:

```
<%

sVirtualDirectory = MSCSAppFramework.VirtualDirectory

%>

<A HREF="/<%=sVirtualDirectory%>/mypage.asp">MyLink</A>
```

Using the VerifyWith Method

You might also want to provide a method to verify that the amount of an order has not been changed between the Order Confirmation page and the Order Acceptance page. This ensures that the last amounts that the user saw are the ones used to process the user's payment. You can do this using the VerifyWith method shown in this example:

```
<%= MSCSAppFramework.VerifyWith(MSCSOrderForm, "_total_total", _
 "_tax_total", "_handling_total", "_shipping_total") %>
```

This results in the following Hypertext Markup Language (HTML) code being generated and provided into the HTML form:

```
<INPUT TYPE=HIDDEN NAME="_VERIFY_WITH" _
 VALUE="_total_total=12345">

<INPUT TYPE=HIDDEN NAME="_VERIFY_WITH" VALUE="_tax_total=66">

<INPUT TYPE=HIDDEN NAME="_VERIFY_WITH" _
 VALUE="_handling_total=77">

<INPUT TYPE=HIDDEN NAME="_VERIFY_WITH" _
 VALUE="_shipping_total=88">
```

When these values are submitted into the next page, you can confirm that the values calculated by the pipeline are the same as those written into the _VERIFY_WITH fields.

DataFunctions

The DataFunctions object is generally used to format data, such as numbers, dates, and currency, based on the specified locale. It also includes functions that can be used to process or convert data from one type to another.

Creating the DataFunctions Object

You can create the DataFunctions object using the PROGID Commerce.DataFunctions. You should store the DataFunctions object in the Application object, as shown here:

```
Set MSCSDataFunctions = _
 Server.CreateObject("Commerce.DataFunctions")

Set Application("MSCSDataFunctions") = MSCSDataFunctions
```

Setting the Defaults

You can set the default locale, which is used if no other locale is provided in the functions, by setting a value in the Locale property. You can also specify the currency symbol that should be used if no currency symbol is provided automatically by setting a value in the CurrencySymbol property, as shown in this example:

```
MSCSDataFunctions.Locale = 1033

MSCSDataFunctions.CurrencySymbol = "$"
```

Getting a List of Available Locales

You can retrieve a list of the locales that are available on your machine through the GetLocaleList method. Using this code returns a SimpleList that contains the LocaleID of every locale on the server:

```
set slLocale = mscsDataFunctions.GetLocaleList
```

Getting Locale Information

Given a LocaleID, you can gather information about the locale, including such data as the country name and abbreviation, native and English language names, currency symbols, native month and day names, and more. You retrieve this information using the GetLocaleInfo method for the object and passing it a parameter that identifies the information you are seeking. Table 8-1 contains a partial list of some of the common parameters you might want to use. The full list is enumerated as LCType constants, which you can find in the *Win32 Platform Software Development Kit*.

Table 8-1. Some LCType Constants

Constant	Hex Value	Long Value	Description
LOCALE_SLANGUAGE	0x2	2	Base language for this locale
LOCALE_SABBREVLANGNAME	0x3	3	Abbreviated language name of this locale (often this is the same as the LOCALE_SLANGUAGE value)
LOCALE_SNATIVELANGNAME	0x4	4	Language as it appears in the native language
LOCALE_SCOUNTRY	0x6	6	Name of the country
LOCALE_SABBREVCTRYNAME	0x7	7	Abbreviation of the country name
LOCALE_SCURRENCY	0x14	20	Local currency symbol

(continued)

Table 8-1. *(continued)*

Constant	Hex Value	Long Value	Description
LOCALE_SDAYNAME1 to LOCAL_SDAYNAME7	0x2A to 0x30	42 to 48	Local day name, starting with Monday through Sunday
LOCALE_SABBREVDAYNAME1 to LOCALE_SABBREVDAYNAME7	0x31 to 0x37	49 to 55	Local abbreviation day name, starting with Monday through Sunday
LOCALE_SMONTHNAME1 to LOCALE_SMONTHNAME12	0x38 to 0x43	56 to 67	Local month name, starting with January through December
LOCALE_SABBREVMONTHNAME1 to LOCALE_SABBREVMONTHNAME12	0x44 to 0x4F	68 to 79	Local abbreviated month name, starting with January through December
LOCALE_SENGLANGUAGE	0x1001	4097	English representation of the language
LOCALE_SENGCOUNTRY	0x1002	4098	English representation of the country name

With the correct parameters and the SimpleList of locales, you can gather and display various information for each locale. The following sample code demonstrates the building of an HTML table that includes the LocaleID, English Language Name, Native Language Name, Country Name and Abbreviation, Currency, Day Names and Abbreviations, and Month Names and Abbreviations values:

```
set slLocale = mscsDataFunctions.GetLocaleList

for i = 0 to slLocale.Count - 1

   Response.Write "<TR>"

   Response.Write "<TD>" & slLocale(i) & "</TD>"

'---------------------

'Write Cells that hold English and Native Language

'---------------------

   Response.Write "<TD>" _
    & mscsDataFunctions.GetLocaleInfo(&H1001, slLocale(i)) _
    &"</TD>"

   Response.Write "<TD>" _
    & mscsDataFunctions.GetLocaleInfo(4, slLocale(i)) & "</TD>"

'---------------------

'Write Cells that hold the Country and Country Abbreviation
```

(continued)

(continued)

```
'---------------------

   Response.Write "<TD>" _
    & mscsDataFunctions.GetLocaleInfo(6, slLocale(i)) & "</TD>"

   Response.Write "<TD>" _
    & mscsDataFunctions.GetLocaleInfo(7, slLocale(i)) & "</TD>"

   '---------------------

   'Write Cell that holds the Currency Symbol

   '---------------------

   Response.Write "<TD>" _
    & mscsDataFunctions.GetLocaleInfo(20, slLocale(i)) & "</TD>"

'---------------------

'Write Cells that hold the Day Names and Abbreviations

'---------------------

   for j = 0 to 6

      Response.Write "<TD>" _
       & mscsDataFunctions.GetLocaleInfo(42+j, slLocale(i)) _
       & " (" _
       & mscsDataFunctions.GetLocaleInfo(49+j, slLocale(i)) _
       & ")</TD>"

   next

'---------------------

'Write Cells that hold the Month Names and Abbreviations

'---------------------

   for j = 0 to 11

      Response.Write "<TD>" _
       & mscsDataFunctions.GetLocaleInfo(56+j, slLocale(i)) _
       & " (" _
       & mscsDataFunctions.GetLocaleInfo(68+j, slLocale(i)) _
       & ")</TD>"

   next

   Response.Write "</TR>"

Next
```

Displaying Localized Currency

When the prices of products are displayed on your Web page, they should be shown in the user's native currency format. The DataFunctions object contains the LocalizeCurrency method that does just this. You should supply the currency value you want displayed, as well as the LocaleID and the currency symbol to use. Of course, the currency symbol for the locale can be determined using the DataFunctions's GetLocaleInfo method, as shown here:

```
Response.Write mscsDataFunctions.LocalizeCurrency(cyValue, _
 lLocale, mscsDataFunctions.GetLocaleInfo(20,lLocale))
```

Based on this code statement, the value 123.45 will be written out in various formats, depending on the locale, as follows:

- 1031 (Germany) = 123,45 DM
- 1033 (United States) = $123.45
- 1034 (Spain) = 123 pta
- 1036 (France) = 123,45 F
- 1040 (Italy) = L. 123
- 2057 (United Kingdom) = £123.45

MessageManager

The MessageManager object is used to provide localized error messages that are reported back primarily from pipeline components. The MessageManager loads an Extensible Markup Language (XML) file that contains a list of the error messages. Each message is an entry in the XML file identified by the message name and language. A separate version of each message should be created in each language.

RC.XML

An example of the source data file that the MessageManager object uses, RC.XML, can be found in the Retail and Supplier sample sites. This file, shown in the following sample, is a good starting point for your own source file:

```
<?xml version="1.0"?>

<MessageManager DefaultLanguage="English">

<Language Name="English" Locale="1033"/>

   <Entry Name="pur_badsku" Type="_Basket_Errors">

       <Value Language="English">Please note that one or more
        items were removed from your order because the product
        is no longer sold.</Value>

   </Entry>

   <Entry Name="pur_badplacedprice" Type="_Basket_Errors">

       <Value Language="English">Please note that prices of
        products in your order have been updated.</Value>

   </Entry>
```

(continued)

(continued)

```
   <Entry Name="pur_discount_changed" Type="_Basket_Errors">

       <Value Language="English">One or more discounts have
        changed.</Value>

   </Entry>

</MessageManager>
```

Creating the MessageManager

You can create the MessageManager object using the PROGID Commerce.MessageManager, as shown here:

```
Set MSCSMessageManager = CreateObject("Commerce.MessageManager")
```

You should create and initialize the MessageManager object in the GLOBAL.ASA file and store it in an Application variable.

Initializing the MessageManager

Initializing the MessageManager requires loading the XML document that holds all of the error messages into the MessageManager, as shown here:

```
Set MSCSMessageManager = CreateObject("Commerce.MessageManager")

sRootPath = Server.MapPath("\" & appframework.VirtualDirectory) _
 & "\"

RCFileName = sRootPath & "rc.xml"

Set oDOMDocument = CreateObject("MSXML.DOMDocument")

oDOMDocument.load RCFileName

Set SchemaNode = _
 oDOMDocument.getElementsByTagName("MessageManager").Item(0)

Set LanguageNodes = SchemaNode.selectNodes("Language")

For Each LanguageNode In LanguageNodes

   LanguageName = _
     LanguageNode.Attributes.getNamedItem("Name").Text

   Locale = LanguageNode.Attributes.getNamedItem("Locale").Text

   Call MSCSMessageManager.AddLanguage(LanguageName, Locale)

Next

Set EntryNodes = SchemaNode.selectNodes("Entry")
```

(continued)

(continued)

```
For Each EntryNode In EntryNodes

   EntryName = EntryNode.Attributes.getNamedItem("Name").Text

   Set ValueNodes = EntryNode.selectNodes("Value")

   For Each ValueNode In ValueNodes

      LanguageName = _
        ValueNode.Attributes.getNamedItem("Language").Text

      EntryValue = ValueNode.Text

      Call MSCSMessageManager.AddMessage(EntryName, _
       EntryValue, LanguageName)

Next

Next

MSCSMessageManager.DefaultLanguage = _
 SchemaNode.Attributes.getNamedItem("DefaultLanguage").Text
```

Getting Messages from MessageManager

When you need to retrieve a message from the MessageManager, you can use the GetMessage method. You must specify the Message key, as shown here:

```
Response.Write  oMessageManager.GetMessage("pur_badplacedprice")
```

In addition, if you want the message in any language other than the default language, you must specify the language name, as shown here:

```
Response.Write oMessageManager.GetMessage("pur_badplacedprice", _
 "Spanish")
```

CacheManager

To provide a more scalable site, Commerce Server 2000 uses the CacheManager to maintain sets of data within the memory cache on the local Web servers. Data is cached in the CacheManager in either Dictionary objects or LRUCache objects.

A typical use of the cached data is the dynamic building of a page based on data from the database. A Product Detail page, for instance, might be generated based on the name, product ID, description, and other supporting information. All of this data must be retrieved from the catalog database. It is then put into HTML code for display on the Web page. Instead of doing this every time the page is accessed for that product, it would be more efficient to store that data in the cache and retrieve it directly from the local memory cache when needed, rather than the database. This can save substantial time in generating the page.

However, to accomplish this task, you need to adjust the manner in which you build the page. Rather than creating HTML directly and wrapping ASP around the HTML as necessary, you need to generate the HTML page entirely within ASP and store it in a server-side variable. This data can be written out once using Response.Write. As an example, the first HTML page fragment shown here would need to be modified to look like the code in the second fragment:

```
<HTML>
<HEAD>
<TITLE>PRODUCT DETAIL</TITLE>
</HEAD>
<BODY>
   <H1>Product Detail</H1>
   <FORM ACTION="_add_to_basket.asp" METHOD=POST>
   <% = sProductID %><BR>
   <% = sProductName %><BR>
   <% = sProductDescription %><BR>
   <% = sProductManufacturer %><BR>
   <IMG SRC="<% = sProductImageURL %>"><BR>
   <% = sProductPrice %><BR>
   <INPUT TYPE=HIDDEN NAME="hdnProductID"
   VALUE="<%=sProductID%>">
   <INPUT TYPE=SUBMIT VALUE="Add to Basket">
   </FORM>
</BODY>
```

```
<%
htmProductDetail = "<HTML><HEAD>" _
   & "<TITLE>PRODUCT DETAIL</TITLE></HEAD>" _
   & "<BODY>" _
   & "<H1>Product Detail</H1>" _
   & "<FORM ACTION=""_add_to_basket.asp"" METHOD=POST>" _
   & sProductID " & "<BR>" _
   & sProductName " & "<BR>" _
```

(continued)

(continued)

```
    & sProductDescription " & "<BR>" _
    & sProductManufacturer " & "<BR>" _
    & "<IMG SRC=""" & sProductImageURL """><BR>" _
    & "<INPUT TYPE=HIDDEN NAME=""hdnProductID"" VALUE=""" _
    & sProductID & """>" _
    & "<INPUT TYPE=SUBMIT VALUE=""Add to Basket"">" _
    & "</FORM>" _
    & "</BODY>"

Response.Write htmProductDetail
%>
```

LRUCache

The LRUCache object is similar to a Dictionary object, in that it stores name and value pairs of data. However, the LRUCache object is designed to work directly with the CacheManager and to store a limited number of elements. When that number is exceeded, the least recently used elements are removed from the cache so that newer elements can be added.

Creating the CacheManager Object

The CacheManager object can be created using the PROGID Commerce.CacheManager, as shown here:

```
Set MSCSCacheManager = _
 Server.CreateObject("Commerce.CacheManager")
```

After it is initialized in the GLOBAL.ASA file, it should be stored in an Application variable.

Initializing the CacheManager

The CacheManager object must be initialized before you can use it. The caches that will be maintained in the CacheManager should be loaded and configured, as shown here:

```
sMachineBaseURL = "http://" _
 & MSCSOptionsDictionary.s_NonSecureHostname _
 & "/" & MSCSAppFramework.VirtualDirectory

' Create CacheManager object
```

(continued)

(continued)

```
Set MSCSCacheManager = _
 Server.CreateObject("Commerce.CacheManager")

MSCSCacheManager.AppUrl = sMachineBaseUrl


Set dDefaultPageConfig = _
 Server.CreateObject("Commerce.Dictionary")

dDefaultPageConfig("ConnectionString") = _
 MSCSOptionsDictionary.s_TransactionConfigConnectionString

dDefaultPageConfig("CacheSize") = 10000

dDefaultPageConfig("TableName") = _
 "CatalogCache_Virtual_Directory"

dDefaultPageConfig("CacheName") = "CatalogCache"

dDefaultPageConfig("AppUrl") = sMachineBaseURL


Set dDefaultPageConfig = _
 Server.CreateObject("Commerce.Dictionary")

dDefaultPageConfig("ConnectionString") = _
 MSCSOptionsDictionary.s_TransactionConfigConnectionString

dDefaultPageConfig("CacheSize") = 10000

dDefaultPageConfig("TableName") = _
 "CatalogCache_Virtual_Directory"

dDefaultPageConfig("CacheName") = "CatalogCache"

dDefaultPageConfig("AppUrl") = sMachineBaseURL


MSCSCacheManager.RefreshInterval("DefaultPageCache") = 0

MSCSCacheManager.RetryInterval("DefaultPageCache") = 5 * 60

MSCSCacheManager.CacheObjectProgId("DefaultPageCache") = _
 "Commerce.LRUCache"

MSCSCacheManager.LoaderProgId("DefaultPageCache") = _
 "Commerce.LRUCacheFlush"

Set MSCSCacheManager.LoaderConfig("DefaultPageCache") = _
 dDefaultPageConfig
```

Adding Data to the Cache

To add data to a cache, you first retrieve the LRUCache from the CacheManager object, based on the cache name. You can then use the LRUCache object's Insert method to add the desired data. You must provide a unique key to identify the data so that it can be retrieved.

As an example, you can build a cache that includes the HTML code that displays a product description, including the name, SKU, description, and other information. You can then give the cache a unique key, using the product ID or SKU that uniquely identifies the product, as shown in the following code sample. If you can't guarantee that the SKU is unique on your system, for instance if you have multiple catalogs that may have duplicate SKUs, you can add the catalog name to the cache name, such as <catalog>_<SKU>.

```
'Build a cache key to uniquely define this HTML in the cache
sCacheKey = sCatalogName & "_" & sProductID
sCacheName = "ProductPageCache"

Set oLRUCache = MSCSCacheManager.GetCache(sCacheName)
Call oLRUCache.Insert(sCacheKey, htmProductDetail)
```

Retrieving Data from the Cache

Once you've loaded data into the cache, you can quickly retrieve and make use of it. This allows you to quickly retrieve a product's Product Detail page, rather than having to dynamically rebuild the page. You can retrieve the data using the LRUCache object's Lookup method. As you can see in this example, if no data has been cached for the given key, the value returned will be Null:

```
sCacheKey = sCatalogName & "_" & sProductID
sCacheName = "ProductPageCache"

Set oLRUCache = MSCSCacheManager.GetCache(sCacheName)
htmProductDetail = oLRUCache.Lookup(sCacheKey)

If isNull(htmProductDetail) then
   'Build the page, because nothing was returned
   'Then store the page HTML code back in the cache
End If
```

GenID

At various times on the site, you'll find that you need to generate IDs or counters. The GenID object assists in allowing you to do just this. It maintains a list of available counters, as well as the next available value, that you can use in a table named Counters in the database.

Note Commerce Server creates and works with one counter, OrderTracking, automatically. This counter is used by the OrderGroup object's SaveAsOrder method to create a unique order number, unless an order number already exists in the order.

Creating the GenID Object

You can create the GenID object using the PROGID Commerce.GenID. After creating the object, you should initialize it, as shown here, specifying the connection string to the database that holds the Counters table:

```
Set MSCSGenID = Server.CreateObject("Commerce.GenID")

MSCSGenID.Initialize _
 MSCSOptionsDictionary.s_BizDataStoreConnectionString

Set Application("MSCSGenID") = MSCSGenID
```

Generating GUIDs

The GenID object allows you to create globally unique identifiers (GUIDs), which you can use to uniquely identify users, organizations, orders, and just about any other type of data. To create a GUID, you can simply call the GenGUIDString method, as shown here:

```
Set sGUID = mscsGenID.GenGUIDString()
```

Initializing Counters

Before you start using a counter, you should initialize it, setting the starting value with the InitializeCounter method. You'll provide the name of the counter and the starting value for that counter, as shown here:

```
MSCSGenID.InitializeCounter("MyCounter", 1000)
```

Getting the Next Counter Value

You can retrieve the next available counter value using the GetCounterValue method. With this method, you'll provide the name of the counter and the number of digits you want returned, as shown here:

```
lValue = CLng(MSCSGenID.GetCounterValue("MyCounter", 10))
```

If the value returned has fewer digits than the value requested, the value will be left-padded with zeroes. This method also increments the counter value stored in the table by one, so that the next value retrieved is the new value.

Component Reference

The following sections summarize the components commonly used in Commerce Server sites. The tables provide a quick reference to the properties and methods of each of the components.

AppFramework

The AppFramework object is designed to assist in working with HTML forms and data. The methods (see Table 8-2) are used to retrieve data from QueryString or Post fields and to generate particular HTML tags. In addition, it is used to identify the virtual directory of the site.

Table 8-2. AppFramework Methods

Method	Description
Options	Returns the HTML code for an <option> tag.
RequestDate	Gets a value from a query string or a posted HTML form, validates it, and converts it to a Date value.
RequestDateTime	Gets a value from a query string or a posted HTML form, validates it, and converts it to a DateTime value.
RequestFloat	Gets a value from a query string or a posted HTML form, validates it, and converts it to a Float-point value.
RequestMoneyAsNumber	Gets a value from a query string or a posted HTML form, validates it, and converts it to a money value, based on the current locale.
RequestNumber	Gets a value from a query string or a posted HTML form, validates it, and converts it to a numeric value.
RequestString	Gets a value from a query string or a posted HTML form, validates it, and cleans it.
RequestTime	Gets a value from a query string or a posted HTML form, validates it, and converts it to a Time value.
VerifyWith	Returns HTML code that contains hidden input fields with values that are used to verify the amounts of an order that is placed. These are used to ensure that the values are not changed during order processing.
VirtualDirectory	Returns the name of the virtual directory of the current site.

CacheManager

The CacheManager object is designed to store Dictionary and LRUCache objects in local Web server memory. Its properties are given in Table 8-3, and its methods are listed in Table 8-4.

Table 8-3. CacheManager Properties

Property Name	Data Type	Description
AppURL	String	Holds the Uniform Resource Locator (URL) of the application.
CacheObjectProgID	String	PROGID of the object used to manage cache data in the object. This identifies the type of objects returned by GetCache.
LoaderConfig	IDispatch	Dictionary that provides configuration data for the Loader component.
LoaderProgID	String	PROGID for the component used to create and populate a data cache.
RefreshInterval	Long	Number of seconds between cache refreshes.
RetryInterval	Long	Number of seconds to wait before retrying to load a cache after a load failure.
WriterConfig	IDispatch	Dictionary that provides configuration data for the Writer component.
WriterProgID	String	PROGID of the component used to write data that has been added to the cache since the last refresh.

Table 8-4. CacheManager Methods

Method	Description
GetCache	Retrieves a data cache object that is associated with the given cache name
RefreshCache	Causes the cache to be immediately refreshed

DataFunctions

The DataFunctions object provides a number of utility functions for converting, displaying, and formatting data on a Web site. Table 8-5 describes the properties of the DataFunctions object, and Table 8-6 gives its methods.

Table 8-5. DataFunctions Properties

Property Name	Data Type	Description
CurrencySymbol	Variant	Symbol displayed with currency when no currency symbol is supplied by another method
Locale	Long	Default locale that defines how currency, date, time, and numeric data are formatted

Table 8-6. DataFunctions Methods

Method	Description
CleanString	Cleans a string by removing white spaces, modifying case, and validating the length
CloneObject	Creates a copy of a SimpleList or Dictionary object
ConvertDateString	Converts a string that contains a date to a Date type, based on the given Locale
ConvertDateTimeString	Converts a string that contains a date and time to a Date type, based on the given Locale
ConvertFloatString	Converts a string that contains a Float number to a Double type, based on the given Locale
ConvertMoneyStringToNumber	Converts a string that contains a Currency value to a Long type, based on the given Locale
ConvertNumberString	Converts a string that contains a number to an Integer type, based on the given Locale
ConvertStringToCurrency	Converts a string that contains a Currency value to a Currency type, based on the given Locale
ConvertTimeString	Converts a string that contains a Time value to a Date type, based on the given Locale
Date	Returns a Date value as a string, formatted based on the given Locale
DateTime	Returns a Date Time value as a string, formatted based on the given Locale
Float	Returns a Float value as a string, formatted based on the given Locale
GetLocaleInfo	Retrieves information about the given Locale
GetLocaleList	Retrieves SimpleList of locales on the server
LocalizeCurrency	Returns a Currency value as a string, formatted based on the given Locale
Money	Returns a Long value as a string, formatted based on the given Locale
Number	Returns a numeric value as a string, formatted based on the given Locale
Time	Returns a Time value as a string, formatted based on the given Locale
ValidateDateTime	Validates a Date Time value based on the provided criteria
ValidateFloat	Validates a Float value based on the provided critieria
ValidateNumber	Validates a numeric value based on the provided criteria

Dictionary

The Dictionary object is used to maintain a set of name and value pairs of variant data, which can include objects or other values. Its properties are described in Table 8-7.

Table 8-7. Dictionary Properties

Property Name	Data Type	Description
Count	Long	Number of elements in the Dictionary object.
Prefix	String	Any key name that begins with this prefix is saved to the database. By default, this is the underscore (_) character.
Value	Variant	The value associated with a key name in the Dictionary.

GenID

The GenID object is used to generate GUIDs and global counter values on a Commerce Server 2000 site. The GenID methods are listed in Table 8-8.

Table 8-8. GenID Methods

Method	Description
GenBase5GUIDString	Generates a Base5 GUID string
GenGUIDString	Generates a GUID string
GetCounterValue	Gets the next available value for a counter and increments the counter
Initialize	Connects the GenID to the database that holds the Counters table
InitializeCounter	Initializes a counter with a starting value

LRUCache

The LRUCache object is used to store values in the cache, keeping those objects in memory for more efficient access. The methods of the LRUCache are described in Table 8-9.

Table 8-9. LRUCache Methods

Method	Description
Flush	Removes the specified element from the cache
FlushAll	Removes all elements from the cache
Insert	Inserts an element into the cache
Lookup	Returns the value of the specified element in the cache
LookupObject	Returns an object from the specified element in the cache
SetSize	Defines the maximum size of the cache

MessageManager

The MessageManager object is used to maintain a list of language-specific error messages used throughout the site. The MessageManager property is given in Table 8-10, and its methods are listed in Table 8-11.

Table 8-10. MessageManager Property

Property Name	Data Type	Description
DefaultLanguage	String	Default message set

Table 8-11. MessageManager Methods

Method	Description
AddLanguage	Adds a new message set to the MessageManager object
AddMessage	Adds a new message to the MessageManager object
GetLocale	Returns the locale for the given message set
GetMessage	Returns the message identified by the specified message key and language

SimpleList

The SimpleList object is used to maintain an array of variant values that can include objects or other values. Its properties are presented in Table 8-12, and its methods are given in Table 8-13.

Table 8-12. SimpleList Properties

Property Name	Data Type	Description
Count	Long	Number of elements in the SimpleList
Item	Variant	References an element, either an object or another variant value

Table 8-13. SimpleList Methods

Method	Description
Add	Adds an item to the SimpleList
Delete	Deletes the specified item from the SimpleList

Part IV

User Management

Part IV of this book covers user management and profiles on the site. Chapter 9 examines those tasks you need to accomplish in providing user authentication and security on the site, including authenticating users and maintaining user accounts. Chapter 10 provides an in-depth discussion of the use of profiles in Commerce Server 2000 to provide access to user, organization, address, and other information.

Chapter 9

User Authentication

When you are working with an e-commerce site, it is important on several levels that you can easily and accurately identify and track the actions of your customers. When a user views his or her basket, you want to make sure it is that user's basket and that no one else can see it. When a purchase is being made, you want to be certain that the person making the purchase is the user you believe it is. You'll want to be able to track what items users are purchasing or browsing.

All of these tasks require the site to detect and, in some cases, authenticate the user. In this chapter, we'll look at the tools that Microsoft Commerce Server 2000 provides that enable you to secure the site, track and identify users, and authenticate users when necessary.

Your first choice in developing your authentication scheme is to determine exactly when you will want users to log in, if at all. You might allow users to shop and make purchases anonymously, or you might want to force users to log into the site immediately on entry. Some sites only require users to log in when making a purchase. The choice is yours, depending on the needs of your site. The topics and techniques discussed in this chapter can be applied to any of these schemes.

At the end of the chapter is a section that summarizes the components of the authentication system and a table that provide a quick reference to the methods of that component.

Authentication in Commerce Server 2000

Authentication in a Commerce Server 2000 site is managed through the use of tickets that identify a user, whether they have been authenticated or not. Commerce Server provides two types of tickets:

- **MSCSProfile tickets** This ticket is provided to users who have not logged into the site.
- **MSCSAuth tickets** This ticket identifies that this user has been authenticated in the site.

Either of these tickets is written to a cookie on the user's machine. Each consists of a specifically encrypted cookie and globally unique identifier (GUID) to uniquely identify the user. If the user's browser does not support or allow cookies, you can modify your site to pass the ticket encrypted as a part of the Uniform Resource Locator (URL).

AuthManager

The AuthManager component is used to manage the user authentications from page to page. You use this component to check if the user is authenticated, issue tickets to the user, and save user information to the cookies. In addition, AuthManager provides support for managing user tickets for users that do not have cookies supported in their browser by passing ticket information encrypted in the URL.

Note Because the AuthManager component checks to see if the user has been authenticated in code, the security that the component enforces can only require authentication when a user accesses an Active Server Page (ASP).

Creating the AuthManager

To use the AuthManager object, you'll first need to create and initialize it, as shown in the following code sample:

```
set mscsAuthManager = Server.CreateObject("Commerce.AuthManager")

mscsAuthManager.Initialize MSCSSiteName
```

Unlike many of the other Commerce Server components, AuthManager must be created and initialized locally on each page. The component needs access to the ASP page's OnStart and OnEnd events. It should not be stored in application or session variables.

Detecting Authentication

Once you have the reference to the AuthManager object, you can provide code on each page where you need it to determine if the user has been authenticated on the site. If not, you can redirect users to the login page. To do this, you'll call the IsAuthenticated method, as shown here, which returns a Boolean indicating whether the user has been authenticated:

```
If Not mscsAuthManager.IsAuthenticated then

   Response.Redirect "AuthFiles/Login.asp"

End If
```

The IsAuthenticated method simply determines if the user has a valid MSCSAuth ticket that is properly encrypted with the user and site information and that has not expired. The IsAuthenticated method does not attempt to reauthenticate the user's ID and password.

In addition to calling the IsAuthenticated method, you can further improve the process by saving the current page to a cookie. You can then redirect users back to the page they were attempting to access before they were forced to log in. The cookie name MSCSFirstRequestedURL is used by the AuthFilter for this purpose and should also be used in your code, as shown here, so that the login page can consistently be used for either authentication scheme.

```
If Not mscsAuthManager.IsAuthenticated then

    Response.Cookies("MSCSFirstRequestedURL") = _
      Request.ServerVariables("SCRIPT_NAME")

    Response.Redirect "AuthFiles/Login.asp"

End If
```

Issuing Authentication Tickets

At an appropriate point, you can issue a ticket to users so that you can track them on your site. The ticket you issue depends on whether or not the user has been authenticated on the site. You'll issue the MSCSAuth ticket for users that have been authenticated and the MSCSProfile ticket for anonymous users. To do this, you'll use the SetAuthTicket and SetProfileTicket methods, respectively. For example, you can issue the MSCSAuth Ticket after the user logs in, as shown here:

```
mscsAuthManager.SetAuthTicket sUserID, True, 60
```

If you are allowing anonymous users to browse the site, you can issue an MSCSProfile Ticket on the first page they access. In the case of an anonymous user, you may need to provide a unique ID to identify the user. Fortunately, you can use the GenID component, shown here, to generate a GUID for this use:

```
Set mscsGenID = Server.CreateObject("Commerce.GenID")

SUserID = mscsGenID.GenGUIDString()

mscsAuthManager.SetProfileTicket sUserID, True
```

Login Authentication

By putting this code together and working in combination with the User Profile object, you can easily accept users' login information and authenticate them based on their user profile. To authenticate the user, follow this basic process:

1. Retrieve user input of UserName and Password.
2. Retrieve User Profile based on the UserName.
3. Retrieve Password from the User Profile.
4. Determine if the password in the User Profile matches the password typed by the user.
5. If the passwords match, issue the MSCSAuth ticket.

Putting this all together provides something like this code segment:

```
sUserID= Request("username")

sPassword= Request("password")

Set MSCSProfileService = Application("MSCSProfileService")

Set mscsProfile = MSCSProfileService.GetProfile(sUserID, _
 "UserObject")

sProfilePWD = mscsProfile("GeneralInfo.user_security_password")

if sPassword = sProfilePwd then

   mscsAuthManager.SetAuthTicket sUserID, True, 60

   Response.Redirect "/" & MSCSSiteName & "/default.asp"

else

   Response.Redirect "login.asp"

End If
```

Supporting No Cookies

You can use the AuthManager to automatically pass the user's ID as a part of the URL and retrieve it from the URL. You can have the user log in, but instead of attempting to issue the MSCSAuth Ticket to the user's cookie, you can pass the user ID to each page. You can automatically append the user ID to the URL using the AuthManager's URLShopperArgs method, as shown here:

```
Dim aNames(0)

Dim aValues(0)

urlPage = "/" & MSCSCommerceSiteName & "/mypage.asp" _
 & mscsAuthManager.URLShopperArgs(aNames,aValues)
```

This results in a QueryString being built that looks something like this:

```
http://localhost/MySite/mypage.asp?MSCSAuth =
 61E4CECF7275066F5D9F898C286503737BFE _
 18DC266F246F2CAA76CC270904C6C316D1B _
 266888E0C634B09033E2993CF0814EA5089 _
 AD14C0E35FBFF79CBEC208
```

It includes the MSCSAuth ticket being issued and placed on the QueryString. The AuthManager's IsAuthenticated method automatically detects the ticket on the QueryString and uses it to determine whether the user is authenticated.

AuthFilter

If you need to apply or enforce security requirements against all types of files and documents, including images, Hypertext Markup Language (HTML) pages, and more, you can do so using Commerce Server 2000's AuthFilter. The AuthFilter is an Internet Server Application Programming Interface (ISAPI) dynamic-link library (DLL) that works with Internet Information Services (IIS) to check a user's credentials. It allows you to provide authentication services against the Active Directory service domain or a custom data source.

You configure AuthFilter through the Commerce Server Manager by following these steps:

1. Open the Commerce Sites folder, and then the site itself, and the Applications folder.
2. Right-click the Web server that you need to configure and select Properties from the shortcut menu.
3. From the Properties dialog box (Figure 9-1), you can apply the AuthFilter by selecting the appropriate option in the Authentication Filter list box. You can select one of these options:
   - **No Filter** AuthFilter is not used.
   - **Windows Authentication** Users are authenticated against the Active Directory or local Security Access Manager (SAM).
   - **Custom Authentication** Users are authenticated against a custom data source, such as SQL Server.
   - **AutoCookie Mode** This automatically generates cookies that store tickets for guest users.

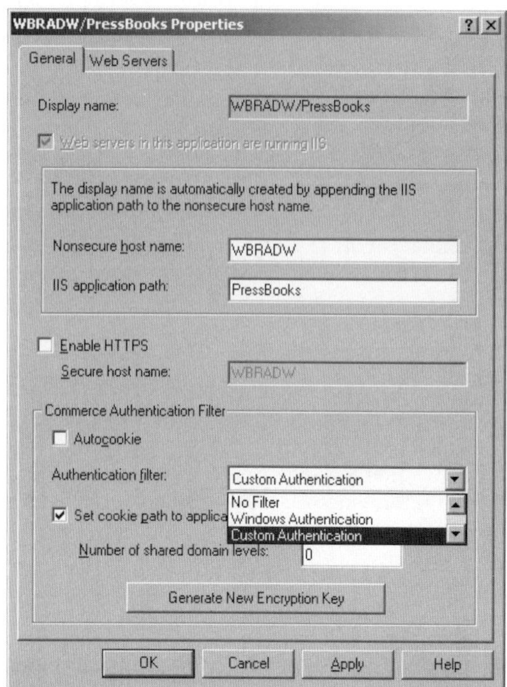

Figure 9-1. *You can configure your site to use the AuthFilter through the Commerce Server Manager.*

When you set up the AuthFilter and a user accesses the site, the AuthFilter performs these actions:

1. **Checks the URL** The AuthFilter verifies that the URL is correct.
2. **Verifies cookie support** Using the AuthFilter requires cookie support in the browser, and AuthFilter checks for cookie support. If the browser doesn't support cookies, the user is redirected to the NOCOOKIE.ASP page.
3. **Checks for valid ticket** AuthFilter checks to see if there is a valid MSCSAuth ticket that has not expired.

 **Note** Using AuthFilter requires that the user's browser allow cookies.

Custom Authentication

When you select Custom Authentication, the AuthFilter is applied to the site and works with IIS. Whenever a user enters the site and accesses any page, the AuthFilter checks to see if that user has a valid MSCSAuth ticket. If so, the user is allowed to proceed. If not, the user is redirected to the login page. The AuthFilter determines the location of the login page by checking the properties of the appropriate CS Authentication resource. In particular, it redirects to the page specified in the Login Form property, which should be located in the virtual directory specified in the AuthFilter Helper Folder.

The actual login page will work and can be written the same way as described earlier. In the case of Custom Authentication, the ISAPI DLL is essentially performing the same task as the AuthManager's IsAuthenticated function. The difference is that the AuthFilter can be applied to all the files in the site, including images, HTML, and ASP files, whereas the AuthManager must be run in an ASP file.

Windows Authentication

By applying the AuthFilter with the Windows Authentication setting, you specify that the user will be authenticated against an account in Active Directory. This configuration works with the IIS to retrieve user information and then automatically validates the user and issues the MSCSAuth ticket.

When a user accesses any page on the site, the AuthFilter ISAPI DLL checks the URL to see if the user name and password have been passed as a part of the query string. If they have, they will be passed in the format proxyuser=<userid>&proxypwd=<password>. If this is the case, the ISAPI DLL strips the user information from the URL, validates the information against Active Directory, and, if successful, issues the MSCSAuth ticket.

From there, the AuthFilter proceeds as it did in the Custom Authentication mode by checking to see if the user has a valid MSCSAuth ticket. If the ticket exists and has not expired, the user is allowed to proceed. If the ticket does not exist, the user is redirected to the login page.

Configuring IIS

The AuthFilter ISAPI DLL works closely with IIS to detect the user name and password on the URL and act accordingly. To support this integration, however, you must properly configure several elements in IIS. For those pages that require authentication, you must ensure that the site uses BASIC Authentication. Those pages should not allow Anonymous Access or Integrated Windows Authentication, so those options must not be selected. In addition, to allow for proper login, the AuthFiles folder should allow Anonymous Access, so you must also establish that setting.

You will set these configurations in the IIS Manager as follows:

1. Open the Web server and select the properties for the appropriate directories.
2. In the Directory Security tab, in the Anonymous Access and Authentication Control section, click Edit.
3. You can then modify the settings for Anonymous Access, Basic Authentication, and Integrated Windows Authentication as required.

Login Page Code

Because of the way that the AuthFilter ISAPI DLL looks for the user name and password, the login page differs slightly from the Custom Authentication login page. In this login page, you can retrieve the Username and Password values that the user has specified. Then, you should redirect the desired page, but after appending the user name and password to the URL QueryString. This is automatically stripped off by the AuthFilter and is not actually displayed in the user's browser. You might also want to confirm that a Profile exists for this user, and not just a valid account, as shown in the following sample:

```
sUserID = request("username")

sUserPWD = request("password")


Set MSCSProfileService = Application("MSCSProfileService")

Set mscsProfile = MSCSProfileService.GetProfile(sUserID, _
 "UserObject")

If mscsProfile Is Nothing Then

   'no profile exists for the specified user

   Response.Redirect "login.asp"

End If


urlReturn = Request.Cookies("MSCSFirstRequestedURL")

if len(urlReturn)=0 Then

   urlReturn = "/" & MSCSSiteName & "/default.asp"

End If

urlReturn = urlReturn & "?proxyuser=" & sUserID & "&proxypwd=" _
 & sUserPWD

Response.Redirect urlReturn
```

Autocookie Support

You might decide that you want to track the way that anonymous users are using your site over a period of time. Commerce Server 2000 supports this capability by providing autocookie support with the AuthFilter. If autocookie support is enabled, the AuthFilter checks to see if users have an MSCSProfile ticket in their cookie. If a valid ticket exists, users are allowed to continue to the page they request. If the MSCSProfile ticket does not exist, users are routed first to the page specified in the Autocookie Form configuration setting, by default AUTOCOOKIE.ASP.

The AUTOCOOKIE.ASP page checks to see if the user's browser supports persistent cookies. If it doesn't, then the user is routed to the NOCOOKIE.ASP page and informed that cookie support is required. If cookies are supported, the page creates a unique ID for the user, which it then uses to issue the MSCSProfile ticket to the user. Finally, the user is rerouted to the page he or she was originally accessing. This entire process will be transparent to the user. Its code is shown here:

```
set mscsAuthManager = Server.CreateObject("Commerce.AuthManager")

MSCSSiteName = CStr(Application("MSCSCommerceSiteName"))
mscsAuthManager.Initialize(MSCSSiteName)

set mscsGenID = Server.CreateObject("Commerce.GenID")
strUsername = mscsGenID.GenGUIDString

mscsAuthManager.SetProfileTicket strUsername, True

urlReturn = Request.Cookies("MSCSFirstRequestedURL")
Response.Redirect urlReturn
```

Single Sign-On Support

If you have a site with several domains or several applications, you may want to avoid forcing your users to log in every time they move between applications or domains. You do this by setting up cookie sharing between your domains or applications. In this way, an MSCSAuth ticket that is stored in the user's cookie is made available to multiple domains or applications.

Sharing Cookies Across Domains

To share a cookie across domains, open the site application's Property dialog box. You can then specify the value for Number Of Shared Domain Levels to be at least two. In this case, you may have several sites that are defined as different domains, such as *www.wingtiptoys.com* and *premium.wingtiptoys.com*. However, if the user logs into one site and then moves to the second, his or her MSCSAuth ticket is still valid and the user ID is accepted.

Sharing Cookies Across Applications

You can also share cookies across multiple applications on the same site. To do this, open the site application's Property dialog box and clear the Set Cookie Path To Application check box. At this point, a user might be able to move between two applications, such as the Web site and the Business Desk, on the same site without being forced to log into both sites.

Integrating with Passport

Microsoft has established a service called Passport that allows users to maintain a single account and password that can be used on multiple sites. A Passport user can specify his or her personal information, including nickname, birthdate, e-mail address, and more. You can easily integrate your Commerce Server 2000 site with Passport and give your users the option of logging in with their Passport credentials.

To integrate your site with Passport, you'll need to retrieve and set up the Passport Software Development Kit (SDK) from the Passport site at *http://www.passport.com/business*. The site also includes directions on installing and configuring Passport on your site, as well as information needed to test the Passport functions. In the following sections, we'll take a look at some of the typical methods you'll use when integrating your site with Passport. However, the SDK provides a great deal more detail and you'll definitely want to give the SDK documentation a closer look.

The Passport Manager

At the core of Passport integration is the Passport Manager object. With this object, you can authenticate a user through Passport and work with his or her Passport profiles. You'll create the passport manager on the page as shown here:

```
Set oPassportMgr = Server.CreateObject("Passport.Manager")
```

Once you have the object instantiated, you can begin working with Passport.

The Passport Factory

To provide greater scalability on the site, you should actually create the Passport Manager object from the Passport Factory. This factory maintains a pool of Passport Manager objects that it then issues as needed to the page. You should create the Passport Factory at the application level in the GLOBAL.ASA file, shown here, so that it is available throughout the site:

```
<OBJECT RUNAT=SERVER SCOPE=APPLICATION PROGID="Passport.Factory"
ID="oPassportFactory">

</OBJECT>
```

Once the object is granted, you'll then retrieve an instance of the Passport Manager on each page. To do this, use the Passport Factory's CreatePassportManager method. You'll then need to initialize the Passport Manager within the local page's context using its OnStartPageASP method, shown in this sample:

```
set oPassportMgr = oPassportFactory.CreatePassportManager

oPassportMgr.OnStartPageASP Request, Response
```

Now that the Passport Manager object is initialized, you can put it to use.

Displaying the Passport Login/Logout Logo

The first step in integrating Passport on your site is to give your customers the option to log into the site with their Passport credentials. Fortunately, the Passport Manager provides a mechanism for doing this automatically using the LogoTag2 method, as shown here:

```
lTimeWindow = 3600

BForceLogin = True

thisURL = "http://" & Request.ServerVariables("SERVER_NAME") _
  & Request.ServerVariables("SCRIPT_NAME")

Response.Write oPassportMgr.LogoTag2(Server.URLEncode(thisURL), _
  lTimeWindow, bForceLogin)
```

The LogoTag2 method returns the image tag with a link to the Passport authentication server. The image displayed is the Login image if the user is not already logged in and the Logout image if the user is already logged in. You'll pass the method the return URL, which is the page to which users are returned once they've been logged in or out. The TimeWindow and ForceLogin parameters help define how the login function works at the Passport server. See the SDK for more details.

You can silently log the user in, if the user has a Passport account, by calling the LoginUser method directly. This redirects users to your site if they are able to silently log in using Passport. Otherwise, the method takes users to the Passport login screen. After users are authenticated, they are redirected to the return URL, as shown here:

```
oPassportMgr.LoginUser thisURL, lTimeWindow, bForceLogin
```

In addition, you might find it useful to determine if the user is already logged in using the IsAuthenticated method, shown here:

```
If Not oPassportMgr.IsAuthenticated(lTimeWindow, bForceLogin) _
 Then

   oPassportMgr.LoginUser thisURL, lTimeWindow, bForceLogin

End If
```

Reading the Passport Profile

Once the user has been authenticated with Passport, you can use the Passport Manager to retrieve profile properties and values. With this, you can determine the user's e-mail address, nickname, and other profile properties. The Passport defines a set of standard properties, shown in Table 9-1, that you can query.

Table 9-1. Standard Properties in a User's Passport Profile

Property Name	Description
Accessibility	Identifies if the user requires site accessibility features (0 = no, 1 = yes)
Bday_Precision	Identifies the precision of the birthdate that will be returned
Birthdate	Returns the birth date or birth year
City	Returns an ID that can map to the user's city; however, this is not an exact match
Country	Returns the country code for the user's country
Gender	Returns the user's sex (Null, M, F, U)
Lang_Preference	The Location ID (LCID) of the user's preferred language
MemberIDHigh	The first half of the user's Passport user ID
MemberIDLow	The second half of the user's Passport user ID
Nickname	The user's nickname
PreferredEmail	The user's e-mail address
PostalCode	The user's postal code
ProfileVersion	Version number for the profile
Region	ID that maps to the user's region
Wallet	Identifies whether the user has a Passport wallet (0 = no, 1 = yes)

You can retrieve a profile value using the Passport Manager, as shown here:

```
Response.Write "Welcome, " & oPassportMgr.Profile("Nickname")
```

You can also save changes to the Passport profile. This is done in a three-part process. The first step is to write the changes into the value, the second is to call the Commit method, and the third is to call the LogoTag2 method. After the Commit method is called, the LogoTag2 method writes the profile changes back to the Passport server when it retrieves the logo HTML image tag, as displayed here:

```
sEmail = Request.Form("Email")

If oPassportMgr.HasProfile Then

   oPassportMgr.Profile("PreferredEmail") = sEmail

   oPassportMgr.Commit

End If

'do some other stuff

Response.Write oPassportMgr.LogoTag2(Server.URLEncode(thisURL))
```

Of course, the methods that have been shown here only go so far. You will definitely want to explore the Passport SDK. In addition, you should take a look at the Passport sitelet, which also demonstrates some techniques for integrating with Passport.

Authentication Components

This section provides a quick reference to the subject component covered in this chapter, along with its properties and methods.

AuthManager

The AuthManager component is created using the PROGID Commerce.AuthManager. This component should be created and initialized locally on each page, as it needs to be able the access the ASP page's OnStart and OnEnd events. Its methods are described in Table 9-2.

Table 9-2. AuthManager Methods

Method Name	Description
GenerateEncryptionKey	Creates an encryption key for use with storing cookie data
GetProperty	Retrieves the specified property from the cookie or query string
GetURL	Builds a URL with a set of name and value pairs
GetUserID	Retrieves the user's ID from the ticket
GetUserIDFromCookie	Retrieves the user's ID from the cookie
Initialize	Initializes the AuthManager object with the Site Name
IsAuthenticated	Returns True or False to determine if the user is authenticated by detecting whether the user has a valid MSCSAuth Ticket
Refresh	Updates the cache site configuration properties
SetAuthTicket	Provides the encrypted MSCSAuth Ticket to the user
SetProfileTicket	Provides an encrypted MSCSProfile Ticket to the user
SetProperty	Adds a name and value pair to the cookie or query string
SetUserID	Saves the User ID property in a ticket
UnInitialize	Removes the site configuration properties from cache
URLArgs	Builds a URL-encoded query string with name and value pairs
URLShopperArgs	Builds a URL-encoded query string with name and value pairs and the user's ticket

Chapter 10
Profiles

Microsoft Commerce Server 2000 introduces the concept of profiles to provide enhanced management of and access to data. A profile is a standard representation of an entity of data that allows you to define exactly what attributes or properties you expect to represent a given entity. These entities might be users, groups, addresses, or anything else you might want to provide.

One of the advantages of the profiling system is that the data that describes an entity can be kept in multiple data stores. For instance, you might maintain user information in a SQL Server database, Active Directory, or another legacy database. As long as the data source is compliant with object linking and embedding database (OLE DB) or Lightweight Directory Access Protocol (LDAP) 3.0, it can be used as a store for profile data.

Through the profiling system, the Web developer doesn't need to worry about exactly where the data is being stored because the system aggregates the data from all of the data sources and presents it as a single object. Whether the data is from the Active Directory or a database, the developer reads and writes through the profile object, which ensures that the data is stored in the proper location.

Another advantage to the profiling system is that the profile data retrieved from the data stores is cached locally on the Web server. This means that after the first time the data is accessed, the profile data is quickly accessible. If you're just reading the data, the system doesn't need to make a round trip to the database server(s).

This chapter includes a section at the end that summarizes the components of profile objects and includes tables that provide a quick reference to their methods and properties.

Defining a Profile Object

So how do you define an entity in the profiling system? How do you identify the data store for the profile object? You manage the profiling system using the Commerce Server Manager (CSM) snap-in. CSM lets you define data stores for the profile system and make those data stores available to the profiling system. Once the data store and fields are defined, you can use the Profile Definition pages in the Business Desk or in CSM to manage the profiles.

The Data Source

At the root of the profile system are its data sources. A data source is any data store that contains some or all of the data for a profile. Any data store can be used as a profile data source as long as that store is accessible via OLE DB (for example, SQL Server, Oracle, and so on) or LDAP (for example, Active Directory).

Partitioned Data Sources

If you need to support larger numbers of users, you can partition the data to reside in various databases. By segregating the data into different partitions, you can distribute the load of accessing the profiles. You should plan on dividing the profile data source into partitions if you have more than 10 million profile entries, and each partition should hold less than 10 million entries. When you use a partitioned data source, the storage devices must have the same schema. For example, if you create a partitioned data source that maps a profile definition to three databases, the table definitions of all three databases must be the same. In addition, you are limited to a maximum of 128 partitions.

The hashing field property in the profile definition identifies the field that is used to determine in which partition the data will be stored. When profile data is stored or retrieved, the profiling system checks with the hashing field to determine which partition holds the data.

Adding a Data Source

To create a new data source, follow these steps:

1. Open Commerce Server Manager and the Profiles resource for your site in the Global Resources folder.
2. Open the Profiles Catalog, right-click on the Data Sources container, and select the New Data Source. This guides you through the steps of creating the new data source.
3. You'll need to specify the Name, Display Name, and Description values for the data source (see Figure 10-1).

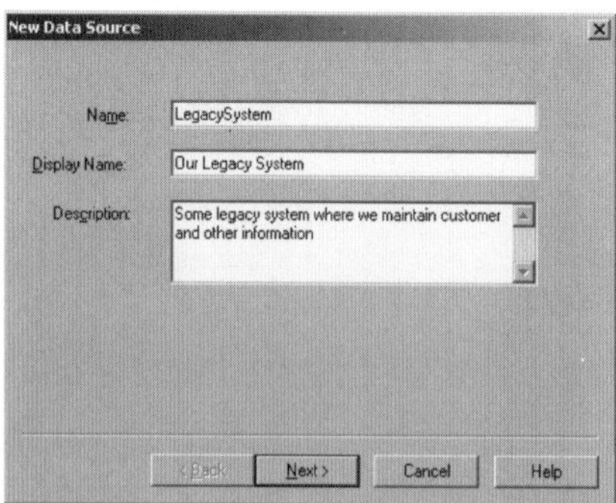

Figure 10-1. *The New Data Source wizard helps you add a new data source to the profile system. The first step is identifying the data source's name and display name.*

4. Identify the type of source as either an LDAPv3 Compliant Source or an OLEDB ANSI Provider.
5. Next, define the partitions of the data source. You'll need at least one. If you are partitioning the data store across multiple servers, select the Partitioned Data Source check box. For each partition, you'll need to provide connection information. If you're accessing an LDAP store, you'll also need to specify credentials, which identify how you'll bind to the LDAP store. Finally, if you're providing more than one partition, you'll need to identify one of the partitions to be the default.

Tip Defining the Data Source does not actually create the data store, whether it is a database or an LDAP store. You'll need to create that before creating the data store.

The Data Object

Once you've established the data source, you need to specify the data object that will hold the profile data. The data object can be either a database table or an LDAP class, depending on the data source. When you create the data object, you'll also provide a Display Name, which is the name you'll see when referring to the data object.

To add a new data object to the profile system, right-click the desired Data Source in CSM and select New, Data Object. From there (Figure 10-2), you'll be able to select from the available data objects in the data store to identify the data object.

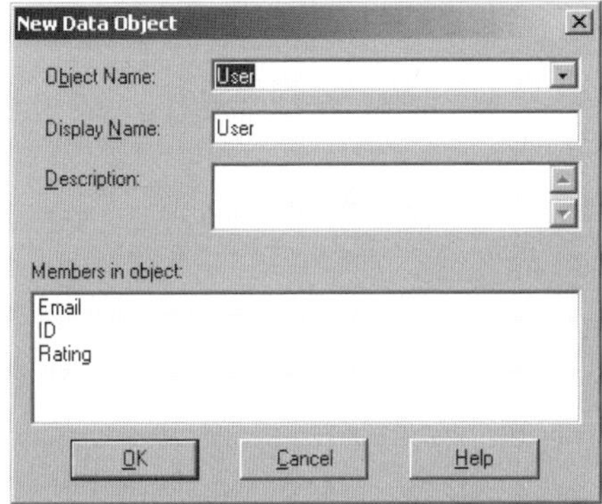

Figure 10-2. *Select from the available database tables or LDAP classes in the data source to create a new data object.*

Tip Creating a new data object does not create the database table or LDAP class. Those objects must already exist.

Data Members

A data member is used to identify the fields in any data object that can be used by the profile system. For instance, you might identify data in a legacy database that you want to include in your profile system. However, you might not want all of those fields available to the profiles. Instead, you might select a smaller list of fields to make available to the profile system. You do this by defining each of the desired fields as data members, so only those will be available (see Figure 10-3).

In addition, when creating a data member, you can provide a display name to use for it. This display name is used when defining properties for the profiles. Therefore, the person maintaining the profiles won't really need to know or understand how the database is structured or how the fields are named.

To make a field available as a data member, perform the following steps:

1. Right-click the appropriate data object in CSM and select New Data Member.
2. Select the field you want to make available from the list of available fields. The fields shown in bold are already data members.
3. Define a Display Name and Description for the data member, and confirm that the correct data type is specified.
4. Make it available by clicking Add.

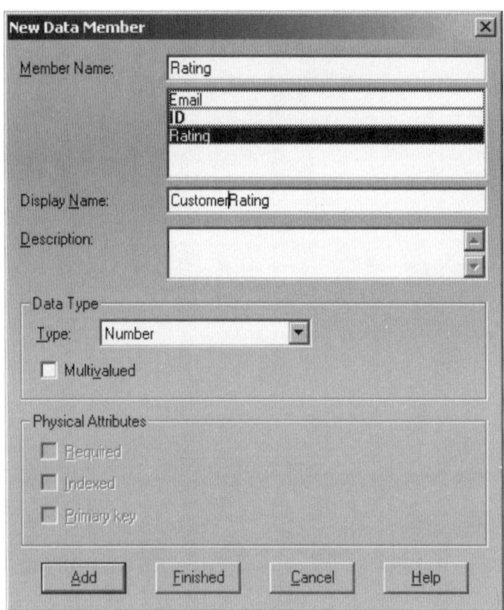

Figure 10-3. *You can make a field available as a data member by selecting it from the list and clicking Add. You can also provide a more friendly display name that will be used by the profile system.*

Profile Definition

Once you have the back-end systems set up to hold your profile data and you've defined what tables, classes, and fields will be available to the profiles, it's time to actually define the different types of profiles. In CSM, you can manage or create profile definitions. You can also manage the profile definitions in the site's Business Desk.

In CSM, open the Global Resources, Profiles (for your site), Profiles Catalog, and Profile Definitions. Selecting any of the profiles in the list will load the profile definition pages. These are the same pages you'll see in the Business Desk. To create a new profile definition, follow these steps:

1. Right-click Profile Definition or any of the profile definitions and then select New Profile.
2. Provide a profile name, display name, and description, and click Next.
3. You can also specify any custom attributes that describe this profile. In most cases, you won't need any.
4. After you've finished the profile, click Finish.

In the Business Desk, open the Users section and select the Profile Designer. A list of the existing profiles is displayed. Select one of the profiles in the list and click the Open button on the toolbar, which loads that profile into the Profile Editor pages. In the CSM, you can find the list of profiles under the Profile Definitions container. By clicking one of the profiles, you'll load the Profile Editor in the right panel. The Profile Editor in both the CSM and Business Desk makes use of the same pages.

Once the profile is created, you can maintain it by adding or modifying the properties that define the profile. For better organization of the profile definition, properties are organized into property groups. From the profile definition editor, you can add new groups or new properties to the profile (see Figure 10-4).

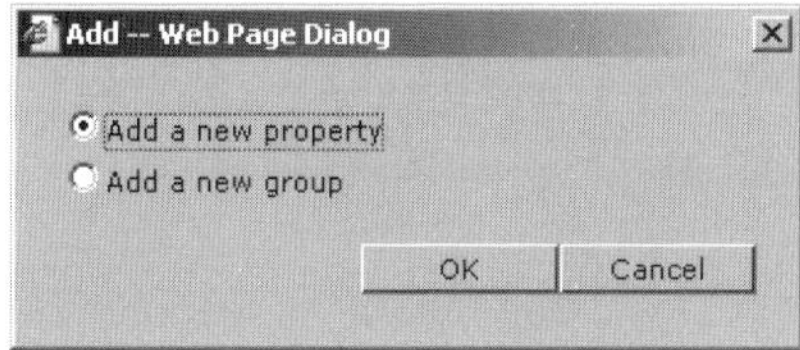

Figure 10-4. *You can add a group or property to a profile by clicking Add and specifying the desired type.*

To add a group to the profile, follow these steps:

1. Click Add and identify that you're creating a new group. A group with a default name will be created.
2. You'll then be able to specify the group name, display name, and description (see Figure 10-5).
3. Once you click Apply, the changes are made to the profile definition.

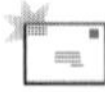

Note The changes are not truly saved until you click Save on the toolbar in either the CSM or Business Desk.

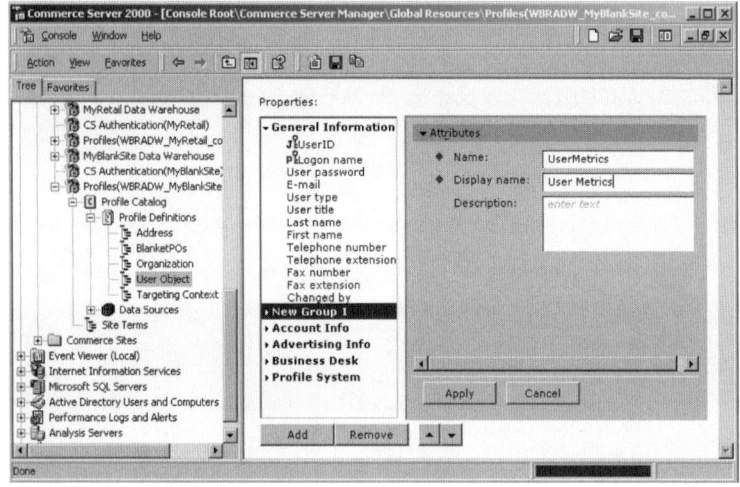

Figure 10-5. *You can add a new group to a profile by clicking Add and specifying that you are creating a group. You then have to fill in the required attributes for the group.*

To add a property to a profile, follow these steps:

1. Click Add and specify that you're adding a new property. The property is added in the group that you currently have selected in the left-hand tree.
2. Fill in the necessary attributes to describe the new profile property (see Figure 10-6).

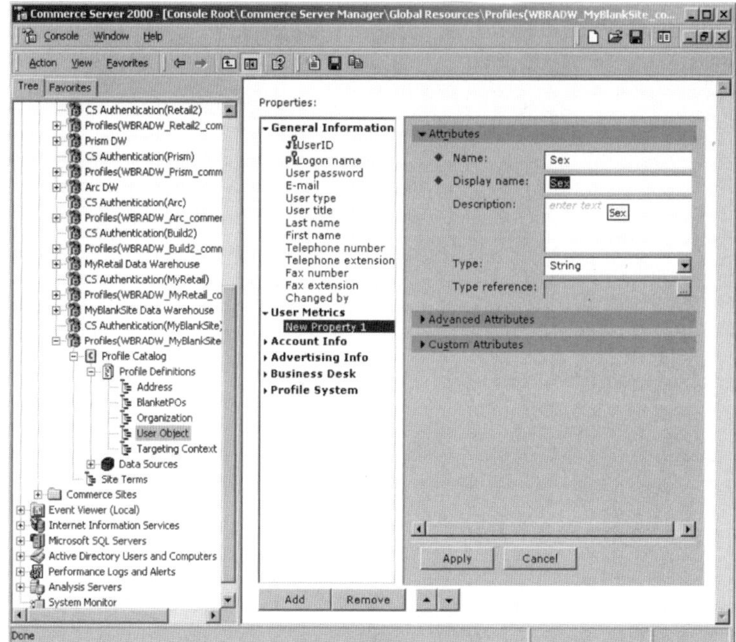

Figure 10-6. *You can add a new property to the profile and then complete the required descriptive attributes for that property.*

A profile property has a set of standard attributes, used to describe the property, which are organized into the following three sections:

- Attributes
- Advanced attributes
- Custom attributes

Attributes

The basic attributes, detailed in Table 10-1, are used to provide the naming and display names, as well as basic data types for the property.

Table 10-1. Property Attributes

Attribute Name	Description
Name	The name of the property. Maximum length is 127 alphanumeric characters, including the underscore.
Display Name	Friendly name that can be displayed for the property and can include spaces. Maximum length is 127 characters.
Description	Description of the property. Maximum length is 127 characters.
Type	Data type of the property. Types available include these: • String • Long String • Number • Decimal • Boolean • Binary • Long Binary • Date/Time • Date • Time • Currency • Password • Site Term • Profile
Type Reference	If you select Site Term or Profile for the type, you'll specify the Site Term or Profile here by clicking the ellipsis (...) button.

Advanced Attributes

The advanced attributes, detailed in Table 10-2, are used to describe the behavior and other more detailed elements of the property.

Table 10-2. Property Advanced Attributes

Attribute Name	Description
Active	Identifies if the property is currently active.
Map To Data	Data member in the data source that is used to store this property value.
Key Type	Type of key that the property is in the profile. Key types include the following: • **Unique Key** This property is unique. • **Primary Key** This property is the primary key for this profile object. • **Join Key** This property is used to join data from multiple data sources. This property must be found in each of the data sources. • **Dual (Primary and Join)** This property is both a Primary and Join key.

(continued)

Table 10-2. *(continued)*

Attribute Name	Description
Required	A value must be provided for this required property when the profile data is created.
Exported	This property is exported to the Data Warehouse.
Defer Cache Load	This property is not loaded when the profile is retrieved, but only when the property itself is accessed.
Multi-Valued	This property contains multiple values. The values are represented in the database as a string, separated with semicolons, such as 3;value1;value2;value3.
Searchable	This property is indexed in the database and is searchable using the Find By method.
RDN	This is the relative distinguished name (RDN) for a directory store.
Hashing Key	This property is the key to distributing profile data across multiple partitions.

When you are mapping the property to the data store, the Data Source Picker dialog box, shown in Figure 10-7, displays the available data members. Any data members that are already selected for another property or that do not match the data type of this property will be unavailable. Only those data members that match the data type and are available will be enabled in the list.

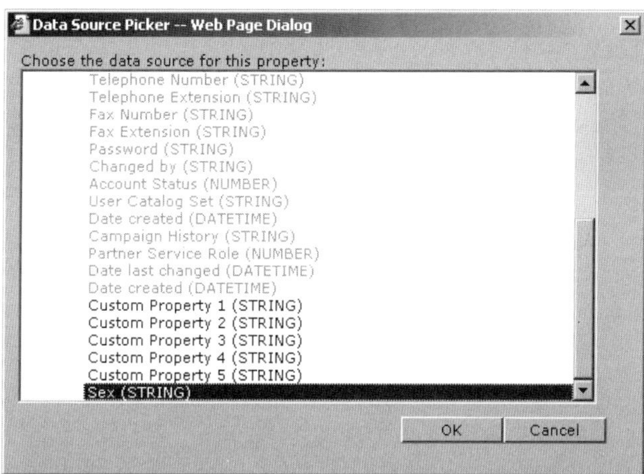

Figure 10-7. *The Data Source Picker dialog box shows the available data members.*

Custom Attributes

In addition to the other attributes, the profile system allows you to define a set of custom attributes that can hold their own data. Table 10-3 lists the custom attributes that are provided as a part of the profile property definition.

Table 10-3. Property Custom Attributes

Attribute Name	Description
sAnonymousAccess	Specifies Anonymous User Access Level
sDelegatedAdminAccess	Specifies Delegated Admin Access Level
sSearchOptions	Specifies if this property should be available for searching
sFeatureID	Specifies the site features that use this property
ShowInList	Specifies if this property should be available in the list
sSiteAdminAccess	Specifies Site Admin Access Level
sUserAccess	Specifies Registered User Access Level

Types of Profiles

The Commerce Server Solution Sites, including the Blank Site, provide several default profile objects. You can use these, modify or expand them, or delete them and create your own. You can see the predefined profile objects in the Profile Definitions area of CSM, including the following:

- **Address** This profile object contains standard address information, such as street, city, state, postal code, country, and more.
- **BlanketPOs** This profile object contains standard purchase order information fields, including Purchase Order ID, Organization, PO Number, and more.
- **Organization** This profile object contains standard information fields about an organization for your site, including Name, Administrative Contact, Receiver, Purchasing Manager, and more.
- **User Object** This profile object contains standard user information, such as user ID, login name, e-mail, first name, last name, password, organization, and more.
- **Targeting Context** This profile object contains a PageGroup property that identifies the page group of a given page, and is used by content selection framework.

If you create a site based on the SupplierAD solution site, you'll also notice this additional profile definition:

- **ADGroup** This profile object contains group account information that is maintained in the Active Directory, such as GroupName, SAMAccountName, group type, members, and more.

Profiles in Action

Now that you have some understanding of the way the profile system is maintained, let's take a look at how it works.

Profile Service

To begin using the Profile system, you'll first need to access it through the ProfileService object. This object can be created and stored in an application variable so that all of the resources can use it. This means that you'll create it in the GLOBAL.ASA file's Application_OnStart event, as shown here:

```
Set mscsAppConfig = Server.CreateObject("Commerce.AppConfig")

Call  mscsAppConfig.Initialize(MSCSCommerceSiteName)

Set dctConfig = mscsAppConfig.GetOptionsDictionary("")

Set mscsProfileService = _
 Server.CreateObject("Commerce.ProfileService")

Call mscsProfileService.Initialize( _
 dctConfig.s_ProfileServiceConnectionString, _
 "Profile Definitions")

Set Application("MSCSProfileService") = mscsProfileService
```

Once the ProfileService object is created, initialized, and stored in the application variable, you can make use of it on any page by retrieving it from the application variable, using the following code:

```
Set mscsProfileService = Application("MSCSProfileService")
```

You'll use the ProfileService object to retrieve a reference to profile objects of any of the types in your profile system. The profile object might be a user, organization, address, or one of the several other objects. There are actually three ProfileService object methods that return a reference to a Profile Object.

CreateProfile

The CreateProfile method is used to create a new profile, which is often a new user profile. When you use this method, you must identify the primary key for the new profile object you're creating and the type of profile object, as shown here:

```
mscsUserProfile = MSCSProfileService.CreateProfile _
 ("MyUserLogon", "UserObject")
```

Once you have the profile object, you can make any necessary changes you might need. For instance, you will want to generate a UserID, which is a globally unique identifier (GUID) that is required for the user profile and is used to match user information with other profile information. Generating a GUID is made easy by the GenID object's GenGUIDString method. You can then save the GUID into the user_id property of the user's profile. You'll save the changes you've made by calling the Update method, as displayed in this sample:

```
Set mscsGenID = Server.CreateObject("Commerce.GenID")

mscsUserProfile("GeneralInfo.user_id").value = _
 mscsGenID.GenGUIDString()

mscsUserProfile.Update
```

GetProfile

You can retrieve a profile quickly and easily using the GetProfile method, shown in the next code sample. This method expects you to pass it the primary key value and the type of profile object you want to retrieve. Optionally, you can also provide a parameter that tells the system to return an error value if an error occurs. The default value is True. If you send a False value, an empty ProfileObject object is returned.

```
mscsProfile = MSCSProfileService.GetProfile("myUserLogon", _
 UserObject", True)
```

GetProfileByKey

At times, you might need to access a user's profile based on a parameter other than the primary key. For instance, you might have the user's customer ID from an Enteprise Resource Planning (ERP) system or other data system, or some other unique identifier for the profile, and you can use that to retrieve the profile. To do this, first define that property as a Primary, Join, or Unique key. Then you'll call the GetProfileByKey method. In this case, you'll identify what field you're matching against, the value of the field you want to match, and the type of profile object you're retrieving, as shown here:

```
mscsProfile = MSCSProfileService.GetProfileByKey("user_id", _
 "{12345678-AAAA-BBBB-CCCC-999999999999}", "UserObject")
```

Note The field you are matching against must be one of the key fields in the profile.

ProfileObject

The ProfileObject is the object that holds the actual data in the profile. You'll use this object to reference the data, retrieve the data for use, or update the profile. This is the single means you have to access the data in the profiles, while maintaining the data abstraction that the profiling system provides.

Accessing the Data

Once you've retrieved the particular profile object, you can begin to work with the data. You access the profile data using the ProfileObject's Fields property, which returns the collection of fields that make up the profile. As previously stated, the properties of the profile are organized into property groups, so to refer to each property, you'll need to specify the group and the property name. The formal syntax to retrieve data from a property is shown here:

```
oProfileObject.Fields("PropertyGroupName").Value("PropertyName")
```

For example, to retrieve the login name from a user profile, you would use the following code:

```
sLogon = oProfileObject.Fields("GeneralInfo").Value("Logon_Name")
```

However, you can use a shortcut to this by appending the PropertyName to the GroupName in the properties field, separated by a period, as shown here:

```
oProfileObject.Fields("PropertyGroupName.PropertyName").Value
```

This would allow you to retrieve the login name in code such as the following:

```
sLogon = oProfileObject.Fields("GeneralInfo.logon_name").Value
```

When you're reading the value from the field, you can even leave off the .Value reference. However, you will need to keep it when writing to the value.

Updating the Data

Just as you can read the profile data, you can make updates to it at any time. To do so, simply write the new data back into the value of the appropriate property. Once you've finished updating the profile, save the changes back to the profile system by calling the ProfileObject's Update method.

BusinessDataAdmin Object

At times, you might need to access the profile definition in your site, perhaps to dynamically build your user profile page. You can do this with the BusinessDataAdmin object, which provides access to the profile definitions catalogs. However, this object is not well documented and you should use caution in working with it, especially when making any modifications to the profile definitions.

To use the BusinessDataAdmin object, you'll need to connect to the business data store, as shown in this sample:

```
Set mscsBizData = _
  Server.CreateObject("Commerce.BusinessDataAdmin")

Call _
  mscsBizData.Connect(dictConfig.s_BizDataStoreConnectionString)
```

At this point, you can retrieve any of the profile definitions, in Extensible Markup Language (XML) format, using the GetProfile method shown here:

```
Set oXMLProfile = oBizData.GetProfile( _
 "Profile Definitions.UserObject")
```

You can preload this information in an application variable as a string, or within a Dictionary object, for quick access throughout the site.

User Object Profile

Of all of the profile objects, you'll make the most use of the User Object, which holds the user information that is used to log in and access user-specific data. The User Object profile properties are detailed in Table 10-4.

Table 10-4. User Object Profile Properties

Profile Property Group	Profile Property
AccountInfo	Org_id Account_status User_catalog_set Date_registered
Advertising	Campaign_history
BusinessDesk	Partner_desk_role
GeneralInfo	User_id Logon_name User_security_password Email_address User_type User_title Last_name First_name Tel_number Tel_extension Fax_number Fax_extension User_id_changed_by
ProfileSystem	Date_last_changed Date_created

In the following sections, we'll take a look at some of the common tasks you'll be performing on the site involving the User Object profile.

Retrieving the Profile

The most common task you'll need to perform is to retrieve the user's profile. You'll do this to authenticate the user or to read various properties that you can use to personalize the site. First you have to retrieve the profile object. You can then read the properties in the profile using the object's Fields property. You'll need to specify both the property group and the property name, in the format PropertyGroup.PropertyName, as shown the following sample:

```
set mscsUser = MSCSProfileService.GetProfile(sLogon, _
 "UserObject")

htmUser = "<form action=""_account.asp"" method=post>"

htmUser = htmUser & "<table border=1>"

htmUser = htmUser _
  & "<tr><td>Email</td><td><input name=""email"" value=""" _
  & mscsUser.Fields("GeneralInfo.email_address") & """></td></tr>"
```

(continued)

(continued)

```
htmUser = htmUser _
 & "<tr><td>First Name</td><td><input name=""firstname" _
 & "  value=""" _
 & mscsUser.Fields("GeneralInfo.first_name") & """></td></tr>"

htmUser = htmUser _
 & "<tr><td>Last Name</td><td><input name=""lastname"" value=""" _
 & mscsUser.Fields("GeneralInfo.last_name") & """></td></tr>"

htmUser = htmUser _
 & "<tr><td>Date Last Changed</td><td>" _
 & mscsUser.Fields("ProfileSystem.date_last_changed") _
 & "</td></tr>"

htmUser = htmUser & "</table>"

htmUser = htmUser & "<input type=submit value=""Save""></form>"
```

Creating a User Account

Of course, you'll need to provide the ability for users to create an account. In this way, they'll be able to easily sign up to use your site. To create the site, you just need to call the CreateProfile method of the ProfileService object and provide the value for the primary key of the profile object. In this case, that's the user login name. You also need to specify that the profile object being created is a User Object, as shown here:

```
set mscsUser = MSCSProfileService.CreateProfile(sLogonName, _
 "UserObject")
```

Editing the Profile

At any time after the profile has been created, you might want to provide your users with the ability to edit their profiles. Of course, then you'll need to provide code that allows your users to save their changes. Do this by writing the property values into the Value property of each field. You'll then have to call the ProfileObject's Update method to save the changes, as shown here:

```
set mscsUser = MSCSProfileService.GetProfile(sLogon, _
 "UserObject")

mscsUser.Fields("GeneralInfo.user_security_password").Value = _
 sPassword

mscsUser.Fields("GeneralInfo.email_address").Value = sEmail

mscsUser.Fields("GeneralInfo.first_name").Value = sFirstName

mscsUser.Fields("GeneralInfo.last_name").Value = sLastName

mscsUser.Update
```

Deleting a Profile

In the rare instance in which you must delete a user profile from the system, you can call the DeleteProfile method. You'll pass the primary key for the profile object to identify the object you want to delete, and the type of object, as shown here:

```
MSCSProfileService.DeleteProfile sLogon, "UserObject"
```

Address Profile Object

The Address Profile object is used to store user addresses. Each user might have one or more addresses. For instance, a user might have a home and work address, plus several other addresses for use in identifying shipping destinations. The standard properties for the Address profile object are detailed in Table 10-5.

Table 10-5. Address Profile Object Properties

Profile Property Group	Profile Property
GeneralInfo	Address_id
	Id
	Last_name
	First_name
	Address_name
	Address_type
	Description
	Address_line1
	Address_line2
	City
	Region_code
	Region_name
	Postal_code
	Country_code
	Country_name
	Tel_number
	Tel_extension
	Locale
	User_id_changed_by
ProfileSystem	Date_last_changed
	Date_created

Searching for an Address in the Address Book

Each user can maintain his or her own list of addresses in an address book, if you allow it. You can retrieve address information for a given user based on the ID property, which holds the value of the user's ID. As with the User Object, you can use the GetProfileByKey method to retrieve these objects.

However, there is an unfortunate limitation to the system. Currently, the ProfileService can only be used to retrieve a single profile object at a time. This means you cannot query the ProfileService to return a set of Address profiles, all of which make up the user's address book. Instead, you'll have to utilize SQL queries to get this information.

You can simply write the SQL query in an ASP page and query the database through Microsoft ActiveX Data Objects (ADO). However, you will get better results by building the SQL query as a stored procedure and using ADO's Command object to execute the procedure and return the recordset, as displayed in this sample:

```
CREATE PROCEDURE dbo.sProc_GetAddressBook

@guidUser nvarchar(255)

AS

SELECT
   *
FROM
   addresses
WHERE
   g_id = @guidUser
GO
```

Calling this stored procedure requires a fairly simple call through ADO using the Command object. However, to make this process more reusable, you can wrap it into a function, as shown here:

```
Sub ExecuteSp(ByVal sConnection, _
   ByVal sStoredProcName, _
   ByRef oRecordset, _
   ByRef oConnection , _
   ByRef varSPParameters())

Const adStoredProc= 4

Dim iParameterCounter

Dim oCommand

Set oCommand = Server.CreateObject("ADODB.Command")
```

(continued)

(continued)

```
'Open Conection to the database, if it's not already open
If oConnection.State <> 1 Then
   oConnection.Open sConnection
End If

'Clears any old connections,
'Sets the active connection to connection string designated.
'Sets command object to the database connection.
'ADO is informed that it is dealing with a stored
'procedure and the parameter collection is set up to pass in.
With oCommand
   .ActiveConnection = Nothing
   .ActiveConnection = oConnection
   .CommandText = sStoredProcName
   .CommandType = adStoredProc
   .Parameters.Refresh

   'This will loop through all the SP's Parameters
   'and fill in their value from the ParamArray.
   For iParameterCounter = 1 To .Parameters.Count - 1
      .Parameters(iParameterCounter).Value = _
        varSPParameters(iParameterCounter - 1)
   Next
   End With
   'Open the recordset
   oRecordset.Open oCommand
End Sub
```

This function can be called from within ASP using code similar to the following:

```
dim aParam()
redim aParam(0)
set conn= server.CreateObject("ADODB.Connection")
set rs    = server.CreateObject("ADODB.Recordset")
```

(continued)

(continued)

```
sConn   = _
 Application("MSCSOptionsDictionary").s_BizDataStoreConnectionString

sProcName  = "sProc_GetAddressBook"

'This is the user's GUID

aParam(0)  = _
 mscsUserProfile.Fields("GeneralInfo.user_id").value

call ExecuteSp(sConn, sProcName, rs, conn, aParam)

If Not rs.EOF Then

   'display the address book

Else

   'address book is empty

End if
```

Organization Profile Object

If you're building a site that will allow corporate customers to build and maintain their own organizations within your site, you might find yourself making use of the Organization profile object. With the default object, your customers can assign their organization members to various roles. In addition, you can identify persons in the organization that have administrative rights and purchase approval rights. This can be handy if you want to delegate the account maintenance tasks to your corporate customers. Of course, you'll have to provide the Web pages that recognize and support these organizations. The standard properties for the Organization profile object are detailed in Table 10-6.

Table 10-6. Organization Profile Object Properties

Profile Property Group	Profile Property
GeneralInfo	Org_id Name Trading_partner_number User_id_admin_contact User_id_receiver Org_catalog_set User_id_changed_by
Purchasing	User_id_purchasing_manager
ProfileSystem	Date_last_changed Date_created

Assigning a User to an Organization

Once you have a user profile and organization profile, you can assign a user to the organization by simply placing the Organization's org_id into the user's org_id property, as shown in this sample:

```
'Get the Organization, based on the Organization Name

'(we assume we have the Organization Name at this point)

Set mscsOrgProfile = _
 MSCSProfileService.GetProfile(sOrgName, "Organization")

'Assign the Organization ID to the User's Profile

'Assume that the user's profile is already loaded into

'mscsUserProfile

mscsUserProfile("AccountInfo.org_id").value = _
 mscsOrgProfile("GeneralInfo.org_id").Value
```

Searching for Users in an Organization

If you are supporting organizations on your site, you might want to allow them to be managed by organization administrators. These users would be able to create, delete, or update user accounts in their organizations. To allow this, you must provide a mechanism to select the users within the organization. As you did in searching for a user's addresses, you do this by building a stored procedure that queries the database and returns a list of users in an organization, as shown here:

```
CREATE PROCEDURE dbo.sProc_GetOrgUsers

   @WhereValue nvarchar(255)

AS

SELECT

*

FROM

   userobject uo

   INNER JOIN organizationobject oo

   ON uo.g_org_id = oo.g_org_id

WHERE

   oo.u_name LIKE @WhereValue
```

As you did in searching for addresses in the user's address book, you call the ExecuteSP function with the name of the stored procedure to retrieve the recordset containing the user information.

However, you might want to expand this process to account for organizations that might have many users. In this case, to make the page more manageable, you should build in some paging for the search results. In this case, you would create three stored procedures that would be used to retrieve data:

- sProc_GetOrgUsersFirst
- sProc_GetOrgUsersNext
- sProc_GetOrgUsersPrevious

sProc_GetOrgUsersFirst

This stored procedure, shown in the following code sample, is used to retrieve the first page of search results, with 10 results displayed per page:

```
CREATE PROCEDURE dbo.sProc_GetOrgUsersFirst
   @WhereValue nvarchar(255)
AS

SELECT TOP 10
   uo.g_user_id, uo.g_org_id, uo.u_user_title,
   uo.u_first_name, uo.u_last_name, uo.u_email_address,
   uo.u_logon_name, uo.i_account_status,
   oo.u_name
FROM
   userobject uo
   INNER JOIN organizationobject oo
   ON uo.g_org_id = oo.g_org_id
WHERE
   oo.u_name LIKE @WhereValue
```

sProc_GetOrgUsersNext

This stored procedure, shown here, is used to retrieve the second and additional search results, displaying 10 results per page:

```
CREATE PROCEDURE dbo.sProc_GetOrgUsersNext
@WhereValue nvarchar(255) ,
@StartValue nvarchar(255)
AS
```

(continued)

(continued)

```
SET NOCOUNT ON
SELECT TOP 10
   uo.g_user_id, uo.g_org_id, uo.u_user_title,
   uo.u_first_name, uo.u_last_name, uo.u_email_address,
   uo.u_logon_name, uo.i_account_status,
   oo.u_name
FROM
   userobject uo
   INNER JOIN organizationobject oo
   ON uo.g_org_id = oo.g_org_id
WHERE
   oo.u_name LIKE @WhereValue
AND
   oo.u_name > @StartValue
ORDER BY
   oo.u_name ASC
```

sProc_GetOrgUsersPrevious

This stored procedure, shown in the following code sample, is used to retrieve a previous page of results based on the current page of results. You'll pass in the first record on the current page. The procedure retrieves the 10 results preceding those on the current page. It sorts the results in descending order and puts them in a temporary table and then retrieves the data from the temporary table, resorting the results in the proper order, ensuring that the proper results are returned.

```
CREATE PROCEDURE dbo.sProc_GetOrgUsersPrevious
@WhereValue nvarchar(255) ,
@StartValue nvarchar(255)
AS

SET NOCOUNT ON
SELECT TOP 10
   uo.g_user_id, uo.g_org_id, uo.u_user_title,
   uo.u_first_name, uo.u_last_name, uo.u_email_address,
   uo.u_logon_name, uo.i_account_status,
   oo.u_name
```

(continued)

(continued)

```
INTO
   #tempOrgUsers
FROM
   userobject uo
   INNER JOIN organizationobject oo
   ON uo.g_org_id = oo.g_org_id
WHERE
   oo.u_name LIKE @WhereValue
AND
   oo.u_name < @StartValue
ORDER BY
   oo.u_name DESC

SELECT
   *
FROM
   #tempOrgUsers
ORDER BY
   u_name ASC
```

Paging the Search Results

Finally, you need to build in ASP code, as shown in the following sample, to display the proper page of search results. You'll need to determine whether this is the first page of results or whether the user clicked Next or Previous to get to this page, by tracking the current and prior page numbers. Based on this information, you can determine which stored procedure should be called to retrieve the page of search results.

```
iThisPage = Request("ThisPage")    'The number of this page
iLastPage = Request("LastPage")    'The number of the prior page
sWhere = Request("OrgName")        'The Search Text provided by user
sValue = Request("StartVal")       'The First or Last Record on prior
                                   'page depending on whether Next
                                   'or Prev was selected
```

(continued)

(continued)

```
Dim aParam()

Set conn   = server.CreateObject("ADODB.Connection")

Set rs     = server.CreateObject("ADODB.Recordset")

sConn   = _
 Application("MSCSOptionsDictionary").s_BizDataStoreConnectionString

If iThisPage = 1 Then

   redim aParam(0)

   aParam(0) = sWhere

   sProcName = "sProc_GetOrgUsersFirst"

ElseIf iThisPage > iLastPage Then

   redim aParam(1)

   aParam(0) = sWhere

   aParam(1) = sValue

   sProcName = "sProc_GetOrgUsersNext"

ElseIf iThisPage < iLastPage Then

   redim aParam(1)

   aParam(0) = sWhere

   aParam(1) = sValue

   sProcName = "sProc_GetOrgUsersPrevious"

End If

call ExecuteSp(sConn, sProcName, rs, conn, aParam)
```

Profile Components

This section provides a quick reference to the profile components covered in this chapter, along with their properties and methods.

ProfileObject

The ProfileObject component is created by the CreateProfile, GetProfile, and GetProfileByKey methods of the ProfileService object. Its properties are described in Table 10-7 and its methods are given in Table 10-8.

Table 10-7. ProfileObject Properties

Property Name	Data Type	Description
Fields	Object	Collection of properties of a profile

Table 10-8. ProfileObject Methods

Method Name	Description
GetProfileXML	Returns an XML segment that details the ProfileObject
Update	Saves the current data, including any changes, for the profile to the profile data store

ProfileService

The ProfileService component is created using the PROGID Commerce.ProfileService. Its properties and methods are described in Tables 10-9 and 10-10, respectively.

Table 10-9. ProfileService Properties

Property Name	Data Type	Description
Errors	Object	Collection of errors that were generated by the last activity of the ProfileService

Table 10-10. ProfileService Methods

Method Name	Description
BindAs	Establishes the user information (user ID and password) used to connect to the profile data stores
CreateProfile	Creates a new ProfileObject object
DeleteProfile	Deletes a profile based on the provided primary key
DeleteProfileByKey	Deletes a profile that matches a set of values
GetProfile	Gets a ProfileObject object based on the provided primary key
GetProfileByKey	Gets a ProfileObject object that matches a set of values provided
GetProfileDefXML	Returns an XML segment that describes a profile definition
Initialize	Connects to the profile data store and establishes a cache for profile schemas
UnBind	Removes the user information (user ID and password) that is used to access the profile data store.

BusinessDataAdmin

The BusinessDataAdmin component is created using the PROGID Commerce.BusinessDataAdmin. Its properties and methods are detailed in Table 10-11 and Table 10-12, respectively.

Caution This object is not well documented and should be used with caution. The object provides the means to manipulate the profiles, and errors in doing so can make the profile unusable.

Table 10-11. BusinessDataAdmin Properties

Property Name	Data Type	Description
BizDataConnection	Object	ADO Connection object to the business data store
m_connBizDataStore	Object	ADO Connection object to the business data store

Table 10-12. BusinessDataAdmin Methods

Method Name	Description
Connect	Connects to the business data store, based on the provided connection string.
CreateDataSource	Creates a data source with properties based on the parameters provided as a part of an XML document.
CreateProfile	Creates a profile with properties based on the parameters provided as a part of an XML document.
DeleteDataSource	Deletes a data source.
DeleteProfile	Deletes a profile.
ExportCatalog	Export a profile catalog to a file in XML format
GetCatalogs	Returns an XML DOM document that includes the catalog of profile resources for the site, as shown in the code sample following this table.
GetDataSource	Returns an XML DOM document that details the data sources in the profile, as shown in the second code sample following this table. This method takes a parameter identifying the source path, such as Profile Definitions.UPM_SQLSource.
GetProfile	Retrieves the definition of a profile in XML format.
GetProfileAttribute	Returns the attribute of the identified profile attribute.
GetProfileDomains	Returns a recordset that lists the Active Directory domains that are used in the profile identified. This method takes a parameter identifying the source path, such as Profile Definitions.UPM_ADSource. (This assumes that you have an LDAP source created named UPM_ADSource.)
GetSourceAttribute	Retrieves the value for the identified data source attribute.

(continued)

Table 10-12. *(continued)*

Method Name	Description
ImportCatalog	Imports a catalog from the XML-formatted document.
SetProfileAttribute	Sets a value for the identified profile attribute.
SetSourceAttribute	Sets a value for the identified data source attribute.
UpdateCatalog	Updates the profile catalog based on the parameters provided in XML format.

This sample shows the XML DOM returned by the GetCatalogs() method on the Retail site:

```
<Document xmlns="urn:schemas-microsoft-com:bizdata-profile-
 schema">
<Catalog name="Profile Definitions" displayName="Profile Catalog"
   description="Profile Definitions">
   <Profile name="Address" displayName="Address"
    description="Addresses"/>
   <Profile name="BlanketPOs" displayName="BlanketPOs"
   description="Blanket Purchase Orders"/>
   <Profile name="Organization" displayName="Organization"
    description="Organization Object"/>
   <Profile name="UserObject" displayName="User Object"
    description="User Object"/>
   <Profile name="TargetingContext" displayName="Targeting
    Context" description="CSF Targeting Context"/>
   <DataSource name="UPM_SQLSource"
    displayName="ProfileService_SQLSource"
    description="Source" sourceType="OLEDB-ANSI"/>
</Catalog>
<Catalog name="Site Terms" displayName="Site Terms">
   <Profile name="MSCommerce" displayName="Site Terms"
    description="Site Terms for Microsoft Commerce Server"
    isProfile="0"/>
</Catalog>
</Document>
```

The following sample shows the XML DOM returned by the GetDataSource method on the Retail site.

```
<Document xmlns="urn:schemas-microsoft-com:bizdata-profile-
 schema">

<Catalog name="Profile Definitions" displayName="Profile Catalog"
 description="Profile Definitions">

<DataSource name="UPM_SQLSource"
 displayName="ProfileService_SQLSource" description="Source"
 sourceType="OLEDB-ANSI">

<SourceInfo name="SQLSource" isDefault="1"
 connStr="Provider=SQLOLEDB;Data Source=WBRADW;Initial
 Catalog=Retail_commerce;User ID=sa;Password=plh;Extended
 Properties=;Network Library=dbmssocn"/>

<DataObject name="Addresses" displayName="Addresses"
 description="Addresses">

<DataMember name="g_address_id" displayName="Address ID"
 description="Address Identifier" memberType="STRING"
 isIndexed="1" isPrimaryKey="1" isRequired="1"/>

<DataMember name="g_id" displayName="ID"
 description="Organization/User Identifier" memberType="STRING"
 isIndexed="1"/>

<DataMember name="i_address_type" displayName="Address Type"
 description="Address / Ship To Address / Bill To Address"
 memberType="NUMBER"/>

<DataMember name="u_address_name" displayName="Address Name"
 description="Name for this address" memberType="STRING"
 isIndexed="1"/>

<DataMember name="u_last_name" displayName="Last Name"
 description="User Last Name" memberType="STRING" isIndexed="1"/>

<DataMember name="u_first_name" displayName="First Name"
 description="User First Name" memberType="STRING" isIndexed="1"/>

<DataMember name="u_Description" displayName="Description"
 description="Description" memberType="STRING"/>

<DataMember name="u_address_line1" displayName="Address Line 1"
 description="First Line of Address" memberType="STRING"/>

<DataMember name="u_address_line2" displayName="AddressLine2"
 description="Second line of address" memberType="STRING"/>

<DataMember name="u_city" displayName="City"
 description="City name" memberType="STRING"/>
```

(continued)

(continued)

```
<DataMember name="u_region_name" displayName="Region Name"
 description="Region or Province name" memberType="STRING"/>
<DataMember name="u_region_code" displayName="Region Code"
 description="Region or Province code" memberType="STRING"/>
<DataMember name="u_postal_code" displayName="Postal Code"
 description="Postal Code" memberType="STRING"/>
<DataMember name="u_country_name" displayName="Country Name"
 description="Country Name" memberType="STRING"/>
<DataMember name="u_country_code" displayName="Country Code"
 description="Country ISO Code" memberType="STRING"/>
<DataMember name="u_tel_number" displayName="Telephone Number"
 description="Telephone Number at this address"
 memberType="STRING"/>
<DataMember name="u_tel_extension" displayName="Telephone Number
 Extension" description="Telephone Number Extension at this
 address" memberType="STRING"/>
<DataMember name="i_locale" displayName="Locale Id"
 description="Locale in which to render the address form."
 memberType="NUMBER"/>
<DataMember name="u_user_id_changed_by" displayName="Changed by"
 description="Changed by" memberType="STRING"/>
<DataMember name="d_date_last_changed" displayName="Date last
 changed" description="Date Last Changed" memberType="DATETIME"
 isIndexed="1"/>
<DataMember name="d_date_created" displayName="Date created"
 description="Date Created" memberType="DATETIME" isIndexed="1"/>
</DataObject>
<DataObject name="BlanketPOs" displayName="BlanketPOs"
 description="Blanket Purchase Orders">
<DataMember name="g_org_id" displayName="Organization Id"
 description="Organization Id" memberType="STRING"/>
<DataMember name="g_po_id" displayName="Purchase Order Id"
 description="GUID referring to the Blanket Purchase Order"
 memberType="STRING" isIndexed="1" isRequired="1"/>
<DataMember name="u_po_number" displayName="PO Number"
 description="Blanket Purchase Order Number" memberType="STRING"
 isIndexed="1" isPrimaryKey="1" isRequired="1"/>
```

(continued)

(continued)

```
<DataMember name="u_description" displayName="Description"
 description="Description" memberType="STRING" isIndexed="1"/>

<DataMember name="g_user_id_changed_by" displayName="Changed by"
 description="Changed By" memberType="STRING"/>

<DataMember name="d_date_last_changed" displayName="Date last
 changed" description="Date Last Changed" memberType="DATETIME"
 isIndexed="1"/>

<DataMember name="d_date_created" displayName="Date created"
 description="Date Created" memberType="DATETIME" isIndexed="1"/>

</DataObject>

<DataObject name="OrganizationObject" displayName="Organization
 Object" description="Organization Object">

<DataMember name="g_org_id" displayName="Organization Id"
 description="Organization Id" memberType="STRING" isIndexed="1"
 isRequired="1"/>

<DataMember name="u_Name" displayName="Name" description="Name"
 memberType="STRING" isIndexed="1" isPrimaryKey="1"
 isRequired="1"/>

<DataMember name="u_trading_partner_number" displayName="Trading
 partner number" description="Trading Partner Number"
 memberType="STRING"/>

<DataMember name="g_user_id_admin_contact"
 displayName="Administrative contact" description="GUID for
 Administrative Contact" memberType="STRING"/>

<DataMember name="g_user_id_receiver" displayName="Receiver"
 description="User Id of the default person to receive products
 shipped from the supplier." memberType="STRING"/>

<DataMember name="u_org_catalog_set" displayName="Organization
 catalog set" description="Organization
 Catalog Set" memberType="STRING"/>

<DataMember name="g_user_id_changed_by" displayName="Changed by"
 description="Changed By" memberType="STRING"/>

<DataMember name="g_user_id_purchasing_manager"
 displayName="Purchasing manager" description="User Id of
 purchasing manager of buying orgainzation." memberType="STRING"/>

<DataMember name="d_date_last_changed" displayName="Date last
 changed" description="Date Last Changed" memberType="DATETIME"
 isIndexed="1"/>
```

(continued)

(continued)

```
<DataMember name="d_date_created" displayName="Date created"
 description="Date Created" memberType="DATETIME"
 isIndexed="1"/>

</DataObject>

<DataObject name="UserObject" displayName="User Object"
 description="User Object">

<DataMember name="u_logon_name" displayName="Logon Name"
 description="Logon Name" memberType="STRING" isIndexed="1"
 isPrimaryKey="1" isRequired="1"/>

<DataMember name="g_org_id" displayName="Organization Id"
 description="Organization Id" memberType="STRING"/>

<DataMember name="g_user_id" displayName="User Id"
 description="User Id" memberType="STRING" isIndexed="1"
 isRequired="1"/>

<DataMember name="u_user_title" displayName="User Title"
 description="User Title" memberType="STRING"/>

<DataMember name="i_user_type" displayName="User Type"
 description="User Type" memberType="NUMBER"/>

<DataMember name="u_last_name" displayName="User Last Name"
 description="Name Desc" memberType="STRING" isIndexed="1"/>

<DataMember name="u_first_name" displayName="User First Name"
 description="Name Desc" memberType="STRING" isIndexed="1"/>

<DataMember name="u_email_address" displayName="Email Address"
 description="Email Address" memberType="STRING" isIndexed="1"/>

<DataMember name="u_tel_number" displayName="Telephone Number"
 description="Telephone Number" memberType="STRING"/>

<DataMember name="u_tel_extension" displayName="Telephone
 Extension" description="Telephone Extension"
 memberType="STRING"/>

<DataMember name="u_fax_number" displayName="Fax Number"
 description="Fax Number" memberType="STRING"/>

<DataMember name="u_fax_extension" displayName="Fax Extension"
 description="Fax Extension" memberType="STRING"/>

<DataMember name="u_user_security_password"
 displayName="Password" description="Password"
 memberType="STRING"/>

<DataMember name="g_user_id_changed_by" displayName="Changed by"
 description="Changed By" memberType="STRING"/>
```

(continued)

(continued)

```
<DataMember name="i_account_status" displayName="Account Status"
 description="Account Status" memberType="NUMBER"/>

<DataMember name="u_user_catalog_set" displayName="User Catalog
 Set" description="User Catalog Set" memberType="STRING"/>

<DataMember name="d_date_registered" displayName="Date created"
 description="Date Created" memberType="DATETIME"/>

<DataMember name="u_campaign_history" displayName="Campaign
 History" description="Campaign History" memberType="STRING"/>

<DataMember name="i_partner_desk_role" displayName="Partner
 Service Role" description="Partner Service Role"
 memberType="NUMBER"/>

<DataMember name="d_date_last_changed" displayName="Date last
 changed" description="Date Last Changed" memberType="DATETIME"
 isIndexed="1"/>

<DataMember name="d_date_created" displayName="Date created"
 description="Date Created" memberType="DATETIME" isIndexed="1"/>

<DataMember name="u_Pref1" displayName="Custom Property 1"
 description="Custom Property 1 for Schema Extension"
 memberType="STRING"/>

<DataMember name="u_Pref2" displayName="Custom Property 2"
 description="Custom Property 2 for Schema Extension"
 memberType="STRING"/>

<DataMember name="u_Pref3" displayName="Custom Property 3"
 description="Custom Property 3 for Schema Extension"
 memberType="STRING"/>

<DataMember name="u_Pref4" displayName="Custom Property 4"
 description="Custom Property 4 for Schema Extension"
 memberType="STRING"/>

<DataMember name="u_Pref5" displayName="Custom Property 5"
 description="Custom Property 5 for Schema Extension"
 memberType="STRING"/>

</DataObject>

</DataSource>

</Catalog>

</Document>
```

Part V

The Catalog System

Part V of this book covers the Catalog Management System, introducing the concepts, tools, and components you'll need to design, implement, and use various catalogs on your site. Chapter 11 provides a discussion of the topics you'll need to know to design a Microsoft Commerce Server 2000 catalog, including how the catalogs are organized and managed in the site. Chapter 12 covers the Commerce Server 2000 components that are used to manage and retrieve catalog information. Chapter 13 demonstrates the variety of ways that you can search the catalogs for information.

Chapter 11

Managing Catalogs

Microsoft Commerce Server 2000 introduces a catalog management system that allows you to better organize and manage the products that you are offering to your customers. The catalog system provides a great deal of flexibility in building and displaying the product listings for customers. In addition, you can display products from multiple catalogs to your users. This allows you to retrieve and display offerings from various vendors seamlessly on your Web site. In this chapter, we'll take a look at how the catalogs are organized. We'll review some important concepts and terms and also see how the catalogs can be managed from within the Business Desk.

Catalog Hierarchy

One of the first things that you'll notice when you walk into a large department store is that the products in the store are grouped and placed in a logical manner. Men's clothing is grouped together in the men's department. Women's clothing is in the women's department. You might also find areas in the store for infants, children, housewares, and jewelry. This way, when you walk into the store looking for a new shirt, diamond necklace, or any other product, you don't need to waste your time searching the entire store. Instead, you know right where to go to find what you're looking for. This makes shopping a faster, simpler, and typically more pleasing experience. And if you've had a good shopping experience, you're more likely to return to shop some more in the future. This organization of products is now standard in most stores.

That same organization can also be found in the hierarchy that Commerce Server 2000 provides for its product catalogs, an example of which is shown in Figure 11-1. A *catalog* is a listing of products that are available to shoppers. The catalog includes all of the information needed to fully describe each product, including its name, price, description, and other pertinent information. Each catalog can be broken into different sections or categories, which are analogous to the departments (men's, women's, children's) in a department store. Categories can also be placed under other categories. For instance, you might have a jewelry category that is further divided into earrings, necklaces, rings, and so on.

A product in the catalog can be placed into any category, but it doesn't need to be entered in any category. Instead, the product can exist at what is referred to as the catalog root. This is particularly useful for products that don't really fit any particular category in the catalog. The product is made up of all the data that describes the item being offered. This can include the price, name, description, manufacturer, and other information. When you are designing the catalog, you also need to provide a unique field that is used to identify the product. This might be the SKU, an ISBN for a book, or just a unique name.

In some cases, a particular product might actually be available in a number of different variations. For instance, you might have a polo shirt available in several sizes (small, medium, large, extra large) and in two colors (blue, white). A medium white shirt is distinct from a large blue shirt, which is different from an extra large blue shirt. These differences are known as product variants. Each variant must be uniquely identified in the catalog as well.

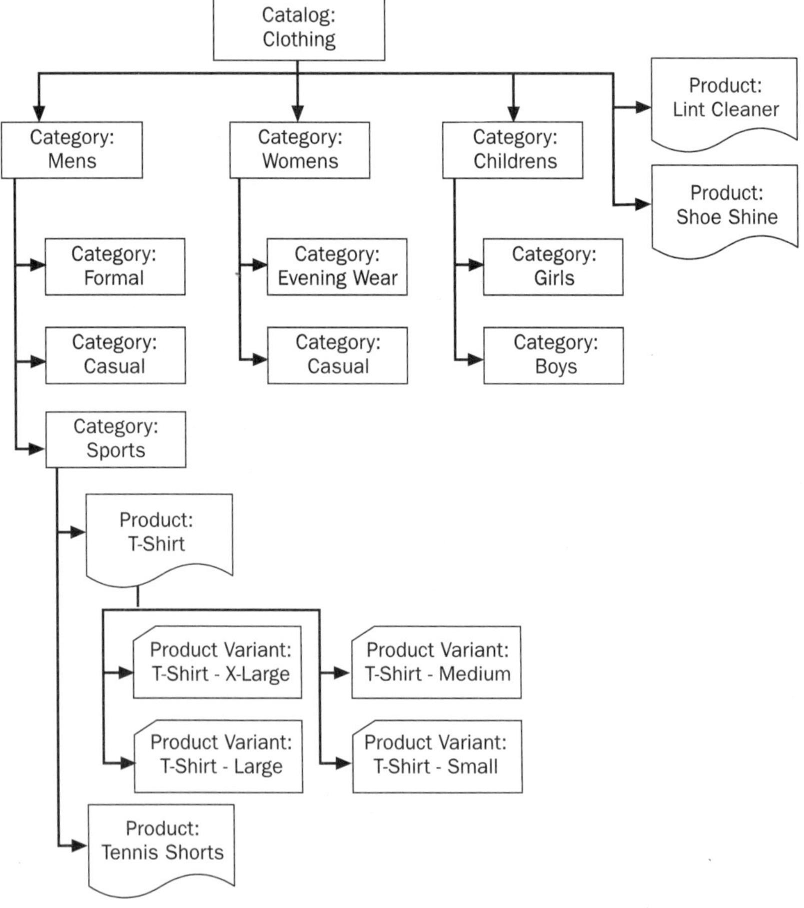

Figure 11-1. *This sample catalog hierarchy is displayed.*

Finally, products in the catalog can be directly related to other products. For instance, you might have a polo shirt that also has a matching pair of pants. When users want to purchase the shirt, you can also provide information about the matching or related products that they might also be interested in. The catalog system maintains a list of all of the related products that you can easily retrieve and display.

Multiple Catalogs

The catalog system provides a great deal of flexibility in arranging your products, and you are not limited to a single category on your site. Instead, you can provide a number of different catalogs for your site. If you are selling products from many different vendors, you might find it helpful to separate each vendor's product listings into a separate catalog, identifying the vendor to which the catalog pertains. You can then use this information when a user places an order to determine which vendor should receive the order for fulfillment.

Note SQL Server 2000 is limited to 256 full text search catalogs. This means that you can only provide up to 256 catalogs on a given Commerce Server 2000 site if you want to provide full-text searching of the catalogs.

Using the Commerce Server 2000 catalog system, you can show products from the available catalogs to your users seamlessly. You won't necessarily need to indicate that the products are from different catalogs.

Custom Catalogs

You can also provide custom views of any existing catalogs. For instance, you might want a particular group of users to automatically receive a discount on all items in a catalog. Rather than creating a whole new catalog, you can define a custom catalog for those users. The custom catalog might include all of the same products, but specify that the prices should be discounted by 10 percent.

Catalog Sets

If you are working with multiple catalogs on your site, you might want to specify which catalogs a given user or group of users is able to view. For instance, you might provide a small selection of items to all users who come to your site, but you might provide a wider selection or other special items to registered users. You might provide one catalog for most users and a separate catalog for special corporate users who might get some special pricing or special items.

Catalog sets are used to group catalogs together. You can give a user or group access to any catalog set, thereby granting them access to all of the catalogs in the set. A catalog can be a member of a number of different catalog sets.

Note Commerce Server 2000 sites typically include two default catalog sets—Registered User Default CatalogSet and Anonymous User Default CatalogSet—that are used to identify catalogs available to users that have registered and logged in and those users who have not logged into the site, respectively. You can add others as appropriate.

Designing the Catalogs

Before you can begin working with the catalog, you'll need to design it, deciding how the information should be organized. You'll need to determine the hierarchy of products and catalogs. First, however, you'll need to determine what types of products you'll be offering and what information you want to maintain about those products.

The catalogs can be designed and developed using the Business Desk for your site, which includes all of the tools and pages needed to create each of the definitions for your catalogs. In addition, you can also import a catalog into your site from a properly formatted Extensible Markup Language (XML) or comma-separated value (.csv) file. As we proceed through the following sections, we'll take a look at how you can use the Business Desk to perform these tasks.

Creating Property Definitions

Before you actually create your catalog, you'll need to decide what products you'll want to store in it. Will you be selling books? Clothing? Compact discs? Computer software? Some other products? Once you've determined what products you'll be selling, you'll need to determine what properties will be used to describe those products. For instance, a book might be described by a number of properties, including the following:

- ISBN
- Title
- Subtitle
- Description
- Author
- Publisher
- Number of pages
- Genre

Meanwhile, a shirt might be described with these properties:

- Name
- Description
- Manufacturer

A shirt's description might also include the following variant properties:

- SKU
- Size
- Color

Once you've identified each of the properties that you'll use to describe the products, you must actually create them. You can do so in the Business Desk's Catalog Designer section. You can view the existing property definitions by clicking View Catalog Definitions on the toolbar and selecting Property Definitions from the resulting drop-down menu. This shows a list of the existing property definitions.

To create a new property definition, click New Property Definition on the toolbar (Figure 11-2). You'll then need to specify the type of property that you are creating. The available types are listed in Table 11-1.

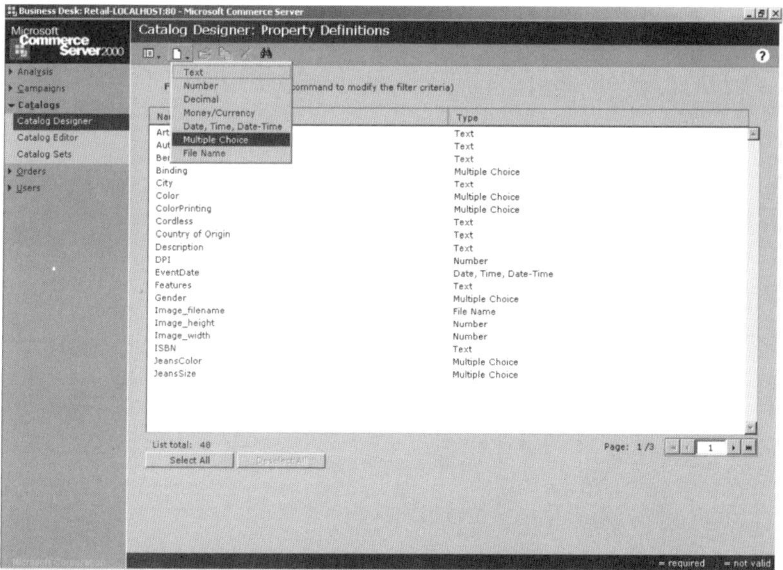

Figure 11-2. *When you're creating a new property definition in the Business Desk, you'll need to specify the type of property.*

Table 11-1. Available Property Definition Types

Property Definition Type	Description
Text	This property can hold any text, such as "some text information."
Number	This property can hold an integer (nondecimal) number, such as 12.
Decimal	This property can store a decimal value, such as 19.50.
Money/Currency	This property holds a currency value, such as 29.99.
Date, Time, Date-Time	This property holds a date or time value, such as April 1, 2001.
Multiple Choice	This property holds one of a specific list of allowable values.
File Name	This property holds a filename, such as the location of an image file, like *http://www.mysite.com/images/image1.jpg*

Each type of property definition has a different set of attributes that are used to describe how that property is displayed and used. For instance, the Text property allows you to specify the minimum and maximum character length of the data in the field (Figure 11-3). The Number property allows you to specify the minimum and maximum values allowed. However, there are several attributes, listed in Table 11-2, that are common to all of the property definitions.

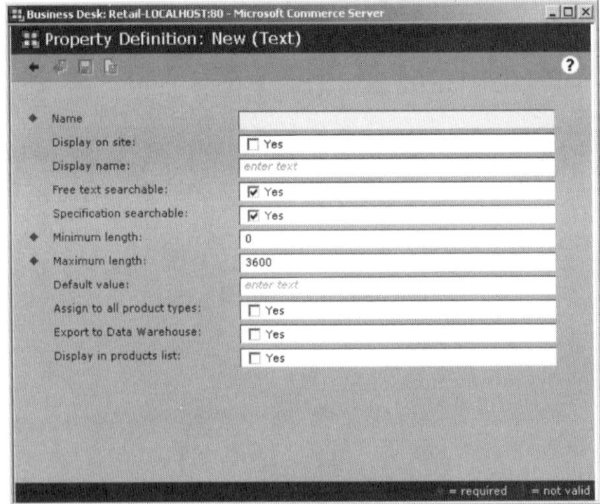

Figure 11-3. *You can add new property definitions from the Business Desk. In this case, we're adding a new text property.*

Table 11-2. Common Property Definition Attributes

Property Definition Attribute	Description
Name	This required attribute is the name of the property. This must be a unique name throughout the list of property definitions.
Display On Site	Select this check box if you want this property to be available to be displayed on the site. This is useful when you are building a dynamic product page that can scan all of the properties and only display those properties that should be publicly viewable.
Display Name	This is the friendly name, which you can use as the label on your site. This value does not need to be unique.
Free Text Searchable	If you want this field to be indexed for free text searching, select this check box. This is only available for property definition types that contain text values.
Specification Searchable	If this field should be available in a specification search, select this check box.
Assign To All Product Types	If this property should appear in every product, select this check box. Typically, only the Name and Description properties are put into every product.
Export To Data Warehouse	If you want the values of these properties to be exported to the Data Warehouse, which means they can be used for analysis and reporting, select this check box.
Display In Products List	If you want this field to appear as one of the columns in the product listing in the Business Desk, select this check box.

When the property definition is saved, the data detailing the definition is saved in the CatalogAttributes database table. The table includes the PropertyName, DataType, and fields to hold default values, minimum values, maximum values, and other attributes of the property.

Note Creating the Multiple Choice property definition type is a bit different. When you create this type of property, you will provide a list of available values to be selected (Figure 11-4). For instance, for a sweatshirt that you're offering in two different colors, you might create a property definition called Sweatshirt Color as a multiple choice and then provide the values Red and Blue. This eliminates any chance that someone else entering data might try and enter a different, invalid value.

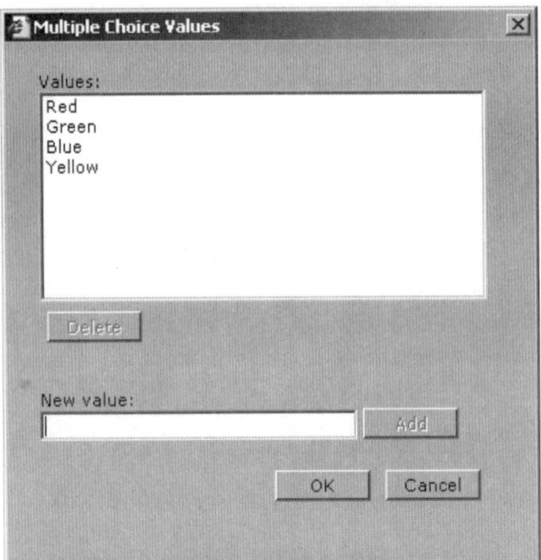

Figure 11-4. *When you create a Multiple Choice property, you must enter a list of available choices for the property.*

When you save the available multiple choice values, they are saved into the CatalogEnumValues database table, which consists of two fields: PropertyName and Value. The combination of those two fields must be unique in the table.

Note The property definitions you create will be available throughout all of the catalogs on your site. For this reason, the name must be unique among all properties for all products in all of the catalogs.

Product Definitions

Once you've defined the properties to describe the products you're selling, you can actually define the products themselves. At this point, you're not going to create actual products. Rather, you're creating the product definition, or identifying which properties you'll use to describe the products.

You can view the existing product definition in the Catalog Designer section of the Business Desk. Click View Catalog Definitions on the toolbar, and then select Product Definitions. You can create a new product definition by clicking New Product Definition on the toolbar.

When you create a product definition, you'll need to specify the product name. You'll also have to identify the properties that will be used to describe each product item (Figure 11-5). For instance, each product has a name and description. If you intend to provide a picture of the product on your site, you can use the image_filename, image_height, and image_width properties to store this information about the product. You might want to store the manufacturer name or other related data. You can select each of these from the Available Properties list box and move them to the Assigned Properties list box by clicking Add.

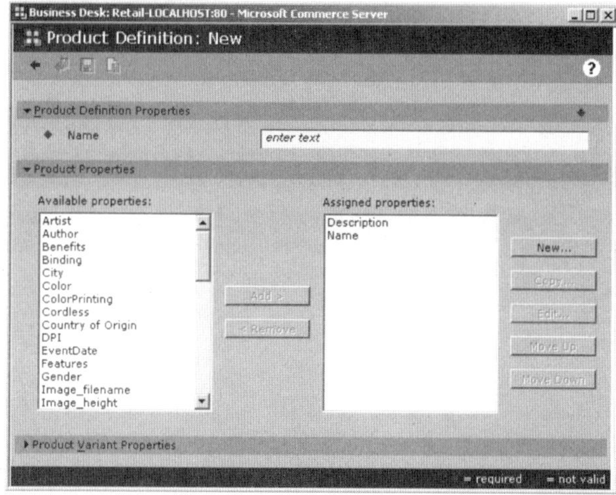

Figure 11-5. *When defining a product in the Business Desk, you'll need to specify which properties will be used to describe the product in the catalog.*

In addition, if this product contains variants, you need to identify the variant properties (Figure 11-6).

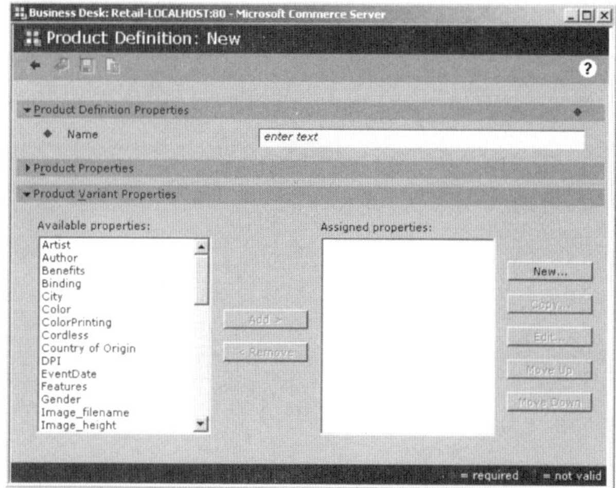

Figure 11-6. *You'll need to define the variant properties for a product, if needed, when you create that product.*

Category Definitions

In most cases, you probably won't provide much detail or additional properties when describing the categories on your site. You may find that the default category definition, Department, is sufficient to meet your needs. However, you can create your own departments and provide any properties that are appropriate to describe the particular category.

Populating Catalogs

Now that you've created the definitions that will be used to describe the products and categories in the catalog, it's time to actually create the catalog and those products.

Creating the Catalog

You can create the catalog by going into the Business Desk and opening the Catalog Editor area. There you'll see a list of the catalogs that have already been created on your site. You can then add additional catalogs. To create a new catalog, click New Catalog on the toolbar, and then select New Catalog from the list that appears.

When you create a catalog, you'll need to define a number of attributes for that catalog, as listed in Table 11-3. The Catalog Name must be unique within your site and the database that will store the catalog data. You'll also need to identify the fields that uniquely identify the products and any product variants in your catalog.

Table 11-3. Catalog Properties That Define Each Catalog on Your Site

Property Name	Required	Description
Name	Yes	This is the name of the catalog. It is used to identify the catalog for display on your site, as well as to retrieve the data from within the catalog.
Start Date	No	This is the first day on which you want this catalog to be available and active.
End Date	No	This is the last day on which you want this catalog to be available and active.
Currency	Yes	This is the type of currency that you'll be using as the primary currency for this catalog.
Unit Of Weight Measure	No	This is the unit used for measuring the weight of products. This is used when displaying the weights and calculating shipping costs based on product weight.
Product Unique ID	Yes	This is the field name that uniquely identifies the products that you are selling on your site.

(continued)

Table 11-3. *(continued)*

Property Name	Required	Description
Product Variant Unique ID	Yes	This is the field name that uniquely identifies the product variants on your site.
Vendor ID	No	You can select from a list of vendors you've set up in BizTalk and add that vendor ID here. This is used to associate these products with that vendor, so that a purchase order can be automatically sent to the vendor.

Notice that all of the products and product variants in the catalog must have the same fields specified as the unique IDs (Figure 11-7). This means that if your catalog includes a variety of items, such as books, CDs, and clothing, they'll all need to have the same unique ID fields.

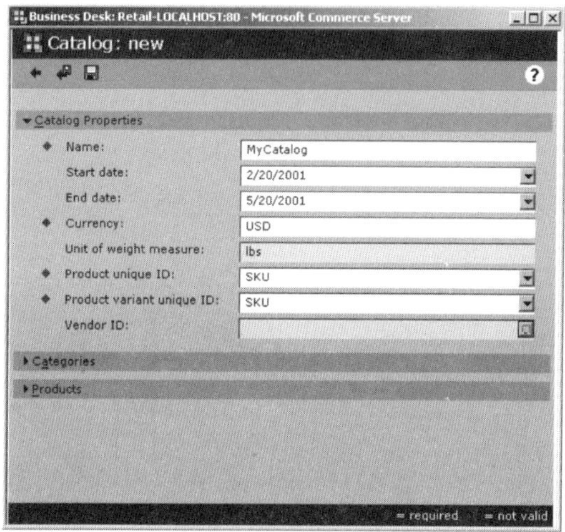

Figure 11-7. *The Business Desk can be used to easily create a catalog in which you place your products.*

Once you've provided the values for these properties, you can save the catalog. When you do so, Commerce Server 2000 creates the following three database tables to hold the data in the catalog:

- **<catalogname>_CatalogHierarchy** This table holds information concerning the hierarchy of categories and products in the catalog.
- **<catalogname>_CatalogProducts** This table holds the data that describes each category and product in the catalog.
- **<catalogname>_CatalogRelationships** This table holds information that defines the relationships between categories and between products.

Adding Categories

Once a catalog has been created and saved, you can begin to set up the catalog hierarchy by adding categories. You can do so by opening the catalog in the Business Desk and opening the Categories section of the Catalog page (Figure 11-8). There you will see any categories that have been added to this catalog.

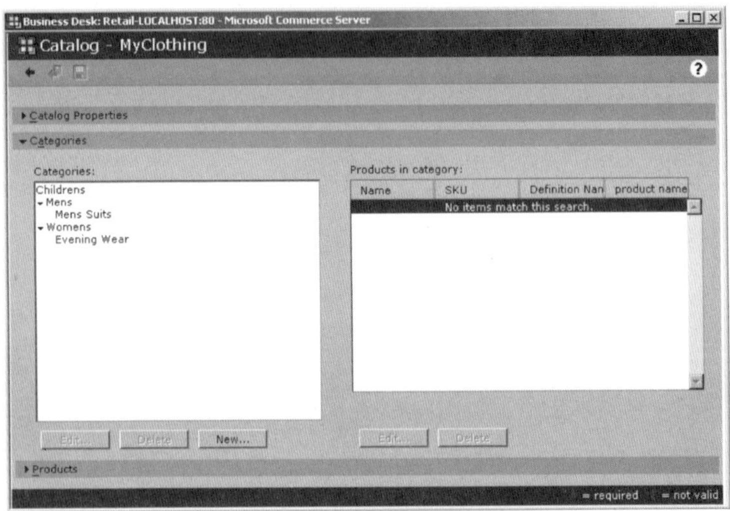

Figure 11-8. *When you open the catalog in Business Desk, you can see the categories in the catalog, as well as a list of products that exist within a selected category. You can also use this area to create new categories.*

Click New to create a new category in the catalog. You'll need to identify the type of category you're creating. In this case, you are presented with a list of the existing category definitions. From there, you need to enter values for the properties that describe the category. The properties that exist depend on those you chose if you created your own category definition. The default Department category contains the properties listed in Table 11-4.

Table 11-4. Department Category Properties

Property Name	Description
Name	This is the name of the category.
Description	This is a longer description for the category.
Image_Filename	If you want an image associated with the category, provide the filename here.
Image_Width	This holds the width of the image you want displayed.
Image_Height	This holds the height of the image you want displayed.

(continued)

Table 11-4. *(continued)*

Property Name	Description
Price	If you want all products in this category to have a default price, you can set it here.
Searchable	If you want this category to be used in a specification search, select this check box.

You must provide a name and description for the category (Figure 11-9). In most cases, you'll want to mark the category as searchable so that you can use it in a specification search, if you check that property when building your specification search pages. The other properties are used less often, but they are there if you need them.

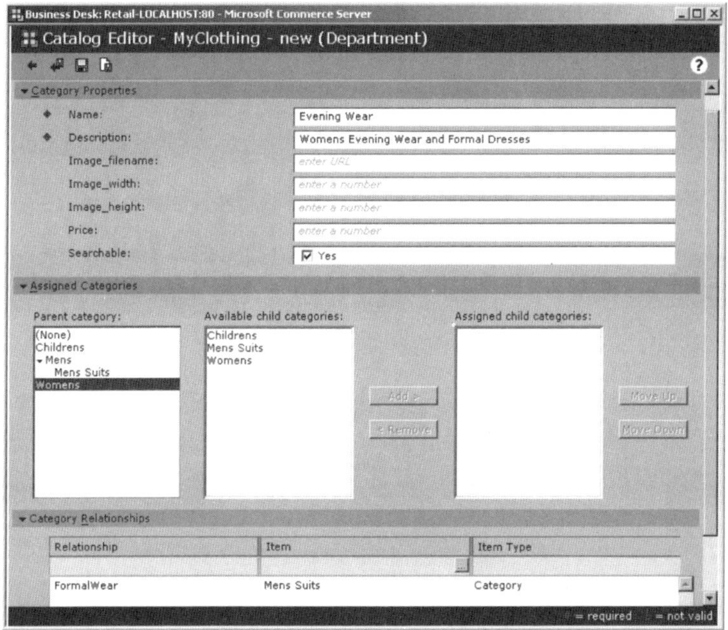

Figure 11-9. *Creating a category requires you to provide property values to describe the category, how it will be used in the site, and how it relates to other categories in the catalog.*

Specifying the Placement of a Category

When creating the category, you can also specify how that category is placed in the hierarchy with other categories in the catalog. You can specify that the Evening Wear category is a child of the Women's category by selecting the Women's category in the Parents list box. You can also define any existing categories as child categories of the current one by selecting them in the Available Child Categories list box and clicking Add to move them to the Assigned Child Categories list box.

Note A category is not restricted to being a child of one parent, so you can select multiple parent categories for a child.

Specifying Relationships Between Categories

In addition to the hierarchy of categories, you can also specify relationships that might exist between any two or more categories. For instance, you might have Men's Formalwear and Women's Formalwear categories. You can establish a relationship between them in the Category Relationships section of the category page. When information about this category is displayed on your site, a message about any related categories can be displayed as well. In this way, you can encourage customers to check out other areas of the site.

Adding Products

At any point, you can begin creating products to enter into the category. This also can be done from within the Business Desk by opening the catalog and opening the Product section, which provides you with a list of all of the products currently in the catalog (Figure 11-10).

Note The columns shown in the Products list box are those that were identified in the property definitions with the Display In Products List check box selected.

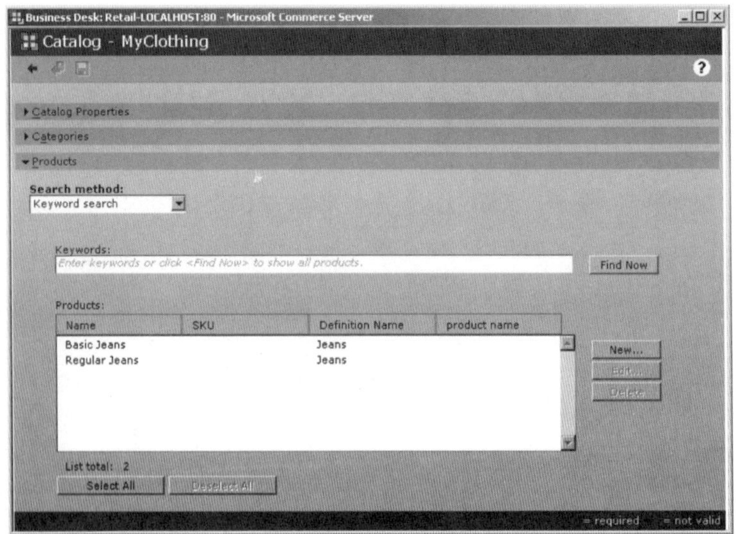

Figure 11-10. *You can list the products in a catalog in the Business Desk by opening the catalog. From here, you can also create a new product.*

To create a new product in this catalog, follow these steps:

1. Click New to open the product page in the Business Desk (Figure 11-11).
2. The page is dynamically built, with fields for each of the properties from the product definition. Those properties that are defined as product properties are listed in the Product Properties section of the page. Provide the requisite data for each of those fields.
3. Those properties that were defined as variant properties can be found in the Product Variants field. To create a product variant, click New and enter a value for each of the variant properties, including the variant price.
4. When you've completed that variant, click Done to save it.

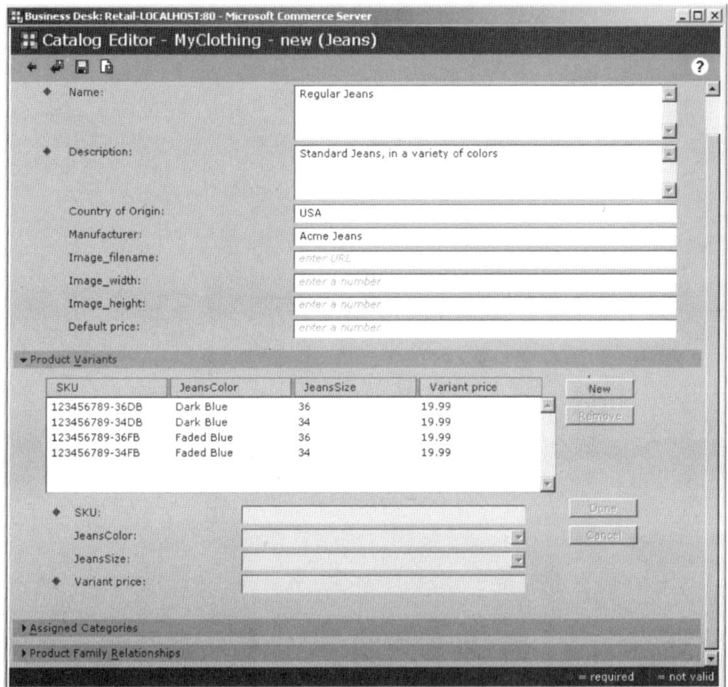

Figure 11-11. *When you create the product, you'll need to provide values for the property fields and also create any required product variants.*

When creating the product, you can also assign that product to be included in any of the categories in your catalog. You are not limited to one category. The list of categories can be found in the Assigned Categories section of the page (Figure 11-12). To assign a product to a catalog, simply highlight the appropriate category and click Add to move the category into the Assigned Categories list box.

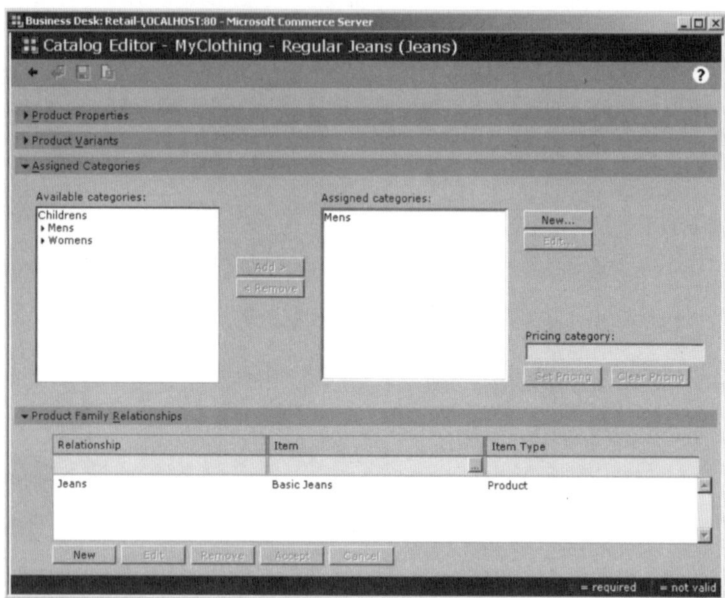

Figure 11-12. *When creating the product, you can assign it to categories in the catalog. You can also create a relationship between this product and any other product in the catalog.*

You can also establish a relationship between the current product and any other product in the catalog. As customers browse your site and pick out this product, you can show them related products that they might be interested in. For instance, if they select a pair of earrings, you might show them a matching necklace or bracelet. To establish that relationship, perform the following steps:

1. In the Product Family Relationships section of the product page, click New.
2. Provide a name for the relationship.
3. Next, click the ellipses button in the Item column to open the Product Picker page (Figure 11-13).
4. Select the product to which this product will be related.
5. When you are finished, click Accept to save the product relationship.

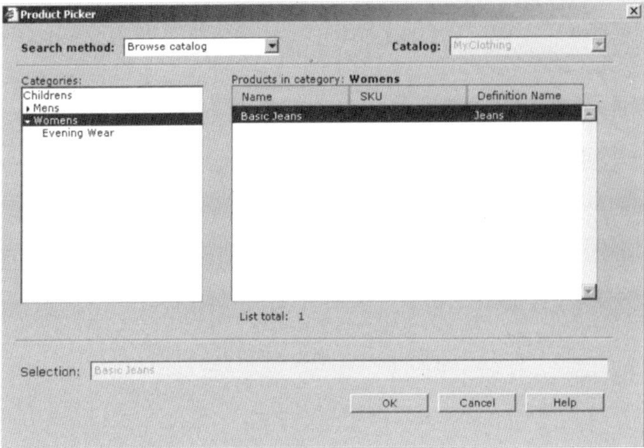

Figure 11-13. *Use the Product Picker to select the product that you are identifying as a part of a relationship.*

Importing Catalogs

Another method of populating a catalog is to import the catalog data from another source. You can do so using the Business Desk's Catalog Editor page. Click Import Catalog on the toolbar. You can then choose to import a catalog from either an XML document or a .csv file.

Importing from XML

When you import a catalog from an XML document, the document should use the format in the CATALOGXMLSCHEMA.XML file. This schema includes specifications for the catalog, categories, products, and properties, so that when the catalog is imported, the catalog name and its category hierarchy are automatically created as well. All that you need to do is identify the location of the XML document you're importing.

Importing from a .csv File

You might, at times, find it necessary to import catalog data from a comma-delimited file. For instance, the file might be extracted from another system that holds product information from one of your suppliers. The supplier might not be able to provide the data in an XML format, but can provide it as a flat, comma-delimited file.

Using the .csv format has some limitations. Because there's no schema, the products cannot be placed in a category hierarchy. Rather, they are all placed at the catalog root. In addition, the products must all have the same product definition. The file must include a unique product ID field and a price field. Finally, the products cannot include any product variants.

When you import a catalog in .csv format, you'll need to specify the location of the file, as well as the name of the unique ID field and the price field, as it appears in the file (Figure 11-14). You'll also have to specify the name of the resulting catalog that will be created.

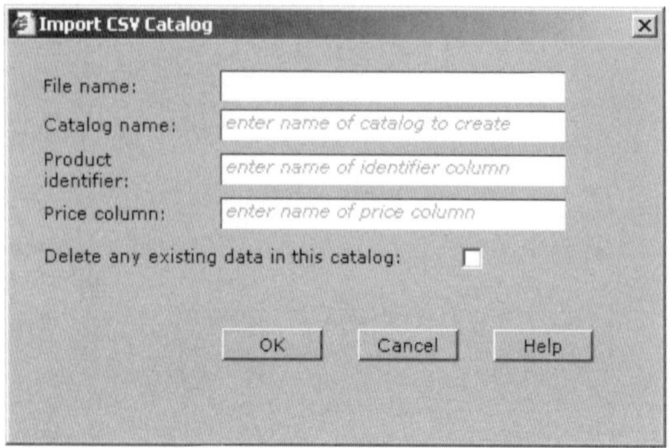

Figure 11-14. *You can import a catalog from a comma-delimited file, but you must specify additional information about the incoming data.*

Catalog Updates Using BizTalk

Microsoft BizTalk Server 2000 provides support in exchanging information and documents between many disparate systems. The server is used to accept, translate, and transmit documents that contain various types of information. Using BizTalk, you can receive a document in a given format, translate that document to a format you need or can use, and then take action on it. For instance, you can receive a document that contains a vendor catalog, in whatever format they can provide. BizTalk can accept that catalog, translate it into the XML format used by Commerce Server 2000, and insert it into the system. You can use BizTalk to take a purchase order from Commerce Server 2000 and send it to a vendor, in the format the vendor needs.

If your site is providing catalogs from other suppliers and allowing users to make purchases from those catalogs, you can automatically receive catalog updates from those suppliers. Those catalogs can be sent via BizTalk and incorporated into the catalog system. To do so, you might follow a process like the following:

1. Define the BizTalk interface to receive the supplier's catalog.

   There are several ways of building this interface through BizTalk or through a Web page that accepts the updated catalog from the supplier.

One such example of building a page that accepts a submitted document from a supplier can be found in the Retail site. The file is named RECEIVESTANDARD.ASP and its code is shown here:

```
Option Explicit

Response.Buffer = True

Dim interchange

Dim SubmissionHandle

Dim PostedDocument

Dim ContentType

Dim CharSet

Dim EntityBody

Dim Stream

Dim StartPos

Dim EndPos

Set interchange = CreateObject( "BizTalk.Interchange" )

ContentType = Request.ServerVariables( "CONTENT_TYPE" )

'
' Determine request entity body character set
' (default to us-ascii)
'

CharSet = "us-ascii"

StartPos = InStr( 1, ContentType, "CharSet=""", 1)

If (StartPos > 0 ) then

   StartPos = StartPos + Len("CharSet=""")

   EndPos = InStr( StartPos, ContentType, """",1 )

   CharSet = Mid (ContentType, StartPos, EndPos - StartPos )

End if

'
' Check for multipart MIME message
```
(continued)

(continued)

```
PostedDocument = ""

if ( ContentType = "" or Request.TotalBytes = 0) then

'

' Content-Type is required as well as an entity body

'

   Response.Status = "406 Not Acceptable"

   Response.Write "Content-type or Entity body is missing _
    & VbCrlf

   Response.Write "Message headers follow below:" & VbCrlf

   Response.Write Request.ServerVariables("ALL_RAW") & VbCrlf

   Response.End

else

   if ( InStr( 1,ContentType,"multipart/" ) > 0 ) then

   '

   ' MIME multipart message. Build MIME header

'

   PostedDocument = MIME-Version: 1.0" & vbCrLf _
      &  " Content-Type: "  & ContentType & vbCrLf & vbCrLf

   PostedDocument = PostedDocument _
      & "This is a multi-part message in MIME format." _
      & vbCrLf

   End if

   '

   ' Get the post entity body

   '

   EntityBody = Request.BinaryRead (Request.TotalBytes )

   '

   ' Convert to UNICODE

   '
```

(continued)

(continued)

```
    Set Stream = Server.CreateObject("AdoDB.Stream")
    Stream.Type = 1                  'adTypeBinary
    Stream.Open
    Stream.Write EntityBody
    Stream.Position = 0
    Stream.Type = 2                  'adTypeText
    Stream.Charset = CharSet
    PostedDocument = PostedDocument & Stream.ReadText
    Stream.Close
    Set Stream = Nothing

    '
    ' Submit document asynchronously to Biztalk Server
    '
    SubmissionHandle = interchange.submit( 1, PostedDocument )

    Set interchange = Nothing

    '
    ' indicate that the message has been received,
    ' but that processing may not be complete
    '

    Response.Status = "202 Accepted"
    Response.End
End if
```

Of course, this code assumes that the BizTalk interchange components are installed locally on the Web server. This process can be simply modified to submit the incoming document to BizTalk through a message queue, as shown in the following code:

```
dim MSMQInfo,MSMQ, MSMQMsg
set MSMQInfo = server.CreateObject("MSMQ.MSMQQueueInfo")
set MSMQMsg = server.CreateObject("MSMQ.MSMQMessage")
```

(continued)

(continued)

```
MSMQInfo.PathName = sQueueName

set MSMQ = MSMQInfo.Open(2,0)         'open as SEND_ACCESS _
                                      'and DENY_NONE

MSMQMsg.Body = PostedDocument

call MSMQMsg.Send(MSMQ)
```

Of course, this assumes that BizTalk has a receive function configured to poll the queue to which we've sent that document. This must be created in BizTalk.

2. Map the supplier's catalog to the Commerce Server 2000 catalog schema.

   The data map could be built using BizTalk Mapper and the transformation would be completed by BizTalk.

3. Perform a preprocessing of the catalog.

   This might be done using an Application Integration Component (AIC) in BizTalk to perform any necessary processing.

4. Insert the catalog into the Commerce Server catalog system.

   This can be done in two ways. The first would be to write an AIC that would call the Commerce Server CatalogManager component's ImportXML method to import the supplier's catalog. The second would be to use a Data Transformation Service (DTS) task in SQL Server 2000 to copy the data from the supplier's catalog to Commerce Server.

5. Perform any postprocessing of the catalog.

   This might be done using an AIC in BizTalk to perform any necessary processing.

Refreshing Catalog Data

Whenever you make changes to the catalog, you should plan on refreshing the catalog system using the Update Catalogs toolbar button. Clicking this button actually causes several things to happen, in the following order:

1. Publish custom catalogs, based on any changes you've made.
2. Refresh/Rebuild free text search indexes.
3. Flush any existing catalog caches.

By performing this action, you ensure that your customers are getting the most up-to-date data on your available offerings.

Exporting Catalog Data

At various times, you might need to export a catalog so that you can send it to vendors, partners, or others. You might simply need to copy the catalog from one server to another. In the Business Desk, you can export the catalog to an XML or a .csv file by clicking the Export Catalog toolbar button. You only need to provide the destination filename to save the file.

Note Your first choice when exporting a catalog should always be to use the XML format. This maintains the entire catalog, including the hierarchy, product and property definitions, and relationships.

Sending Catalog Data

If you have integrated BizTalk Server with your Commerce Server 2000 site and have vendors or trading partners connected through BizTalk, you can automatically send them catalog updates. You do this by clicking Send Catalog on the toolbar. This packages the current catalog using BizTalk and transmits it to your partner. The actual method of this transmission is determined and controlled by BizTalk.

Catalog Sets

Once you've built several catalogs, you may want to put them in groups so that you can more easily define which catalogs can be seen by which users. For instance, you might want only a limited selection of your products available to users who have not registered on your site. The expanded offering might be used as an incentive to convince users to register. Perhaps your site offers corporate customers a different selection of items or different pricing. To achieve this, you can place catalogs in a catalog set and define for any given user, or group of users, which catalog set to use to display products.

To view the catalog sets that are on your site, open the Catalog Sets section of the Business Desk. To create a new catalog set, perform the following steps:

1. Click New Catalog Set on the toolbar.
2. Provide Name and Description values for the new catalog set (Figure 11-15).
3. Specify which of the existing catalogs should be available in this catalog set. You can move catalogs from the Available Catalogs list box to the Assigned Catalogs list box to include them in the set. You can also simply select the Add All Catalogs check box to make sure the set includes all of the existing catalogs.

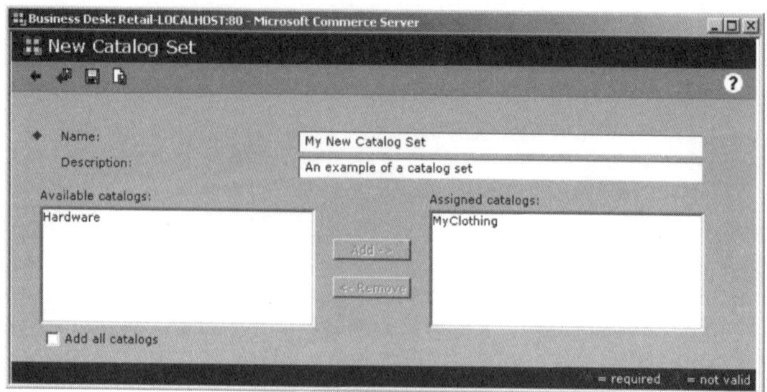

Figure 11-15. *When you create a catalog set in the Business Desk, you'll need to provide a name and identify the catalogs to be placed in the set.*

Retrieving a User's Catalog Set

As a default, Commerce Server 2000 provides two catalog sets, both of which include all of the catalogs in your site. These two sets are Anonymous User Default CatalogSet and Registered User Default CatalogSet, used to determine the catalogs available for anonymous users and registered users, respectively. Using the code found in the file CATALOG.ASP of the Retail site, you can check to see if the current user has a catalog set assigned. If so, you use the indicated catalog set. If not, you can use the appropriate default catalog set, as shown in this sample:

```
'-----------------------------------
' mscsUserCatalogsetID
'
' Description:
'  This method looks up the catalogsetid for the user.
'
' Parameters:
'  none
'
' Returns:
'  CatalogSet
'
' Notes :
'  It works by first looking at the user properties...
'  if there is no user-level default, it will look for an
'  org-level catalogset.
```
(continued)

(continued)

```
'  Else, the method will return a catalogID as specified in
'  RegisteredUserDefaultCatalogSet or
'  AnonymousUserDefaultCatalogSet
'  (This code simulates CatalogSets::mscsUserCatalogsetID
'  w/o any object creation)
'--------------------------------------

Function mscsUserCatalogsetID()
   Dim rsUser, rsOrg
   Dim org_id

   Set rsUser = GetCurrentUserProfile()

   If Not rsUser Is Nothing Then
      mscsUserCatalogsetID = _
       rsUser.Fields.Item(USER_CATALOGSET).Value
        If IsNull(mscsUserCatalogsetID) Then
'  Get the user's org profile.
          org_id = rsUser.Fields.Item(USER_ORGID).Value

          If Not IsNull(org_id) Then
'  Set rsGetProfile's bForceDBLookUp to False
'  to avoid a database look-up.
            Set rsOrg = _
             rsGetProfileByKey(FIELD_ORG_ORG_ID, _
             org_id, PROFILE_TYPE_ORG, False)
              If Not rsOrg Is Nothing Then
                mscsUserCatalogsetID = _
                 rsOrg.Fields.Item(ORG_CATALOGSET).Value
              End If
          End If
        End If
   Else
      mscsUserCatalogsetID = Null
   End If
```

(continued)

(continued)

```
    If IsNull(mscsUserCatalogsetID) Then
' Get the catalog set to fall back if no catalog set
' was specified at user/org level.
        If m_UserType = AUTH_USER Then
            mscsUserCatalogsetID = _
              dictConfig.s_AuthenticatedUserDefaultCatalogSet
        Else
            mscsUserCatalogsetID = _
              dictConfig.s_AnonymousUserDefaultCatalogSet
        End If
    End If
End Function
```

Catalog Schema

When you're importing or exporting a catalog using XML or retrieving a catalog through BizTalk, you'll be using the Commerce Server Catalog XML Schema, CATALOGXMLSCHEMA.XML. You can find a copy of this schema in the \Program Files\Microsoft Commerce Server directory. This schema specifies the product, property, and category definitions, as well as each category and product entry in the catalog. The schema itself is shown in the following code sample:

```
<?xml version="1.0"?>
<Schema name="MSCommerceCatalogCollection"
    xmlns="urn:schemas-microsoft-com:xml-data"
    xmlns:dt="urn:schemas-microsoft-com:datatypes" >
    <!--Model is open (default)-->
    <AttributeType name="name" dt:type="string" required='yes'/>
    <AttributeType name="id" dt:type="id" required='yes'/>
    <AttributeType name="dataType" dt:type="enumeration"
    dt:values="string number bignumber datetime money
    real float currency
    boolean enumeration filename " required='yes'/>
    <AttributeType name="value"/>
    <AttributeType name="parentCategories" dt:type="idrefs"/>
```

(continued)

(continued)

```
<ElementType name="MSCommerceCatalogCollection">
  <element type="CatalogSchema" minOccurs="1" maxOccurs="1"/>
  <element type="Catalog" minOccurs="0" maxOccurs="*"/>
</ElementType>

<ElementType name="PropertiesDefinition">
  <element type="Property" minOccurs="0" maxOccurs="*"/>
</ElementType>

<ElementType name="CatalogSchema">
  <element type="PropertiesDefinition" minOccurs="0"
   maxOccurs="1"/>
  <element type="Definition" minOccurs="0" maxOccurs="*"/>
  <element type="AttributeDefinition" minOccurs="0"
   maxOccurs="*"/>
</ElementType>

<ElementType name="AttributeDefinition">
  <attribute type="name"/>
  <attribute type="dataType"/>
</ElementType>

<ElementType name="PropertyValue">
  <AttributeType name="displayName" dt:type="string"
   required='yes'/>
  <attribute type="displayName"/>
</ElementType>

<ElementType name="Property" model="open">
  <AttributeType name="DefaultValue" dt:type="string"/>
  <AttributeType name="MinValue" dt:type="string"/>
  <AttributeType name="MaxValue" dt:type="string"/>
  <AttributeType name="IsFreeTextSearchable"
   dt:type="boolean"/>
```

(continued)

(continued)

```
      <AttributeType name="IncludeInSpecSearch"
       dt:type="boolean"/>

      <AttributeType name="DisplayOnSite" dt:type="boolean"/>

      <AttributeType name="DisplayName" dt:type="string"/>

      <AttributeType name="AssignAll" dt:type="boolean"/>

      <AttributeType name="ExportToDW" dt:type="boolean"/>

      <AttributeType name="DisplayInProductsList"
       dt:type="boolean"/>

      <attribute type="DefaultValue"/>

      <attribute type="MinValue"/>

      <attribute type="MaxValue"/>

      <attribute type="IsFreeTextSearchable"/>

      <attribute type="IncludeInSpecSearch"/>

      <attribute type="DisplayOnSite" />

      <attribute type="DisplayName" />

      <attribute type="AssignAll"/>

      <attribute type="ExportToDW"/>

      <attribute type="DisplayInProductsList"/>

      <attribute type="name"/>

      <attribute type="dataType"/>

      <attribute type="id"/>

      <element type="PropertyValue" minOccurs="0" maxOccurs="*"/>
   </ElementType>

   <ElementType name="Definition">
      <AttributeType name="properties" dt:type="idrefs"/>

      <AttributeType name="variantProperties" dt:type="idrefs"/>

      <AttributeType name="DefinitionType" required= "yes"
       dt:type="enumeration" dt:values="product category "/>

      <attribute type="name"/>

      <attribute type="DefinitionType"/>
```

(continued)

(continued)

```
    <attribute type="properties"/>

    <attribute type="variantProperties"/>

  </ElementType>

  <ElementType name="Catalog">

    <AttributeType name="currency" required='yes'/>

    <AttributeType name="locale" dt:type="string"/>

    <AttributeType name="startDate" dt:type="string"/>

    <AttributeType name="endDate" dt:type="string"/>

    <AttributeType name="productUID" required= "yes"
     dt:type="string"/>

    <AttributeType name="variantUID" required= "yes"
     dt:type="string"/>

    <AttributeType name="weight_measuring_unit"
     dt:type="string"/>

    <element type="Category" minOccurs="0" maxOccurs="*"/>

    <element type="Product" minOccurs="0" maxOccurs="*"/>

    <attribute type="name"/>

    <attribute type="currency"/>

    <attribute type="locale"/>

    <attribute type="startDate"/>

    <attribute type="endDate"/>

    <attribute type="productUID"/>

    <attribute type="variantUID"/>

    <attribute type="weight_measuring_unit"/>

  </ElementType>

  <ElementType name="Field">

    <AttributeType name="fieldID" dt:type="idref" />

    <AttributeType name="fieldValue" dt:type="string"
     required='yes'/>
```

(continued)

(continued)

```
    <attribute type="fieldID"/>
    <attribute type="fieldValue"/>
  </ElementType>

  <ElementType name="Category">
    <AttributeType name="isSearchable" dt:type="string"/>
    <AttributeType name="listprice" dt:type="string"/>

    <attribute type="listprice"/>
    <attribute type="id"/>
    <attribute type="name"/>
    <attribute type="parentCategories"/>
    <attribute type="Definition"/>
    <attribute type ="isSearchable" />
    <element type="Field" minOccurs="1" maxOccurs="*"/>
    <element type="Relationship" minOccurs="0" maxOccurs="*"/>
  </ElementType>

  <ElementType name="Product">
    <AttributeType name="pricingCategory" />
    <AttributeType name="listprice" dt:type="string"
     required="yes"/>

    <attribute type="listprice"/>
    <attribute type="id"/>
    <attribute type="Definition"/>
    <attribute type="pricingCategory"/>
    <attribute type="parentCategories"/>
    <element type="Field" minOccurs="1" maxOccurs="*"/>
    <element type="Relationship" minOccurs="0" maxOccurs="*"/>
    <element type="ProductVariant" minOccurs="0" maxOccurs="*"/>
  </ElementType>
```

(continued)

(continued)

```
    <ElementType name="ProductVariant">

      <AttributeType name="listprice" dt:type="string"
       required="yes"/>

      <attribute type="listprice"/>

      <element type="Field" minOccurs="1" maxOccurs="*"/>

    </ElementType>

    <ElementType name="Relationship">

      <AttributeType name="description" dt:type="string" />

      <AttributeType name="relation" required ="yes"
       dt:type="idref"/>

      <attribute type="name"/>

      <attribute type="description"/>

      <attribute type="relation"/>

    </ElementType>

</Schema>
```

Chapter 12

Catalog Management System

Microsoft Commerce Server 2000 has a catalog management system containing a number of components that you can use to display and search catalogs and products on your commerce site (see Figure 12-1). This chapter covers the components used to build the pages necessary to open and display the catalogs, categories, and products. At the end of the chapter is a section that summarizes the components of the catalog management system and tables that provide a quick reference to the properties and methods of each of the components.

The components of the catalog management system are organized in a nested fashion. Both the CatalogManager and CatalogSets components are used to identify catalogs within the system. You'll use the CatalogManager to gain access to the catalog system itself. Once in the system, you can then access an individual catalog in the ProductCatalog component. From the ProductCatalog component, you can use the Category component to retrieve category information or the Product component to get product information.

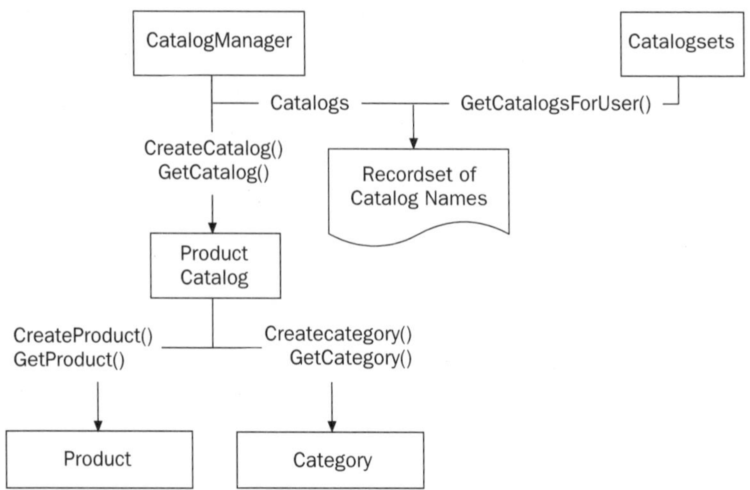

Figure 12-1. *The Commerce Server 2000 catalog system is made up of several interrelated COM components.*

Retrieving Catalog Information on the Web Site

On the actual Web site, you'll primarily be concerned with retrieving the appropriate set of catalogs for the current user and allowing that user to browse the catalogs. In addition, to help users better find the products they're looking for, you might need to support several different options in searching the catalogs. We'll cover the catalog search techniques in Chapter 13, "Catalog Searching." In this section, we concentrate on how to retrieve and display catalog, category, and product information using the CatalogManager, CatalogSets, and ProductCatalog objects.

Note The various catalog components don't just provide you with the means to access and display the catalogs on your site; they also provide a means for you to administer the catalogs. These components are used by the Business Desk to create and edit catalogs, categories, products, and their definitions. In addition, the components provide the functionality to import, export, and publish the catalogs to the site.

CatalogManager

To access any catalog information, you begin by creating a reference to the CatalogManager object. This object is used as the primary source for retrieving information or references to any catalog on the site. Typically, you should establish a reference to this object and initialize it in the GLOBAL.ASA file, then store that reference in an application variable, as shown in the following code sample. Doing this allows all users to make use of the same CatalogManager object from every page. This means that you don't need to re-create and initialize the object on every page for every user, greatly increasing the scalability and performance of the site.

```
Set mscsCatalogManager = _
 Server.CreateObject("Commerce.CatalogManager")

Call mscsCatalogManager.Initialize( _
 MSCSOptionsDictionary.s_CatalogConnectionString, True)

Set Application("MSCSCatalogManager") = mscsCatalogManager
```

Using this object, we can retrieve a list of the catalogs on the site. We might want to display the list of catalogs, so that users can decide which catalogs they want to browse. You can retrieve the list of catalogs using the Catalogs property of the component. This function returns a recordset that lists each of the catalogs and information about each, as shown in Table 12-1.

Table 12-1. Retrieving the List of Catalogs from a Sample Site That Includes the Books Sample Catalog Returns This Information

Field Name	Description	Sample Value
CatalogName	Name of the catalog	Books
Locale	Locale ID as a base for this catalog	8
StartDate	First date when a catalog should be available	12/8/1999
EndDate	Last date when a catalog should be available	12/8/2006
VariantID	Name of the field that will hold the unique ID for product variants	ISBN
ProductID	Name of the field that will hold the unique ID for each product	Title
Currency	The currency type for this catalog	USD
WeightMeasure	The unit of measure for the product weights	Lbs
Timestamp	Timestamp that marks when the catalog was created in the database	<binary>
CatalogID	The catalog ID	1
CustomCatalog	Specifies if this is a custom catalog	False
FreeTextIndexCreated	Date and time when the free text index for this catalog was last updated	2/24/2001 1:17:05 PM
ProductTableUpdated	Date and time when the product data in this catalog was last updated	2/24/2001 1:16:29 PM

Based on that recordset, we can then display a list of all of the available catalogs on the Web site, as shown here:

```
set rsCatalogs = MSCSCatalogManager.Catalogs

htmCatalogs="<h4>Catalogs</h4>"

do while not rsCatalogs.EOF

   htmCatalogs = htmCatalogs & "<A HREF=""catalog.asp?cat=" _
    & rsCatalogs("CatalogName") & """>" _
    & rsCatalogs("CatalogName") & "</a><br>"

   rsCatalogs.movenext

loop
```

CatalogSets

On your site, however, you might not want to show all catalogs to each user. Rather, you might want to determine which catalogs a user should have access to and only show those. You can do this using the CatalogsSets object, which allows you to retrieve a set of catalogs based on the current user's profile. The user profile holds a property that identifies the catalog set. If the user is not logged in or does not have a catalog set specified, then you can use a default catalog set.

The CatalogSets object can be created in the GLOBAL.ASA file as the application is started and then stored in an application variable, as shown in the next code sample. This allows all users on all pages to use the same object, which reduces the time and load on the server that would otherwise be required to create and initialize multiple copies of the object.

```
set mscsCatalogSets = server.CreateObject("Commerce.CatalogSets")

call _
 mscsCatalogSets.Initialize( _
 MSCSSiteConfig.s_CatalogConnectionString, true)

set Application("MSCSCatalogSets") = mscsCatalogSets
```

As with the CatalogManager object, you can use this object to retrieve a recordset that contains a list of catalogs on the site. You can retrieve all of the catalogs using the following code:

```
set rsCatalogs = mscsCatalogSet.GetCatalogs()
```

You can also retrieve just the catalogs that are available to the user by calling the GetCatalogsForUser method, shown in the next sample. With this method, you must provide a reference to the ProfileService object, the current user's ID, and a default catalog set ID to use if the user does not have an identified catalog set.

```
const _ANONUSER_DEFAULTCATALOGSET = _
 "{11111111-1111-1111-1111-11111111111}"

const REGUSER_DEFAULTCATALOGSET = _
 "{22222222-2222-2222-2222-222222222222}"


'Assume that user is registered...

guidDefaultCatalogSetID = REGUSER_DEFAULTCATALOGSET

set rsCatalogs = _
 mscsCatalogSet.GetCatalogsForUser(MSCSProfileService, _
 m_userid, guidDefaultCatalogSetID)
```

The resulting recordset contains only a single field, CatalogName. Each record provides the name of a catalog to which the user has access, as shown here:

```
htmCatalogs="<h4>Catalogs</h4>"

do while not rsCatalogs.EOF

   htmCatalogs = htmCatalogs & "<A HREF=""catalog.asp?cat=" _
    & rsCatalogs("CatalogName") & """>" _
    & rsCatalogs("CatalogName") & "</a><br>"

   rsCatalogs.movenext

loop
```

ProductCatalog

Once you've retrieved a list of catalogs, you can use those to browse to and open a selected catalog. Likewise, you might want to provide a default catalog that is automatically opened if no other catalog is selected. To open a catalog, you can call the CatalogManager's GetCatalog method, specifying the catalog name, as shown here:

```
set mscsCatalog = MSCSCatalogManager.GetCatalog(sCatalogName)
```

This returns a ProductCatalog object, which you can use to navigate the categories and products in the catalog. This object is your key to finding information about the products and categories in your catalog. You can use the ProductCatalog object to retrieve lists of categories and products. The object's RootCategories and RootProducts methods provide lists of categories and products that can be found at the root of the catalog, and not within any categories. You can set a reference to the Category and Product objects using the GetCategory() and GetProduct() methods.

Categories

To allow your customers to browse through your site, you'll need to list the categories, including the base categories and all of the child categories, in the catalog. You'll need to provide a means to navigate from the parent to the child categories.

Root Categories

The first categories that you'll want to show are likely the root categories, or those with no parent categories. These categories are typically the starting point for browsing through the catalog. You can retrieve and display the root categories using the ProductCatalog's RootCategories property, shown here:

```
set rsCategories = mscsCatalog.RootCategories
```

This property returns a recordset containing the list of categories at the root of the catalog, as well information about each, as listed in Table 12-2. This recordset includes a collection of fields that describes the categories. The fields returned include fields for the products as well as the category, as this data is maintained in the same table, <catalogname>_CatalogProducts.

Table 12-2. Fields Provided in the Recordset Returned by the RootCategories Property of the ProductCatalog Object

Field Name	Description	Sample Value
CategoryName	The name of the category	Business Software
OID	The ID of this object, used to relate this to other objects	7
DefinitionName	The name of the definition that describes this category	Department
IsSearchable	Identifies whether the category is marked as searchable, to be used in specification searches	-1
Cy_list_price	From the product definition	0
PricingCategoryOID	From the product definition	[NULL]
TimeStamp	Timestamp that identifies when the data was last updated	<binary>
OriginalPrice	From the product definition	0
I_ClassType	Identifies the type of this record	1
ParentOID	ID of the parent object (-1 indicates that this is a root category)	-1
ProductID	The ID of this object	Business Software
VariantID	The ID of the object's variant	ISBN
Title	From the product definition	[NULL]
ISBN	From the product definition	[NULL]
Description	Description of the category	Business Software

(continued)

Table 12-2. *(continued)*

Field Name	Description	Sample Value
Image_filename	Image filename associated with the category	[NULL]
Image_height	Height of the image associated with the category	[NULL]
Image_width	Width of the image associated with the category	[NULL]
Author	From the product definition	[NULL]
Name	From the product definition	[NULL]
Pagecount	From the product definition	[NULL]
Producturl	From the product definition	[NULL]
Publication Year	From the product definition	[NULL]
Publisher	From the product definition	[NULL]
Reading Level	From the product definition	[NULL]
CatalogName	Name of the catalog in which this category is located	Books

Once you've retrieved the recordset, you can use it to display the list of categories on the Web page, as shown here:

```
htmCategories="<h4>Categories</h4>"

do while not rsCategories.EOF

   htmCategories = htmCategories & "<A HREF=""category.asp?cat=" _
    & sCatalogName & "&ctg=" & rsCategories("CategoryName") _
    & """>" & rsCategories("CategoryName") & "</a><BR>"

   rsCategories.movenext

loop
```

Category Object

Once you have the name of a category, you can use it to retrieve the Category object. This Category object can then be used to retrieve other information about the category. You'll use this object to retrieve the parents and children of the selected category. To retrieve the Category object, use the GetCategory method of the ProductCatalog, shown here:

```
Set mscsCategory = mscsCatalog.GetCategory(sCategoryName)
```

Child Categories

If the user selects a category, you'll need to display the child categories within that category. This allows your customers to walk through the hierarchy of the categories. You'll retrieve a recordset that lists each of the categories that is a child of the current category, as shown here:

```
set rsCategories = mscsCategory.ChildCategories
```

You can then use that recordset to display the list of categories.

ParentCategories

At times, you might find it necessary to provide a link back to the parent categories of the current category. In this case, you can retrieve a recordset that lists all of the parents of the current category, using the ParentCategories property, as follows:

```
set rsCategories = mscsCategory.ParentCategories
```

RelatedCategories

When users select a category, you might want to provide a list of related categories that might also be of interest to them. In this way, you can attract their attention to categories that they might not otherwise look into. You can retrieve a recordset containing a list of categories related to the current category through the RelatedCategories property, as shown here:

```
set rsCategories = mscsCategory.RelatedCategories
```

Products

As customers begin to navigate through the catalog, you'll need to display the products that are available in that category.

Retrieving Products at the Root of a Catalog

As with the categories, you'll need to determine if there are any products available at the root of the catalog that haven't been placed in any given categories. You can retrieve a recordset of products that are available at the root using the ProductCatalog's RootProducts property, as shown here:

```
set rsProducts = mscsCatalog.RootProducts
```

This recordset contains data about each of the products, as listed in Table 12-3, and a collection of fields that describes the products. The fields returned include fields for the categories as well as the product, as this data is maintained in the same table, <catalogname>_CatalogProducts.

Table 12-3. Fields Provided in the Recordset Returned by the RootProducts Property of theProductCatalog Object

Field Name	Description	Sample Value
CategoryName	From the category definition	[NULL]
OID	The ID of this object, used to relate this to other objects	64
DefinitionName	The name of the definition that describes this product	SDKBook
IsSearchable	From the category definition	[NULL]
Cy_list_price	The list price of the product	19.99

(continued)

Table 12-3. *(continued)*

Field Name	Description	Sample Value
PricingCategoryOID	ID of the pricing category	[NULL]
TimeStamp	Timestamp that identifies when the data was last updated	<binary>
OriginalPrice	Original price of the product	19.99
I_ClassType	Identifies the type of this record	4
ParentOID	ID of the parent object (-1 indicates that this is a root product)	-1
ProductID	The ID of this object	*Microsoft Age of Empires II: The Age of Kings: Inside Moves*
VariantID	The ID of the object's variant	ISBN
Title	Book Title	*Microsoft Age of Empires II: The Age of Kings: Inside Moves*
ISBN	Book ISBN	0-7356-0513-0
Description	Book Description	<Description omitted for space>
Image_filename	Image filename associated with the product	Boxshots/press/2388.gif
Image_height	Height of the image associated with the product	120
Image_width	Width of the image associated with the product	120
Author	Book's author	Microsoft Corporation
Name	Book name	*Microsoft Age of Empires II: The Age of Kings: Inside Moves*
Pagecount	Number of pages in the book	280
Producturl	URL for the product	*http://mspress.microsoft.com / prod/books/2388.htm*
Publication Year	Year of book publication	1999
Publisher	Book publisher	Microsoft Press
Reading Level	Level of the book	All levels
CatalogName	Name of the catalog in which this product is located	Books

Once you've retrieved the recordset, you can use it to display the list of products on the site. You can then build a link so that the customer can get a detailed view of the products, as shown in the following sample:

```
htmProducts = "<h4>Products</h4>" & htmProducts

do while not rsProducts.EOF

   htmProducts = htmProducts & "<A HREF=""product.asp?cat=" _
    & sCatalogName & "&id=" & rsProducts("ProductID") & """>" _
    & rsProducts("Name") & "</a><br>"

rsProducts.movenext

loop
```

Retrieving Products in a Category

As you maneuver through the catalog hierarchy, you'll need to retrieve a list of the products in any given catalog. You can do so using the Products property of the Category object, as shown here:

```
set rsProducts = mscsCategory.Products
```

With the resulting recordset, you can build the list of available products.

Product Object

Once you have the ID of a selected product, you can retrieve the product from the catalog. You retrieve the Product object from the ProductCatalog by calling the GetProduct method, shown here:

```
Set mscsProduct = mscsCatalog.GetProduct(sProductID)
```

From this object, you can then retrieve the information concerning the individual product.

Displaying Product Properties

Once you've retrieved the Product object from the catalog, you can use it to gather detailed information about that product. From there, you'll be ready to build the product display. If you have only one type of product, you can build a display specifically for that individual product. If you have several types of products, you might build a more complex page that automatically detects the product type and routes the display to the required page. You can also build the page dynamically, displaying all of the necessary fields. Doing this requires checking the product definition to identify the properties that should be displayed on the site.

The first step in displaying this data is to retrieve the Product object from the ProductCatalog. With the Product object, you can retrieve a recordset containing a list of the product properties using the Product's GetProductProperties method, as shown here:

```
set mscsProduct = mscsProductCatalog.GetProduct(sProductID)

set rsProductData = mscsProduct.GetProductProperties
```

To then identify the properties that should and should not be displayed on the page, you'll need to examine the Product Definition. To do so, first retrieve the name of the definition from the DefinitionName field in the Product properties recordset. You can then retrieve a recordset that contains the definition data from the CatalogManager object, using the GetDefinitionProperties method, as seen here:

```
sProductDefinition = rsProductData("DefinitionName")

set rsProductProperties = _
 MSCSCatalogManager.GetDefinitionProperties(sProductDefinition)
```

Once you have that recordset, you can loop through the list of properties. From each property, you can get the attributes that describe that property. You get that information from the CatalogManager object's GetPropertyAttributes method, which is shown in this code sample:

```
htmProduct = "<table width=""100%"">"

do until rsProductProperties.EOF

   sPropertyName = rsProductProperties("PropertyName")

   set rsPropertyAttributes = _
    MSCSCatalogManager.GetPropertyAttributes(sPropertyName)
```

This returns a recordset with the property's attributes, with which you can determine whether the property should be shown on the page by checking the value of the DisplayOnSite field. If the value is True, then it should be shown. You can get the name to display on the site from the DisplayName field in the property attributes, as shown in the next code sample. Otherwise, you can just use the property name itself.

```
   if rsPropertyAttributes("DisplayOnSite") then

      if IsNull(rsPropertyAttributes("DisplayName")) _
       or rsPropertyAttributes("DisplayName") = "" then

         sDisplayName = sPropertyName

      else

         sDisplayName = rsPropertyAttributes("DisplayName")

      end if

   end if
```

Now that you've determined that the property should be shown on the site and what label it should be given, you can now retrieve the value of the property from the product recordset, as shown here:

```
    sValue = rsProductData(sPropertyName)

    if not IsNull(sValue) and not IsNull(sDisplayName) then

        htmProduct = htmProduct & "<tr><td><b>" & sDisplayName _
         & "</b></td>"

        htmProduct = htmProduct & "<td>" & sValue & "</td></tr>"

    end if

    rsProductProperties.MoveNext

loop
```

Displaying Variant Product Properties

If the product you are about to display contains variants, you can retrieve the variant data and display each of the variations using the Product object's Variants property, as shown in the next code sample. This property returns a recordset that contains each of the variations for the current product. With that recordset, you can display the variants and provide a means for your customer to choose the appropriate product.

```
set rsVariants = mscsProduct.Variants

htmVariants = "<table>"

htmVariants = htmVariants & "<tr>"

for each fldVariant in rsVariants.Fields

    if lcase(htmVariants.name) <> "cy_list_price" then

        htmVariants = htmVariants & "<th> _
         & fldVariant.Name & "</th>"

    end if

next

htmVariants = htmVariants & "<th>Price</th></tr>"

do while not rsVariants.EOF

    htmVariants = htmVariants & "<tr>"

    for each fldVariant in rsVariants.Fields

        if lcase(fldVariant.Name) <> "cy_list_price" then

            htmVariants = htmVariants & "<td>" _
             & fldVariant.Value & "</td>"

        end if

    next
```

(continued)

(continued)

```
    htmVariants = htmVariants & "<td>" _
     & rsVariants("cy_list_price") & "</td>"

    htmVariants = htmVariants & "</tr>"

    rsVariants.MoveNext

Loop

htmVariants = htmVariants & "</table>"
```

Note Each of the variant properties should be displayed on the site, as these are the means by which your customers can differentiate between the variations.

Listing Related Products

If a product is related to other products in the catalog, you might want to also list those related products to the shopper. It's useful for buyers to know that there are, in fact, related products that they might be interested in. In this way, you can attempt to cross-sell these products. You can retrieve a recordset of related products from a product's RelatedProducts property, as shown in the next code sample. You can use this recordset to display the appropriate list of products, if any, on the page.

```
set rsRelated = mscsProduct.RelatedProducts

htmRelated = "<h4>Related Products</h4>"

if rsRelated.Eof then

    htmRelated = htmRelated & "No Related Products<P>"

else

    do while not rsRelated.EOF

        htmRelated = htmRelated & "<A HREF=""product.asp?cat=" _
         & sCatalogName & "&id=" & rsRelated("ProductID") _
         & """>" & rsRelated("Name") & "</a><br>"

        rsRelated.MoveNext

    loop

end if
```

Catalog Component Reference

The following sections summarize the components that comprise the catalog management system. The tables provide a quick reference to the properties and methods of each of the components.

CatalogManager

The CatalogManager component can be created using the PROGID Commerce.CatalogManager. Its properties are shown in Table 12-4, and its methods are displayed in Table 12-5.

Table 12-4. CatalogManager Properties

Property Name	Data Type	Description
Catalogs	Recordset	Lists each catalog and its respective properties
CategoryDefinitions	Recordset	Lists the names of each category definition in the system
CustomCatalogs	Recordset	Lists the names of the custom catalogs in the system, including the base catalog name
ProductDefinitions	Recordset	Lists the names of the product definitions in the system
Properties	Recordset	Lists the name of each property in the system

Table 12-5. CatalogManager Methods

Method Name	Description
AddDefinitionProperty	Adds a property to the specified definition
AddDefinitionVariantProperty	Adds a variant's property to the specified definition
AddPropertyValue	Adds a multiple-choice value to the list of available values
CreateCatalog	Creates a catalog
CreateCategoryDefinition	Creates a category definition
CreateProductDefinition	Creates a product definition
CreateProperty	Creates a property
DeleteCatalog	Deletes a catalog
DeleteDefinition	Deletes a definition
DeleteProperty	Deletes a property
ExportCSV	Exports the specified catalog to a comma-delimited file
ExportXML	Exports the specified catalog to an Extensible Markup Language (XML) document

(continued)

Table 12-5. *(continued)*

Method Name	Description
FreeTextSearch	Executes a free text search of all catalogs in the system
GetCatalog	Retrieves a catalog
GetDefinitionProperties	Retrieves properties of a definition
GetPropertyAttributes	Retrieves attributes of a definition property
GetPropertyValues	Retrieves a list of available choices for a multiple-choice property
ImportCSV	Imports a catalog from a comma-delimited file
ImportXML	Imports a catalog from an XML document
Initialize	Initializes the object, establishing the connection information to the database
Query	Executes a query in the system
RemoveDefinitionProperty	Removes a property from the specified definition
RemovePropertyValue	Removes a value from the list of available values in a multiple-choice property
RenameDefinition	Renames a definition
RenameProperty	Renames a property
SetDefinitionProperties	Saves the changed properties of a definition
SetDefinitionAttributes	Saves the changes of a property's attributes

CatalogSets

The CatalogSets component can be created using the PROGID Commerce.CatalogSets. The methods of the CatalogSets component are shown in Table 12-6.

Table 12-6. CatalogSets Methods

Method Name	Description
CreateCatalogSet	Creates a catalog set
DeleteCatalogSet	Deletes a catalog set
GetCatalogs	Retrieves a list of all catalogs in the system
GetCatalogSetIDForUser	Retrieves the catalog set ID, which is a globally unique identifier (GUID) for the specified user
GetCatalogSetInfo	Retrieves a recordset with information concerning the catalog set
GetCatalogSets	Retrieves a list of catalog sets
GetCatalogsForUser	Retrieves a list of catalogs available to a user
GetCatalogsInCatalogSet	Retrieves a list of catalogs in the specified catalog set

(continued)

Table 12-6. *(continued)*

Method Name	Description
GetCatalogsNotInCatalogSet	Retrieves a list of catalogs not in the specified catalog set
Initialize	Initializes the CatalogSets object with database connection information
RemoveCatalogFromCatalogSets	Removes a catalog from the catalog set
UpdateCatalogSet	Saves changes to a catalog set

Category

The Category component is a dependent object, and can only be created using the ProductCatalog's CreateCategory or GetCategory methods. The properties of the Category component are shown in Table 12-7. Table 12-8 lists the Category component methods.

Table 12-7. Category Properties

Property Name	Data Type	Description
AncestorCategories	Recordset	List of categories anywhere above the current category in the catalog hierarchy
CatalogName	String	Name of the current catalog
CategoryName	String	Name of the current category
ChildCategories	Recordset	List of the categories that are children of the current category
DescendantProducts	Recordset	List of products that are anywhere below the current category in the catalog hierarchy
GetCategoryProperties	Recordset	Contains information describing the current category
ParentCategories	Recordset	List of the parents of the current category
Products	Recordset	List of products within the current category
RelatedCategories	Recordset	List of categories related to the current category
RelatedProducts	Recordset	List of products related to the current category

Table 12-8. Category Methods

Method Name	Description
AddChildCategory	Adds specified category as a child to the current category
AddParentCategory	Adds specified category as a parent of the current category
AddProduct	Adds specified product to the current category
AddRelationshipToCategory	Establishes a relationship between the specified category and the current category

(continued)

Table 12-8. *(continued)*

Method Name	Description
AddRelationshipToProduct	Establishes a relationship between the specified product and the current category
RemoveChildCategory	Removes specified category as a child of the current category
RemoveParentCategory	Removes specified category as a parent of the current category
RemoveProduct	Removes specified product from the current category
RemoveRelationshipToCategory	Removes a relationship between the specified category and the current category
RemoveRelationshipToProduct	Removes a relationship between the specified product and the current category
SetCategoryProperties	Saves new properties to the current category

Product

The Product component is a dependent object that can only be created using the ProductCatalog's CreateProduct or GetProduct methods. The Product component properties are displayed in Table 12-9, and its methods are listed in Table 12-10.

Table 12-9. Product Properties

Property Name	Data Type	Description
AncestorCategories	Recordset	List of categories anywhere above the current product in the catalog hierarchy
CatalogName	String	Name of the current catalog
GetProductProperties	Recordset	Contains the properties that describe the current product
ParentCategories	Recordset	List of categories that are parents of the current product
PricingCategory	String	Name of the pricing category of the current product
ProductID	String	Unique ID of the current product
RelatedCategories	Recordset	List of categories with a relationship to the current product
RelatedProducts	Recordset	List of products with a relationship to the current product
Variants	Recordset	Contains records describing the variants of the current product

Table 12-10. Product Methods

Method Name	Description
AddRelationshipToCategory	Establishes a relationship between the specified category and the current product
AddRelationshipToProduct	Establishes a relationship between the specified product and the current product
CreateVariant	Creates a variant of the current product
DeleteVariant	Deletes a variant of the current product
GetVariantProperties	Retrieves the properties of a variant of the current product
RemoveRelationshipToCategory	Removes a relationship between the specified category and the current product
RemoveRelationshipToProduct	Removes a relationship between the specified product and the current product
SetProductProperties	Saves the properties of the current product
SetVariantProperties	Saves the properties of the variants of the current product

ProductCatalog

The ProductCatalog component is a dependent object that only can be created using the CatalogManager's CreateCatalog or GetCatalog methods. The properties of the ProductCatalog component are shown in Table 12-11, and its methods are given in Table 12-12.

Table 12-11. ProductCatalog Properties

Property Name	Data Type	Description
BaseCatalogName	String	Name of the catalog that the current catalog is based on, if this is a custom catalog
CatalogName	String	Name of the current catalog
IdentifyingProductProperty	String	Name of the property that uniquely identifies each product
IdentifyingVariantProperty	String	Name of the property that uniquely identifies each product variant
RootCategories	Recordset	List of the root categories, which have no parent categories
RootProducts	Recordset	List of the root products, which are not in any category
SearchableCategories	Recordset	List of the categories marked as searchable

Table 12-12. ProductCatalog Methods

Method Name	Description
AddSpecificationSearchClause	Adds a constraint clause to the ongoing specification search
BeginSpecificationSearch	Begins the specification search
CreateCategory	Creates a category in the current catalog
CreateCustomCatalog	Creates a custom catalog based on the current catalog
CreateProduct	Creates a product in the current catalog
DeleteCategory	Deletes a category from the current catalog
DeleteCustomCatalog	Deletes a custom catalog based on the current catalog
DeleteProduct	Deletes a product from the current catalog
GenerateCustomCatalog	Builds a custom catalog from the current catalog
GetCatalogAttributes	Retrieves a recordset of attributes describing the current catalog
GetCategory	Retrieves a Category object for the specified category
GetCategoryCustomPrice	Returns the price for the specified category in the custom catalog
GetCustomCatalogAttributes	Retrieves a recordset of attributes describing the custom catalog
GetProduct	Retrieves a Product object for the specified product
GetProductVariant	Retrieves a recordset containing the properties of a product variant
GetSpecificationSearchClauses	Retrieves a recordset with the search or constraint clauses in the current specification search
GuaranteedSpecificationSearch	Runs a specification search, removing constraints, until at least one match is found
PerformSpecificationSearch	Runs a specification search
RegenerateFreeTextSearchIndex	Rebuilds the free text index for the current catalog
RemoveSpecificationSearchClause	Removes the last specification search clause that was applied
SetCatalogAttributes	Saves the attributes for the current catalog
SetCategoryCustomPrice	Saves a price for the specified category in the custom catalog
SetCustomCatalogAttributes	Saves the attributes for a custom catalog

Chapter 13

Catalog Searching

Providing your customers with the ability to browse through catalogs is a good step toward helping them find what might interest them on your site. The hierarchical nature of the catalogs provides an easy way for users to scroll through the products for which they are searching. However, this typically isn't enough. Sometimes, your users won't be able to decide which category in the catalog a product might be in. You'll need to provide your customers with a means to find the desired products quickly and easily. Users will expect to be able to come to your site, search the catalog, and quickly find the products they want. If they can't, they'll go elsewhere.

Microsoft Commerce Server 2000 provides several means for searching the catalogs, including the following:

- Free-text searches, or keyword searches
- Property searches (or parametric searches)
- Specification searches, or step searches

This chapter takes a look at how you can provide each of these search mechanisms on your site. Both the free-text and parametric searches act across multiple catalogs on your site. The specification search is applied only to a specific catalog, and then to a particular category within that catalog.

Free-Text Search

The free-text search is the easiest and most direct way of performing a search on your site. In addition, it's probably the most straightforward search to develop and place on the site. In this search, your site accepts text that the user provides and then searches for that text throughout the catalogs on your site. Users can search all of the catalogs or a limited number of catalogs. You can set which fields are returned and the number of records returned.

The FreeTextSearch Method

You set up your site to perform a free-text search using the CatalogManager object's FreeTextSearch method. This method returns a recordset containing the results of the search. It accepts the following parameters that allow you to control how the free-text search is performed:

- **strPhrase** This is the search phrase or keywords to be searched for within the catalogs.
- **strCatalogsToSearch** This is a comma-delimited list of catalogs to search. If you don't provide an entry, all the catalogs in the site are searched.
- **eClassTypeRequired** This identifies the types of objects that should be returned. The values are listed in the CatalogClassTypeEnum enumeration of the CatalogManager component. The values can be combined with logical OR operators or added together to provide a single parameter to be passed. The values are as follows:
    - **cscCategoryClass (1)** Returns categories
    - **cscProductVariantClass (2)** Returns product variants
    - **cscProductClass (4)** Returns products
    - **cscProductFamilyClass (8)** Returns product families
    - **cscProductFamilyForVariantsClass (16)** Returns the family for a product variant
    - **cscProductVariantsForFamily (32)** Returns the product variants for a product family
- **strPropertiesToReturn** This is a comma-delimited list of properties that should be returned in the resulting recordset. If more than one catalog is being searched, you must specify the list of properties to be returned.
- **strPropertiesToSortOn** This is a comma-delimited list of properties used to sort the returned results.
- **fSortAscending** This Boolean identifies whether the sorting should be in ascending order. If the value for this parameter is False, the sort is in descending order.
- **lStartingRecord** This is the number of the first record that should be returned. If the value of this parameter is 1, the results start with the first record. You can use this value, in conjunction with the next parameter, to set up a page of results.
- **lRecordsToRetrieve** This is the maximum number of records that should be returned in this recordset. This allows you to create a page of results. You can move to another page by changing the Starting Record parameter.
- **plTotalRecordsInQuery** This value is returned by the call and identifies how many records match the search criteria.

The free-text search is performed based on the full text index, which is built in Microsoft SQL Server. Commerce Server 2000 establishes the full text index on those properties that are identified as *free-text searchable* in the catalog. When the search is performed, it returns results if the values in those properties match the search phrase.

Note Free-text searches in Commerce Server 2000 are performed using the full-text indexing that SQL Server provides. A full-text catalog is built for each product catalog in Commerce Server. SQL Server 2000 has a limitation of 256 full-text catalogs that can be created on a server. This effectively limits your site to 256 Commerce Server product catalogs.

As changes are made to the catalog data, you will need to rebuild the free-text indexes within SQL Server. When you're working within Business Desk, you can do this by clicking Update Catalogs on the toolbar. Among its other functions, this calls the ProductCatalog's RegenerateFreeTextSearchIndex method, resulting in the rebuilding of the free-text indexes.

Using FreeTextSearch

To start the free-text search, you'll first have to provide your customer with the ability to enter the search phrase, as shown in Figure 13-1. That phrase can be submitted to the results page, where the search is performed. The results page will probably include a set of variables for the parameters of the search. You can then execute the FreeTextSearch method, as shown in the following code sample:

```
sCatalogs = "Books"
lClassType = 1 + 2 + 4 'cscCategoryClass
 '+ cscProductVariantClass
 '+ cscProductClass
sReturnProperties = "ISBN,Title,Author"
sSortProperty = "Title"
bSortAscending=true
lStartRecord=1
lNumberRecords=20

search = request("search")

set rsResults = MSCSCatalogManager.FreeTextSearch(search, _
 sCatalogs, lClassType, _
 sReturnProperties, sSortProperty, bSortAscending, _
 lStartRecord, lNumberRecords, lReturnedRecords)
```

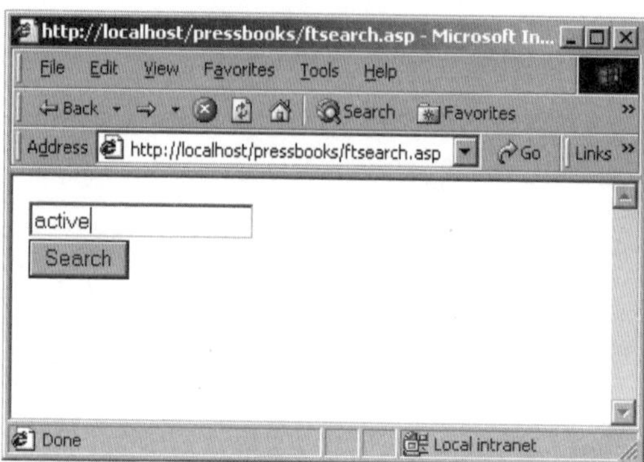

Figure 13-1. *You'll need to provide a field for the shopper to enter the search text to be used in the free-text search.*

Once the FreeTextSearch method returns its results in a recordset, you can go about displaying the results to the customer, as shown in the following code sample and Figure 13-2.

```
htmResults = ""

If rsResults.BOF and rsResults.EOF Then

   htmResults = "<h3>No Results were returned</h3>"

   htmResults = htmResults & "Keyword search: " & search & "<BR>"

Else

   htmHeader="<tr>"

   for each fld in rsResults.Fields

      htmHeader = htmHeader & "<th>" & fld.name & "</th>"

   next

   htmHeader = htmHeader & "</tr>"

   do while not rsResults.EOF

      htmResults = htmResults & "<tr>"

      for each fld in rsResults.Fields

         if not isnull(fld.value) then

            htmResults = htmResults & "<TD>" & fld.value & "</td>"

         else

            htmResults = htmResults & "<TD> </td>"

         end if

      next
```

(continued)

(continued)

```
        htmResults = htmResults & "</TR>"

        rsResults.MoveNext

    loop

    htmResults = "<table border=1 cellspacing=1 cellpadding=2>" _
     & htmHeader & htmResults & "</table>"

    htmResults = "Keyword Search: " & search & "<BR>" _
     & "Matches found: " & lReturnedRecords & "<BR>" _
     & htmResults

End If
```

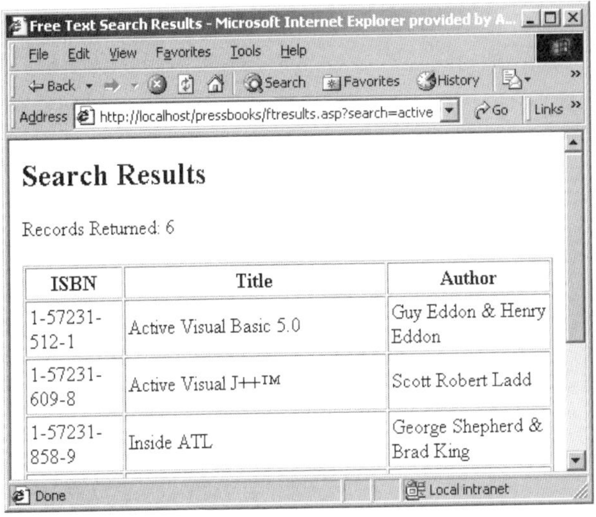

Figure 13-2. *The results of the free-text search can be displayed on the page, and you can take action as necessary.*

With that done, you've completed the basic tasks of providing the free-text search functionality on your site, so your customers can easily perform a quick search of your catalogs.

Property Search

At times, you might need to provide a stronger or more detailed search function for your users, but still not force them to step through a specification search. For instance, your users might know specific information about a product they are looking for. However, simply providing that information in a free-text search can return more results than they are looking for. For instance, if you have a Books catalog, a user might know the name of the author, and maybe a word in the book's title. You can provide a form on which users can specify what values in each of these fields they want to search for. This is known as *property searching* and is also sometimes called *parametric searching*.

The Property Search Page

The first step in providing parametric search functionality is to provide the form on which users will enter their search criteria, such as the one shown in the following code sample and Figure 13-3. You might need to develop a separate form for each type of product for which they might search.

```
sTitle = request("title")

sAuthor = request("author")

sPublisher = request("publisher")

htmForm = "<form action=""qry_search.asp"" method=get>"

htmForm = htmForm & "<table>"

htmForm = htmForm & "<tr><td>Title</td><td>" _
 & "<input name=Title value=""" _
 & sTitle & """></td></tr>"

htmForm = htmForm & "<tr><td>Author</td><td>" _
 & "<input name=Author value=""" _
 & sAuthor & """></td></tr>"

htmForm = htmForm & "<tr><td>Publisher</td><td>" _
 & <input name=Publisher " _
 & "value=""" & sPublisher & """></td></tr>"

htmForm = htmForm & "</table>"

htmForm = htmForm & "<input type=submit value=""Search"">"

htmForm = htmForm & "</form>"
```

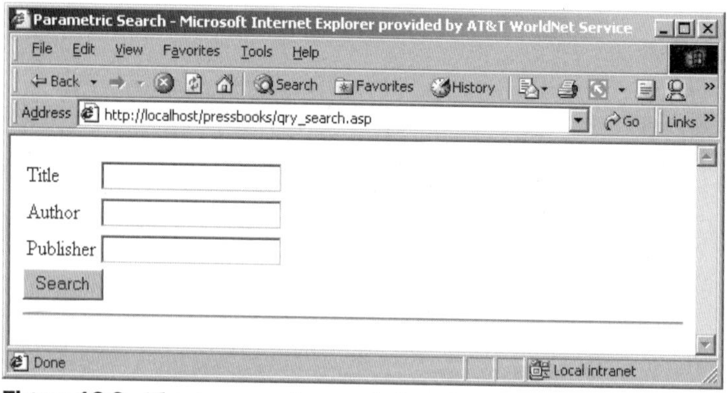

Figure 13-3. *This parametric search form has been built to provide entry fields for the Books catalog.*

The Query Method

Once you've gathered the user's search parameters, you can then build and run the search. To run the search, you'll call the CatalogManager's Query method, which accepts the following parameters:

- **strPhrase** This is the phrase to be searched for within the catalogs.
- **strCatalogsToSearch** This is a comma-delimited list of catalogs to search. If you don't provide an entry, all the catalogs in the site are searched.
- **eClassTypeRequired** This identifies the types of objects that should be returned. The values are listed in the CatalogClassTypeEnum enumeration of the CatalogManager component. The values can be combined with logical OR operators or added together to provide a single parameter to be passed. The values are as follows:
    - **cscCategoryClass (1)** Returns categories
    - **cscProductVariantClass (2)** Returns product variants
    - **cscProductClass (4)** Returns products
    - **cscProductFamilyClass (8)** Returns product families
    - **cscProductFamilyForVariantsClass (16)** Returns the family for a product variant
    - **cscProductVariantsForFamily (32)** Returns the product variants for a product family
- **strPropertiesToReturn** This is a comma-delimited list of properties that should be returned in the resulting recordset. If more than one catalog is being searched, you must specify the list of properties to be returned.
- **strPropertiesToSortOn** This is a comma-delimited list of properties used to sort the returned results.
- **fSortAscending** This Boolean identifies whether the sorting should be in ascending order. If the value for this parameter is False, the sort is in descending order.
- **lStartingRecord** This is the number of the first record that should be returned. If the value of this parameter is 1, the results start with the first record. You can use this value, in conjunction with the next parameter, to set up a page of results.
- **lRecordsToRetrieve** This is the maximum number of records that should be returned in this recordset. This allows you to create a page of results. You can move to another page by changing the Starting Record parameter.
- **plTotalRecordsInQuery** This value is returned by the call and identifies how many records match the search criteria.

Using Property Search

The search string is a combination of the entries that your user provides, just as though a SQL WHERE clause was being built. Once the search phrase is established, you can provide the other parameters that define how the search is run, including the properties to be returned, the number of records to return, and the sorting information. The Query method, shown in the following code sample, returns a recordset that you can use to display the results to your customer (see Figure 13-4).

```
sSearch = ""

if len(sAuthor)>0 then

   sSearch = sSearch & "author LIKE '%" & sAuthor & "%' AND "

end if

if len(sTitle)>0 then

   sSearch = sSearch & "title LIKE '%" & sTitle & "%' AND "

end if

if len(sPublisher)>0 then

   sSearch = sSearch & "publisher LIKE '%" & sPublisher & "%' AND "

end if

if len(sSearch)>0 then

   sSearch = left(sSearch, len(sSearch)-5)

   sCatalogs = "Books"

   iClassType = 4 + 8

   sProperties = "Title, Author, Publisher"

   sSortProperties = "Title, Author"

   bSortAscending = True

   lStartingRecord = 1

   lMaxRecords = 20

   set rsResults = MSCSCatalogManager.Query(sSearch, sCatalogs, _
    iClassType, sProperties, sSortProperties, bSortAscending, _
    lStartingRecord, lMaxRecords, lRecordsReturned)
```

(continued)

(continued)

```
do while not rsResults.EOF
    htmResults = htmResults & "<tr>"
    for each fld in rsResults.Fields
        htmResults = htmResults & "<td>" & fld.value & "</td>"
    next
    htmResults = htmResults & "</tr>"
    rsResults.MoveNext
loop
if len(htmResults)>0 then
    htmResults = "<table border=1 cellspacing=1 _
     cellpadding=2>" & htmResults & "</table>"
    htmResults = "<h4>Records Returned: " & lRecordsReturned _
     & "</h4>" & htmResults
else
    htmResults = "<h4>No Matching Records</h4>"
end if
end if
```

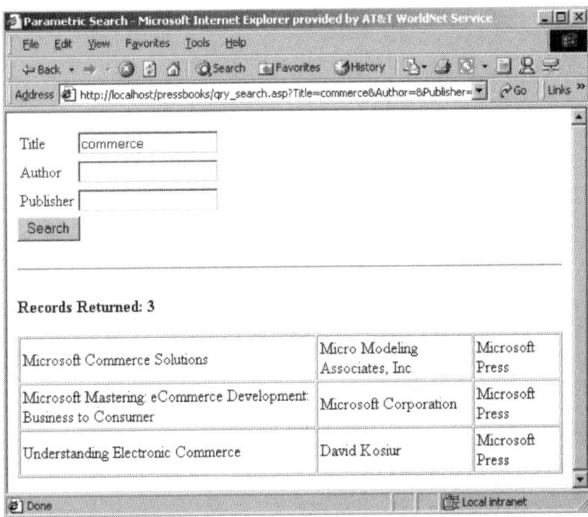

Figure 13-4. *Performing a parametric search provides results that you can display and act on as necessary.*

Specification Search

At times, your customers might want to be able to build a more detailed search. Perhaps a keyword search or parametric search provides too many results, or perhaps users are not quite sure what keywords they should use to find what they're looking for. The specification or step search will allow them to better search on the products they're looking for.

Selecting the Catalog

The specification search is performed on just one catalog. If your site contains more than one catalog, your customers will need to select which catalog they want to search to start the specification search.

Searchable Categories

When the categories are created within the catalog, you can specify which of them are searchable. The searchable categories are those that will be available in the specification search and allow users to scroll through the search in those categories. You can retrieve the list of categories that are searchable by calling the SearchableCategories method of the ProductCatalog, as shown in the following code sample:

```
set rsSearchCategories = mscsProductCatalog.SearchableCategories

htmSearchCategories = ""

do while not rsSearchCategories.Eof

   urlSearchCtg = "search_step.asp?cat=" _
    & sCatalogName & "&ctg=" & rsSearchCategories("Name")

   htmSearchCategories = htmSearchCategories _
    & "<a href='" & urlSearchCtg & "'>" _
    & rsSearchCtgs("Name") & "</a><br>"

   rsSearchCategories.MoveNext

loop
```

Step Search

Once you've selected the category that you are going to search, you can begin the process of building the specification search. This can be a potentially iterative process. Each step through the process, you can add additional search clauses to narrow the results to a more manageable number.

Beginning the Specification Search

You'll start the specification search process by initializing the search. You'll do this by retrieving the ProductCatalog and calling the BeginSpecificationSearch method, as shown in the following code, specifying the name of the category that you'll be searching. The method also returns two parameters. The first is a recordset that includes all the fields being returned by the search, as well as the distinct values in each field. For instance, if you have a color field that has, in various records, the values Blue, Green, Green, Red, Yellow, Blue, this recordset would contain a field named Color. The value of that field would be a variant array with the values Blue, Green, Red, Yellow, which you can use to help better filter a search. The second parameter that the method returns is the number of matches that are currently being returned in the category. Finally, as a result of the function call, the method returns a handle that you'll use to identify this search in other specification search function calls.

```
sCatalogName = request("cat")

sCategoryName = request("ctg")

set mscsProductCatalog = _
 MSCSCatalogManager.GetCatalog(sCatalogName)

hSearch = _
 mscsProductCatalog.BeginSpecificationSearch(sCategoryName, _
 rsProperties, iMatches)
```

Examining the Properties Being Returned

Next you'll take a look at each of the properties being returned. As you do so, you perform two tasks. The first task is to identify all those fields for which the user has not yet provided a value by checking to see if a value was passed in as a part of a POST or QueryString for each field. Those fields that have not been selected are displayed later to allow the user to further filter the search results. You place this list of fields in an array that can be used at a later point, as shown in the following code:

```
iFields=0

htmFilter = "The following filters have been applied:<P>"

If rsProperties Is Nothing Then

   htmFilter = "No Searchable Properties"

Else

   for each fld in rsProperties.Fields

      sValue = request(fld.name)

      if sValue = "" or lcase(sValue) = "no preference" then

'this property has not been selected yet as a filter,

'let's keep track of it since we'll need to display it later

         redim preserve aFields(iFields)

         aFields(iFields) = fld.name
```

(continued)

(continued)

```
        iFields = iFields + 1
        else
```

The second task is to identify those properties for which the user has specified a value as a filter. As you retrieve each of these values, you'll build the search clause and add it to the specification search. To do this, you call the AddSpecificationSearchClause method, shown in the following code sample, passing it the clause as well as the handle of this search, which was previously returned by the BeginSpecificationSearch method.

```
            set rsAttributes = _
              MSCSCatalogManager.GetPropertyAttributes(fld.name)
            select case rsAttributes("DataType")
            case 5, 6, 8, 9 'string, datetime, filepath, enumeration
               sValue = "'" & sValue & "'"
            end select
            htmFilter = htmFilter & fld.name & " = " & sValue _
             & "<BR>"
            mscsProductCatalog.AddSpecificationSearchClause _
             fld.name & " = " & sValue, hSearch
        end if
    next
end if
```

Performing the Specification Search

Now that you've applied all of the specification search clauses, you can run the search. There are actually two methods that will run the search: the PerformSpecificationSearch and GuaranteedSpecificationSearch methods. The PerformSpecificationSearch exactly applies each of the search clauses. You can specify the maximum number of records to return, as well as which columns you want returned. You'll also need to pass the handle of the specification search as a parameter. This method returns a recordset with the results.

If that recordset does not contain any results, you might want to call the GuaranteedSpecificationSearch method (see the following code sample), which is nearly the same as the PerformSpecificationSearch method. The one difference is that if no records are returned, it removes the last specification search clause applied and run the search again. It continues to remove all the search clauses until at least one record is returned.

```
sColumns = "Name, ISBN, Author"

iSearchType = 4 + 8           'Product + ProductFamily

iMaxRecords = 20

set rsResults = _
 mscsProductCatalog.PerformSpecificationSearch(hSearch, _
 iSearchType, iMaxRecords, iMatches, rsNewProperties, sColumns)

if rsResults.Bof And rsResults.Eof then

'no results returned, so use the GuaranteedSpecificationSearch

   set rsResults = _
    mscsProductCatalog.GuaranteedSpecificationSearch(hSearch, _
    iSearchType, iMaxRecords, iMatches, rsNewProperties, _
    sColumns)

end if
```

Displaying the Results

Once you have the search results in a recordset, you can display the results in whatever format you need (see the following code sample), similar to those shown in Figure 13-5.

```
if rsResults.bof and rsResults.eof then

   htmResults = "<h3>No Matches Returned</h3>"

else

   htmResults = "<h3>Number of Matches Found: " & iMatches _
    & "</h3>"

   htmResults = htmResults _
    & "<TABLE border=1 cellspacing=2 cellpadding=1><tr>"

   for each fld in rsResults.Fields

     htmResults = htmResults & "<th>" & fld.name & "</th>"

   next

   htmResults = htmResults & "</tr>"
```

(continued)

(continued)

```
   do while not rsResults.EOF
      htmResults = htmResults & "<tr>"
      for each fld in rsResults.Fields
         if not isnull(fld.value) then
            htmResults = htmResults & "<td>" & fld.value & "</td>"
         else
            htmResults = htmResults & "<td> [NULL] </td>"
         end if
      next
      htmResults = htmResults & "</tr>"
      rsResults.MoveNext
   loop
   htmResults = htmResults & "</table>"
end if
```

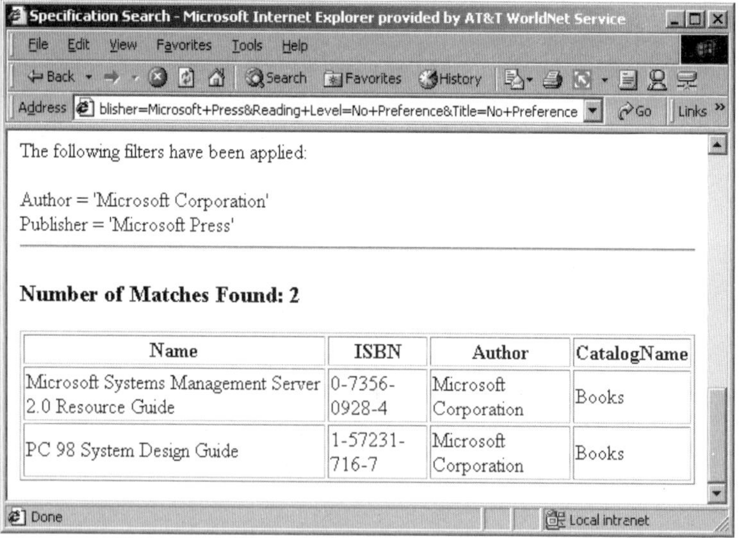

Figure 13-5. *The results of a specification search can be displayed for the user to choose from.*

Displaying the Filter Fields

Finally, you'll need to provide your users with a way to further filter the results. You can build a set of list boxes that hold each distinct value for each property that is being searched to help users pare down results that return too many records. From there, you can allow the users to select a value they want to be able to filter on, as shown in Figure 13-6. These values can be resubmitted to the same form, and the specification search can be rerun with the added filter values (see the following code sample).

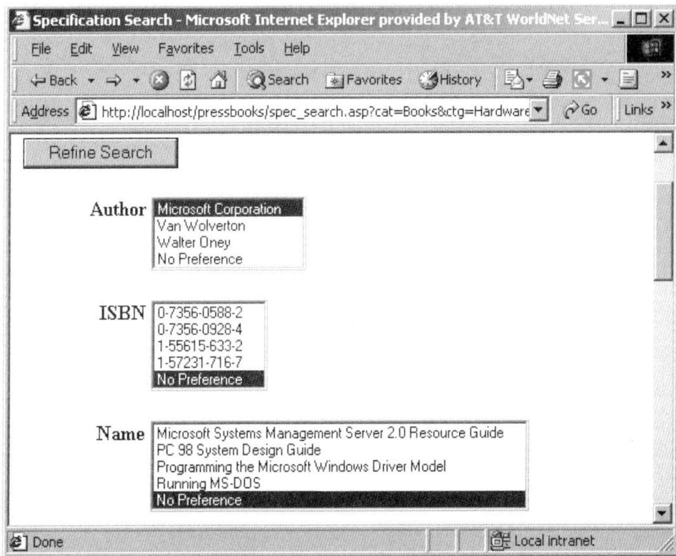

Figure 13-6. *The specification search should provide a list of the fields that can be used to refine the search, along with the available entries for each field.*

```
htmFields = "<form action=""spec_search.asp"" method=get>"

htmFields = htmFields _
 & "<input type=hidden name=""cat"" value=""" _
 & sCatalogName & """>"

htmFields = htmFields _
 & "<input type=hidden name=""ctg"" value=""" _
 & sCategoryname & """>"

htmFields = htmFields _
 & "<input type=submit value=""Refine Search""><P>"

htmFields = htmFields & "<Table>"
```

(continued)

(continued)

```
for i = lbound(aFields) to ubound(aFields)
   sListName = aFields(i)
   aValues = rsProperties(sListName)
   set rsAttributes = _
    MSCSCatalogManager.GetPropertyAttributes(sListName)
   if rsAttributes("DataType") = 4 then
      'boolean, show TRUE and FALSE
      for j = lbound(aValues) to ubound(aValues)
         if aValues(j)=0 then
            aValues(j)="False"
         else
            aValues(j)="True"
         end if
      next
   end if
'Add "No Preference" option to the value lists
   if ubound(aValues)>0 then
      redim preserve aValues(ubound(aValues)+1)
      aValues(ubound(aValues)) = "No Preference"
   end if

   htmFields = htmFields & "<tr valign=top><td align=right>" _
    & "<strong>" & sListName & "</strong></td><td>"
   htmFields = htmFields & "<SELECT NAME=""" & sListName _
    & """ SIZE=" & ubound(aValues)+1 _
    & " style=""font-size:xx-small"">"
   for j = lbound(aValues) to uBound(aValues)
      if aValues(j) = "No Preference" then
         htmFields = htmFields & "<OPTION SELECTED VALUE=""" _
          & aValues(j) & """>" & aValues(j)
      else
         htmFields = htmFields & "<OPTION VALUE=""" _
          & aValues(j) & """>" & aValues(j)
      end if
```

(continued)

(continued)

```
   next

   htmFields = htmFields & "</SELECT><p>"

   htmFields = htmFields & "</td></tr>"

next

htmFields = htmFields & "</table>"

htmFields = htmFields & "<input type=submit" _
 & "value=""Refine Search""><BR>"

htmFields = htmFields & "</form>"
```

Part VI

Transactions and Processing

Part VI of this book covers transactions and order processing on your site, from utilizing the basket to completing an order. Chapter 14 provides an introduction to the the OrderGroup and OrderForm objects that are used to maintain the basket and orders on the site, as well as the components that are used to work with those items. Chapter 15 demonstrates in detail the many tasks involved in processing orders on your Microsoft Commerce Server 2000 site, from placing items in the basket to completing and processing the purchase. Chapter 16 introduces the Commerce Server 2000 pipelines that are used to process orders and other information in an efficient and scalable manner. Chapter 17 demonstrates how to build your own custom pipeline components and functionality to use in your pipelines.

Chapter 14

Order Basics

At the core of your e-commerce site is the ability to accept orders, allowing customers to purchase items from your catalogs. This chapter starts to look at the order processing system in Microsoft Commerce Server 2000, including the OrderForm object, which holds the items being processed in the basket, and the OrderGroup object, which can contain multiple OrderForm objects.

The OrderForm

The OrderForm is a special implementation of the Dictionary object that is used to collect and contain all order-related information, including data about the shopper, addresses, payment information, and each of the items included in the order. Each of the entries in the OrderForm can contain either a specific value or a Dictionary or SimpleList object.

OrderForm Structure

The OrderForm is organized with a fairly consistent structure, which includes SimpleLists and Dictionaries to hold data and basic order data values, as represented in Figure 14-1.

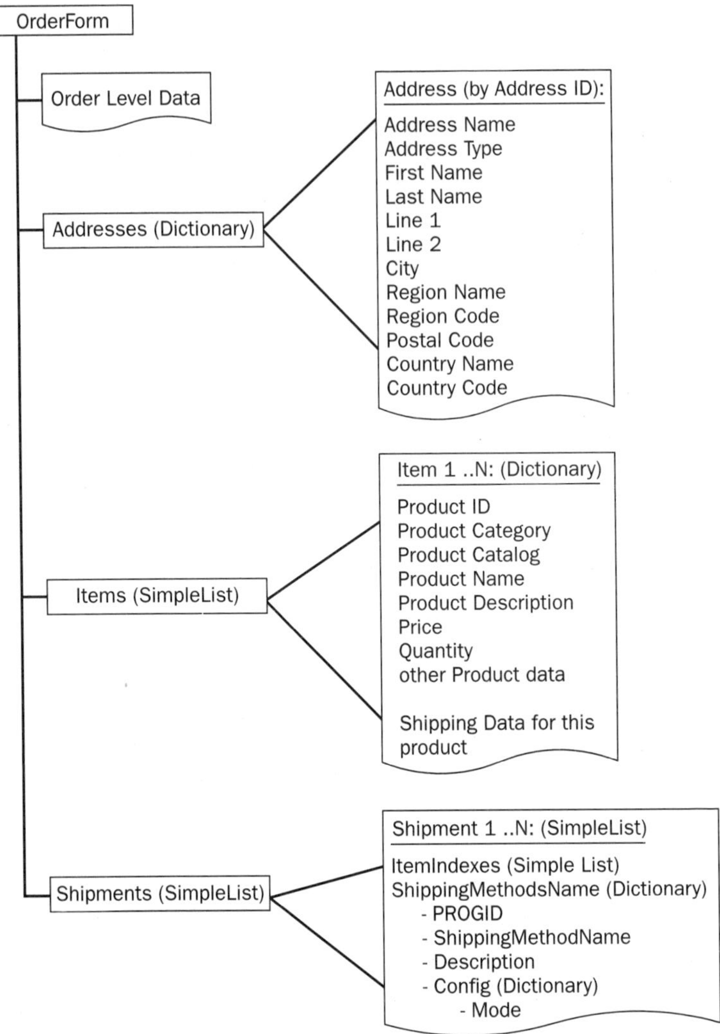

Figure 14-1. *The OrderForm structure includes objects to hold data and order-related data values.*

If you want another look at the OrderForm, the following XML document shows an order that has been completed in the Retail Solution Site in XML format, which is used to more accurately render the information in the OrderForm.

```
<user_last_name>Wist</user_last_name>
<payment_method>credit_card</payment_method>
<billing_amount>184.61</billing_amount>
<user_id>{6961497D-FC92-4561-8568-36D4E7FE0C0C}</user_id>
<user_org_id>{1BD08BDB-B3FC-46D5-B44E-0BB5F9CD3485}</user_org_id>
- <shipments>
 - <shipments..1>
  - <ItemIndexes>
     <ItemIndexes..1>0</ItemIndexes..1>
     <ItemIndexes..2>1</ItemIndexes..2>
     <ItemIndexes..3>2</ItemIndexes..3>
    </ItemIndexes>
   - <shipping_method_name>
    - <__lbrace__00000000-0000-0000-0000-001982001992__rbrace__>
     - <config>
        <mode>0</mode>
       </config>
       <progid>commerce.stepwiseshipping</progid>
       <shipping_method_name>MyShippingSubtotal</
        shipping_method_name>
       <description />
      </__lbrace__00000000-0000-0000-0000-001982001992__rbrace__>
    </shipping_method_name>
    <shipping_address_id>{260F01E4-DEF7-416B-8BD4-
     F9B52EAF74F1}</shipping_address_id>
    <shipping_method_id>{00000000-0000-0000-0000-
     001982001992}</shipping_method_id>
   </shipments..1>
  </shipments>
<cc_name>Wist Brad</cc_name>
```


(continued)

(continued)


```
<g_UserIDChangedBy>{6961497D-FC92-4561-8568-
 36D4E7FE0C0C}</g_UserIDChangedBy>
<_Verify_With />
<saved_cy_oadjust_subtotal>169.97</saved_cy_oadjust_subtotal>
<user_first_name>Brad</user_first_name>
<_Purchase_Errors />
<saved_cy_total_total>184.61</saved_cy_total_total>
<billing_address_id>{260F01E4-DEF7-416B-8BD4-
 F9B52EAF74F1}</billing_address_id>
<order_id>AUTC6DVJXLD28HG20UH82AB527</order_id>
<_Basket_Errors />
- <__itemids>
   <__1__>1</__1__>
   <__2__>1</__2__>
   <__3__>1</__3__>
  </__itemids>
<d_DateCreated>3/4/2001 9:54:40 AM</d_DateCreated>
<orderform_id>{73BADBBA-B84F-4F90-B8F1-8E5BAB1019B3}
 </orderform_id>
<billing_currency>USD</billing_currency>
<d_DateLastChanged>7/27/2001 5:13:41 PM</d_DateLastChanged>
<user_org_name>WistHome</user_org_name>
- <Addresses>
  - <__lbrace__260F01E4-DEF7-416B-8BD4-F9B52EAF74F1__rbrace__>
     <region_code>VA</region_code>
     <last_name>Wist</last_name>
     <address_type>0</address_type>
     <address_line1>123 Here St</address_line1>
     <g_UserIDChangedBy>{6961497D-FC92-4561-8568-
      36D4E7FE0C0C}</g_UserIDChangedBy>
```


(continued)

(continued)


```
    <user_id_changed_by>{6961497D-FC92-4561-8568-
     36D4E7FE0C0C}</user_id_changed_by>
    <region_name>Virginia</region_name>
    <address_line2 />
    <country_code>US</country_code>
    <id>{6961497D-FC92-4561-8568-36D4E7FE0C0C}</id>
    <d_DateCreated>7/27/2001 5:13:23 PM</d_DateCreated>
    <d_DateLastChanged>7/27/2001 5:13:42 PM</d_DateLastChanged>
    <first_name>Brad</first_name>
    <address_name>Here</address_name>
    <postal_code>55555</postal_code>
    <city>Hereville</city>
   </__lbrace__260F01E4-DEF7-416B-8BD4-F9B52EAF74F1__rbrace__>
  </Addresses>
- <Items>
  - <Items..1>
    <product_category />
    <cy_placed_price>49.99</cy_placed_price>
    <vendor_qual />
    <cy_unit_price>49.99</cy_unit_price>
    <product_catalog>Books</product_catalog>
    <vendorID>Books</vendorID>
    <shipping_method_name>MyShippingSubtotal</
     shipping_method_name>
    <description>With this MICROSOFT MASTERING learning system,
     you'll discover how to deliver your products or services
     over the Web by buildin</description>
    <g_UserIDChangedBy>{6961497D-FC92-4561-8568-
     36D4E7FE0C0C}</g_UserIDChangedBy>
    <shipping_address_id>{260F01E4-DEF7-416B-8BD4-
     F9B52EAF74F1}</shipping_address_id>
```


(continued)

(continued)


```
    <d_DateCreated>3/4/2001 9:54:40 AM</d_DateCreated>
    <cy_lineitem_total>49.99</cy_lineitem_total>
    <lineitem_id>1</lineitem_id>
    <d_DateLastChanged>7/27/2001 5:13:42 PM</d_DateLastChanged>
    <lineitem_uid>{5D7FBF8E-E25F-4345-978D-373345EDC832}
     </lineitem_uid>
    <shipping_method_id>{00000000-0000-0000-0000-
     001982001992}</shipping_method_id>
    <placed_price>4999</placed_price>
    <saved_product_name>Microsoft Mastering: eCommerce
     Development:Business to Consumer</saved_product_name>
    <product_catalog_base>Books</product_catalog_base>
    <vendor_qual_value />
    <product_id>Microsoft Mastering: eCommerce Development:
     Business to Consumer</product_id>
    <Quantity>1</Quantity>
   </Items..1>
  </Items>
<changeditems>False</changeditems>
<cc_type>VISA</cc_type>
<total_lineitems>3</total_lineitems>
<user_email_address>brad@wisthome.com</user_email_address>
```

Note Tag names in the preceeding XML document have been modified to make the XML data more representative of the data. For instance, the__rbrace__ and __lbrace__ names are used to represent the { and } characters. Typically, any name that is preceeded by two underscores(__) is a name that I created in my code in order to create the tag. An example of this is the __1__, __2__, and __3__ tags in the __itemsids element.

Naming

There are two types of fields that are created in the OrderForm. The basic, persistent fields are shown in the previous code sample. These are the fields that are maintained and stored in the database. However, there are also nonpersistent fields that exist for the life of the OrderForm in memory, but are not stored in the database. By default, these fields are prefixed with the underscore character (_), as in _product_description, _cy_iadjust_regularprice, and more. These are placed into the OrderForm, typically through the various pipeline components, usually for performing calculations.

Note Those OrderForm fields that should be saved once the order is completed are typically copied to new keys in the order without the leading underscore in the CopyFields stage of the "total" pipelines. The CopyFields component in this stage is a scriptor component that copies the values of the desired keys. For more information on pipeline components, see Commerce Server 2000 Help or the Commerce Server 2000 SDK.

OrderForm Fields

Some of the standard fields that you will likely find in the OrderForm include the following:

- **_Basket_Errors** SimpleList of basket errors that are retrieved from the MessageManager and are written into the OrderForm from the pipeline in the event of an error while working with the basket
- **_cc_expmonth** Credit card expiration month
- **_cc_expyear** Credit card expiration year
- **_cc_number** Credit card number
- **_cy_handling_total** Total handling charges
- **_cy_oadjust_subtotal** Subtotal of all the items in the list
- **_cy_shipping_total** Total shipping charges
- **_cy_tax_included** Total taxes included in the cost of the items
- **_cy_tax_total** Total tax charges
- **_cy_total_total** Total cost of the order
- **_payment_auth_code** Authorization code for payment acceptance
- **_Purchase_Errors** SimpleList of purchase errors that are retrieved from the MessageManager and written into the OrderForm during the purchase process from the pipeline
- **_Verify_With** Dictionary of values that are used to verify that the amounts of the order have not changed since the last time the shopper viewed them
- **cc_name** Name on the credit card
- **cc_type** Type of credit card
- **order_id** Unique ID for the order
- **order_number** Reference number for the order that is automatically generated when the OrderGroup's SaveAsOrder method is called, unless it already exists within the order
- **shipments** SimpleList of Dictionary objects that detail the shipments made to fulfill this order
- **shopper_id** Unique ID of the shopper

Note A "cy" at the beginning of the field name denotes that the field holds a currency value.

Items

Within the OrderForm there is a SimpleList containing all the items added to the order. Each item is an entry in the SimpleList and a Dictionary object. The Item dictionary contains all of the information needed about the item to determine its cost, including the following:

- **_cy_iadjust_currentprice** Current price of the item, which reflects the price minus any discounts.
- **_cy_iadjust_regularprice** Regular price of the item.
- **_cy_oadjust_adjustedprice** Total cost for this line item, current price multiplied by the quantity.
- **_cy_tax_included** Amount of tax included in the item's cost.
- **_cy_tax_total** Total tax for this item.
- **_n_unadjusted** Number of items not included in a discount.
- **_product_*** Data from the product's Catalog table. Typically, this includes all data from the _CatalogProducts table. Each field is copied to a field in the OrderForm prefixed with _product_. In this case, the field name "description" appears in the OrderForm as _product_description.
- **cy_placed_price** Price of the item when it was added to the basket.
- **delete** Key that indicates this item should be removed from the OrderForm (if the value is 1).
- **discounts_applied** Dictionary of IDs of the discounts applied to this item.
- **list_price** List price of the item.
- **quantity** Number of this item in the order.

Addresses

Addresses that are associated with the order are stored within a Dictionary, with the key for each item in the Dictionary as the address's globally unique identifier (GUID). Addresses can include any number of fields, depending on what you want to represent. If you're developing an international site, remember that different countries have different postal code formats, regions, and other differences. The fields in the addresses dictionary can include the following:

- **address_line1** First line of street address
- **address_line2** Second line of street address
- **address_name** Name of this address, useful in identifying it as a part of the user's address book
- **address_type** Type of address, useful in identifying an address as a shipping or billing address, if you make the distinction in your address book
- **city** City name
- **country_code** The International Organization for Standardization (ISO) standard code for the country
- **d_DateCreated** The date the address was created

- **d_DateLastChanged** The date the address was last changed
- **g_userIDChangeBy** Unique ID for the user
- **id** Unique ID of the address
- **first_name** First name to use with this address
- **last_name** Last name to use with this address
- **postal_code** Postal code or zip code for the address
- **region_code** Region or state code or abbreviation
- **region_name** Name of the region or state associated with this address
- **user_id_changed_by** ID of the user who last changed this address

Note The addresses are also stored at the OrderGroup level.

Shipments

The OrderForm includes a Dictionary entry that contains a list of shipments made in association with the order. Each shipment entry includes fields such as these:

- **ItemIndexes** SimpleList of line item indexes that are part of this shipment
- **shipping_address_id** Unique ID that identifies the address to which this shipment is sent
- **shipping_method_id** Unique ID that identifies the shipping method
- **shipping_method_name** Dictionary that holds a list of shipping methods, including configuration details and other data about the tools used in working with the shipments

The OrderGroup

Commerce Server 2000 allows a user to build an order from multiple catalogs, and automatically divides those orders based on the catalogs from which the items originate. This is done so that the orders can automatically be split and transmitted to your trading partners, if they are associated with the particular catalog. These trading partners must be set up within BizTalk Server to be available as the trading partner for a catalog in Commerce Server 2000. Each OrderForm is named based on the trading partner name. There is also an OrderForm named Default that is used for all items purchased that are not from a trading partner.

The OrderGroup object is the means by which the multiple OrderForms are maintained as a part of the same order. You use the OrderGroup to load (LoadBasket and LoadOrder methods) and save (SaveAsBasket and SaveAsOrder methods) the orders. The object provides the primary means of access to each of the OrderForms, and it also provides the methods to add and remove items from the selected OrderForms. You'll see all of this in action in Chapter 15, "Order Processing."

OrderGroup Contents

The OrderGroup also maintains data outside of the individual OrderForms at the OrderGroup level. This data includes high-level information, such as the total cost of the order, summed from all of the OrderForms. The XML document in the following code sample shows the contents of the OrderGroup object (the OrderForms are not shown for brevity's sake), as it exists once the order has been completed in the Retail Solution Site. You'll note that a number of these fields in the OrderGroup can also be found in the OrderForms as well.


```
- <OrderGroup>
  <user_last_name>Wist</user_last_name>
  <saved_cy_shipping_total>6.99</saved_cy_shipping_total>
  <order_status_code>4</order_status_code>
  <user_id>{6961497D-FC92-4561-8568-36D4E7FE0C0C}</user_id>
  <g_UserIDChangedBy>{6961497D-FC92-4561-8568-
   36D4E7FE0C0C}</g_UserIDChangedBy>
  <saved_cy_oadjust_subtotal>169.97</saved_cy_oadjust_subtotal>
  <user_first_name>Brad</user_first_name>
  <ordergroup_id>{F22178C0-08B6-4858-9BD0-D5D83E8ACB89}
   </ordergroup_id>
  <saved_cy_total_total>184.61</saved_cy_total_total>
  <saved_cy_tax_total>7.65</saved_cy_tax_total>
  <saved_cy_handling_total>0</saved_cy_handling_total>
  <d_DateCreated>3/4/2001 9:54:39 AM</d_DateCreated>
  <d_DateLastChanged>7/27/2001 5:13:41 PM</d_DateLastChanged>
  <order_number>1002</order_number>
  <billing_currency>USD</billing_currency>
  <saved_cy_tax_included>0</saved_cy_tax_included>
  <user_org_name>WistHome</user_org_name>
- <Addresses>
  - <__lbrace__260F01E4-DEF7-416B-8BD4-F9B52EAF74F1__rbrace__>
      <region_code>VA</region_code>
      <last_name>Wist</last_name>
      <address_type>0</address_type>
```


(continued)

(continued)


```
    <address_line1>123 Here St</address_line1>
    <g_UserIDChangedBy>{6961497D-FC92-4561-8568-
     36D4E7FE0C0C}</g_UserIDChangedBy>
    <user_id_changed_by>{6961497D-FC92-4561-8568-
     36D4E7FE0C0C}</user_id_changed_by>
    <region_name>Virginia</region_name>
    <address_line2 />
    <country_code>US</country_code>
    <id>{6961497D-FC92-4561-8568-36D4E7FE0C0C}</id>
    <d_DateCreated>7/27/2001 5:13:23 PM</d_DateCreated>
    <d_DateLastChanged>7/27/2001 5:13:42 PM</d_DateLastChanged>
    <first_name>Brad</first_name>
    <address_name>Here</address_name>
    <postal_code>55555</postal_code>
    <city>Hereville</city>
   </__lbrace__260F01E4-DEF7-416B-8BD4-F9B52EAF74F1__rbrace__>
  </Addresses>
+ <OrderForms>
  </OrderForms>
  <total_lineitems>3</total_lineitems>
  <order_create_date>7/27/2001 5:13:41 PM</order_create_date>
</OrderGroup>
```


Order Status Codes

The OrderGroup includes a field named Order_Status_Code. This code identifies the current state of the order. By default, the following values are available for this field:

- **1 – Basket** This order is still in the basket. The shopper has not finished the shopping process.
- **2 – Saved Order** This order has been saved as a template.
- **4 – New Order** This order has been created and submitted for processing.

Additional status codes can be created, but they should be assigned values that are powers of two. These can be created in the Business Desk, through the Orders – Data Codes section (see Figure 14-2). The values are stored in the Decode table of the database.

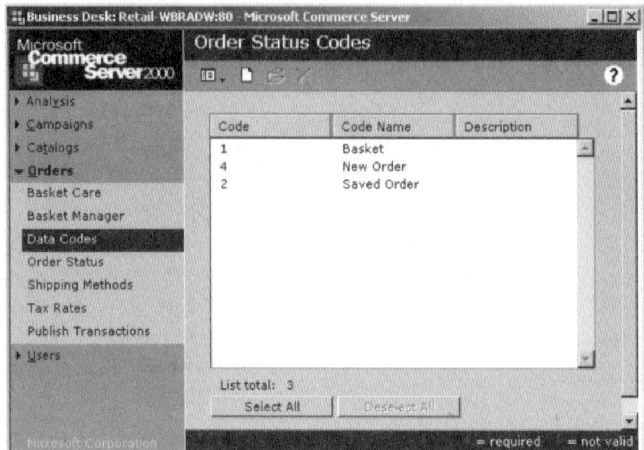

Figure 14-2. *The order status codes can be maintained in the Business Desk.*

Addresses in the OrderGroup

The OrderGroup also contains an Addresses dictionary that holds all of the addresses associated with the order. The OrderGroup's GetAddress and SetAddress methods are used to retrieve and save these addresses with the order.

Order Templates

Some of your customers might place similar orders on a periodic (or not so periodic) basis. This might be particularly true for corporate customers. For instance, if your site is an office supply site, the buying agent for a corporation might regularly order the same group of supplies, or your corporate customer might order a standard package of supplies for any new employee.

Rather than forcing the buyer to re-create that same order every time it needs to be placed, a properly designed Commerce Server 2000 site allows the buyer to create the order once and save it as a template to be reused whenever needed. The OrderGroup provides you with the ability to create an order and save it as a template using the SaveAsTemplate method. The template can be retrieved simply by using the LoadTemplate method, or the items in a template can be added to the current order using the AddItemsFromTemplate method.

A template is similar to an existing user's basket, except that it is given a different status in the database, a name, and a different ID. Whereas a user's basket is identified by the user's GUID, a new GUID is generated for a template, and the user can provide a name to identify the template. In addition, the Order Status Code field in the database is set to 2 for template, rather than 1 for basket.

Managing OrderGroups

Commerce Server 2000 provides the OrderGroupManager object to perform higher level OrderGroup management functions, such as searching for and deleting

OrderGroups. The object is supported in some of its functions by the SimpleFindSearchInfo and SimpleFindResultInfo objects, which are used to provide criteria for search and delete tasks.

Searching OrderGroups

You have the following three means by which to search for orders that have been completed in the system:

- Searching using the OrderGroupManager's Find method
- Searching using the OrderGroupManager's SimpleFind method
- Searching using ActiveX Data Objects (ADO) queries directly against the Order tables

Although all three of these are potential options, the following sections focus on the first two approaches.

Searching Using SQL with Find

You can generate and use SQL search criteria to perform the search using the OrderGroupManager's Find method. This method accepts SQL search criteria at the OrderGroup, OrderForm, and Item levels of an order. In addition, it can search based on an order's date and time and status information. The Find method includes parameters that cover all of these options, and more, including the following:

- **OrderGroupCriteriaArray** Variant array that includes SQL search clauses used to identify desired OrderGroup data
- **OrderFormCriteriaArray** SQL search clause used to identify desired OrderForm data
- **LineItemCriteriaArray** SQL search clause used to identify desired LineItem data
- **SearchDateTimeColumn** Column name that holds a date and time value for the OrderGroup that is used to perform a date and time filter on the search
- **SearchDateTimeStart** Earliest date and time to return as a part of the result set
- **SearchDateTimeEnd** Latest date and time to return as a part of the result set
- **StatusFilter** The order status code on which to search or filter the result set
- **JoinOrderFormInfo** If True, this indicates that the result set should include data from the OrderFormHeader table
- **JoinLineItemInfo** If True, this indicates that the result set should include data from the OrderFormLineItems table
- **Columns** Comma-delimited list of the column names that should be returned, in addition to the default columns
- **OrderGroupSortColumn** Name of the column that should be used to sort the results

- **SortDirection** Order in which the result set should be sorted. This parameter accepts asc or desc as values.
- **PageSize** Number of records returned as a part of the result set (default is 20)
- **PageNumber** Page number of the result set that is returned
- **OutTotalRecordsFound** Total number of records found that match the search criteria

The following code sample can be used to perform a quick search, based on the criteria that the user's first name is Brad and the order number is greater than 1000.

```
asOrderGroup = array("user_first_name = 'brad'", _
 order_number > 1000")

asOrderForm = ""

asLineItem = ""

set rs = mscsOrderGrpMgr.Find(asOrderGroup, asOrderForm, _
 asLineItem,,,,,,,,,,,,lRecords)
```

Note By not providing any values for the search criteria, you retrieve a list of all of the orders within the database.

The result of the Find method is a recordset that includes the desired data, which you can then display on your site as you choose.

Searching Using SimpleFind

You can also perform a search by building the search criteria into the SimpleFindSearchInfo and SimpleFindSearchResult objects. These objects are designed to help you specify the criteria by providing properties for each potential search option. The available properties for these objects are discussed in the section titled "Order Components," later in this chapter.

The following code sample demonstrates a search using the SimpleFind method that retrieves the data for a user whose first name is Brad with the order number of 1002.

```
set SearchInfo = _
  server.CreateObject("Commerce.SimpleFindSearchInfo")

set ResultInfo = _
  server.CreateObject("Commerce.SimpleFindResultInfo")

SearchInfo.user_firstname = "Brad"

SearchInfo.order_number = "1002"


set rs = _
  mscsOrderGrpMgr.SimpleFind(SearchInfo,ResultInfo,lRecords)
```

The SimpleFind method returns a recordset that includes the results of the search that was applied.

Deleting OrderGroups

Orders can be deleted from the database using two methods:

- Delete OrderGroup using the DeleteOrderGroupFromDisk method
- Delete OrderGroup using the SimpleDelete method

Deleting with the DeleteOrderGroupFromDisk Method

An order can be deleted based on its OrderGroup ID using the OrderGroupManager's DeleteOrderGroupFromDisk method. This method accepts only the OrderGroup ID as a parameter and removes just one OrderGroup from the system, as shown in the following code sample:

```
Call mscsOrderGroupManager.DeleteOrderGroupFromDisk( _
"{F22178C0-08B6-4858-9BD0-D5D83E8ACB89}")
```

Deleting with the SimpleDelete Method

You can delete a set of Orders based on any provided criteria in the SimpleFindSearchInfo and SimpleFindResultInfo objects. For instance, you can delete all OrderGroups on the system that belong to any user whose first name is Brad, as shown in the following sample code. Of course, you should be careful to ensure that you are only deleting the orders you want because, as in this case, there could be several users who match the criteria.

```
set SearchInfo = _
  server.CreateObject("Commerce.SimpleFindSearchInfo")

set ResultInfo = _
  server.CreateObject("Commerce.SimpleFindResultInfo")

SearchInfo.user_firstname = "Brad"

Call mscsOrderGrpMgr.SimpleDelete(SearchInfo,ResultInfo)
```

Note The Basket and the Order

Items that a customer selects are stored in two different areas, depending on which part of the purchase process they are in. Until the purchase has been completed, the OrderForm data is stored in the Basket. This means that the order is saved in the BasketGroup table in the database. The data is saved by the SaveAsBasket method of the OrderGroup object.

Once the purchase is completed, the order can be saved into the Order tables, specifically the OrderFormHeader, OrderFormLineItems, OrderGroup, and OrderGroupAddresses tables, in the database. The data is stored using the SaveAsOrder method of the OrderGroup object.

Order Components Reference

The following sections detail the various components used as a part of the order processing system in Commerce Server 2000. You'll see these components put to use in the next chapters.

OrderForm

The OrderForm is a special implementation of the Dictionary object that is used to hold an individual order's data. Its methods are listed in Table 14-1.

Table 14-1. OrderForm Methods

Method Name	Description
AddItem	Adds an item to the Items SimpleList of the OrderForm
ClearItems	Clears the Items SimpleList of the OrderForm
ClearOrderForm	Clears the OrderForm completely

OrderGroup

The OrderGroup object is the means of access to the OrderForms that make up an order. Its properties are described in Table 14-2, and its methods are detailed in Table 14-3.

Table 14-2. OrderGroup Properties

Property Name	Data Type	Description
LogFile	String	Name and path of the log file used by the pipeline to log information.
SavePrefix	String	Prefix that will prevent fields from being saved to the database. Typically, this is the underscore character (_).
Value	Variant	The value of an OrderGroup key.

Table 14-3. OrderGroup Methods

Method Name	Description
AddItem	Adds an item to the identified OrderForm
AddItemsFromTemplate	Adds items from a template to the OrderGroup
AddOrderForm	Adds an OrderForm, with all of its contents and items, to the OrderGroup
AddXMLAsOrderForm	Adds an XML document that represents an OrderForm to the OrderGroup
AggregateOrderFormValues	Calculates a value based on the value of keys in every OrderForm and saves that value at the OrderGroup level
Clear	Removes all OrderForms from the OrderGroup
GetAddress	Retrieves an address from the OrderGroup Addresses dictionary

(continued)

Table 14-3. *(continued)*

Method Name	Description
GetItemInfo	Retrieves an item from the identified OrderForm based on a line item index
GetOrderFormAsXML	Converts an OrderForm to an XML document
GetOrderFormValue	Retrieves the value of a key in the identified OrderForm
Initialize	Initializes the OrderGroup object, specifying the database connection string and the user ID
LoadOrder	Loads a completed order from the database as an OrderGroup
LoadTemplate	Loads a saved order (template) from the database as an OrderGroup
LoadBasket	Loads a basket from the database as an OrderGroup
PurgeUnreferenceAddresses	Removes any addresses from the OrderGroup that are not referenced in the shipping addresses
PutItemValue	Puts a value in a key of an item
PutOrderFormValue	Puts a value in a key of an OrderForm
RemoveItem	Removes an item from the identified OrderForm based on the ItemIndex.
RemoveOrderForm	Removes an identified OrderForm from the OrderGroup
RunPipe	Runs the identified pipeline
SaveAsBasket	Saves OrderGroup as a basket
SaveAsOrder	Saves OrderGroup as an order
SaveAsTemplate	Saves OrderGroup as a template
SetAddress	Saves an address in the OrderGroup, based on an Address Dictionary object
SetAddressFromFields	Saves an Address in the OrderGroup, based on address fields in a provide Fields object
SetShippingAddress	Saves the shipping address for the order based on the Address ID provided

OrderGroupManager

The OrderGroupManager object is used to manage OrderGroups. It also provides search capabilities for OrderGroups. The properties of the OrderGroupManager object are given in Table 14-4. Table 14-5 lists the object's methods.

Table 14-4. OrderGroupManager Properties

Property Name	Data Type	Description
OrderFormHeaderColumns	Variant	Comma-delimited column names from the OrderFormHeader database table
OrderFormLineItemsColumns	Variant	Comma-delimited column names from the OrderFormLineItems database table
OrderGroupColumns	Variant	Comma-delimited column names from the OrderGroup database table

Table 14-5. OrderGroupManager Methods

Method Name	Description
DeleteOrderGroupFromDisk	Removes the OrderGroup from the database
Find	Retrieves a recordset of OrderGroups, based on the search criteria provided as a SQL query
FindTemplatesForUser	Retrieves a recordset of templates as OrderGroups for the identified user
Initialize	Initializes the object by providing the database connection string
SimpleDelete	Deletes the OrderGroup entries that meet the provided criteria in the SimpleFindSearchInfo and SimpleFindResultInfo objects
SimpleFind	Retrieves a recordset of the OrderGroup, based on the search criteria provided by the SimpleFindSearchInfo and SimpleFindResultInfo objects

SimpleFindResultInfo

The SimpleFindResultInfo object is used to define the results returned from the SimpleFind method. Its properties are listed in Table 14-6.

Table 14-6. SimpleFindResultInfo Properties

Property Name	Data Type	Description
Columns	Variant	Comma-delimited list of columns to return as a part of the result set.
JoinLineItemInfo	Boolean	If True, indicates that data from the OrderFormLineItems table should be returned.
JoinOrderFormInfo	Boolean	If True, indicates that data from the OrderFormHeader table should be returned.
OrderGroupSortColumn	Variant	Name of the column that is used to sort the result set.
PageNumber	Long	Number of the page to be returned as a part of the result set.
PageSize	Long	Number of records to be returned in each page of the result set (default is 20).
SortDirection	Variant	Identifies the sort order to be used in returning the result set. Acceptable values include asc and desc.

SimpleFindSearchInfo

The SimpleFindSearchInfo object is used to build search criteria for use in the SimpleFind and SimpleDelete methods. Any properties that are not set will not be a part of the search criteria. The SimpleFindSearchInfo properties are listed in Table 14-7.

Table 14-7. SimpleFindSearchInfo Properties

Property Name	Data Type	Description
Description	Variant	Value to use to search on the product description
Order_number	Variant	Value to use to search on the order number
Ordergroup_id	Variant	Value to use to search on the OrderGroup ID
Po_number	Variant	Value to use to search on the PO number
Product_id	Variant	Value to use to search on the product ID
SearchDateTimeColumn	Variant	Name of the column that holds a date and time value for the order
SearchDateTimeEnd	Variant	Latest date and time value to return as a part of the result set
SearchDateTimeStart	Variant	Earliest date and time value to return as a part of the result set
StatusFilter	Long	Value to use to filter the result set on the order status code
User_firstname	Variant	Value to use to search on the user's first name
User_id	Variant	Value to use to search on the user ID
User_lastname	Variant	Value to use to search on the user's last name
User_org_id	Variant	Value to use to search on the user's organization ID
User_org_name	Variant	Value to use to search on the user's organization name

Chapter 15

Order Processing

As your shopper moves through the purchase process, there are a number of common tasks that you'll need to perform. You'll use the OrderGroup, OrderForm, Dictionary, SimpleList, and other objects to aid in processing the order. In addition, you'll probably have to write some SQL stored procedures and perform queries using ActiveX Data Object (ADO). You'll certainly make use of pipelines, which are covered in the next few chapters, to assist in processing the order through the system.

Creating the OrderGroup Object

As Chapter 14, "Order Basics," pointed out, the OrderGroup object is the central element to working with orders in your system. The first step in working with the object is to create and initialize it. You'll create the object using the PROGID Commerce.OrderGroup and initialize it by providing the database connection string to the database that holds the order information (see the following code sample). You also provide a user ID that you are using to open the order. Typically, this is the user ID of the currently logged in user. However, if this user is an administrator, he or she can open another user's order and must specify that user's ID.

```
Set mscsOrderGroup = Server.CreateObject("Commerce.OrderGroup")

mscsOrderGroup.Initialize _
 mscsOptionsDictionary.s_TransactionConfigConnectionString, _
 mscsUserProfile("generalinfo.user_id").value
```

Working with the Basket

There are a number of tasks that you'll need to complete when working with the user's basket or shopping cart, which are detailed in the following sections.

Creating a New Basket

You can create a new basket by loading and initializing an OrderGroup. If there are no OrderForms in the OrderGroup, you can create a default OrderForm. To do so, you'll create an OrderForm object and then add it to the OrderGroup using the AddOrderForm method, shown in the following code sample:

```
if mscsOrderGroup.Value.orderforms.count = 0 then
    set mscsOrderForm = server.CreateObject("Commerce.OrderForm")
    call  mscsOrderGroup.AddOrderform(mscsOrderForm,"default")
    mscsOrderGroup.SaveAsBasket
    mscsOrderGroup.LoadBasket
end if
```

Retrieving a Basket

You can retrieve the shopper's current basket by using the OrderGroup's LoadBasket method, shown here:

```
Call  mscsOrderGroup.LoadBasket()
```

The basket is identified by the user's ID in the database, and that ID is used to retrieve the basket. That ID was specified when the OrderGroup object was initialized.

Retrieving the OrderForm from the OrderGroup

At times, you might need to retrieve an individual OrderForm from the OrderGroup. The OrderForms within the OrderGroup are identified by name of the trading partner with which they're associated. If the OrderForm is not associated with a trading partner, the name will be default, as shown here:

```
Set mscsOrderForm = mscsOrderGroup("OrderForms").Value("default")
```

Another syntax that performs the same function is the following:

```
Set mscsOrderForm = mscsOrderGroup.Value.OrderForms("default")
```

This is because the OrderGroup is another special implementation of the Dictionary object, and values are retrieved in the same manner as all of the rest of the keys in a Dictionary.

You can also identify the number of OrderForms that are in the OrderGroup using this code:

```
lCount = mscsOrderGroup.Value.OrderForms.Count
```

Displaying the Basket

Building a basket page entails retrieving the data from each OrderForm and listing them on the page. Of course, you must recognize that many of the values you might want to display are added to the OrderForm through various pipeline components. In particular, item data is completed by being retrieved from the database or being calculated. For instance, the line item subtotal (_cy_oadjust_adjustedprice) is calculated based on the quantity of items (quantity) being ordered and the current price (_cy_iadjust_currentprice) of the item.

Note Any key in the order that begins with the underscore character (_) needs to be created after the OrderGroup is loaded, because these values are not persisted in the database. Typically, these values are completed through the pipelines.

Displaying a Single OrderForm Basket

To start, you can directly build a page that displays the order entry by retrieving the desired values and retrieving each of the items from the order. You'll start by retrieving the Basket from the OrderGroup object, as shown in the following code sample:

```
set mscsOrderGroup = Server.CreateObject("Commerce.OrderGroup")

mscsOrderGroup.Initialize Application("sTransactionCS"), _
 m_UserGUID

mscsOrderGroup.LoadBasket
```

You'll then run the basket pipeline, which is covered in more detail in the following chapters. For now, you'll have to accept this at face value. The pipeline helps populate some of the calculated keys in the OrderForm, using the code shown here:

```
Call RunPipe("basket", mscsOrderGroup)
```

Then, you'll retrieve the default OrderForm and parse through it to get the item values that you want to display, as shown in in the following code sample:

```
Set mscsOrderForm = mscsOrderGroup.Value.OrderForms("default")

htmlItems = "<table><tr>" _
   & "<th>Product ID</th>" _
   & "<th>Description</th>" _
   & "<th>Qty</th>" _
   & "<th>Price</th>" _
   & "<th>Total</th>" _
   & "<th>Remove</th>" _
   & "</tr>"
```

(continued)

(continued)

```
For i = 1 to mscsOrderForm.Items.Count

   Set item = mscsOrderGroup.GetItemInfo(i-1, "default")

   htmItems = htmItems & "<tr>" _
    & "<td>" & item("_product_name") & "</td>" _
    & "<td>" & item("_product_description") & "</td>" _
    & "<td>" & item("quantity") & "</td>" _
    & "<td>" & _
      mscsDataFunctions.LocalizeCurrency( _
      item("_cy_iadjust_currentprice"),"1033","$") _
      & "</td>" _
    & "<td>" & _
      mscsDataFunctions.LocalizeCurrency( _
      item("_cy_oadjust_adjustedprice"),"1033","$") _
      & "</td>" _
    & "<td><a href=""_removeitem.asp?i=" & i-1 _
      & """>Remove</a></td>" _
    & "</tr>"

next
```

Note In the previous code, as well as other code in this chapter, the LocalizeCurrency method is used to display the local currency. In this code, the locale is hard-coded as 1033. In your code, you should provide a locale for the individual user. See Chapter 8, "Common Components," for more info on the DataFunctions' LocalizeCurrency method.

Finally, you can retrieve the order-level data, which in the case shown in the following code, is the subtotal for the order. You can then display the entire basket contents.

```
htmItems = htmItems & "<tr>" _
   & "<td colspan=5 align=right><hr width=100></td>" _
   & "</tr>"

htmItems = htmItems & "<tr>" _
   & "<td colspan=4 align=right>SubTotal</td>" _
   & "<td>" & _
      mscsDataFunctions.LocalizeCurrency( _
      mscsOrderForm("_cy_oadjust_subtotal"),"1033","$") _
      & "</td>" _
   & "</tr>"

htmItems = htmItems & "</table>"

htmPage = "<HTML><HEAD></HEAD><BODY>" _
   & htmItems _
   & "</BODY></HTML>"

Response.Write htmPage
```

Displaying a Multiple OrderForm Basket

Of course, if you're attempting to display items that are listed in separate OrderForms within the OrderGroup, you'll have to parse through each OrderForm to retrieve the items from each. You'll also need to retrieve the OrderForm values, such as the subtotal and other values, for each OrderForm and aggregate those as well. To accomplish this, you can modify the previous code to loop through each OrderForm in the OrderGroup and gather the selected data, as shown in the following code:

```
set mscsOrderGroup = Server.CreateObject("Commerce.OrderGroup")

mscsOrderGroup.Initialize Application("sTransactionCS"), _
 m_UserGUID

mscsOrderGroup.LoadBasket


Call RunPipe("basket", mscsOrderGroup)

htmItems = "<table><tr>" _
   & "<th>Product ID</th>" _
   & "<th>Description</th>" _
   & "<th>Qty</th>" _
   & "<th>Price</th>" _
   & "<th>Total</th>" _
   & "<th>Remove</th>" _
   & "</tr>"

cySubTotal = 0.0

For each OrderFormName in mscsOrderGroup.Value.OrderForms

   Set mscsOrderForm = _
    mscsOrderGroup.Value.OrderForms("OrderFormName")

For i = 1 to mscsOrderForm.Items.Count

   Set item = mscsOrderGroup.GetItemInfo(i-1, "default")

   htmItems = htmItems & "<tr>" _
         & "<td>" & item("_product_name") & "</td>" _
         & "<td>" & item("_product_description") & "</td>" _
         & "<td>" & item("quantity") & "</td>" _
         & "<td>" & _
   mscsDataFunctions.LocalizeCurrency( _
   item("_cy_iadjust_currentprice"),"1033","$") _
   & "</td>" _
            & "<td>" & _
   mscsDataFunctions.LocalizeCurrency( _
   item("_cy_oadjust_adjustedprice"),"1033","$") _
   & "</td>" _
   & "<td><a href=""_removeitem.asp?o=" & OrderFormName _
   & "i=" & i-1 & """>Remove</a></td>" _
            & "</tr>"

next
```
(continued)

(continued)

```
cySubTotal = cySubTotal + mscsOrderForm("_cy_oadjust_subtotal")

Next

htmItems = htmItems & "<tr>" _
      & "<td colspan=5 align=right><hr width=100></td>" _
      & "</tr>"

htmItems = htmItems & "<tr>" _
      & "<td colspan=4 align=right>SubTotal</td>" _
      & "<td>" & _
      mscsDataFunctions.LocalizeCurrency( _
      cySubTotal,"1033","$") _
      & "</td>" _
      & "</tr>"

htmItems = htmItems & "</table>"

htmPage = "<HTML><HEAD></HEAD><BODY>" _
      & htmItems _
      & "</BODY></HTML>"

Response.Write htmPage
```

Running a Pipeline

To populate the nonpersistent and calculated values in the order, you'll run an appropriate Order Processing Pipeline by calling the RunPipe method of the OrderGroup object, as shown here:

```
Call mscsOrderGroup.RunPipe(sPath & sPipeFile, _
 "Commerce.MtsPipeline", dContext)
```

Note Building and running pipelines is covered in more detail in Chapter 16, "Pipelines," and Chapter 17, "Building Custom Pipeline Components."

Adding an Item to the Basket

To add an item to the user's basket, you'll first build a Dictionary object that holds all of the desired item data. At a minimum, you must provide the following fields:

- product_catalog
- product_id
- product_variant_id (if this product is a variant)
- quantity

You'll then call the OrderGroup's AddItem method, providing the Item Dictionary and the name of the OrderForm to which the item should be added, as seen here:

```
set dItem = Server.CreateObject("Commerce.Dictionary")

dItem.product_id = _
 "Microsoft Age of Empires II: The Age of Kings: Inside Moves"

dItem.quantity = iQty

dItem.product_catalog = sCatalogName

dItem.product_catalog_base = sCatalogName

mscsOrderGroup.AddItem dItem, "default"

mscsOrderGroup.SaveAsBasket
```

Removing an Item from the Basket

If a user wants to remove an item from his or her basket, you'll need to provide a means to do so. To do this, you specify the index value for the line item in the RemoveItem method of the OrderGroup, as shown in the following code:

```
set mscsOrderGroup = Server.CreateObject("Commerce.OrderGroup")

mscsOrderGroup.Initialize Application("sTransactionCS"), _
 m_UserGUID

mscsOrderGroup.LoadBasket

iLineItem = Request.QueryString("i")

Call mscsOrderGroup.RemoveItem(i, "default")

mscsOrderGroup.SaveAsBasket
```

Removing All Items from the Basket

A user might want to empty his or her basket completely, removing all of the items. This can be done by calling the RemoveItem method without specifying a line item index, as shown in in the following code:

```
set mscsOrderGroup = Server.CreateObject("Commerce.OrderGroup")

mscsOrderGroup.Initialize Application("sTransactionCS"), _
 m_UserGUID

mscsOrderGroup.LoadBasket

Call mscsOrderGroup.RemoveItem(,"default")

mscsOrderGroup.SaveAsBasket
```

Aggregating Items in the Basket

A shopper might add an item to the basket more than once. You can leave the item in the basket multiple times, but you might want to combine those line items so that the item only appears once in the basket. Of course, you'll need to modify the quantity for the item to reflect each of the instances of the item in the OrderForm.

The first thing you'll do is retrieve the Basket and OrderForm for which you'll be aggregating values. You'll also need a Dictionary object that will hold each of the items being processed, as shown in in the following code. Each item will be held in the Dictionary with a unique key, based on the product_id.

```
set mscsOrderGroup = Server.CreateObject("Commerce.OrderGroup")

mscsOrderGroup.Initialize Application("sTransactionCS"), _
 m_UserGUID

mscsOrderGroup.LoadBasket

Set mscsOrderForm = mscsOrderGroup.Value.OrderForms("default")

set dItem = createobject("Commerce.Dictionary")

set slItems = createobject("Commerce.SimpleList")
```

You'll then loop through each item in the OrderForm. If the item has not yet been added to the temporary Item Dictionary, you'll add it, as shown here:

```
i = 0

For Each Item In mscsOrderForm.items

    If IsNull(dItem(Item.product_id)) Then

    'this is a new product, just add the dictionary to it

     i = i + 1

     Item.lineitem_id = i

     Set dItem(Item.product_id) = Item
```

If the item has already been added, you'll increment the quantity in the item in the temporary Item Dictionary by the amount in the current instance of the product, as shown in the following code:

```
    Else

     'this product exists, add the quantities

     Set d = dItem(Item.product_id)

     d.quantity = cint(d.quantity) + cint(Item.quantity)

     Set dItem(Item.product_id) = d

    End If

Next
```

After you've parsed through each of the items in the Basket, you'll build a SimpleList of each of the aggregated items, as shown in in the following code. This list is then saved back into the OrderForm, replacing the existing Items SimpleList.

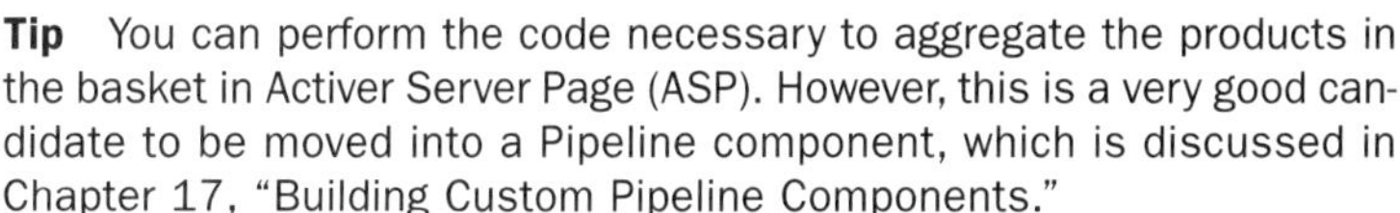

```
For Each vItem In dItem

   slItems.Add dItem(vItem)

Next

Set mscsOrderForm.items = slItems

mscsOrderGroup.SaveAsBasket
```

Tip You can perform the code necessary to aggregate the products in the basket in Activer Server Page (ASP). However, this is a very good candidate to be moved into a Pipeline component, which is discussed in Chapter 17, "Building Custom Pipeline Components."

Saving the Basket

When you make a change to the basket, you must remember to call the SaveAsBasket method of the OrderGroup, shown here, to save those changes to the database:

```
mscsOrderGroup.SaveAsBasket
```

Otherwise, when you leave the current page and the OrderGroup object goes out of scope, the changes are lost.

Processing the Order

Once shoppers have finished adding items to their basket, it is time to process and accept the order. Before the order can be completed, a number of tasks must be accomplished to gather the needed information, including the following:

- Get shipping and billing address information
- Select shipping method
- Calculate shipping, handling, and tax charges
- Get payment information
- Confirm the order

Adding Addresses

Chapter 10, "Profiles," discussed the use of an address book, which allows users to select an address they have already created and use it for shipping or billing. In gathering the shipping and billing addresses for users, you should allow them to select from their address book, but you should also provide a means for them to enter a new address. In either case, the process of adding the address to the order is the same, with a small difference.

The first step is to gather the address and place it in a Dictionary object with the desired fields, as shown in the following sample. If the address is an existing one, you can retrieve it from the Address profile object.

```
const BOTH_ADDRESS = 0

const SHIPPING_ADDRESS = 1

const BILLING_ADDRESS = 2

Set dAddress = server.CreateObject("Commerce.Dictionary")

'Identifies the Address ID, if existing Address

guidAddress = Request.QueryString("AddressID")

'Identifies the Type of Address

iAddressType = Request.QueryString("AddressType")

if len(guidAddress)>0 then

   'got an Address ID, so we can retrieve the Address from the
    'Profile

   bNewAddress=False

   set mscsAddressProfile = _
     mscsProfileServer.GetProfile(guidAddress, "Address")

   dAddress.Address_Line1 = _
     mscsAddressProfile("GeneralInfo.Address_Line1").value

   dAddress.Address_Line2 = _
     mscsAddressProfile("GeneralInfo.Address_Line2").value

   dAddress.City = mscsAddressProfile("GeneralInfo.City").value

   dAddress.Region_Code = _
     mscsAddressProfile("GeneralInfo.Region_Code").value

   dAddress.State_Name = _
     mscsAddressProfile("GeneralInfo.State_Name").value

   dAddress.Postal_Code = _
     mscsAddressProfile("GeneralInfo.Postal_Code").value

   dAddress.Country_Code = _
     mscsAddressProfile("GeneralInfo.Country_Code").value

   dAddress.Country_Name = _
     mscsAddressProfile("GeneralInfo.Country_Name").value

   dAddress.Last_Name = _
     mscsAddressProfile("GeneralInfo.Last_Name").value
```

(continued)

(continued)

```
    dAddress.First_Name = _
     mscsAddressProfile("GeneralInfo.First_Name").value
```

If the address is a newly entered one, you can pass the address values into the processing form through the QueryString or a Hypertext Markup Language (HTML) post and retrieve them from the Request object. The one difference is that you must generate an Address ID for the new address so that it can be properly referenced in the order. You can do this using the Commerce Server GenID object's GenGUIDString method, shown here:

```
else

    'This is a newly entered address

    'it's being passed in through the QueryString from another
     'page

    bNewAddress=true

    set mscsGenID = Application("MSCSGenID")

    guidAddress = mscsGenID.GenGUIDString

    dAddress.Address_Line1 = Request.QueryString("Address_Line1")

    dAddress.Address_Line2 = Request.QueryString("Address_Line2")

    dAddress.City = Request.QueryString("City")

    dAddress.Region_Code = Request.QueryString("Region_Code")

    dAddress.State_Name = Request.QueryString("State_Name")

    dAddress.Postal_Code = Request.QueryString("Postal_Code")

    dAddress.Country_Code = Request.QueryString("Country_Code")

    dAddress.Country_Name = Request.QueryString("Country_Name")

    dAddress.Last_Name = Request.QueryString("Last_Name")

    dAddress.First_Name = Request.QueryString("First_Name")

end if

dAddress.Address_Type = iAddressType
```

You'll then have to retrieve the user's basket, as shown in here, which you've done on other pages.

```
set mscsOrderGroup = Server.CreateObject("Commerce.OrderGroup")

mscsOrderGroup.Initialize Application("sTransactionCS"), _
 mscsUserProfile("GeneralInfo.user_id").value

mscsOrderGroup.LoadBasket
```

If this address can be used as a shipping address, you'll save it to the order using the OrderGroup's SetAddress method. You'll then identify it as a shipping address using the SetShippingAddress method (see the following code). This method assigns the shipping address to the specified items in the selected OrderForms. If you don't specify the items or the OrderForm, it is assigned to all items in all OrderForms in the order.

```
if iAddressType = BOTH_ADDRESS _
 or iAddressType = SHIPPING_ADDRESS Then

   mscsOrderGroup.SetAddress(guidAddress, dAddress)

   mscsOrderGroup.SetShippingAddress(guidAddress,True)

end if
```

If this address is to be used as the billing address, you can save it to the order using the OrderGroup's SetAddress method. You can also identify it on each OrderForm as the billing address by saving it to a key, in this case billing_address_id, on each OrderForm using the OrderGroup's PutOrderFormValue method, as shown here:

```
if iAddressType = BOTH_ADDRESS _
 or iAddressType = BILLING_ADDRESS Then

   mscsOrderGroup.SetAddress(guidAddress, dAddress)

   mscsOrderGroup.PutOrderFormValue("billing_address_id", _
    guidAddress)

end if
```

The Solution Sites that Microsoft developed identify addresses as being one of three potential types, as follows:

- Neutral: 0
- Shipping: 1
- Billing: 2

Adding Shipping Types and Charges

You'll have to provide a way for your users to select the shipping method they want to use, if more than one method is available. Typically, sites provide a standard shipping option and an express shipping option. Of course, the rates for each would depend on the shipping service being used.

The first step in providing shipping support is to build a page that displays the shipping methods supported by your site. You can retrieve this list using the ShippingMethodManager object's GetInstalledMethodList method, shown in the following code. This returns a recordset that lists the shipping methods that have been installed for this site. Once you have that recordset, you can display it so that shoppers can select the method they wish to use.

```
Set mscsShipMgr = _
  Server.CreateObject("Commerce.ShippingMethodManager")

Call mscsShipMgr.Initialize( _
  mscsOptionsDictionary.s_TransactionConfigConnectionString)

aShipCols = Array("shipping_method_id", _
 "shipping_method_name", "description")

Set rsShippingMethods = _
 mscsShipMgr.GetInstalledMethodList("enabled=1", _
 "shipping_method_name", aShipCols)

htmShipMethods = "<FORM ACTION=""_setship.asp"" METHOD=POST>" _
 & "<table>"

do while not rsShippingMethods.Eof
 htmShipMethods = htmShipMethods & "<TR>" _
   & "<TD><INPUT TYPE=radio NAME=""shipping_method_id""" _
     & "" VALUE=""" _
     & rsShippingMethods("shipping_method_id") & """></TD>" _
   & "<TD>" & rsShippingMethods("shipping_method_name") _
   & "</TD>" _
   & "<TD>" & rsShippingMethods("description") & "</TD>" _
   & "</TR>"

 rsShippingMethods.MoveNext

loop

htmShipMethods = htmShipMethods _
 & "</TABLE><INPUT TYPE=SUBMIT></FORM>"

htmPage = "<HTML><HEAD></HEAD><BODY>" _
   & htmShipMethods _
   & "</BODY></HTML>"

Response.Write htmPage
```

Once the user has selected the shipping method, you can pass it into a processing page that saves that method to each item in the order (see the following code). The shipping method should be noted for each item in the order. This is used by the shipping components in the pipeline to define the separate shipments and the shipping costs.

```
set mscsOrderGroup = Server.CreateObject("Commerce.OrderGroup")

mscsOrderGroup.Initialize Application("sTransactionCS"), _
 mscsUserProfile("GeneralInfo.user_id").value

mscsOrderGroup.LoadBasket

sSelectedMethodID = Request.Form("shipping_method_id")
```

(continued)

(continued)
```
Set mscsShipMgr = _
  Server.CreateObject("Commerce.ShippingMethodManager")

Call mscsShipMgr.Initialize( _
  mscsOptionsDictionary.s_TransactionConfigConnectionString)

aShipCols = Array("shipping_method_id", _
  "shipping_method_name", "description")

Set rsShippingMethods = _
  mscsShipMgr.GetInstalledMethodList("shipping_method_id='" _
  & sSelectedMethodID & "'", _
  "shipping_method_name", aShipCols)

sSelectedMethodName = rsShippingMethods("shipping_method_name")

Call mscsOrderGrp.PutItemValue("shipping_method_id", _
  sSelectedMethodID, True)

Call mscsOrderGrp.PutItemValue("shipping_method_name", _
  sSelectedMethodName, True)
```

Note The method shown of retrieving the shipping method name can probably be improved, potentially through the use of a stored procedure that retrieves the data directly. This is left for you to implement if you wish.

Adding Handling Charges

You can set up your site to apply handling charges to an order if you wish. Most commonly, handling charges are applied by a pipeline component. If you want to apply handling charges in your code, you'll save the handling charges for the order in the _cy_handling_total key in the order, as shown here:

```
mscsOrderForm("_cy_handling_total") = "10.00"
```

Adding Taxes

Taxes are generally applied by using a pipeline component that calculates taxes for the order. There are a number of third-party tax calculation components that are available for use on your site. These components are better suited to tracking and applying the variety of tax laws throughout the world than anything you're likely to develop for your own site.

Note Microsoft Commerce Server 2000 provides a sample tax calculation pipeline component that can be used for development purposes. However, this component should be replaced in a production environment with the third-party component of your choice.

The calculated tax for an order is saved in the _cy_tax_total key of the OrderForm.

Calculating the Total Cost of the Order

Of course, you'll also need to calculate the total cost of an order. This is another process that is appropriately handled by a pipeline component, in this case, DefaultTotalCy. This component sums the values from the following keys:

- _cy_oadjust_subtotal
- _cy_shipping_total
- _cy_handling_total
- _cy_tax_total

It then puts the calculated total into the _cy_total_total key. This is the final cost of the order and the amount charged to the user.

Getting Payment Information

If you're going to accept payment on your site by credit card, you'll need to provide a form to gather payment information. Table 15-1 lists the minimum fields you need to provide information for, as well as the fields in the OrderForm.

Table 15-1. Minimum Data Required to Accept and Validate Credit Card Information

Required Information	Field in OrderForm
Type of credit card (VISA, MasterCard, American Express, and so on)	cc_type
Credit card number	_cc_number
Expiration month	_cc_expmonth
Expiration year	_cc_expyear
Name on credit card	cc_name

When a credit card is authorized for payment, you'll save the authorization code in the OrderForm's _payment_auth_code field.

You should note that the credit card number is, by default, not persisted in the database. However, you might notice on the Internet that some sites maintain the last four or five digits of the credit card number with the data for verification purposes. You can do this using code similar to the following:

```
mscsOrderForm("cc_savedigits") = _
 right(mscsOrderForm("_cc_number"), 5)
```

Credit card authorization is generally performed using a pipeline component. There are a number of third-party components that perform credit card validation and authorization to process payments. When selecting the component that is right for you, check with your bank to see what systems they can work with.

Note Commerce Server 2000 provides a sample credit card validation pipeline component, but this component does not accept and process credit card payments. You should replace it with an appropriate third-party component that performs credit card acceptance, authorizations, and validation.

Getting Order Confirmation

After you have gathered all of the payment information and calculated all of the pricing for the order, you should display all of this information to the user one last time. You then ask the user to confirm the order. Until the user does so, the order should not be processed and payment should not be accepted and authorized.

The process of displaying this information is much like that shown previously for displaying the basket. However, this page also retrieves values for the shipping and billing addresses, as well as the calculated shipping, handling, tax, and total amounts.

Once the order is confirmed by the user, you typically run the order through the final pipeline process that includes the components that accept and authorize the payment. In the Solution Sites, this is done with the CHECKOUT.PCF pipeline.

Verifying the Order Amounts

When you display the order confirmation page, as previously described, you should also generate verification fields that can be submitted when users confirm their purchase. These fields should contain the values that have been shown to the user, such as the order total. These fields are submitted to the processing page and used to verify that the calculated amounts have not changed, for any reason, from what the user last saw and confirmed. If the values have changed, the order confirmation screen should be redisplayed. This ensures that the payment is authorized only for the amount that the user confirmed.

You can easily generate the Verification fields using the AppFramework component's VerifyWith method, as follows:

```
htmVerifyWith = mscsAppFrameWork.VerifyWith(mscsOrderForm, _
  "_cy_total_total")
```

This results in hidden fields being built for the form based on the key that you've specified for the OrderForm, such as the following:

```
<INPUT TYPE=HIDDEN NAME="_VERIFY_WITH"
  VALUE="_cy_total_total=123.45">
```

Saving Data from the OrderForms

When you have finished processing an order, you'll want to save some of the data so that it can be persisted in the database. This data is needed when you display an order receipt or report on previous orders. You don't want to regenerate these values, as some of the pricing might change and you want to see the calculated values as they were when the purchase was made. The CopyFields scriptor component in the TOTAL.PCF pipeline is used to copy the fields from the key names that are prefixed with the underscore character (_). In addition, it copies values from the user and organization profiles to the order. If you want to save fields beyond those in the default scriptor, you can modify the script to copy additional fields. The original scriptor code is provided in the following code:

```
Function MSCSExecute(config, orderform, context, flags)
   Dim objProfileService, user_id, objUserProfile, org_id,  _
    objOrgProfile

   MSCSExecute = 1

   'Copy some lineitem-level fields
   Dim item
   For Each item In orderform.value("items")
    item.value("cy_unit_price") = _
     item.value("_cy_iadjust_regularprice")
    item.value("cy_lineitem_total") = _
     item.value("_cy_oadjust_adjustedprice")
    item.value("description") = _
     Mid(item.value("_product_description"), 1, 127)
   item.value("saved_product_name") = _
    item.value("_product_name")
   Next

   'Copy some orderform-level fields
   orderform.value("saved_cy_oadjust_subtotal") = _
    orderform.value("_cy_oadjust_subtotal")
   orderform.value("saved_cy_total_total") = _
    orderform.value("_cy_total_total")
   orderform.value("saved_shipping_discount_description") = _
    orderform.value("_shipping_discount_description")
   ' *************************************************
   ' Copy some fields from the user profile
   ' *************************************************
   ' Get the ProfileService from the context
   If Not IsObject(context.ProfileService) Then Exit Function
   Set objProfileService = context.ProfileService
   If objProfileService Is Nothing Then Exit Function

   ' Get the user's profile
```
(continued)

(continued)

```
    user_id = orderform.user_id

    If IsNull(user_id) Then Exit Function

  Set objUserProfile = objProfileService.GetProfileByKey( _
   "user_id", user_id, "UserObject", False)

    If objUserProfile Is Nothing Then Exit Function

    ' Copy some user fields

    orderform.Value("user_first_name") = _
      objUserProfile.Fields.Item("GeneralInfo.first_name")

    orderform.Value("user_last_name") = _
      objUserProfile.Fields.Item("GeneralInfo.last_name")

    orderform.Value("user_email_address") = _
      objUserProfile.Fields.Item("GeneralInfo.email_address")

    orderform.Value("user_tel_number") = _
      objUserProfile.Fields.Item("GeneralInfo.tel_number")

    orderform.Value("user_fax_number") = _
      objUserProfile.Fields.Item("GeneralInfo.fax_number")

    ' Get the user's org profile, if avail

    org_id = objUserProfile.Fields.Item("AccountInfo.org_id")

    If IsNull(org_id) Then Exit Function

    Set objOrgProfile = _
     objProfileService.GetProfileByKey("org_id", _
     org_id, "Organization", False)

    If objOrgProfile Is Nothing Then Exit Function

    ' Copy some org fields

    orderform.Value("user_org_id") = org_id

    orderform.Value("user_org_name") = _
      objOrgProfile.Fields.Item("GeneralInfo.name")

End Function
```

Saving an Order

Once the processing of an order is completed, it is ready to be saved as a new order with the OrderGroup's SaveAsOrder method. This method, shown here, saves the data in the OrderGroup into the various Order tables in the database:

```
call mscsOrderGroup.SaveAsOrder(lOrderNumber)
```

In addition, if you provide a variable as the parameter, it returns the value of the Order Tracking Number for the order.

If the OrderGroup already has an order_number key, a new tracking number is not generated. However, if the key does not exist, it is created. A number is retrieved from the Counters table in the database from an entry named OrderTracking.

If you want to use an Order Number from another system, perhaps an external Enterprise Resource Planning (ERP) system, you can retrieve the order number and write it into the OrderGroup's order_number key as follows:

```
oOrderGroup("order_number") = lOrderNumber
```

Postorder Processing

Once the order has been completed, there might be additional tasks that you want to complete to finish the order processing. Each of these items is optional, but each can be useful, depending on the system you have in place. For instance, you might want to send an e-mail to confirm the purchase to the user. You also might want to submit the order to BizTalk to be automatically transmitted to your suppliers. You can do this in two ways: by submitting the order directly to BizTalk or by placing the order in a queue and having BizTalk retrieve the order from the queue.

Sending E-Mail for an Order

If you want to send an order confirmation e-mail to your user, you can do so using Collaboration Data Objects (CDO) for Microsoft Windows 2000. This functionality allows you to send Simple Mail Transfer Protocol (SMTP) e-mail from your Web server, and can be configured to send it through any available SMTP server. In this case, you might create a SendMail function, as shown in the following code, that you can use in various places throughout your site.

```
function SendMail(sTo, sFrom, sSubject, sBody)

   Dim iMsg

   Set iMsg = CreateObject("CDO.Message")

   Dim iConf

   Set iConf = CreateObject("CDO.Configuration")

   Dim Flds

   Set Flds = iConf.Fields

  Flds.Item( _
   "http://schemas.microsoft.com/cdo/configuration/sendusing") _
        = 2 ' cdoSendUsingPort

   Flds.Update

   Set iMsg.Configuration = iConf
```

(continued)

(continued)

```
    iMsg.To             = sTo

    iMsg.From           = sFrom

    iMsg.Subject        = sSubject

    iMsg.TextBody       = sBody

    iMsg.Send

end function
```

With this function, you can send an e-mail to the current user by calling the function and passing the user's e-mail address, as well as the contents of the e-mail, as shown here:

```
Call SendMail(mscsUserProfile( _
 "GeneralInfo.Email_address").value, _
 "customerservice@mysitename.com", _
 sSubject, _
 sBody)
```

Submitting an Order to BizTalk

When the order is completed, you may wish to automatically transmit the appropriate contents to your suppliers. This is an excellent use for BizTalk Server. You can submit the order as an Extensible Markup Language (XML) document from Commerce Server to BizTalk. The first step is converting the order from the internal Commerce Server 2000 representation to an XML document. You'll do this using the DictionaryXMLTransforms object. This process requires three steps:

1. Create the DictionaryXMLTransforms Object, as shown here:

   ```
   Set mscsXMLTransforms = _
     Server.CreateObject("Commerce.DictionaryXMLTransforms")
   ```

2. Load the appropriate XML schema for the Commerce Server order using the GetXMLFromFile method. The POSCHEMA.XML file that accompanies the Solution Sites provides an excellent starting point for this document. You can modify it as needed to include additional fields:

   ```
   sFilePath = Server.MapPath("\" & _
    mscsAppFrameWork.VirtualDirectory) & "\poschema.xml"

   Set mscsXMLSchema =  _
    mscsXMLTransforms.GetXMLFromFile(sFilePath)
   ```

3. Generate the XML document that contains the order using the GenerateXMLForDictionaryUsingSchema method, shown here:

   ```
   Set mscsOrderformXML = _
    mscsXMLTransforms.GenerateXMLForDictionaryUsingSchema( _
    mscsOrderForm, mscsXMLSchema)

   sXML = mscsOrderformXML.xml
   ```

Submit Using BizTalk Interchange

Once you have converted the OrderForm into an XML document, you can submit it to BizTalk using the Interchange object. This will work if the BizTalk objects are loaded locally on the Web server. You can start by reading the BizTalk configuration settings from the App Default Configuration (see the following code). These must be set using Commerce Server Manager (see Figure 15-1).

```
'---------------------

'Set the BizTalk document routing information

'---------------------

sDocName = mscsOptionsDictionary.s_BizTalkOrderDocType

sSourceQualifierID = _
 mscsOptionsDictionary.s_BizTalkSourceQualifierID

sSourceQualifierValue = _
 mscsOptionsDictionary.s_BizTalkSourceQualifierValue
```

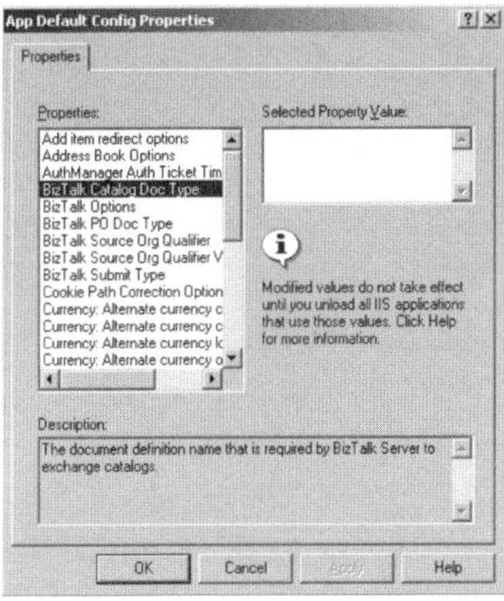

Figure 15-1. *You can establish the BizTalk integration using the BizTalk configuration entries in the App Default Config module in Commerce Server Manager.*

You can then use the BizTalk Interchange object to submit the order directly to BizTalk, as shown here:

```
'---------------------

'Get the BizTalk object and submit the XML file

'---------------------

Set btsInterchange = Server.CreateObject("BizTalk.Interchange")
```

(continued)

(continued)

```
oRes = btsInterchange.Submit(iBIZTALKOPENNESS, _
    sXML, _
    sDocName, _
    sSourceQualifierID, _
    sSourceQualifierValue, _
    sVendorQual, _
    sVendorQualValue)
```

Submitting an Order Using Microsoft Message Queue Service

If you don't have the BizTalk components on your Web server, or you have a Web farm established that is served by a single BizTalk setup, you will probably find it more advantageous to simply put the order, in its XML format, into a queue. BizTalk can set up receive functions to monitor the queues on each of the Web servers. As orders are placed in the queue, BizTalk can retrieve them and act on them.

To submit the order from the queue, you'll start by defining the Microsoft Message Queue Service (MSMQ) queue that you are going to use in the MSMQQueueInfo object, as shown here:

```
sQueueName = ".\Private$\mybiztalkQ"

set MSMQInfo = server.CreateObject("MSMQ.MSMQQueueInfo")

MSMQInfo.PathName = sQueueName
```

You'll then establish a connection to the queue using the MSMQQueueInfo object's Open method, shown here:

```
set MSMQ = MSMQInfo.Open(2,0) 'open as SEND ACCESS and DENY NONE
```

Next, you'll define the Message Queue message that you want to send and call its Send method, passing the Queue object, as shown here:

```
set MSMQMsg = server.CreateObject("MSMQ.MSMQMessage")

MSMQMsg.Body = sXML

call MSMQMsg.Send(MSMQ)
```

Displaying a Receipt

Once your users have completed their purchase, it's typical to provide them with a receipt or at least give them the ability to display one on their own, if they wish. Displaying an order receipt is very similar to displaying the basket. The difference is that you'll retrieve it using the LoadOrder method, shown in the following code, providing the OrderGroupID as a parameter to identify the order to load.

```
set mscsOrderGroup = Server.CreateObject("Commerce.OrderGroup")

mscsOrderGroup.Initialize Application("sTransactionCS"), _
  mscsUserProfile("GeneralInfo.user_id").value

mscsOrderGroup.LoadOrder( _
 "{F22178C0-08B6-4858-9BD0 D5D83E8ACB89}")
```

In addition, you won't run this OrderGroup through any pipelines. Instead, you'll used the values that have been saved to the database. For instance, Table 15-2 shows a list of some of the item and order values that have been renamed so that they're saved in the completed order. You'll use the new saved names to display the values on the receipt page.

Table 15-2. Temporary Keys in the Order Basket and Their Corresponding Keys in the Completed Order

Basket Key Name	Completed Order Key Name
Item._cy_iadjust_regularprice	Item.cy_unit_price
Item._cy_oadjust_adjustedprice	Item.cy_lineitem_total
Item._product_description	Item.description
Orderform._cy_oadjust_subtotal	Orderform.saved_cy_oadjust_subtotal
Orderform._cy_total_total	Orderform.saved_total_total

In this case, you would build the receipt page similarly to the basket page, as the following code shows.

```
htmItems = "<table><tr>" _
   & "<th>Product ID</th>" _
   & "<th>Description</th>" _
   & "<th>Qty</th>" _
   & "<th>Price</th>" _
   & "<th>Total</th>" _
   & "</tr>"

cySubTotal = 0.0

For each OrderFormName in mscsOrderGroup.Value.OrderForms

   Set mscsOrderForm = _
  mscsOrderGroup.Value.OrderForms("OrderFormName")

   For i = 1 to mscsOrderForm.Items.Count

    Set item = mscsOrderGroup.GetItemInfo(i-1, "default")

    htmItems = htmItems & "<tr>" _
     & "<td>" & item("product_id") & "</td>" _
     & "<td>" & item("description") & "</td>" _
     & "<td>" & item("quantity") & "</td>" _
     & "<td>" _
     & mscsDataFunctions.LocalizeCurrency( _
      item("cy_unit_price"),"1033","$") _
     & "</td>" _
     & "<td>" _
     & mscsDataFunctions.LocalizeCurrency( _
      item("cy_lineitem_total"),"1033","$") _
     & "</td>" _
     & "</tr>"

   next
```

(continued)

(continued)

```
   cySubTotal = cySubTotal + _
    mscsOrderForm("saved_cy_oadjust_subtotal")

Next

htmItems = htmItems & "<tr>" _
 & "<td colspan=5 align=right><hr width=100></td>" _
 & "</tr>"

htmItems = htmItems & "<tr>" _
 & "<td colspan=4 align=right>SubTotal</td>" _
 & "<td>" _
 & mscsDataFunctions.LocalizeCurrency( _
   cySubTotal,"1033","$") _
 & "</td>" _
 & "</tr>"

htmItems = htmItems & "</table>"


htmPage = "<HTML><HEAD></HEAD><BODY>" _
 & htmItems _
 & "</BODY></HTML>"


Response.Write htmPage
```

Order Templates

Commerce Server 2000 provides the ability to save an existing basket so that it can be used as the basis for creating or populating baskets. These saved baskets are referred to as templates. There are several tasks you can accomplish with templates, including the following:

- Saving a template
- Loading a template
- Loading items from a template into a basket

Saving an Order Template

To save a template, you'll use the OrderGroup's SaveAsTemplate method and provide a name for the template (see the following code). Your user can use this name to identify the template at a later point.

```
set mscsOrderGroup = Server.CreateObject("Commerce.OrderGroup")

mscsOrderGroup.Initialize Application("sTransactionCS"), _
 mscsUserProfile("GeneralInfo.user_id").value

mscsOrderGroup.LoadBasket


sTemplateName = Request.QueryString("SavedName")

mscsOrderGroup.SaveAsTemplate(sTemplateName)
```

Loading an Order Template

Your users can list the current templates in the database using a query similar to the following:

```
CREATE PROCEDURE sProc_GetTemplates

AS

SELECT

   saved_order_name, ordergroup_id

FROM

   BasketGroup

WHERE

   order_status_code = 2

GO
```

Of course, this query does not identify if the user is permitted to retrieve the template. You should modify the query to apply such a security measure.

Once you have the ordergroup_id of the desired template, you can load it as the current basket using the LoadTemplate method (see the following code). You'll have to provide the ID of the template as a parameter of the method.

```
sTemplateID = Request.QueryString("TemplateID")

set mscsOrderGroup = Server.CreateObject("Commerce.OrderGroup")

mscsOrderGroup.Initialize Application("sTransactionCS"), _
 mscsUserProfile("GeneralInfo.user_id").value

mscsOrderGroup.LoadTemplate(sTemplateID)
```

Adding Items from a Template

Once you have the ordergroup_id of the desired template, you can load the items of the template into the current basket using the OrderGroup's AddItemsFromTemplate method and providing the ID of the template as a parameter, as shown here:

```
sTemplateID = Request.QueryString("TemplateID")

set mscsOrderGroup = Server.CreateObject("Commerce.OrderGroup")

mscsOrderGroup.Initialize Application("sTransactionCS"), _
   mscsUserProfile("GeneralInfo.user_id").value

mscsOrderGroup.LoadBasket

mscsOrderGroup.AddItemsFromTemplate(sTemplateID)
```

Once this is done, your users will be able to continue shopping as normal and complete their purchases when they desire.

Order Processing Components Reference

The following sections detail some of the components used as a part of the order processing system in Commerce Server 2000 that are covered in this chapter.

DictionaryXMLTransforms

The DictionaryXMLTransforms object provides support in converting between Dictionary objects and XML documents. Its methods are listed in Table 15-3.

Table 15-3. DictionaryXMLTransforms Methods

Method Name	Description
GenerateSampleXMLInstanceFromDictionary	Creates an instance of an XML document based on the given Dictionary object
GenerateXMLForDictionaryUsingSchema	Creates an instance of an XML document based on the given Dictionary object transformed by the given XML schema
GetXMLFromFile	Creates an XML document from the given file
ReconstructDictionaryFromXML	Creates a Dictionary object based on the provided XML document that complies with the provided XML schema

ShippingMethodManager

The ShippingMethodManager is used to manage the shipping methods that are available on your site. This object's methods are described in Table 15-4.

Table 15-4. ShippingMethodManager Methods

Method Name	Description
CreateMethodInstance	Creates an empty instance of a shipping method
DeleteMethodInstance	Deletes the current instance of a shipping method
GetComponentConfig	Retrieves a Dictionary object that contains the configuration for the shipping component that implements the current shipping method
GetInstalledMethodList	Retrieves a recordset that holds data about the available shipping methods

(continued)

Table 15-4. *(continued)*

Method Name	Description
GetMethodInfo	Retrieves a recordset that holds data about the current shipping method
Initialize	Initializes the object and connects it to the database that holds the ShippingConfig table
LoadMethodInstance	Loads a shipping method
SaveMethodConfig	Saves configuration information about the current shipping method
SetCachableComponentConfig	Saves configuration and other information about the current component
SetMethodConfig	Sets configuration settings for the current shipping method

Chapter 16

Pipelines

To more efficiently perform a series of tasks on an order or other sets of data, Microsoft Commerce Server 2000 employs the use of pipelines. You can think of these as a basic production line, where a product, in this case an OrderForm, is routed through a specific set of processes to produce the final outcome. By defining the exact steps and applying components that will perform the task at each stage of the process, the system can efficiently focus on doing exactly what it needs to do well. It can then effectively and efficiently perform those tasks.

For example, you can provide a component that is specifically targeted to calculate the taxes on an order. The taxes that must be applied depend on a number of factors, such as the location of your business, the location of the buyer, the products being sold, and more. You might need to apply sales taxes, value-added taxes, and local or regional taxes as well. Rather than attempting to develop the code to do this on your own, you can purchase a tax component that does all of this and then plug it into a pipeline at the appropriate stage to calculate taxes.

The pipeline represents this defined series of steps. It is completely configurable and extensible so you can define any stages within it. For each stage in a particular pipeline, you can assign any components that you wish. To build a custom component, see Chapter 17, "Building Custom Pipeline Components." For additional information on pipeline components, see Commerce Server 2000 Help or the Commerce Server 2000 SDK.

Types of Pipelines

Commerce Server 2000 contains three basic types of pipelines:

- Content Selection Pipeline
- Direct Mailer Pipeline
- Order Processing Pipeline

Each of these pipelines is used for a different purpose, contains different stages, and typically uses different components for each stage.

Content Selection Pipeline

The Content Selection Pipeline is designed to select content targeted for the particular user. The content being selected might be advertisements or discounts to be applied. The selection process can involve a number of factors based on the campaigns that have been established for the site and might reflect user profile attributes, content attributes, and other external factors, such as time of day or season of the year.

There are two basic types of content selection pipelines:

- Content Selection Pipeline
- Event Processing Pipeline

Content Selection Pipeline

The Content Selection Pipeline (CSP) is used to select content for the site. Whether it is used to select advertising or discount content, the basic stages are the same. Table 16-1 provides a list of the default stages, as well as the components available for each.

Table 16-1. Stages and Components in the Standard CSP

CSP Stage	Advertising Application Pipeline Components	Discount Application Pipeline Components
Load Context	InitCSFPipeline LoadHistory	InitCSFPipeline LoadHistory
Filter	FilterContent	FilterContent
Initial Score	AdvertisingNeedOfDelivery	Not applicable
Score	HistoryPenalty EvalTargetGroups	ScoreDiscounts HistoryPenalty EvalTargetGroups
Select	SelectWinners	SelectWinners
Record	RecordHistory SaveHistory RecordEvent IISAppendToLog	RecordHistory SaveHistory RecordEvent IISAppendToLog
Format	FormatTemplate	FormatTemplate

Event Processing Pipeline

The Event Processing Pipeline (EPP) is used to record event information in the database to ensure that the site maintains a record of when content is selected or other events occur. Table 16-2 provides a list of the stages in the basic pipeline, as well as the available components for each.

Table 16-2. Stages and Components in the Basic EPP

EPP Stage	Advertising Application Pipeline Components	Discount Application Pipeline Components
Load Context	None	None
Record	RecordEvent IISAppendToLog	RecordEvent IISAppendToLog
Format	None	None

Direct Mailer Pipeline

The Direct Mailer Pipeline (DMP) is used to configure and send bulk e-mails to a large number of users from your site. Table 16-3 provides a list of the stages in the basic pipeline, as well as the components that are available for use in each.

Table 16-3. Stages and Components Available in the Basic DMP

DMP Stage	Pipeline Components
Throttle	ThrottleDMLPerformance
Preprocess Recipient	VerifyRecipientData
Filter Recipient	None
Create Cookies	CreateUPMCookie
Compose E-Mail	ComposeDMLMessage AddAttachments
Send E-Mail	VerifyMessageBody SendPrecomposedMessage
Postprocess Recipient	None

Order Processing Pipeline

The Order Processing Pipelines (OPPs) are used to process an order, filling out the OrderForm based on the selected products and users and completing the purchase process. The OPP is typically divided into separate pipeline files based on the purpose of the file and the point in the process at which it should be used. These files are as follows:

- Product Pipeline
- Plan Pipeline
- Purchase Pipeline

Product Pipeline

The Product Pipeline is used to retrieve basic product information and set it and other basic information in the OrderForm. Its stages and components are listed in Table 16-4.

Table 16-4. Stages and Components Available in the Basic Product Pipeline

Pipeline Stage	Pipeline Components
Product Info	QueryCatalogInfo QueryProdInfoADO RequiredProdInfo
Shopper Information	DefaultShopperInfo
Item Price	DefaultItemPriceCy, DefaultItemPrice RequiredItemPriceCy, RequiredItemPrice
Item Adjust Price	ItemPromo SaleAdjust RequiredItemAdjustPriceCy, RequiredItemAdjustPrice

(continued)

Table 16-4. *(continued)*

Pipeline Stage	Pipeline Components
Inventory	FlagInventory LocalInventory

Plan Pipeline

The Plan Pipeline contains stages and components to process the order completely, as listed in Table 16-5, with the exception of completing the purchase and accepting payment.

Table 16-5. Stages and Components Available in the Basic Plan Pipeline

Pipeline Stage	Pipeline Components
Product Info	QueryCatalogInfo QueryProdInfoADO RequiredProdInfo
Merchant Information	None
Shopper Information	DefaultShopperInfo
Order Initialization	RequiredOrderInitCy, RequiredOrderInit
Order Check	RequiredOrderCheck
Item Price	DefaultItemPriceCy, DefaultItemPrice RequiredItemPriceCy, RequiredItemPrice
Item Adjust Price	ItemPromo SaleAdjust RequiredItemAdjustPriceCy, RequiredItemAdjustPrice
Order Adjust Price	DBOrderPromoADO OrderDiscount RequiredOrderAdjustPriceCy, RequiredOrderAdjustPrice
Order Subtotal	DefaultOrderSubtotalCy, DefaultOrderSubtotal RequiredOrderSubtotalCy, RequiredOrderSubtotal
Shipping	DefaultShippingCy, DefaultShipping FixedShipping LinearShipping ShippingDiscountAdjust ShippingMethodRouter Splitter TableShippingADO RequiredShippingCy, RequiredShipping
Handling	DefaultHandlingCy, DefaultHandling FixedHandling LinearHandling TableHandlingADO RequiredHandlingCy, RequiredHandling

(continued)

Table 16-5. *(continued)*

Pipeline Stage	Pipeline Components
Tax	DefaultTaxCy, DefaultTax SampleRegionalTax SimpleCanadaTax SimpleJapanTax SimpleUSTax SimpleVATTax RequiredTaxCy, RequiredTax
Order Total	DefaultTotalCy, DefaultTotal RequiredTotalCy, RequiredTotal
Inventory	FlagInventory LocalInventory

Purchase Pipeline

The Purchase Pipeline contains stages and components, listed in Table 16-6, that allow you to complete the purchase and accept payment.

Table 16-6. Stages and Components Available in the Basic Purchase Pipeline

Pipeline Stage	Pipeline Components
Purchase Check	ValidateCCNumber
Payment	DefaultPayment RequiredPayment
Accept	ExecuteProcess MakePO POToFile SaveReceipt SendSMTP SQLItemADO SQLOrderADO

Existing Pipelines

The Solution Sites ship with a number of prebuilt pipelines. These pipeline components provide excellent examples of pipelines that have been developed to meet particular needs in a site.

Order Processing Pipelines

There are several OPPs that ship with the Solution Sites, including the following:

- Basket
- Checkout
- Product
- Receive PO
- Total

Basket Pipeline

The Basket Pipeline is designed to process the order through the stages necessary to populate the OrderForm with the data required to be displayed in the basket. These stages and components are shown in Table 16-7.

Table 16-7. Basket Pipeline Stages and Components

Pipeline Stage	Pipeline Component
Product Info	QueryCatalogInfo RequiredProdInfo
Merchant Information	None
Shopper Information	None
Order Initialization	RequiredOrderInitCy
Order Check	RequiredOrderCheck
Item Price	DefaultItemPriceCy RequiredItemPriceCy
Item Adjust Price	RequiredItemAdjustPriceCy
Order Adjust Price	OrderDiscount RequiredOrderAdjustPriceCy
Order Subtotal	DefaultOrderSubtotalCy RequiredOrderSubtotalCy
Inventory	None

Checkout Pipeline

The Checkout Pipeline is designed to include the stages and components needed to complete the purchase by accepting payment, as shown in Table 16-8.

Table 16-8. Checkout Pipeline Stages and Components

Pipeline Stage	Pipeline Component
Purchase Check	Commerce.Splitter
Payment	Scriptor – Payment Info ValidateCreditCard DefaultPayment RequiredPayment
Accept	RecordEvent IISAppendToLog

Product Pipeline

The Product Pipeline is used to retrieve product-specific information through the pipeline. It includes just the Product Info stage and accompanying components, as shown in Table 16-9.

Table 16-9. Product Pipeline Stages and Components

Pipeline Stage	Pipeline Component
Product Info	QueryCatalogInfo RequiredProdInfo

ReceivePO

The ReceivePO Pipeline is designed to process a purchase order that was submitted to the site. Based on the purchase order data, the order is processed, completed, and accepted with the stages and components as shown in Table 16-10.

Table 16-10. ReceivePO Pipeline Stages and Components

Pipeline Stage	Pipeline Component
Product Info	Scriptor: Fixup product_variant_id QueryCatalogInfo RequiredProdInfo
Order Initialization	None
Order Check	RequiredOrderCheck
Item Price	DefaultItemPriceCy RequiredItemPriceCy
Item Adjust Price	RequiredItemAdjustPriceCy
Order Adjust Price	Scriptor: Use Submitted Prices RequiredOrderAdjustPriceCy
Order Subtotal	DefaultOrderSubTotalCy RequiredOrderSubTotalCy
Order Total	Scriptor: MyTotal RequiredTotalCy
Accept	None

Total Pipeline

The Total Pipeline is designed to include the stages and components, shown in Table 16-11, required to calculate the total charges for the order, including shipping, handling, taxes, and the order total.

Table 16-11. Total Pipeline Stages and Components

Pipeline Stage	Pipeline Component
Shipping	Commerce.Splitter Commerce.ShippingMethodRouter ShippingDiscountAdjust
Handling	DefaultHandlingCy RequiredHandlingCy
Tax	SampleRegionalTax RequiredTaxCy
Order Total	DefaultTotalCy RequiredTotalCy
CopyFields	CopyFields

Content Selection Pipelines

The Content Selection Pipelines are used to identify and select content, either advertising or discounts, for use in the site.

Advertising Pipeline

The Advertising Pipeline is designed to select advertising content on the site, based on the advertising campaigns that have been created for the site. The pipeline includes the stages and components shown in Table 16-12. Campaigns are discussed in more detail in Chapter 18, "Campaign Management."

Table 16-12. Advertising Pipeline Stages and Components

Pipeline Stage	Pipeline Component
Load Context	InitCSFPipeline Load History
Filter	FilterContent
Initial Score	AdvertisingNeedOfDelivery
Scoring	HistoryPenalty EvalTargetGroups
Select	SelectWinners
Record	RecordEvent IISAppendToLog RecordHistory SaveHistory
Format	FormatTemplate

Discounts Pipeline

The Discounts Pipeline is designed to select discounts available for use on the site that will be shown. The pipeline includes the stages and components shown in Table 16-13.

Table 16-13. Discounts Pipeline Stages and Components

Pipeline Stage	Pipeline Component
Load Context	InitCSFPipeline Load History
Filter	FilterContent
Initial Score	None
Scoring	HistoryPenalty ScoreDiscounts EvalTargetGroups
Select	SelectWinners
Record	RecordEvent IISAppendToLog RecordHistory SaveHistory
Format	FormatTemplate

RecordEvent Pipeline

The RecordEvent Pipeline is designed, with the stages and components shown in Table 16-14, to record events of interest in the content selection system.

Table 16-14. RecordEvent Pipeline Stages and Components

Pipeline Stage	Pipeline Component
Load Context	None
Record	RecordEvent IISAppendToLog
Format	None

Pipeline Objects

In Commerce Server 2000, pipelines are processed using one of several potential objects. Your choice of object will depend on the purpose of the pipeline, the components being used in the pipeline, and the current state of the site. The following objects are available:

- MicroPipe
- MtsPipeline
- MtsTxPipeline
- OrderPipeline
- PooledPipeline
- PooledTxPipeline

Some of these objects support transactions. Others support component object pooling within the pipeline for greater scalability. Table 16-15 summarizes the features that each supports. Each component is described in more detail in the following sections.

Table 16-15. Pipeline Object Types and the Features Supported by Each

Pipeline Object	Supports Transacted Pipelines	Supports Object Pooling	Content Selection Pipelines	Execute Single Component
MicroPipe				X
MtsPipeline				
MtsTxPipeline	X			
OrderPipeline			X	
PooledPipeline		X		
PooledTxPipeline	X	X		

MicroPipe

The MicroPipe object is used to execute a single component without executing an entire pipeline configuration file. This is loaded using the PROGID Commerce.MicroPipe.

MtsPipeline

The MtsPipeline object is used to run an OPP that does not require transactional support. This component is provided for backward compatibility with Microsoft Site Server 3. In addition, this component should be used while debugging problems, as it is not cached. This object is loaded using the PROGID Commerce.MtsPipeline.

MtsTxPipeline

The MtsTxPipeline object is used to run an OPP that requires transactional support. This component is provided for backward compatibility with Site Server 3. In addition, this component should be used while debugging problems, as it is not cached. This object is loaded using the PROGID Commerce.MtsTxPipeline.

OrderPipeline

The OrderPipeline object is used to run CSPs. It does not support transactions, and components for the CSPs do not support transactions either. This object is loaded using the PROGID Commerce.OrderPipe.

PooledPipeline

The PooledPipeline is used to run an OPP that does not require transactional support and uses components that support object pooling. By executing the pipeline as a PooledPipeline, you gain scalability and performance, particularly for those components that are designed to be poolable. This is loaded using the PROGID Commerce.PooledPipeline.

PooledTxPipeline

The PooledPipeline is used to run an OPP that requires transactional support and uses components that support object pooling. By executing the pipeline as a PooledTxPipeline, you gain scalability and performance, particularly for those components that are designed to be poolable. This is loaded using the PROGID Commerce.PooledPipeline.

Running a Pipeline

With Commerce Server 2000, you can run a pipeline file in a number of different ways. The OrderGroup object provides a method to execute the pipeline. It runs the pipeline indirectly, providing some front-end processing, and then sends each OrderForm in the OrderGroup through the pipeline, using one of the other identified pipeline components. In addition, you can run a pipeline directly from the Pipeline component. If you want to run a CSP, you can execute the pipeline using the OrderPipeline component.

Pipeline Parameters

Each of the pipelines that are executed expect two common parameters:

- **Order Dictionary** The Order Dictionary contains the information that is being directly processed by the pipeline. For the OPPs, this is an OrderForm.
- **Context Dictionary** The Context Dictionary is used to pass additional information into the pipeline that might be needed during the processing. For instance, the Context Dictionary can be used to pass in the MessageManager, Cache, CatalogManager, and other objects. In addition, you might use the Context Dictionary to pass in other information, such as database connection strings, configuration settings, and more.

These parameters are required no matter which type of pipeline is being executed and which component is being used to process the pipeline.

Configuring a Pipeline Dictionary

You'll likely find it useful to build a Dictionary object that contains a reference to the pipeline files you have in your system. This way, you can define the path for the pipeline files, as well as a pointer to each pipeline. You can also also save this Pipeline Dictionary in an application variable to reference it throughout the site, as shown here:

```
set dPipeline = server.CreateObject("Commerce.Dictionary")

sPath = server.MapPath("\" & mscsAppFramework.VirtualDirectory) _
 & "\pipeline\"

dPipeline.Path = sPath

dPipeline.Basket = sPipelineDir & "basket.pcf"

dPipeline.Total = sPipelineDir & "total.pcf"

Set Application("MSCSPipeline") = dPipeline
```

In this way, when you need to reference the pipeline information, you can retrieve the Dictionary from the application and use the pipeline name to retrieve the necessary data.

Running Through the OrderGroup

The most common method of executing a pipeline is through the OrderGroup object, by calling its RunPipe method (see the following code). When you execute this method, you provide the name and path of the pipeline file, the component you'll use to actually execute the pipeline, and the Context Dictionary to be passed to the pipeline.

```
Function RunPipe(sPipeName, mscsOrderGroup)
   Dim dContext
   Dim dPipeline
   Dim sPath
   Dim sPipeFile

   Set dPipeline = Application("MSCSPipeline")

   Set dContext = server.CreateObject("Commerce.Dictionary")
   Set dContext.MessageManager = _
    Application("mscsMessageManager")
   Set dContext.DataFunctions = _
    Application("mscsDataFunctions")
   Set dContext.CatalogManager = _
    Application("mscsCatalogManager")
   Set dContext.CacheManager = _
    Application("mscsCacheManager")
   dContext.LanguageCode = sLanguage

   sPath = dPipeline.Path
   sPipeFile = dPipeline(sPipeName)
   RunPipe = mscsOrderGroup.RunPipe(sPath & sPipeFile, _
    Commerce.PooledTxPipeline", dContext)
End Function
```

Runing Through the Pipeline Component

You can execute a pipeline directly using one of the Commerce Server 2000 pipeline components. To execute the pipeline, you'll first need to load it and then execute it. All of the pipeline components, except the OrderPipeline, can be run using the Execute method. The OrderPipeline component uses the OrderExecute method, as shown here:

```
Function RunPipeline(sPipeName, dOrder, sPipeComponent)
   Dim mscsPipeline
   Dim dContext
   Dim dPipeline
```
(continued)

(continued)

```
Set dPipeline = Application("MSCSPipeline")

Set dContext = server.CreateObject("Commerce.Dictionary")

Set dContext.MessageManager = _
 Application("mscsMessageManager")

Set dContext.DataFunctions = Application("mscsDataFunctions")

Set dContext.CatalogManager = _
 Application("mscsCatalogManager")

Set dContext.CacheManager = Application("mscsCacheManager")

dContext.LanguageCode = sLanguage

sPath = dPipeline.Path

sPipeFile = dPipeline(sPipeName)

Select Case LCASE(sPipeComponent)

   Case "mts"

      Set mscsPipeline = _
       Server.CreateObject("Commerce.MTSPipeline")

   Case "mtstx"

      Set mscsPipeline = _
       Server.CreateObject("Commerce.MTSTxPipeline")

   Case "pooled"

      Set mscsPipeline = _
       Server.CreateObject("Commerce.PooledPipeline")

   Case "pooledtx"

      Set mscsPipeline = _
       Server.CreateObject("Commerce.PooledTxPipeline")

   Case "order"

      Set mscsPipeline = _
       Server.CreateObject("Commerce.OrderPipeline")

End Select

mscsPipeline.LoadPipe sPath & sPipeFile

If lcase(sPipeComponent) = "order" Then

   RunPipeline = mscsPipeline.OrderExecute(1, dOrder, _
    dContext, 0)

else
```

(continued)

(continued)

```
        RunPipeline = mscsPipeline.Execute(1, dOrder, dContext, 0)
    end if
End Function
```

Running a Single Pipeline Component

You can execute a single pipeline component using the MicroPipe object. To run the component, you'll need to call the SetComponent and specify the component's PROGID. You then call the Execute method to process the component (see the following code), passing it Order and Context Dictionaries with the information needed for the component.

```
Set mscsMicroPipe = Server.CreateObject("Commerce.MicroPipe")
mscsMicroPipe.SetComponent  "Commerce.RequiredProdInfo"
lResult = mscsMicroPipe.Execute(dOrder, dContext, 0)
```

Using the Pipeline Editor

Commerce Server 2000 provides the Pipeline Editor, which can be used to create and edit pipelines. It can be launched by clicking the Start menu, selecting Programs, selecting Microsoft Commerce Server 2000, and then selecting Pipeline Editor. This loads the pipeline, represented as a pipe with links for each stage and components as pipe joints, as shown in Figure 16-1.

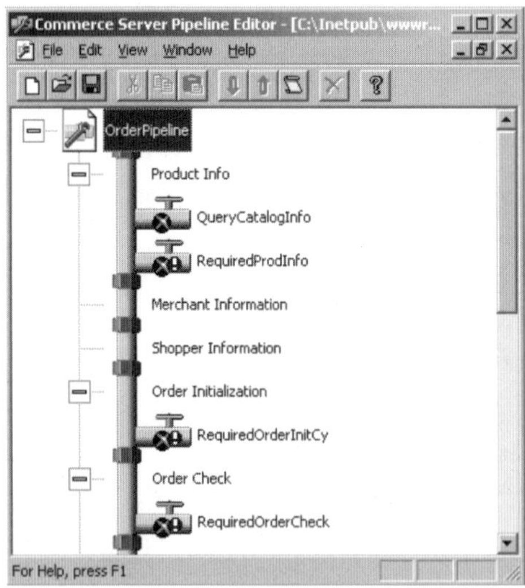

Figure 16-1. *The Commerce Server 2000 Pipeline Editor represents the pipeline visually with a pipe and joints.*

Opening a Pipeline

You can open a pipeline file by double-clicking its icon. You can also open it through the Pipeline Editor from the File menu, by clicking Open.

Creating a New Pipeline

You can create a new pipeline from the File menu by selecting New. You are presented with the Choose A Pipeline Template dialog box (Figure 16-2), from which you choose a template as a basis for the new pipeline. By selecting a template and clicking OK, you establish a new pipeline based on the chosen template.

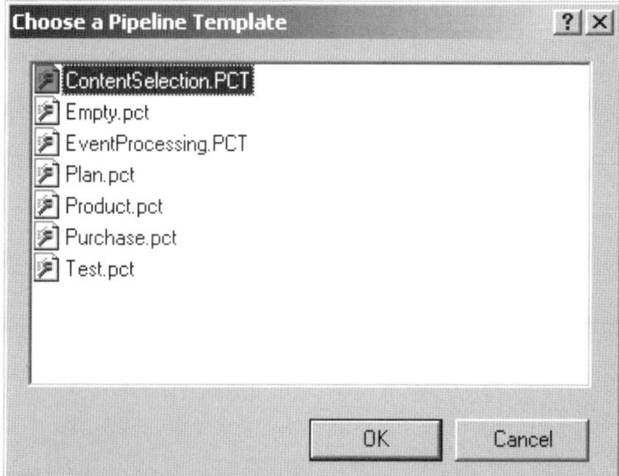

Figure 16-2. *Choose a template to begin creating a new pipeline.*

The following templates exist in the system:

- **ContentSelection** Basic CSP
- **Empty** An empty pipeline with no stages or components
- **EventProcessing** Basic EPP
- **Product** Basic Product Pipeline
- **Plan** Basic Plan Pipeline
- **Purchase** Basic Purchase Pipeline
- **Test** Simple pipeline with one stage and no components defined

These templates include the stages and components that were previously described for each, as a default. They can then be modified as required.

Viewing Pipeline Properties

You can view the properties of a pipeline by right-clicking on the pipeline name in the editor and selecting Properties. You are presented with the Pipeline Properties dialog box (Figure 16-3), where you can modify the pipeline settings, including the following:

- **Label** The label that displays as the pipeline name in the editor.
- **Transaction Compatibility** Identifies whether the pipeline requires transactional pipelines, nontransactional pipelines, or either.
- **Currency Mode** Identifies whether the pipeline will support currency and integer values or only currency values.
- **Supply A Currency LCID** You can select this check box to supply a Locale ID. Providing the Locale ID as 0 allows the pipeline to use the default on the server. Otherwise, the provided Locale ID is used.
- **Supply The Number Of Decimal Places Used For Currency Rounding** If the Currency (High-Precision) is selected as the currency mode, this check box and text box are enabled. You can use them to specify the number of decimal places that will be maintained for tracking currency.
- **Description** This text box holds a description of the pipeline.

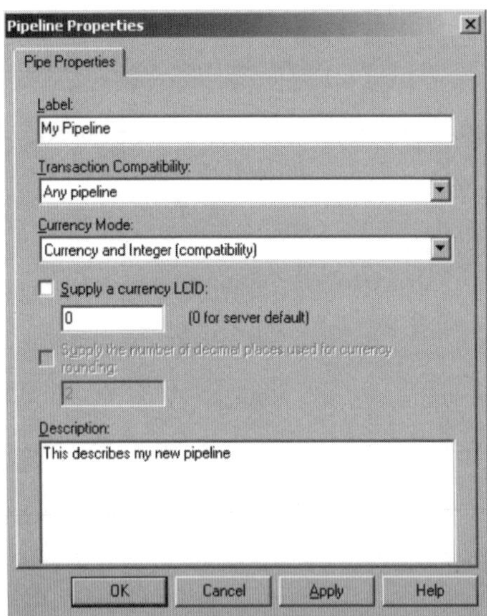

Figure 16-3. *Modify pipeline settings using the Pipeline Properties dialog box.*

Adding a Stage

With a pipeline open, you can add a stage by right-clicking on any stage and selecting Insert Stage from the shortcut menu. If you have existing stages in the pipeline, you'll need to specify whether the stage should be added before or after the current stage, as shown in Figure 16-4.

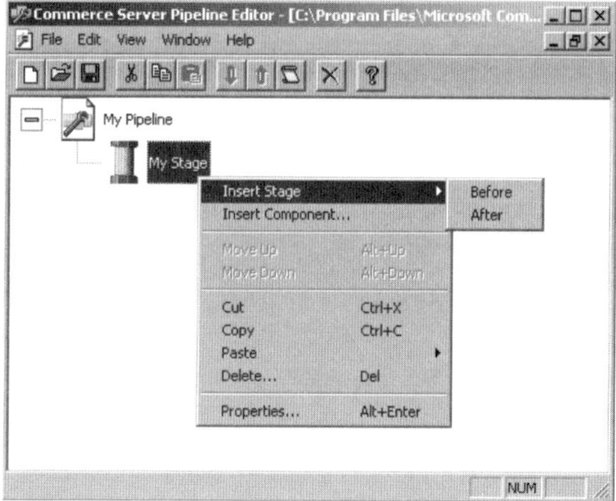

Figure 16-4. *You can add a stage to the pipeline via the Insert Stage command on the shortcut menu.*

Viewing Stage Properties

You can view the properties of any stage by right-clicking the desired stage and selecting Properties. You'll see the Stage Properties dialog box that holds the properties of the stage, as shown in Figure 16-5. These include the following:

- **Label** Holds the name of the stage.
- **Description** Holds a description for the stage.
- **GUID** A globally unique identifier (GUID) that uniquely identifies this stage.
- **Mode** For backward compatibility with Microsoft Site Server 2, this value should be set to 1, the default.
- **Error Level** Used as the threshold for the stage. If any component reports an error result equal to or higher than this number, the stage stops running and generates an error. Typically, this value should be left as 2.

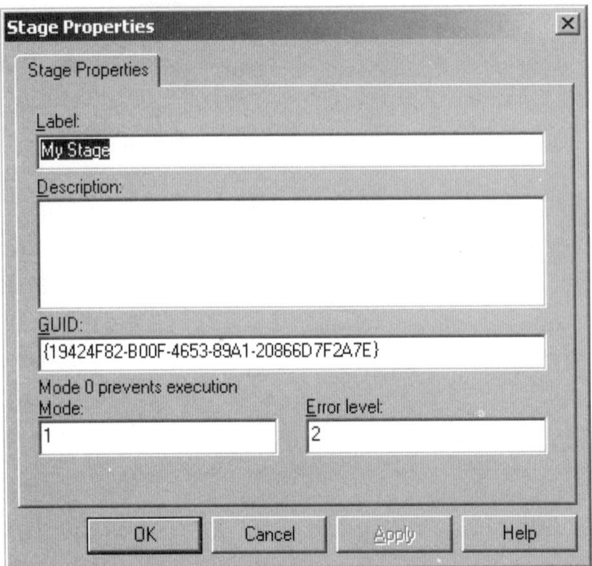

Figure 16-5. *View the properties of the stage in the Stage Properties dialog box.*

Removing a Stage

To remove a stage, you can highlight the stage and press DELETE or right-click and select Delete. This removes the stage and any components that are installed for the stage.

Adding a Component

You can add a component within any stage by right-clicking on the stage and selecting Insert Component from the shortcut menu. If you right-click a component within that stage, you can select Insert Component, but you have to specify whether the component will be inserted before or after the highlighted component. You'll then be presented with the Choose A Component dialog box (Figure 16-6) that lists the available components for this stage.

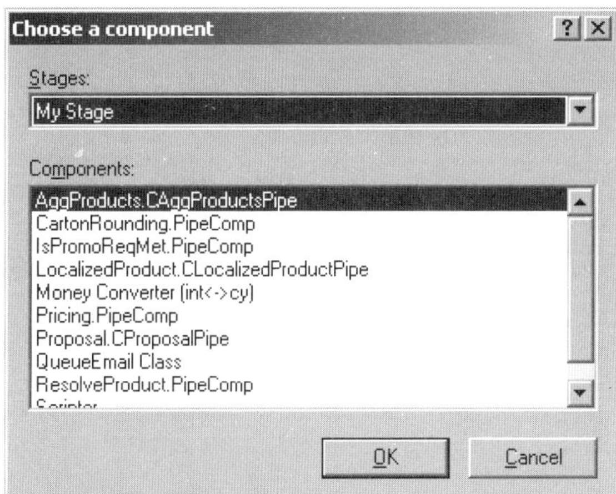

Figure 16-6. *The Choose A Component dialog box lists the available components for a stage.*

Component Properties

You can view the properties of a component by right-clicking the component and selecting Properties. Each component has at least two tabs in the Component Properties dialog box. The Component Properties tab (Figure 16-7) is used to display general properties about the component, including the following:

- **Label** This is the name of the component as shown in the pipeline.
- **Class ID** This is the Class ID of the pipeline component.
- **Program ID** This is the PROGID of the component.
- **Required** This check box is selected if the component is required in the pipeline and must be executed correctly.
- **Description** This is a description of the pipeline component.

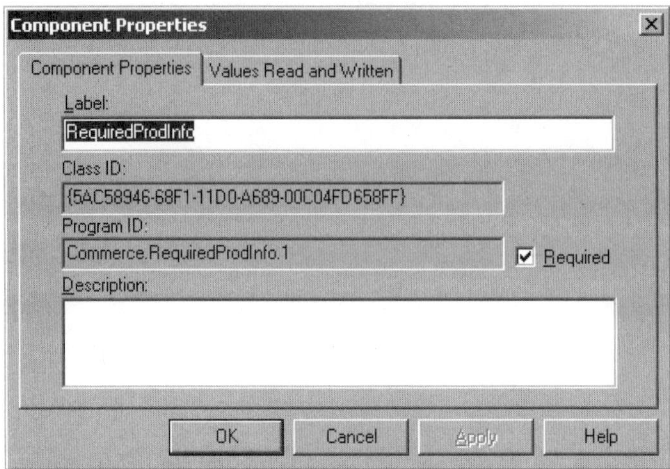

Figure 16-7. *The Component Properties tab is used to display general properties about the component.*

The Values Read And Written tab, shown in Figure 16-8, is used to identify the values that will be read from the Order and Context Dictionaries and the values that will be written in the Order Dictionary. These lists are useful in identifying what this component needs to see to execute correctly.

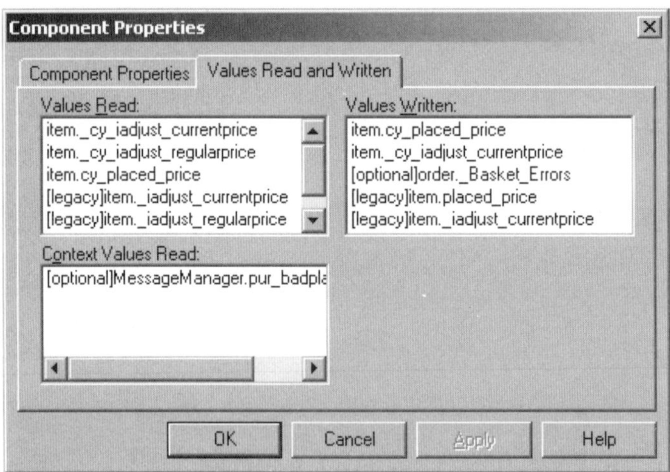

Figure 16-8. *The Values Read And Written tab is used to identify dictionary values.*

Removing a Component

To remove a component, you can highlight the desired component and press DELETE or right-click the component and select Delete.

Saving a Pipeline

To save a pipeline, from the File menu, select Save. If this is the first time you're saving the file, you'll need to specify a filename.

Pipeline Components Reference

The following sections provide a reference for the pipeline objects that are detailed in this chapter.

MicroPipe

The MicroPipe object is used to execute a single pipeline component without processing a pipeline file. Its methods are listed in Table 16-16.

Table 16-16. MicroPipe Methods

Method Name	Description
Execute	Executes the current pipeline component
SetComponent	Loads a pipeline component
SetLogFile	Specifies a file used to log pipeline events

MtsPipeline

The MtsPipeline object is used to process a pipeline that does not require transactional support. This object does not support pipeline component pooling. Table 16-17 describes this object's methods.

Table 16-17. MTSPipeline Methods

Method Name	Description
Execute	Executes the current pipeline
LoadPipe	Loads a pipeline from the pipeline file
SetLogFile	Specifies a file used to log pipeline events

MtsTxPipeline

The MtsTxPipeline object is used to process a pipeline that requires transactional support. This object does not support pipeline component pooling. Its methods are displayed in Table 16-18.

Table 16-18. MTSTxPipeline Methods

Method Name	Description
Execute	Executes the current pipeline
LoadPipe	Loads a pipeline from the pipeline file
SetLogFile	Specifies a file used to log pipeline events

OrderPipeline

The OrderPipeline object is used to process a CSP. This object does not provide transactional support, nor does it support pipeline component pooling. Table 16-19 lists the object's methods.

Table 16-19. OrderPipeline Methods

Method Name	Description
LoadPipe	Loads a pipeline from the pipeline file
OrderExecute	Executes the current pipeline
SetLogFile	Specifies a file used to log pipeline events

PooledPipeline

The PooledPipeline object is used to process a pipeline that does not require transactional support. This object supports pipeline component pooling. Table 16-20 lists the methods of the PooledPipeline object.

Table 16-20. PooledPipeline Methods

Method Name	Description
Execute	Executes the current pipeline
LoadPipe	Loads a pipeline from the pipeline file
SetLogFile	Specifies a file used to log pipeline events

PooledTxPipeline

The PooledTxPipeline object is used to process a pipeline that does not require transactional support. This object supports pipeline component pooling. The object's methods are described in Table 16-21.

Table 16-21. PooledTxPipeline Methods

Method Name	Description
Execute	Executes the current pipeline
LoadPipe	Loads a pipeline from the pipeline file
SetLogFile	Specifies a file used to log pipeline events

Chapter 17

Building Custom Pipeline Components

You will frequently need some functionality in the pipeline that is not available in the pipeline components that ship with Microsoft Commerce Server 2000. One thing you can do is find a third-party component that meets your needs, and often this is definitely the best course of action. For instance, you'll probably want to purchase components to validate and authorize credit card payments or handle tax calculations, as these tasks involve very complicated procedures and requirements.

However, there are many times that you might want to write your own components to specifically meet the needs of your site. For instance, you might want to provide a component that integrates with some of your legacy systems. Examples might include applying special discounts for premium or special users or linking inventory data with your Enterprise Resource Planning (ERP) system.

There are several ways to provide this custom functionality in your site. You can write the functionality in script and place it in a scriptor component. This component is ideal for use in fairly simple, straightforward tasks.

You could also develop a custom pipeline component. These components can be written in Microsoft Visual Basic or Microsoft Visual C++. You can expect to get better performance from the components than with similar functionality in script. In addition, you gain the greater functionality that these languages provide.

Custom Pipeline Strategies

There are a number of common techniques that you'll use, regardless of whether the component is based on a scriptor or your own component.

Using Context Dictionary Values

From the scriptor or your custom component, a Context Dictionary object is passed in as a parameter to the MSCSExecute method. This dictionary object contains any number of values or objects that might be useful. Typical objects that might be found in the Context Dictionary include the following:

- MessageManager object
- CacheManager object
- CatalogManager object
- DataFunctions object
- Database Connection Strings

In addition, other helpful values can easily be added to the dictionary to support the needs of your pipeline code. Any changes you make to the Context Dictionary are passed back to the calling application.

Using Order Dictionary Values

The Order Dictionary object contains the data you will be working directly on. When working with an Order Processing Pipeline, the Order Dictionary contains the OrderForm and all of its contents. You can then manage the data within the order as necessary. Any changes you make to the order are returned back to the calling application.

Returning Results

When a pipeline component is executed, it should return one of the three following values that indicate the success or failure of the component:

- **1 – Success** This code executed without any errors.
- **2 – Warning** This code executed with some problems, but the problems were not so significant that processing of the pipeline should be halted.
- **3 – Error** Critical problems were encountered in this component and pipeline processing should be halted.

You might want to define constants for your scripts, as shown here, to make the code more readable:

```
const PIPE_GOOD = 1

const PIPE_WARN = 2

const PIPE_ERROR = 3
```

Reporting Errors

If an error occurs, you will identify it based on the return code. However, this doesn't identify the particular error that occurred. The OrderForm has two

SimpleLists that can be used to pass error messages back to the calling application. These SimpleLists can be found in the following dictionary keys:

- **_Basket_Errors** Used to identify errors during the basket processing phases of order management
- **_Purchase_Errors** Used to identify errors during the order purchase phases of order management

When an error occurs, you'll add the appropriate key that corresponds to an error in the MessageManager's RC.XML source file. In this way, the calling application can use the MessageManager to retrieve the description of the error that matches the user's language requirements, as seen here:

```
Set slBasketErrors = oOrderForm("_Basket_Errors")

Call  slBasketErrors.Add("pur_aggregate_items")

Set OrderForm("_Basket_Errors") = oBasketErrors
```

Scriptor Components

A scriptor component is a simple component that can be written in either VBScript or JavaScript. The script can be maintained either internally in the scriptor component or in an external file that can be referenced by the scriptor component. You'll identify the location of the script in the properties dialog box of the scriptor component, which can be seen in Figure 17-1.

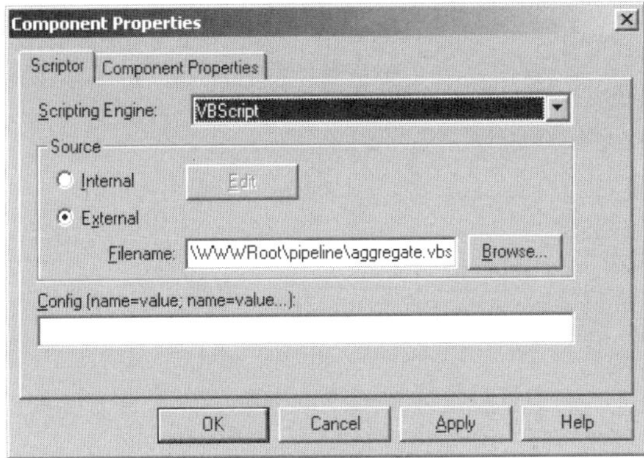

Figure 17-1. *When you create a scriptor component, you can define whether the component will maintain the script code internally or reference an external file with the script code.*

Internal

The Scriptor component provides an internal editor where you can write the script code. The editor, shown in Figure 17-2, is fairly rudimentary, but will support your needs in creating the component.

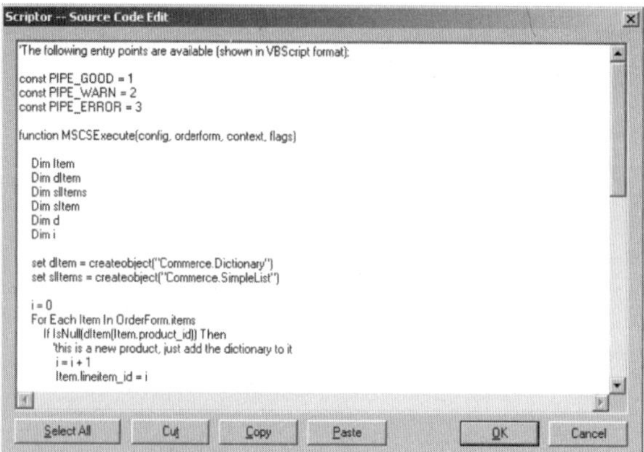
Scriptor -- Source Code Edit
'The following entry points are available (shown in VBScript format):
const PIPE_GOOD = 1
const PIPE_WARN = 2
const PIPE_ERROR = 3
function MSCSExecute(config, orderform, context, flags)
Dim Item
Dim dItem
Dim slItems
Dim sItem
Dim d
Dim i
set dItem = createobject("Commerce.Dictionary")
set slItems = createobject("Commerce.SimpleList")
i = 0
For Each Item In OrderForm.items
If IsNull(dItem(Item.product_id)) Then
'this is a new product, just add the dictionary to it
i = i + 1
Item.lineitem_id = i
Select All
Cut
Copy
Paste
OK
Cancel

Figure 17-2. *The scriptor component provides an internal editor to contain and manage the script.*

An advantage of the internal script code is that it is easier to deploy, as the code goes along with the scriptor component. However, it can be less convenient to make modifications. In addition, if you want to provide the same functionality in multiple pipelines, you'll need to duplicate the code several times, making it more difficult to maintain.

External

The scriptor can also reference an external script file. The script code is exactly the same as the internal code, except that it is located in a separate file, which can make it easier to maintain. It also provides the ability to use the code in multiple scriptor components in multiple pipelines by specifying the exact path to the scriptor file as the external filename for the scriptor.

Script Contents

The standard script you write contains the following three basic methods:

- MSCSOpen
- MSCSClose
- MSCSExecute

MSCSOpen

The MSCSOpen method, shown here, is used to initialize any values or components as the scriptor is initiated:

```
sub MSCSOpen(config)

end sub
```

MSCSClose

The MSCSClose method, displayed here, is used to clean up any values or components as the scriptor is completed:

```
sub MSCSClose()

end sub
```

MSCSExecute

The MSCSExecute method is the main method you'll use in the scriptor. It provides the primary entry point for the processing of the scriptor. It receives the OrderForm and Context Dictionaries as parameters. It also includes parameters for the Config and Flags parameters, but these are not used in this example:

```
const PIPE_GOOD = 1
const PIPE_WARN = 2
const PIPE_ERROR = 3

function MSCSExecute(config, orderform, context, flags)
   Dim Item
   Dim dItem
   Dim vItem
   Dim slItems
   Dim d
   Dim i

   set dItem = createobject("Commerce.Dictionary")
   set slItems = createobject("Commerce.SimpleList")

   i = 0

'First, loop through all items in the OrderForm
   For Each Item In OrderForm.items
      If IsNull(dItem(Item.product_id)) Then
'If this is the first time you've seen the Item, add it to a
'dictionary to hold all new items.
         i = i + 1
         Item.lineitem_id = i
         Set dItem(Item.product_id) = Item
```

(continued)

(continued)

```
      Else
'This item has already been in once, so just add the
'quantity to the quantity in the holding dictionary
         Set d = dItem(Item.product_id)
         d.quantity = cint(d.quantity) + cint(Item.quantity)
         Set dItem(Item.product_id) = d
      End If
   Next

'Go through each item in the holding dictionary
'and put it in the SimpleList
   For Each vItem In dItem
      slItems.Add dItem(vItem)
   Next
'Put the SimpleList of items in the Items SimpleList of the
   'OrderForm
   Set OrderForm.items = slItems


   if Err.number then
      MSCSExecute = PIPE_ERROR
      Set slBasketErrors = OrderForm("_Basket_Errors")
      Call slBasketErrors.Add("pur_aggregate_items")
      Set OrderForm("_Basket_Errors") = oBasketErrors
   else
      MSCSExecute = PIPE_GOOD
   end if
End Function
```

You can provide any script code that you want in the scriptor component, including additional functions and other values.

Pipeline Components

In addition to the scriptor components, you might want to build the code into a custom pipeline component that is developed in Visual C++ or Visual Basic.

Language Choice

Your choice of language for developing a custom component will depend on a number of factors, including your experience with Visual Basic and Visual C++. Because Visual Basic only supports apartment-threaded components, and not free-threaded components, these components will not perform as well as the Visual C++ components, in general.

If you are creating pipelines that will be established to run globally, such as by storing the pipelines in an application variable, Visual Basic components can't be used in MtsOrderPipeline or MtsTxOrderPipelines objects. They will need to be run using the OrderPipeline object. However, the MtsOrderPipeline and MtsTxOrderPipelines support Visual Basic components easily when the are created on each page where they are used.

Tip To provide efficient performance by Visual Basic components, select the Unattended Execution and Retained In Memory check boxes in the Project Properties dialog box, as shown in Figure 17-3.

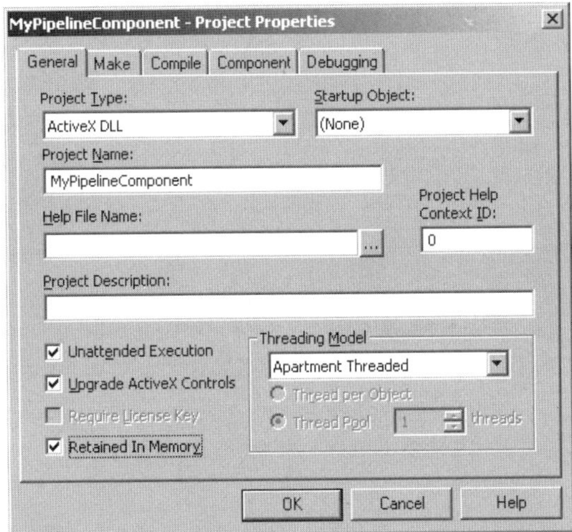

Figure 17-3. *Visual Basic pipeline components should have the Unattended Execution and Retained In Memory check boxes enabled.*

Interfaces

Any pipeline component that you build can implement a number of interfaces, but the one interface that must be provided is the IPipelineComponent; all other interfaces are optional. However, you should also implement the IPipelineComponentDescription interface, at minimum.

IPipelineComponent

The IPipelineComponent interface must be implemented in your pipeline component because it is used to execute the pipeline component. It contains the following methods that you'll need to code for:

- **EnabledDesign** Used to define the mode in which the component is run, either design mode or execution mode. Execution mode is the default. Design mode is more error-tolerant and can be useful in designing and testing the component.
- **Execute** Provides the main functionality of the component. This event is triggered when the pipeline executes the component.

IPipelineComponentDescription

The IPipelineComponentDescription is used to provide a list of values that are read and written by the pipeline component. The values specified in the events of this interface appear in the Component Properties dialog box in the Values Read And Written tab, shown in Figure 17-4. In this way, users of the pipeline can identify the values that must be present in the appropriate dictionary and understand which values are being written back to the Order Dictionary.

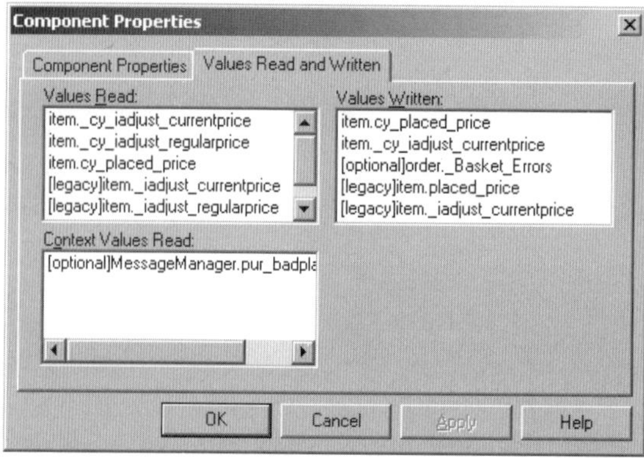

Figure 17-4. *Each pipeline component should advertise the values that it will be working with in both the Order and Context dictionaries.*

The IPipelineComponentDescription interface includes the following methods:

- **ContextValuesRead** Uses a SAFEARRAY variant to identify the keys from the Context Dictionary that will be used by this component
- **ValuesRead** Uses a SAFEARRAY variant to identify the keys from the Order Dictionary that will be used by this component
- **ValuesWritten** Uses a SAFEARRAY variant to identify the keys in the Order Dictionary that will be created or updated by this component

IPipelineComponentAdmin

The IPipelineComponentAdmin interface is used to provide design time support for the component within the pipeline editor. Dictionary objects are used to maintain the configuration settings by the events of this interface. These methods include the following:

- **GetConfigData** Retrieves a Dictionary object that contains configuration settings for the component
- **SetConfigData** Creates a Dictionary object that contains configuration settings for the component

These events are called from the user interface that is used in the pipeline editor to manage these settings and save and retrieve them.

ISpecifyPipelineComponentUI

The ISpecifyPipelineComponentUI interface is used to identify the component that provides the user interface to manage the configuration settings for the pipeline component. The component to which this interface refers must implement the IPipelineComponentUI interface. ISpecifyPipelineComponentUI provides the following method:

- **GetPipelineComponentUIProgID** Specifies the PROGID of the component that implements the IPipelineComponentUI that will be used as the user interface for managing the properties of this pipeline component

IPipelineComponentUI

The IPipelineComponetUI interface is used to display a dialog box that manages the properties of the pipeline component in the pipeline editor. The interface provides the following method:

- **ShowProperties** Called by the pipeline editor to display a dialog box that manages the component properties

ISpecifyPropertyPages

The ISpecifyPropertyPages interface is a standard Win32 object linking and embedding (OLE) interface that is used by components that support property pages in the pipeline editor. The editor can use this interface to utilize the property pages as a part of the component Properties dialog box. The interface includes this method:

- **GetPages** Returns an array of Class IDs (CLSIDs) that indicate which property pages will be displayed in the properties dialog

IPersistDictionary

The IPersistDictionary interface is used to save or read data from a Dictionary object. The interface provides the following methods:

- **GetProgID** Returns the PROGID of the object
- **InitNew** Initializes settings before loading values from the Dictionary
- **IsDirty** Identifies if any values have changed and need to be saved

- **Load** Loads data values from the Dictionary
- **Save** Saves data values to the Dictionary

IPersistStreamInit

The IPersistStreamInit interface is a standard Win32 OLE interface that allows the object to use stream-based persistence. The pipeline components use this interface to save or load the pipeline configuration files. This interface provides the following methods:

- **GetClassID** Returns the CLSID of the object
- **GetSizeMax** Returns the number of bytes in the stream needed to save the persisted data
- **InitNew** Initializes settings before saved values are loaded
- **IsDirty** Identifies if any values have changed and need to be saved
- **Load** Loads the data values from the stream
- **Save** Saves the data values to the stream

Visual Basic Pipeline Component Wizard

You can develop your own components to support your needs simply by implementing the interfaces described in the previous sections. However, the Commerce Server 2000 Software Development Kit (SDK) includes a Visual Basic Pipeline Component Wizard that creates the initial pipeline component. You can use that starting component and then plug in your own code to get the results you want.

You can find the Visual Basic Pipeline Component Wizard in the Commerce Server 2000 SDK in the \Tools\VB Pipe Wizard directory. The wizard file is named PIPELINE COMPONENT WIZARD.VBZ. By double-clicking on this file, you can launch the Visual Basic Pipeline Component Wizard, which creates the base pipeline component.

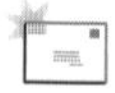

Note Before you start using the Pipeline Wizard, you must register the support DLL, PIPELINECOMPWIZARD.DLL, which can be found in the same directory as the wizard.

Step 1: Support Transactions

Once you launch the Visual Basic Pipeline Component Wizard, you step through six dialog boxes, supplying information that is used to build the sample code base for your pipeline component. In the first step, you'll identify if the pipeline component should support transactions, as shown in Figure 17-5. If it does, the pipeline component can be run in transactional pipelines.

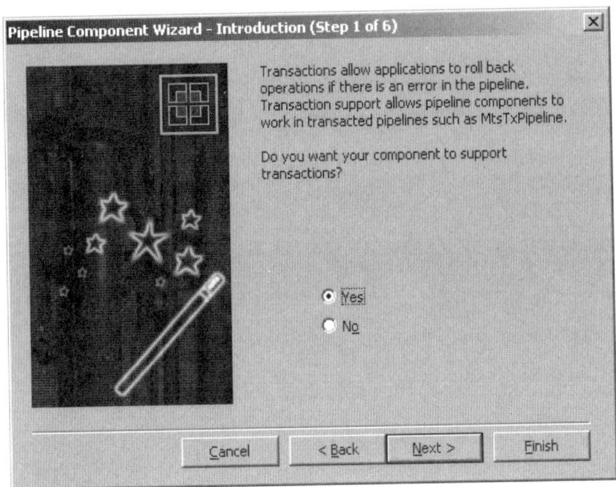

Figure 17-5. *Do you want your component to support transactions?*

When you select Yes on the Introduction wizard page, the wizard automatically implements the MTS Object Control that is used to support transactions. The code that is inserted by selecting Yes is shown here:

```
Implements ObjectControl

' For storing the transaction context supplied by COM+
Dim g_objCtx As ObjectContext

Private Sub ObjectControl_Activate()

   Set g_objCtx = GetObjectContext()

End Sub

Private Function ObjectControl_CanBePooled() As Boolean

   ObjectControl_CanBePooled = False

End Function

Private Sub ObjectControl_Deactivate()

   Set g_objCtx = Nothing

End Sub
```

Step 2: Shipment Processing

The next step in the wizard is to identify whether you need shipment processing code in your component. Unless your component is specifically dealing with shipments, you'll likely select No in the Transaction Support wizard page, as shown in Figure 17-6.

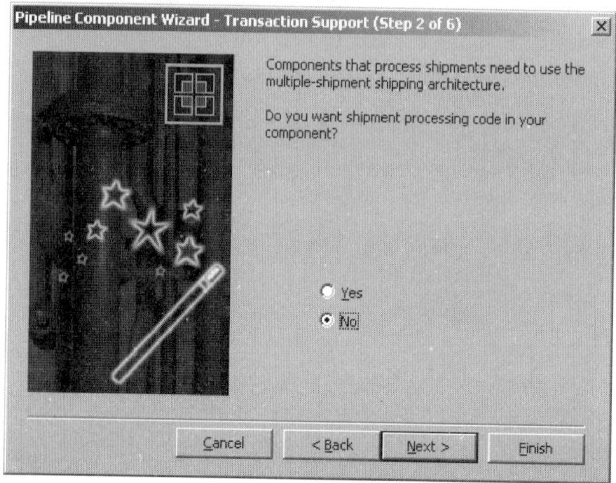

Figure 17-6. *Do you want shipment processing code in your component?*

If you select Yes here, the wizard inserts the basic logic you'll need to process through the multiple shipments. Of course, you'll have to fill in all of the details yourself. The following code is inserted into the IPipelineComponent_Execute method if you select Yes:

```
' Shipping components iterate over a list of shipments to process

Dim objShipment As CDictionary

Dim objShipmentsToProcess As CSimpleList

Dim objAddresses As CDictionary 'Ship-to addresses

Set objShipmentsToProcess = _
 objPipeCtx.Value("shipments_to_process")

For Each objShipment In objShipmentsToProcess

' Your code for handling shipping addresses goes here

Next
```

Step 3: Pipeline Component Properties

You can create a set of properties that will be persisted and used to manage the way in which the pipeline component works in the Shipping Support page of the Pipeline Component Wizard, displayed in Figure 17-7. If you establish a set of properties, you'll probably want to build a user interface that can be used from within the pipeline editor to maintain values for the properties. The Pipeline Component Wizard creates this code for you.

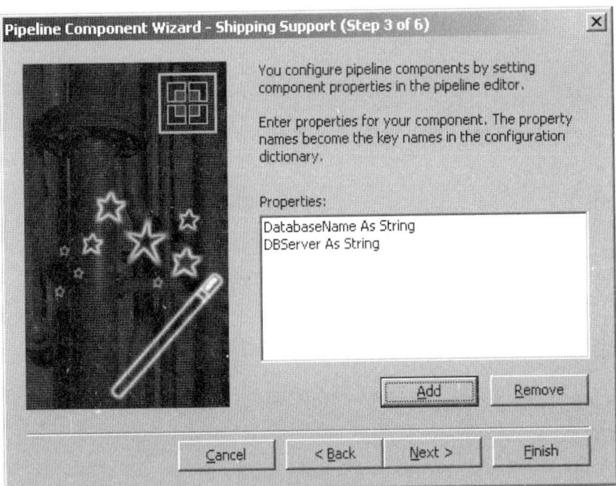

Figure 17-7. *Enter properties for your component in the Shipping Support wizard page.*

When you click Add, you'll be able to create properties for the component in the Add Property dialog box (see Figure 17-8), in which you'll specify the property name and data type. The data types supported include the following:

- Boolean
- Byte
- Currency
- Date
- Double
- Integer
- Long
- String
- Variant

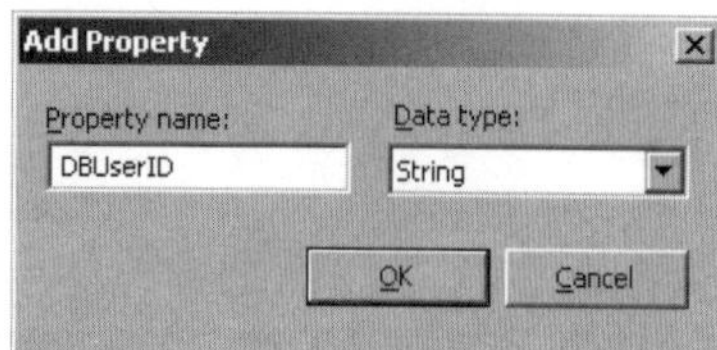

Figure 17-8. *Add a pipeline component property in the Add Property dialog box.*

When a property is created, code is added in several places in the component to save and load the properties from persistent storage, as shown in this code sample:

```
Private m_strDBConnection As String

Private Function IPersistDictionary_GetProgID() As String

 IPersistDictionary_GetProgID = "MySamplePipe.CMySamplePipeComp"

End Function

Private Sub IPersistDictionary_InitNew()

 fIsDirty = False

End Sub

Private Function IPersistDictionary_IsDirty() As Long

 IPersistDictionary_IsDirty = fIsDirty

End Function

Public Property Let DBConnection(ByVal strValue As String)
 m_strDBConnection = strValue
End Property

Public Property Get DBConnection() As String
 DBConnection = m_strDBConnection
End Property

Private Function IPipelineComponentAdmin_GetConfigData() As Object

 Dim objDict As MSCSCoreLib.CDictionary
 Set objDict = CreateObject("Commerce.Dictionary")
```
(continued)

(continued)

```
 objDict.Value("DBConnection") = m_strDBConnection

 Set IPipelineComponentAdmin_GetConfigData = objDict

End Function

Private Sub IPersistDictionary_Save(ByVal objDict As Object, _
 ByVal fSameAsLoad As Long)

 objDict.Value("DBConnection") = m_strDBConnection

 fSameAsLoad = False

End Sub

Private Function _
 ISpecifyPipelineComponentUI_GetPipelineComponentUIProgID() _
 As String

 ISpecifyPipelineComponentUI_GetPipelineComponentUIProgID = _
  "MySamplePipeUI.CMySamplePipeCompUI"

End Function

Private Sub IPipelineComponentAdmin_SetConfigData(ByVal objDict _
 As Object)

 m_strDBConnection = objDict.Value("DBConnection")

End Sub

Private Sub IPersistDictionary_Load(ByVal objDict As Object)

 m_strDBConnection = objDict.Value("DBConnection")

End Sub
```

Note Regardless of whether or not properties are created for the component, the wizard still implements the interfaces IPersistDictionary and IPipelineComponentAdmin.

In addition to that code, a second project is created to handle the form that will be displayed from the pipeline editor. This project includes a base class that is used to interact with the pipeline component and a Visual Basic form that is used to display and edit component properties, as can be seen in Figure 17-9.

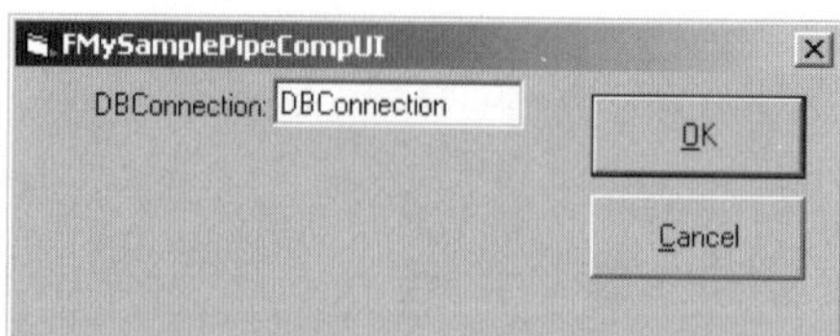

Figure 17-9. *The Pipeline Component UI Visual Basic form is used to display and edit component properties.*

The code created to work with this user interface can be found in the class of this project, as shown in the following sample:

```
Option Explicit

Implements IPipelineComponentUI

Private Sub IPipelineComponentUI_ShowProperties( _
 ByVal pdispComponent As Object)

 On Error GoTo HandleError

 'Use IPipelineComponentAdmin Interface to get configuration
'information

 Dim pdispPCA As IPipelineComponentAdmin

 Set pdispPCA = pdispComponent

 'Populate a dictionary with component configuration

 Dim dictConfig As CDictionary

 Set dictConfig = pdispPCA.GetConfigData

 Dim FMySamplePipeCompUIObj As New FMySamplePipeCompUI

 'Display the properties for the user to edit

 FMySamplePipeCompUIObj.txtDBConnection.Text = _
  dictConfig.Value("DBConnection")

 FMySamplePipeCompUIObj.Show 1

 If FMySamplePipeCompUIObj.fOk Then

 'Save entered values into the dictionary

   dictConfig.Value("DBConnection") = _
     CStr(FMySamplePipeCompUIObj.txtDBConnection.Text)
```
(continued)

(continued)

```
'Update the component with new configuration information
   pdispPCA.SetConfigData dictConfig
 End If

 Set pdispPCA = Nothing
 Set dictConfig = Nothing
 Exit Sub

HandleError:
 MsgBox Err.Description & " " & Err.Number
End Sub
```

Step 4: Project Properties

Next, in the Component Properties wizard page (see Figure 17-10), you need to specify the Visual Basic project, class, and form filenames. These are the names of the files under which the components are saved. In addition, the class and form names are used as references within the code to those elements.

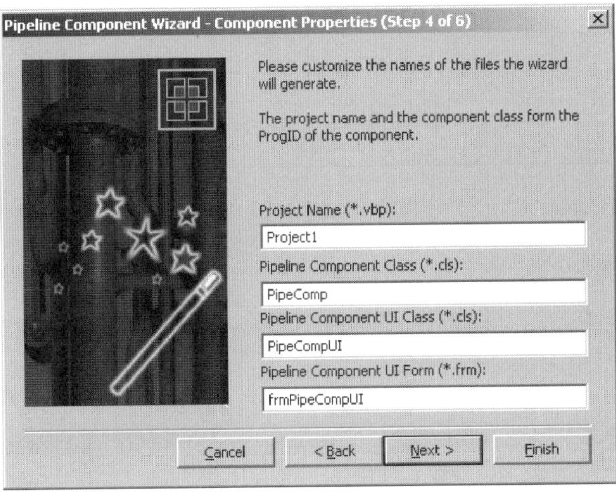

Figure 17-10. *Name the project, class, and form files in the Component Properties wizard page.*

Step 5: Project Directory

Once you've named the forms, you'll need to identify the directory in which the project files will be created and saved in the Project, Class, And Form Names page shown in Figure 17-11.

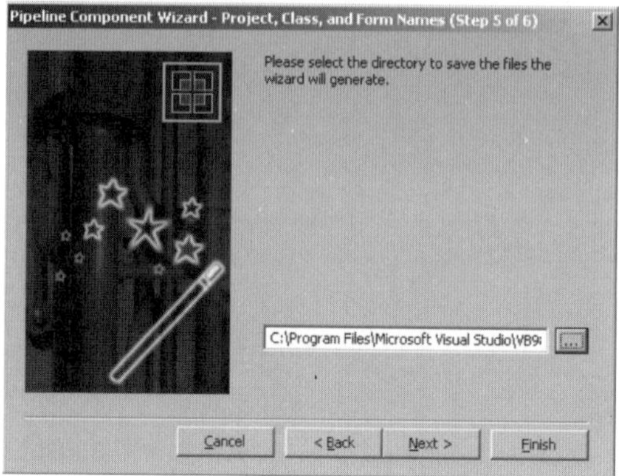

Figure 17-11. *Project files will be saved into this directory.*

Step 6: Finish

Now that you've gathered all of the data needed, in the Select Directory page (see Figure 17-12), you'll simply click Finish to complete the process. Once you click Finish, the projects, classes, and forms are created and saved in Visual Basic. You'll be left in the Visual Basic Integrated Development Environment (IDE), ready to begin coding.

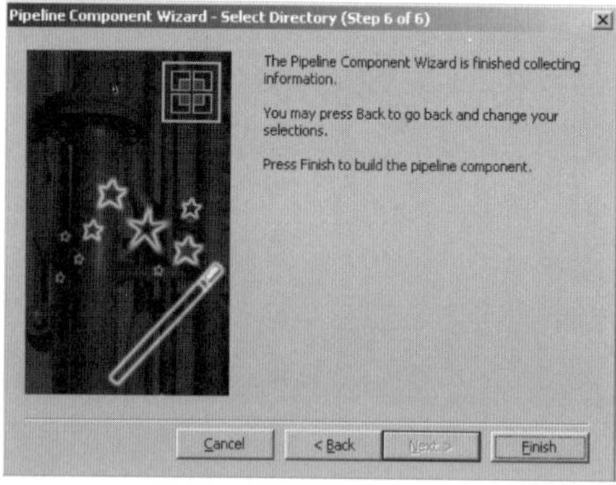

Figure 17-12. *Click Finish to allow the wizard to build your projects.*

Resulting Base Code

In addition to the code shown in the previous sections, the Visual Basic Pipeline Component Wizard inserts code to support the pipeline functionality. The set of code shown here is used as the basis for the functionality needed to execute a pipeline task by implementing the IPipelineComponent interface:

```
Private Sub IPipelineComponent_EnableDesign(
 ByVal fEnable As Long)

End Sub


Private Function IPipelineComponent_Execute(ByVal objOrderForm
 As Object, ByVal objContext As Object, ByVal lFlags As Long)
 As Long

Dim objPipeCtx As CDictionary 'Pipe Context

Dim objItems As CSimpleList 'Items

Dim objMsgMgr As Object 'Message Manager


' Return 1 for Success

IPipelineComponent_Execute = 1


' Initialize the Pipe Context and Order Form


Set objPipeCtx = objContext

Set objOrderForm = objOrderForm


' Initialize the Message Manager and get the Items from the Order
 'Form

Set objMsgMgr = objPipeCtx.Value("MessageManager")

Set objItems = objOrderForm.Value("Items")


End Function
```

In addition, the wizard provides code to implement the IPipelineComponentDescription interface, which is used to report to the pipeline editor what Order and Context Dictionary values are read and written:

```
Private Function
  IPipelineComponentDescription_ContextValuesRead()
 As Variant

 IPipelineComponentDescription_ContextValuesRead = Array("None")


End Function
```

(continued)

(continued)

```
Private Function IPipelineComponentDescription_ValuesRead()
 As Variant

 IPipelineComponentDescription_ValuesRead = Array("None")

End Function

Private Function IPipelineComponentDescription_ValuesWritten()
 As Variant

 IPipelineComponentDescription_ValuesWritten = Array("None")

End Function
```

As mentioned previously in this chapter, the IPipelineComponent interface is required, and the IPipelineComponentDescription interface is optional. However, at a minimum, both should be implemented in every pipeline component.

Active Template Library Pipeline Wizard

You can build a pipeline component in an Active Template Library (ATL) C++ component. You can manually create and code the necessary interfaces, but fortunately, Commerce Server 2000 provides an ATL Pipeline Wizard in the SDK that can be used to automatically create the base C++ project and files.

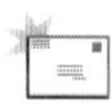

Note Before you can use the ATL Pipeline Wizard, you must register the supporting DLL, COMMERCEDLG.DLL, on the development machine. This can be found in the SDK, in the \Tools\ATL Pipe Wizard directory.

Step 1: Creating the C++ ATL Project

When you want to create the application, you'll start by launching Visual C++. In the IDE, you'll create a new workspace by opening the File menu and selecting New. You'll be presented with the New dialog box, as shown in Figure 17-13, where you'll identify that the workspace you're creating is an ATL project.

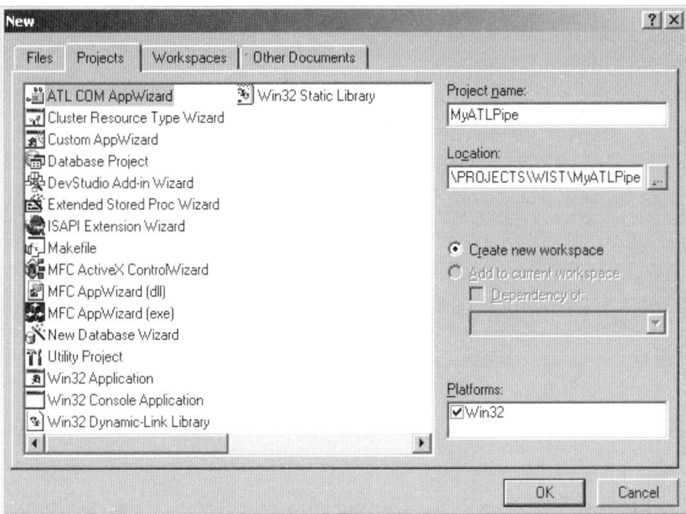

Figure 17-13. *Create an ATL project in the Projects tab of the New dialog box.*

Step 2: Creating a DLL

Next, you'll specify that you are going to create a DLL in the ATL COM AppWizard page, shown in Figure 17-14.

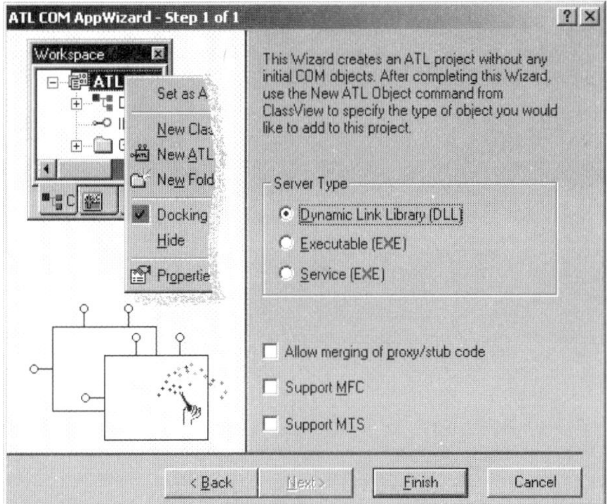

Figure 17-14. *Create an ATL COM application by selecting the Dynamic Link Library (DLL) option.*

Step 3: Completing the ATL COM Application

Finally, you'll confirm the ATL application creation options you've selected in the New Project Information dialog box seen in Figure 17-15.

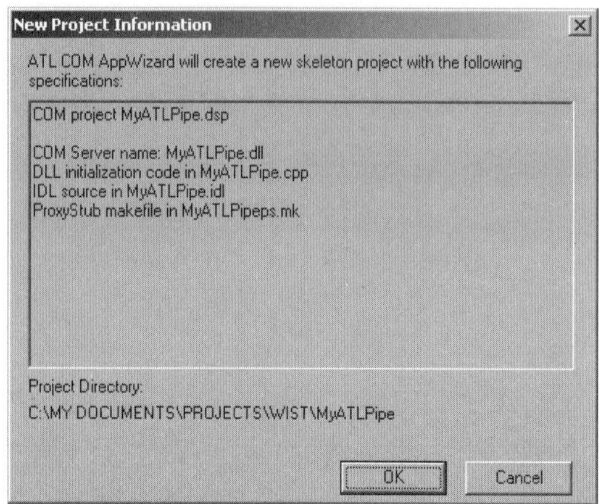

Figure 17-15. *Finish creating an ATL COM application in the New Project Information dialog box.*

Step 4: Adding an ATL Object

Once the project workspace is created, you'll insert the pipeline interfaces by opening the Insert menu and selecting New ATL Object in the IDE. You'll be presented with the ATL Object Wizard dialog box, shown in Figure 17-16, that will include the Pipeline Component object in the list. Click Pipeline Component and then click Next.

Figure 17-16. *Add the ATL Pipeline Component object with the ATL Object Wizard.*

Step 5: ATL Pipeline Component Names

You'll provide the name of the C++ files in the ATL Object Wizard Properties dialog box (see Figure 17-17). The names assigned here are the basis for identifying the file, class, and interface names in the project.

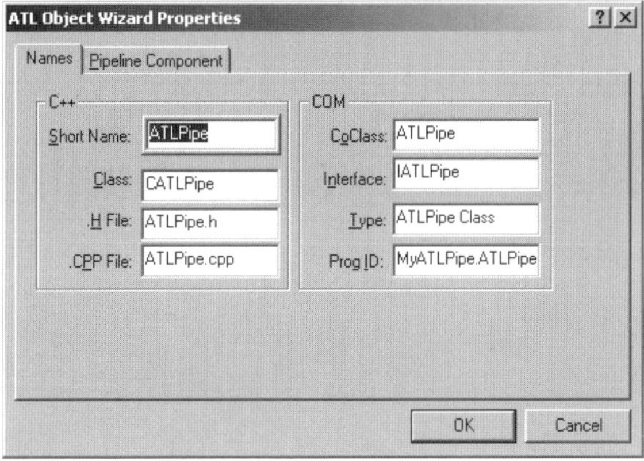

Figure 17-17. *Specify the application, class, and interface names in the ATL Object Wizard Properties dialog box.*

Step 6: ATL Pipeline Component Interfaces

In the Pipeline Component tab of the ATL Object Wizard Properties dialog box, shown in Figure 17-18, you'll also specify the interfaces and other code settings that you want to add to your project. The IPipelineComponent interface is automatically implemented. At a minimum, you should plan on implementing the IPipelineComponentDescription interface. If you want to support transactions in the component, you should also implement the IObjectControl interface.

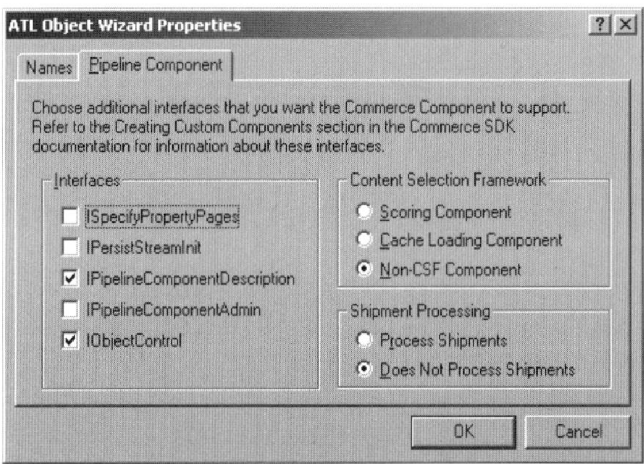

Figure 17-18. *Select the interfaces and other code settings for the application.*

Component Header Code

Once the wizard is completed, you'll find the .h header file that includes the base code definitions, as listed here:

```
// ATLPipe.h : Declaration of the CATLPipe

#ifndef __ATLPIPE_H_
#define __ATLPIPE_H_

#include "resource.h" // main symbols
#include "computil.h"
#include "pipeline.h"
#include "pipecomp.h"
#include "pipe_stages.h"
#include "mtx.h"

#define PIPECOMP_STATUS_OK 0
#define PIPECOMP_STATUS_WARN 1
#define PIPECOMP_STATUS_FAIL 2
/////////////////////////////////////////////////////////////////////////////
// CATLPipe
class ATL_NO_VTABLE CATLPipe :
public CComObjectRootEx<CComMultiThreadModel>,
public CComCoClass<CATLPipe, &CLSID_ATLPipe>,
public ISupportErrorInfo,
public IPipelineComponent,
public IDispatchImpl<IPipelineComponentDescription,
 &IID_IPipelineComponentDescription, &LIBID_MYATLPIPELib>,
public IObjectControl,
public IDispatchImpl<IATLPipe, &IID_IATLPipe,
 &LIBID_MYATLPIPELib>
{
public:
CATLPipe()
```
(continued)

(continued)

```
{

}
BEGIN_COM_MAP(CATLPipe)
COM_INTERFACE_ENTRY(IATLPipe)
COM_INTERFACE_ENTRY2(IDispatch, IATLPipe)
COM_INTERFACE_ENTRY(IPipelineComponent)
COM_INTERFACE_ENTRY(IPipelineComponentDescription)
COM_INTERFACE_ENTRY(ISupportErrorInfo)
COM_INTERFACE_ENTRY(IObjectControl)
END_COM_MAP()
// ISupportsErrorInfo
STDMETHOD(InterfaceSupportsErrorInfo)(REFIID riid);
// IATLPipe
public:
// IPipelineComponent
STDMETHOD(Execute)(
        IDispatch* pdispOrder,
        IDispatch* pdispContext,
        LONG lFlags,
        LONG* plErrorLevel);
STDMETHOD (EnableDesign) (BOOL fEnable);

// IPipelineComponentDescription
STDMETHOD(ContextValuesRead)(VARIANT *pVarRead);
STDMETHOD(ValuesRead)(VARIANT *pVarRead);
STDMETHOD(ValuesWritten)(VARIANT *pVarWritten);

static HRESULT WINAPI UpdateRegistry(BOOL bRegister)
```

(continued)

(continued)

```
{
   HRESULT hr = _Module.UpdateRegistryFromResource(IDR_ATLPIPE,
    bRegister);
   if (SUCCEEDED(hr))
   {
      // TODO: Add stage affinities here
       hr = RegisterCATID(GetObjectCLSID(),
         CATID_MSCSPIPELINE_COMPONENT);
       hr = RegisterCATID(GetObjectCLSID(),
         CATID_MSCSPIPELINE_ANYSTAGE);
   }
   return hr;
};

// IObjectControl
public:
STDMETHOD(Activate)();
STDMETHOD_(VOID, Deactivate)();
STDMETHOD_(BOOL, CanBePooled)();
};
#endif //__ATLPIPE_H_
```

Component Base Code

Once the wizard is completed, you'll also find the .cpp file that contains the basic code elements, based on the interfaces you've implemented, as seen in the following code:

```
// ATLPipe.cpp : Implementation of CATLPipe

#include "stdafx.h"
#include "ATLPipe.h"

/////////////////////////////////////////////////////////////////////////////
// CATLPipe

STDMETHODIMP CATLPipe::InterfaceSupportsErrorInfo(REFIID riid)

{
static const IID* arr[] =
```

(continued)

(continued)

```
{
   &IID_IATLPipe,
};
for (int i=0;i<sizeof(arr)/sizeof(arr[0]);i++)
{
   if (InlineIsEqualGUID(*arr[i],riid))
      return S_OK;
}
return S_FALSE;
}

//
// IPipelineComponent Methods
//
STDMETHODIMP CATLPipe::Execute (
  IDispatch* pdispOrder,
  IDispatch* pdispContext,
  LONG lFlags,
  LONG* plErrorLevel)
{
HRESULT hRes = S_OK;
// TODO: Add code that performs the main operations for this
component

 return hRes;
}

STDMETHODIMP CATLPipe::EnableDesign(BOOL fEnable)
{
 return S_OK;
}

//
// IPipelineComponentDescription Methods
//
STDMETHODIMP CATLPipe::ContextValuesRead(VARIANT *pVarRead)
```

(continued)

(continued)

```
{
// TODO: Add your own values to the array

int cEntries = 1;

// allocate the safearray of VARIANTs
SAFEARRAY* psa = SafeArrayCreateVector(VT_VARIANT, 0, cEntries);

// Populate the safearray variants
VARIANT* pvarT = (VARIANT*)psa->pvData;
V_BSTR(pvarT) = SysAllocString(L"Example Context Value Read");
V_VT(pvarT) = VT_BSTR;

// set up the return value to point to the safearray
V_VT(pVarRead) = VT_ARRAY | VT_VARIANT;
V_ARRAY(pVarRead) = psa;

return S_OK;
}

STDMETHODIMP CATLPipe::ValuesRead(VARIANT *pVarRead)
{
// TODO: Add your own values to the array

int cEntries = 1;

// allocate the safearray of VARIANTs
SAFEARRAY* psa = SafeArrayCreateVector(VT_VARIANT, 0, cEntries);

// Populate the safearray variants
VARIANT* pvarT = (VARIANT*)psa->pvData;
V_BSTR(pvarT) = SysAllocString(L"Example Value Read");
V_VT(pvarT) = VT_BSTR;
// set up the return value to point to the safearray
V_VT(pVarRead) = VT_ARRAY | VT_VARIANT;
V_ARRAY(pVarRead) = psa;

return S_OK;
```

(continued)

(continued)

```
}

STDMETHODIMP CATLPipe::ValuesWritten(VARIANT *pVarWritten)
{
// TODO: Add your own values to the array

int cEntries = 1;

// allocate the safearray of VARIANTs
SAFEARRAY* psa = SafeArrayCreateVector(VT_VARIANT, 0, cEntries);

// Populate the safearray variants
VARIANT* pvarT = (VARIANT*)psa->pvData;
V_BSTR(pvarT) = SysAllocString(L"Example Value Written");
V_VT(pvarT) = VT_BSTR;

// set up the return value to point to the safearray
V_VT(pVarWritten) = VT_ARRAY | VT_VARIANT;
V_ARRAY(pVarWritten) = psa;

return S_OK;
}

STDMETHODIMP CATLPipe::Activate()
{
return E_NOTIMPL;
}

VOID CATLPipe::Deactivate()
{
return;
}
BOOL CATLPipe::CanBePooled()
{
return 0;
}
```

Pipeline Component Registration

Regardless of the language you used in building the pipeline component, you'll need to register the component on the Web server before it can be used. You can do this as with any other component, using the REGSVR32.EXE application. This can be found in the \Winnt\System32 directory and can be called using this syntax:

```
regsvr32  c:\inetpub\wwwroot\mysite\pipelines\mypipe.dll
```

Registering the component makes it available for use, but it does not provide stage affinity, where the component is identified as being run under a given stage in the pipeline. This information is maintained in the Registry keys, under the component's CLSID, in a key called *implemented categories*. The CLSIDs of the pipeline stages that this component supports are listed within this key. Your method of providing this support will depend on the language you used to create the component.

ATL Component Stage Affinity Registration

If you built the pipeline component using C++ ATL, you will insert code in the .h header file of your component that calls the RegisterCATID function, as shown in the next code sample. You'll make the call as many times as necessary to register the component for each supported stage.

```
static HRESULT WINAPI UpdateRegistry(BOOL bRegister)

{

HRESULT hr = _Module.UpdateRegistryFromResource(
 IDR_ATLPIPE, bRegister);

if (SUCCEEDED(hr))

{

// TODO: Add stage affinities here

hr = RegisterCATID(GetObjectCLSID(),
 CATID_MSCSPIPELINE_COMPONENT);

hr = RegisterCATID(GetObjectCLSID(),
 CATID_MSCSPIPELINE_ANYSTAGE);

}

return hr;

};
```

Stage Affinity Registration with Pipe Registration Wizard

If you build a pipeline component using Visual Basic, you'll need to register the component using the Pipe Registration Wizard. Follow the steps outlined in the following sections.

Step 1: Selecting a Component

The first step in registering the component is selecting the pipeline component that you're registering. You'll do this in the Pipeline Component Registration Wizard page shown in Figure 17-19.

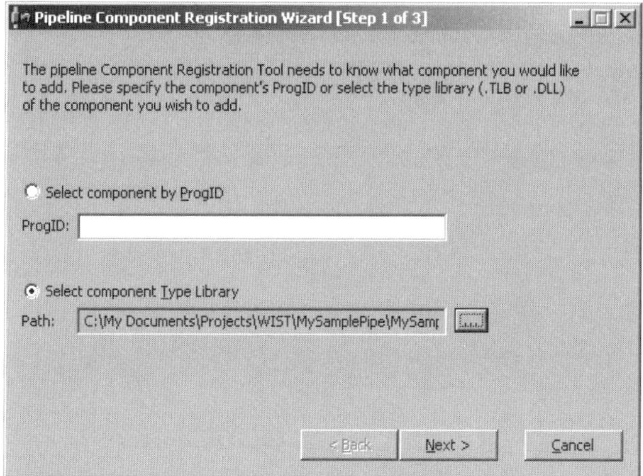

Figure 17-19. *Select the component that you're registering either by PROGID or by type library.*

Step 2: Selecting Pipeline Stages

The next step is to identify the stages that the component will support. You'll be presented with a list of all available stages. From this Available Categories list, move those stages that the component will support into the Selected Categories list, as shown in Figure 17-20.

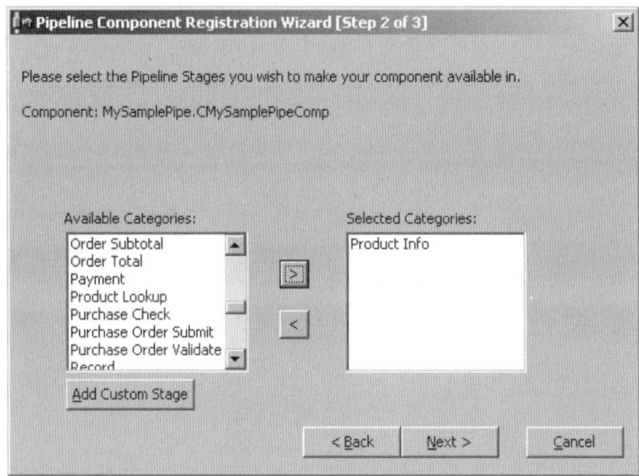

Figure 17-20. *Select the stages supported by the pipeline component from the Available Categories list.*

Step 3: Registering and Exporting

Now, you'll need to identify whether you want to register the pipeline component, export the registration data to a .reg file, or both in the Pipeline Component Wizard Registration page, as shown in Figure 17-21. You might find it useful to both register the component and export the registration data. The registration data can be used to transport the component to other systems more easily. This is discussed further in the following section.

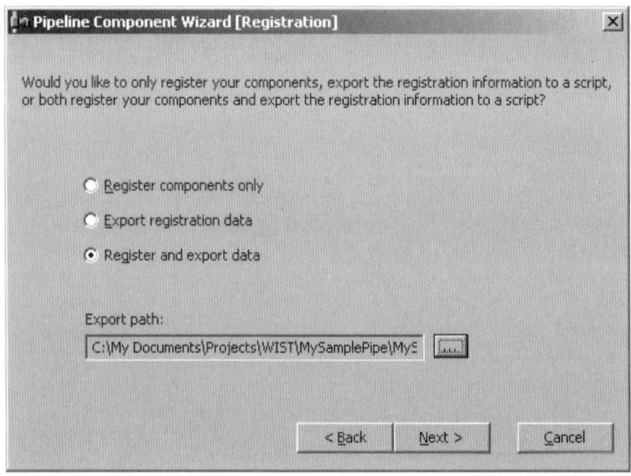

Figure 17-21. *Identify whether you want to register the component, export the registration data, or both.*

Step 4: Finishing

When you've completed the wizard, you'll see the Finished page, as displayed in Figure 17-22, which provides a summary of the actions taken by the Pipeline Registration Wizard.

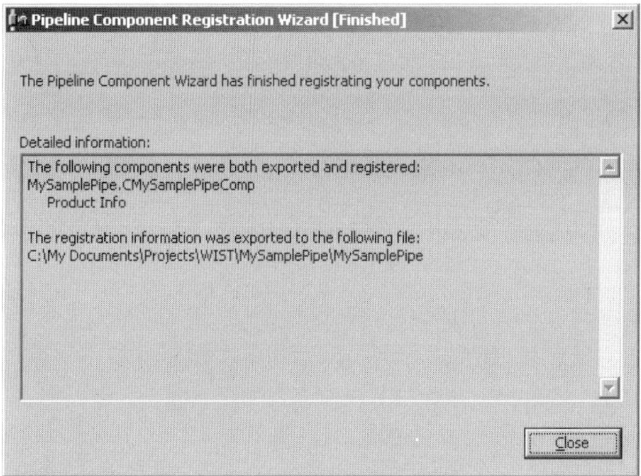

Figure 17-22. *You've now completed the Pipeline Registration Wizard. This Finished dialog box gives you a summary report of the actions taken.*

Registry Files

If you need to deploy your component from development to the production Web server, you can go through the process just described. Alternatively, you can create Registry files with a .reg extension and use these to transport the Registry settings to the server. In this case, you'll need to ensure that you correctly identify the location of the pipeline component in the file. This location should be where the file can be found on the new system. You can simply double-click the file to execute it and specify that you want to merge the data into the Registry. The following code contains an example of this type of Registry file:

```
Windows Registry Editor Version 5.00

[HKEY_CLASSES_ROOT\Pricing.PipeComp]
@="Pricing.PipeComp"

[HKEY_CLASSES_ROOT\Pricing.PipeComp\Clsid]
@="{41AAD88A-DD6B-4ED0-A9AB-9E1A63479745}"

[HKEY_CLASSES_ROOT\TypeLib\{842D21C3-77E6-4A20-8B96-
 1235C12C8F47}]
```

(continued)

(continued)

```
[HKEY_CLASSES_ROOT\TypeLib\{842D21C3-77E6-4A20-8B96-
 1235C12C8F47}\8.0]

@="Pricing"

[HKEY_CLASSES_ROOT\TypeLib\{842D21C3-77E6-4A20-8B96-
"1235C12C8F47} \8.0\0]

[HKEY_CLASSES_ROOT\TypeLib\{842D21C3-77E6-4A20-8B96-
 1235C12C8F47}\8.0\0\win32]

@="C:\\INETPUB\\WWWROOT\\MYSITE\\PIPELINES\\MyPipe.dll"

[HKEY_CLASSES_ROOT\TypeLib\{842D21C3-77E6-4A20-8B96-
 1235C12C8F47} \8.0\FLAGS]

@="0"

[HKEY_CLASSES_ROOT\TypeLib\{842D21C3-77E6-4A20-8B96-
 1235C12C8F47}\8.0\HELPDIR]

@=" C:\\INETPUB\\WWWROOT\\MYSITE\\PIPELINES"

[HKEY_CLASSES_ROOT\CLSID\{41AAD88A-DD6B-4ED0-A9AB-9E1A63479745}]

@="Pricing.PipeComp"

"AppID"="{41AAD88A-DD6B-4ED0-A9AB-9E1A63479745}"

[HKEY_CLASSES_ROOT\CLSID\{41AAD88A-DD6B-4ED0-A9AB-9E1A63479745}
 \Implemented Categories]

[HKEY_CLASSES_ROOT\CLSID\{41AAD88A-DD6B-4ED0-A9AB-9E1A63479745}
 \Implemented  Categories\{0DE86A53-2BAA-11CF-A229-00AA003D7352}]

[HKEY_CLASSES_ROOT\CLSID\{41AAD88A-DD6B-4ED0-A9AB-9E1A63479745}
 \Implemented  Categories\{0DE86A57-2BAA-11CF-A229-00AA003D7352}]

[HKEY_CLASSES_ROOT\CLSID\{41AAD88A-DD6B-4ED0-A9AB-9E1A63479745}
 \Implemented  Categories\{40FC6ED5-2438-11CF-A3DB-080036F12502}]

[HKEY_CLASSES_ROOT\CLSID\{41AAD88A-DD6B-4ED0-A9AB-9E1A63479745}
 \Implemented  Categories\{CF7536D0-43C5-11D0-B85D-00C04FD7A0FA}]

[HKEY_CLASSES_ROOT\CLSID\{41AAD88A-DD6B-4ED0-A9AB-9E1A63479745}
 \Implemented  Categories\{D2ACD8E0-43C5-11D0-B85D-00C04fD7A0fA}]

[HKEY_CLASSES_ROOT\CLSID\{41AAD88A-DD6B-4ED0-A9AB-9E1A63479745}
 \InprocServer32]
```

(continued)

(continued)

```
@=" C:\\INETPUB\\WWWROOT\\MYSITE\\PIPELINES\\MyPipe.dll"

"ThreadingModel"="Apartment"

[HKEY_CLASSES_ROOT\CLSID\{41AAD88A-DD6B-4ED0-A9AB-
 9E1A63479745}\ProgID]

@="MyPipe.PipeComp"

[HKEY_CLASSES_ROOT\CLSID\{41AAD88A-DD6B-4ED0-A9AB-
 9E1A63479745}\Programmable]

[HKEY_CLASSES_ROOT\CLSID\{41AAD88A-DD6B-4ED0-A9AB-
 9E1A63479745}\TypeLib]

@="{842D21C3-77E6-4A20-8B96-1235C12C8F47}"

[HKEY_CLASSES_ROOT\CLSID\{41AAD88A-DD6B-4ED0-A9AB-
 9E1A63479745}\VERSION]

@="8.0"
```

Part VII

Content Selection Framework

Part VII of this book covers the content selection framework in Microsoft Commerce Server 2000 that is used to select and target content for individual users based on a variety of criteria. Chapter 18 provides detailed coverage of the use and management of campaigns—Advertising, Discount, and Direct Mail—on your site. Chapter 19 dives into the process for selecting content for an individual user, based on selection criteria that you define. Chapter 20 covers the use of the Predictor Service to make predictions and suggestions for users and to predict information about users, based on data that you've collected on your site.

Chapter 18

Campaign Management

Establishing a catalog and opening your e-commerce site likely will not be the end of your work on the site. Just as with any brick-and-mortar store, you might find times when you need to provide advertising for items in your catalog so that the products have more visibility and exposure. In addition, you might decide to put some products on sale or make special offers to encourage shoppers to buy more products. And of course, you'll need to let your users know that you're making these offers. All of these things fall under the umbrella of campaigns in Microsoft Commerce Server 2000.

At the end of the chapter is a section that summarizes the components of the campaign management system and tables that provide a quick reference to the properties and methods of each of the components.

Campaigns in the Business Desk

The primary means of managing the ongoing campaigns in your site is the Business Desk, in the Campaigns section (see Figure 18-1). The Campaigns section contains the following areas:

- **Campaign Manager** Used to create and manage the campaigns
- **List Manager** Used to access and manage lists that are created as a result of reports generated in the Business Analytics section
- **Campaign Expressions** Used to create and manage expressions that help select the targets of campaigns
- **Target Group** Used to group target expressions to create a more selective target for campaigns
- **Reference Tables** Used to manage tables that are used to administer campaigns

You manage the following three reference tables in this section:

- **Content Sizes** Used to specify the size of campaign content, such as ads or discounts, that will be displayed on your site
- **Industry Codes** Provides a reference to ensure that two ads of the same industry are not shown on the same page
- **Page Groups** Specifies groups of pages that are used to define and select campaign content

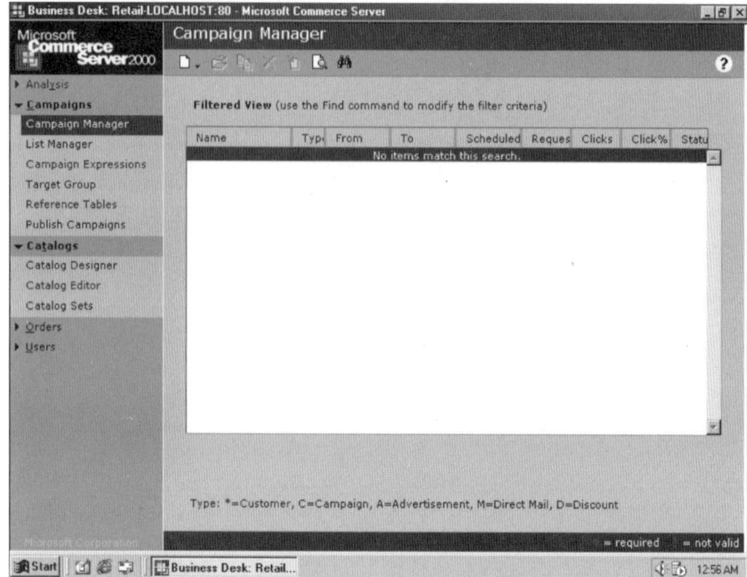

Figure 18-1. *The Business Desk's Campaigns section is where you'll create and manage campaigns for your site.*

Campaign Expressions and Targets

To select content that will be displayed for any given user or set of users, you build expressions that select those users to whom the content will be shown. You can create two types of expressions: target expressions and catalog expressions. Target expressions are used to specify targets for content, whether the target is based on a user or a set of pages. Catalog expressions are used to define products or categories in your catalogs to which a discount may be applied.

Creating a Target Expression

To create a new target expression, follow these steps:

1. Open Business Desk for your site.
2. Open the Campaigns section of the Business Desk.
3. Click Campaign Expressions in the Campaigns section.
4. From the toolbar on the Campaign Expressions page, click View Campaign Expressions and select the type of expression you wish to create (see Figure 18-2). Select Target Expressions.

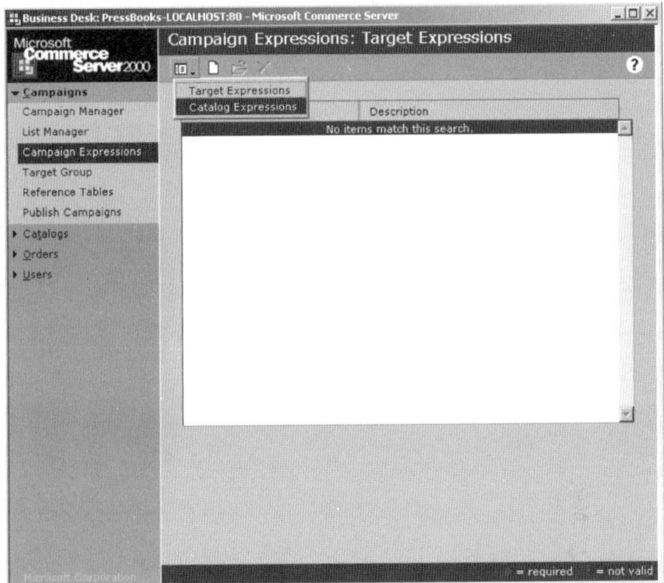

Figure 18-2. *You can select the property to use in building the condition that will be a part of the expression.*

5. Click the New Target Expression toolbar button. This loads the Target Expressions dialog box.
6. In the Target Expressions dialog box, specify a name and, if desired, a description.
7. Build the target conditions using the list boxes in the center of the dialog box by clicking New.
8. Select the property that will be used as the basis for the condition (see Figure 18-3) from the first list box. This property, in combination with the matching criteria and value provided in the next two steps, will be used to build the expression that will be evaluated.
9. In the second list, specify the condition comparison.

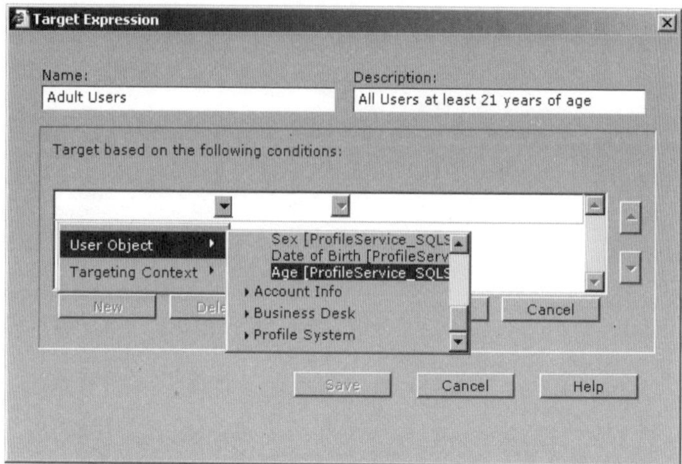

Figure 18-3. *You can identify the properties and matching criteria that will make up the expression in the Target Expression dialog box.*

10. In the text box to the right, specify the value to which the property is being compared. If the property you select is based on a site term, as defined in the profile (see Chapter 10, "Profiles," for more details on doing this), you can click the ellipses button to the right of the box. You can then choose the site term from the Choose a Site Term dialog box shown in Figure 18-4.

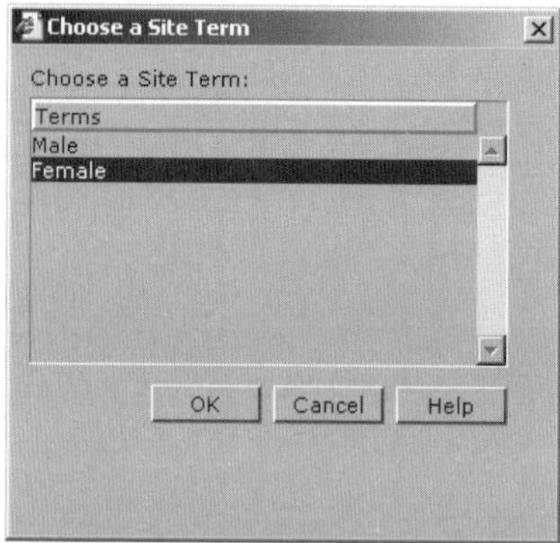

Figure 18-4. *If you're building the condition based on a site term, you can choose the site term from a dialog box.*

11. Click Apply to apply this condition to the expression.
12. Add more conditions as a part of the expression, as desired.
13. Click Save to save the expression.

When you're done with this process, you'll have created an expression that you can use to select the content to be displayed on the site.

Creating a Catalog Expression

To create a catalog expression, follow these steps:

1. Open Business Desk for your site.
2. Open the Campaigns section of the Business Desk.
3. Click Campaign Expressions in the Campaigns section.
4. From the toolbar on the Campaign Expressions page, click View Campaign Expressions and select the type of expression you wish to create (see Figure 18-2). Select Catalog Expressions.
5. Click New Catalog Expression on the toolbar and select whether you'll be creating the expression from the Product Picker dialog box, to build an expression identifying a list of products or a particular product, or building an expression based on properties of products (see Figure 18-5).

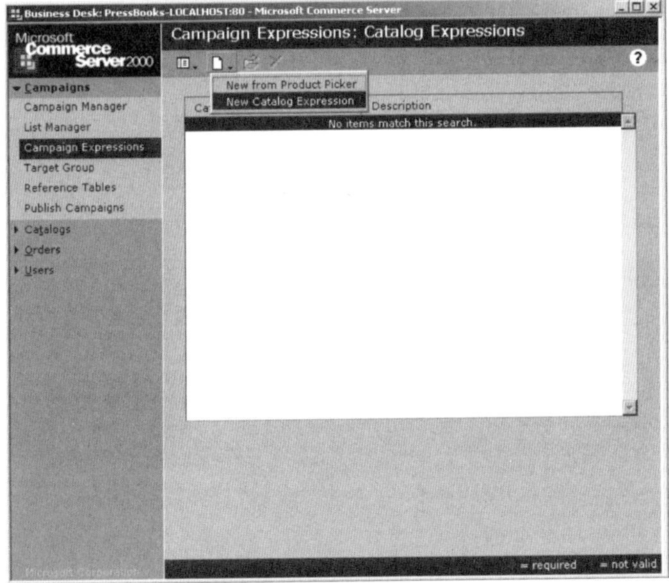

Figure 18-5. *Indicate how you will be creating the new catalog expression from the product picker as a new expression.*

6. If you choose to create an expression from the Product Picker dialog box, you'll be presented with a dialog box (see Figure 18-6) to choose the product. You can choose an individual product or categories of products. Click OK when you've selected the products you want to include in this expression.

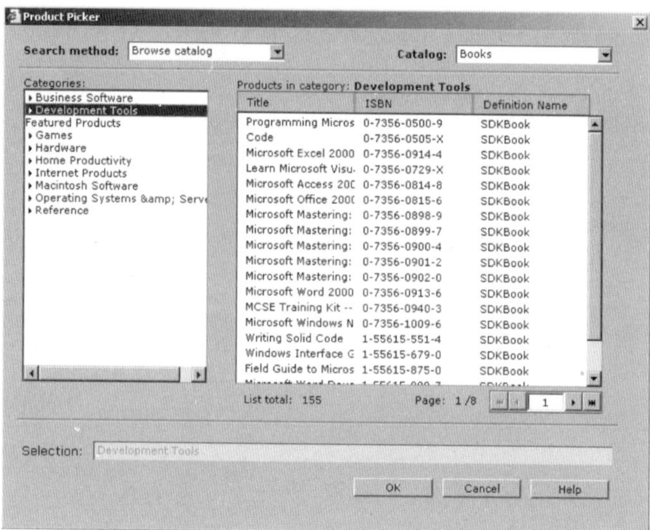

Figure 18-6. *The product picker is used to select categories of products or individual products to include as a part of this catalog expression.*

7. If you choose to create a catalog expression based on product properties, you will build an expression in the Catalog Expression dialog box (see Figure 18-7).

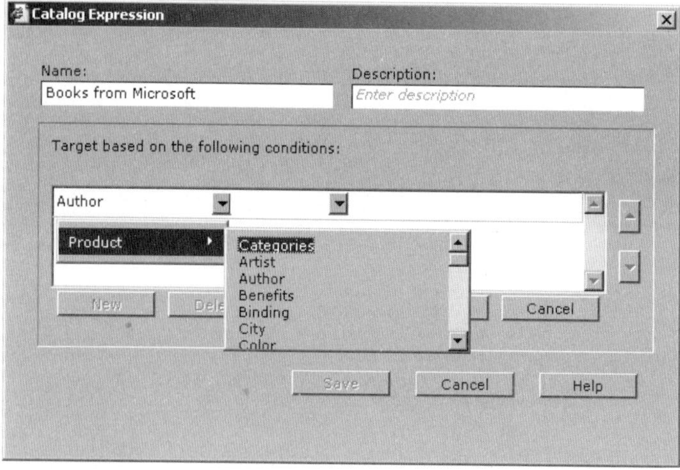

Figure 18-7. *The Catalog Expression dialog box is used to build an expression based on product properties.*

8. In this dialog box, you can build the selection expression. Start by specifying a name for the expressions.

9. Next, indicate the product property that you're going to use as a part of the condition in the first list box.
10. Second, identify the type of condition or comparison being created.
11. Finally, provide the value being used in the condition in the text box.
12. Click Apply to apply this condition to the expression.
13. Click Save to save the expression.

Once you have created and saved the catalog expression, it is available to be used in campaigns.

Target Groups

At times, creating an expression might not enable you to exactly target your intended audience. You might want to focus an ad on a group that is defined by more than one expression, or you might target a discount toward a group of users, but exclude a subset of those users. In these cases, you can use the target groups to combine different expressions and reach just the audience you want.

To create a new target group, you'll follow these steps:

1. Open Business Desk for your site.
2. Open the Campaigns section of the Business Desk.
3. Click Target Group in the Campaigns section.
4. Click New Target Group on the toolbar. This loads the Target Group page (see Figure 18-8).

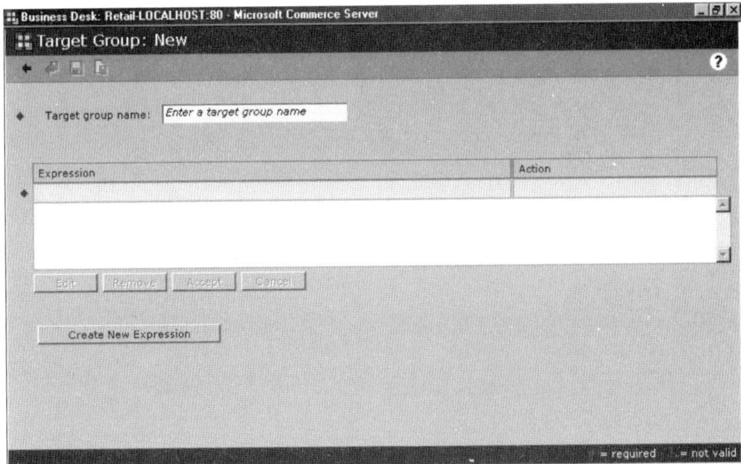

Figure 18-8. *You can combine expressions to more accurately direct content to the proper audience by creating target groups.*

5. Provide a name for this target group.

6. Click New to add an expression to this group. Select an expression from the Expression drop-down list box, which contains a list of all of the campaign expressions you've created.
7. Select an action from the Action drop-down list box. Available actions include Target, Require, Exclude, and Sponsor. These are explained in greater detail later.
8. Click Accept to include this expression and action in the group.
9. Click one of the Save buttons in the toolbar to save this target group.

Actions in the Target Group

When you apply expressions in a target group, you need to define an action that specifies the impact that expression will have on selecting content. There are four actions that can be selected, as follows:

- **Target** If this expression is met, the content selection score is increased. If not, the content selection score is not changed. However, the content is still eligible to be displayed for the current user. This is used to make it more likely that the content will be shown for a given user, but it is available to other users who don't meet this criteria.
- **Require** This expression must be satisfied for the content to be eligible for display to the current user. For instance, you might want an ad to be shown only to women, so you will require that the value for the user's sex is Female.
- **Exclude** If this expression is met, the content will not be eligible for the current user. This is used to exclude some users who would otherwise be eligible. For instance, you might be targeting an ad for women, but want to exclude any user who is not at least 18 years of age.
- **Sponsor** If this expression is satisfied, the content is eligible for display and no other content is eligible, unless that content also has an expression with an action of Sponsor.

By combining expressions and combining them with the available actions, you can target your content to an audience that is as narrow or broad as you desire.

Campaign Management

Once you've created the expressions and target groups that you can use to target your campaigns, you can begin to create actual campaigns. To create a campaign, you'll follow the basic steps, as outlined here:

1. Open Business Desk for your site.
2. Open the Campaigns section of the Business Desk.
3. Click Campaign Manager in the Campaigns section. This loads the Campaign Manager page (see Figure 18-9). This page shows you the campaigns that are in existence and allows you to create more.

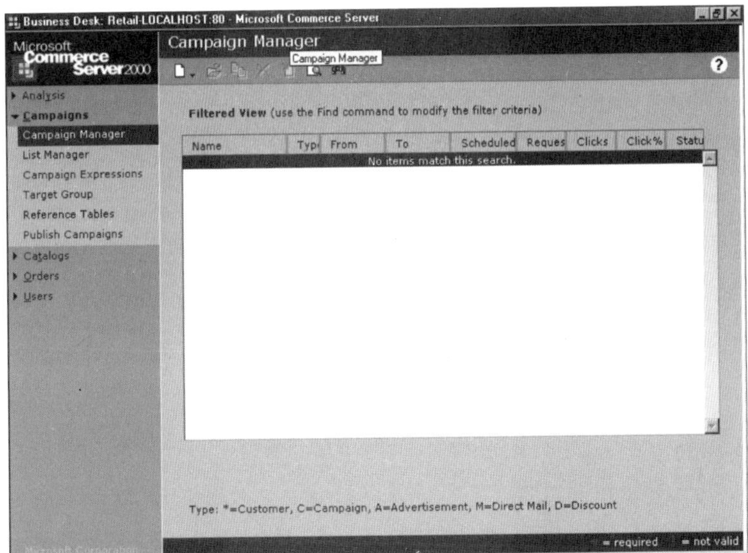

Figure 18-9. *The Campaign Manager page in the Business Desk shows the existing campaigns and their current performance. New campaigns can be created from here as well.*

4. Create a customer for the campaign. A customer can have a number of different campaigns in existence. Some will be active and some inactive at any given time.
5. Create a campaign for that customer.
6. Create the campaign content, such as the ad, direct mail, or discount.

Steps 4 through 6 are presented in greater detail in the following sections.

In addition to using the Campaign Management page to create and manage your campaigns, you can also use it to get a quick look at how the campaigns are performing. As you see in Figure 18-9, the page provides a summary of the number of requests and clicks that each item has received.

Creating a Customer

Before you can create a campaign, you'll need to define the customer that the campaign is being run for. This might be a company that is paying for advertising on your site, or a supplier that is running a special offer. It could also be just you, for campaigns that are not paid for by others. To create a customer, follow these steps:

1. Click New Campaign Item on the toolbar and select New Customer from the list. This loads the New (Customer) page (see Figure 18-10).

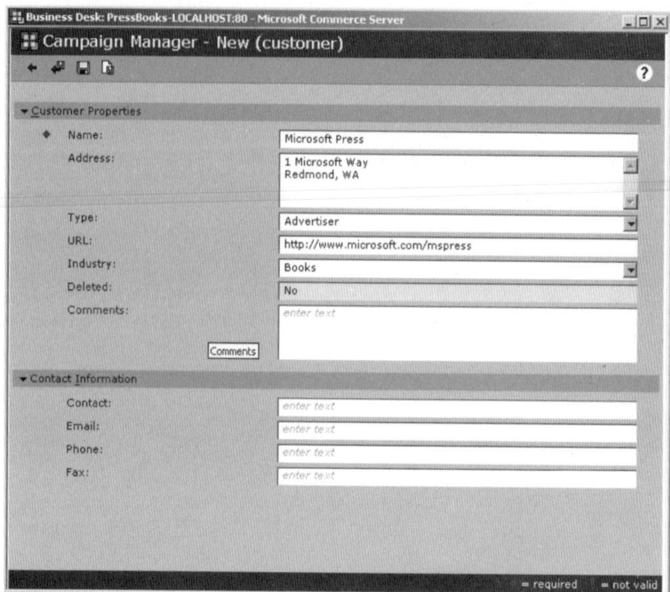

Figure 18-10. *In the Campaign Manager New (Customer) page, you can define administrative information about the customer.*

2. Provide a customer name in the Name text box. This is the only field that is required.
3. Identify the type of customer from the Type drop-down list. Available selections are Advertiser, Agency, and Self.
4. Specify the industry to which this customer applies, if any, from the Industry drop-down list. This field is used to ensure that two ads from the same industry are not shown on the same page.
5. Complete the remaining information fields as desired.
6. Click the Save toolbar button to save the customer record.

Creating a Campaign

Once a campaign customer is created, you can create a campaign for that customer from the Campaign Manager page. To do so, you'll follow these steps:

1. Select the customer on the Campaign Manager page.
2. Click New Campaign Item on the toolbar and select New Campaign from the list. This loads the Campaign page (see Figure 18-11).
3. Give the campaign a name in the Campaign Name text box.

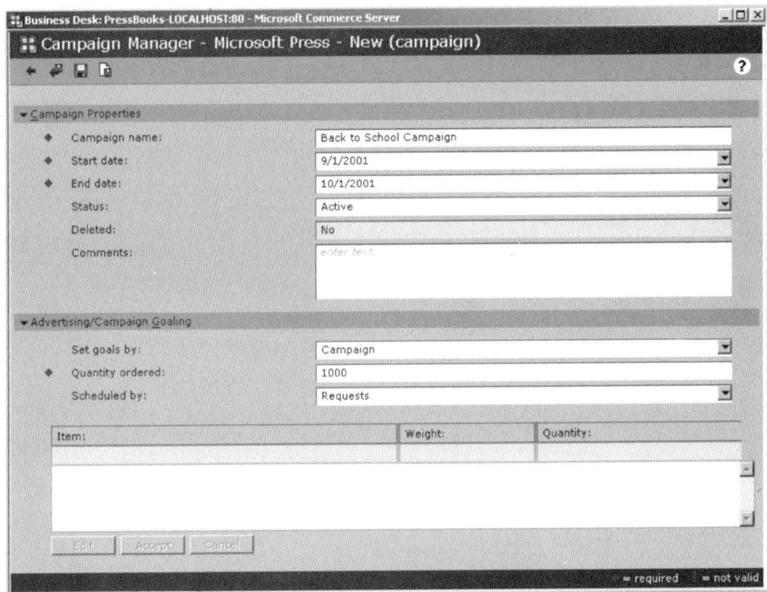

Figure 18-11. *The Campaign page is used to create and edit campaigns.*

4. Specify the start and end dates for the campaign in the Start Date and End Date text boxes. By default, the start date will be the current date, and the end date will be one month from the current date. This campaign will only be available between the dates specified.
5. The campaign's Status field should be set to Active. Otherwise, the campaign is not available to be used on the site.
6. In the Advertising/Campaign Goaling section, specify whether goals will be met at the campaign level or the advertising level. If you select Campaign, all of the ads in the campaign will contribute toward meeting the defined goal. If you select Advertising Items, goals are defined at the advertising item level.
7. If you selected Campaign goals, you can define the quantity of items ordered. If you selected Advertising Item goals, this field is unavailable.
8. Define how the advertising will be counted in the Scheduled By drop-down list box by selecting Requests or Clicks. Selecting Requests counts the ad toward meeting the goal every time it is displayed. Selecting Clicks counts the ad toward meeting the goal only when the user clicks on the ad.
9. Change the Weight and Quantities settings for individual ad items, if desired, by selecting them in the Item list. Ad items will not be available until they've been created (see the "Creating an Ad" section, later in this chapter). If you are setting the goals at the campaign level, the Weight text box allows you to spread the desired quantity across the available ad items in proportion to the weights you've defined. If you are setting goals by advertising item, you can directly adjust the quantities for each ad.

10. When you're done creating or modifying the campaign, click Save on the toolbar to save this campaign.

When you've completed the preceeding steps, you will have a campaign ready to be used on your site. However, you'll still need to specify the content used in that campaign, as demonstrated in the next several sections.

Creating an Ad

You can build an ad that will be shown on your pages and define the pages on which the ad will be shown, as well as who should see it, using the Campaign Manager. To do so, follow these steps:

1. In the Campaign Manager page, click the rightpointing arrow to the left of the campaign customer that you'll be creating this ad for. This expands the Campaigns list for this customer.
2. Select the campaign for which this ad will be created by single-clicking it (see Figure 18-12).

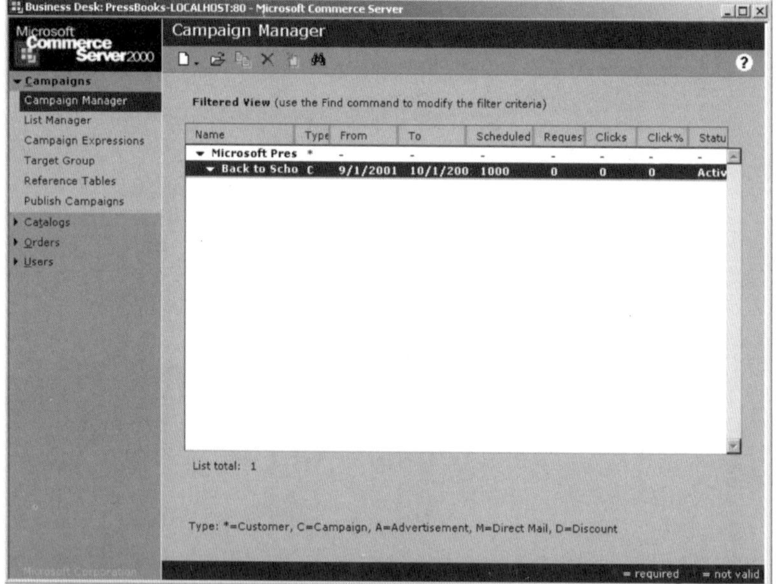

Figure 18-12. *You can expand the list of campaigns for a customer by clicking the icon to the left of the customer in the table. Then, select the campaign you want to work on to create campaign items.*

3. Click the New Campaign Item toolbar button and select New Ad from the list. This loads the Campaign Ad page.

4. In the Ad Properties section of the page (see Figure 18-13), provide a name for the ad.
5. Set the Status to Active. Unless the status is active, the ad will not be available for selection and display on the site.
6. You can select the Type setting for the ad as either a Paid Ad or a House Ad.
7. Specify the Weight setting for the ad. This is used in determining a score for the ad when selecting content to be displayed. The higher the number, the more likely that this ad will be shown, as compared to other available ads with lower weights.

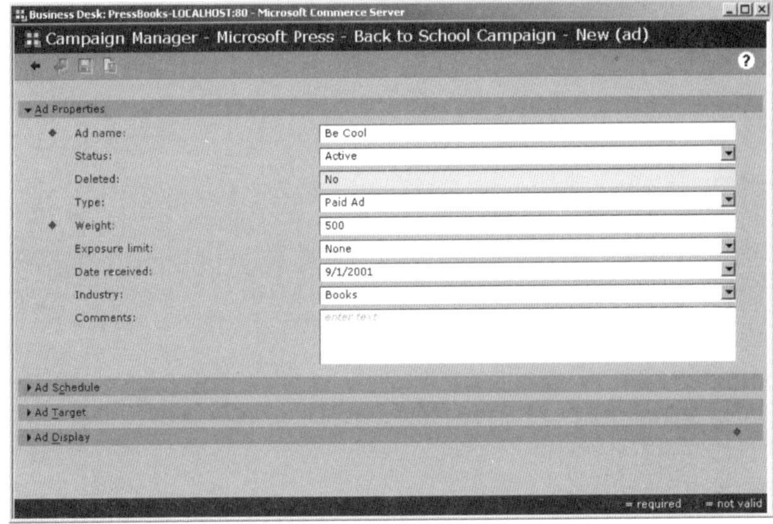

Figure 18-13. *Provide a name for your ad on the Ad Properties page.*

Tip Typically, for a paid ad, you'll provide a weight equal to the number of request or click goals set for the campaign. For a house ad, you should leave the weight as 1. This makes ads with higher goals more likely to be shown on the site.

8. Select an Exposure Limit setting for the ad. This limits the number of times a user on the site sees the same ad during the same session. You can select the limit from the drop-down list or specify that it is unlimited.
9. In the Ad Schedule section of the page (see Figure 18-14), schedule the ad for the time and days for which you want it to be available. This allows you to only show ads during a particular period of the day or on certain days of the week.

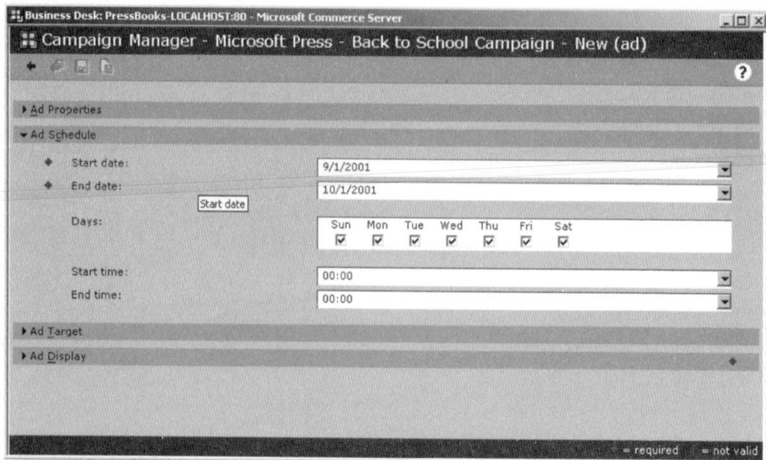

Figure 18-14. *The Ad Schedule section of the Campaign Ad page is used to schedule the advertisement for display at selected times or days.*

10. In the Ad Target section of the page (see Figure 18-15), specify the pages on which the ad may appear. You can also make the ad available on any page by selecting the Show On All Page Groups check box. To select a particular page group, clear the check box, select the group in the Available list box and click Add to move the group to the Assigned list box.

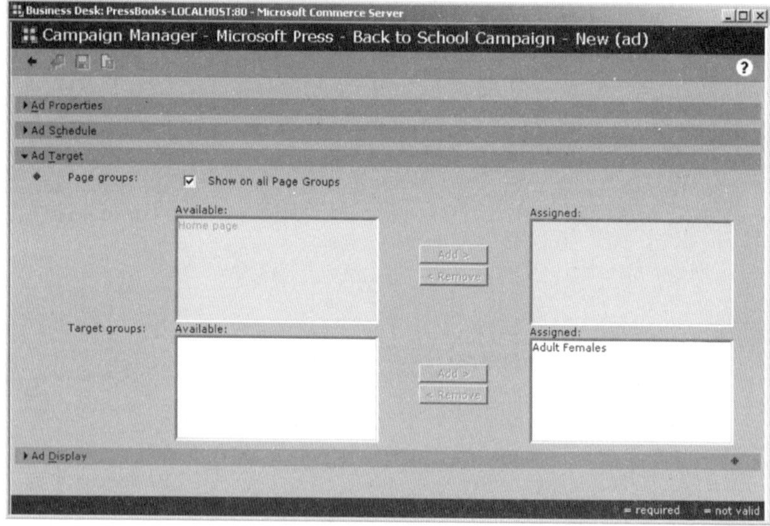

Figure 18-15. *The Ad Target section of the Campaign Ad page is used to define the content targeting information, so that the ad will be shown on the pages and to the users that you choose.*

11. You can also specify the target groups that will be used to identify recipients of the ad. To select a particular target group, select the group in the Available list box and click Add to move the group to the Assigned list box.
12. In the Ad Display section of the Campaign Ad page (see Figure 18-16), specify the size of the ad that will be displayed.

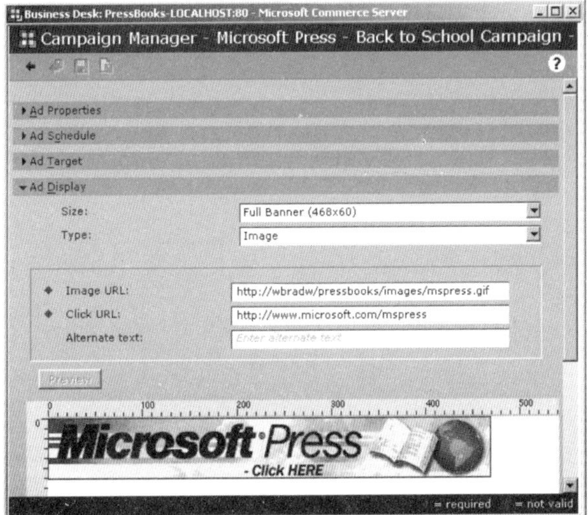

Figure 18-16. *The Ad Display section of the Campaign Ad page is used to specify the actual ad content to be displayed.*

13. Specify the type of ad being displayed from the Type drop-down list. Available selections are as follows:
    - **Image** A graphic ad
    - **Text** A text ad
    - **HTML** A Hypertext Markup Language (HTML) ad, text defined by some HTML code
    - **Non-Clickable Image** An image that does not have a link Uniform Resource Locator (URL)
    - **Buy Now** An image ad that allows the user to immediately purchase the advertised item
    - **Windows Media Services** An ad made up of video and/or audio
    - **Left Vignette** An ad with text and an image to the left
    - **Right Vignette** An ad with text and an image to the right
    - **Top Vignette** An ad with text and an image above it

14. Specify the ad size. The sizes available are those that are defined in the reference tables. By default, the following sizes are available:
    - **Full Banner** 468 × 60 pixels
    - **Full Banner With Nav Bar** 392 × 72 pixels
    - **Link Exchange** 440 × 40 pixels
    - **Half Banner** 234 × 60 pixels
    - **Square Bottom** 125 × 125 pixels
    - **Button #1** 120 × 90 pixels
    - **Button #2** 120 × 60 pixels
    - **Micro Button** 88 × 31 pixels
    - **Vertical Banner** 120 × 240 pixels
15. Provide necessary ad properties that define the display, depending on the type of ad being created. Some of these properties will include the following:
    - **Image URL** URL of the image that will be a part of the ad. Used in the Image, Non-Clickable Image, Buy Now, and Vignette ads.
    - **Click URL** URL of the page where shoppers will navigate if they click the ad. Used in the Image, Text, Buy Now, Windows Media Services, and Vignette ads.
    - **Alternate Text** Alternate text to display if the image cannot be shown. Used in the Image, Non-Clickable Image, Buy Now, and Vignette ads.
    - **Text** Text to be shown as a part of the ad. Used in the Text and Vignette ads.
    - **HTML Text** HTML code that will make up the ad. Used in the HTML ads.
    - **Window Width** Width of the dialog box that will be displayed as a part of the Buy Now process. Used in the Buy Now ads.
    - **Window Height** Height of the dialog box that will be displayed as a part of the Buy Now process. Used in the Image, Non-Clickable Image, Buy Now, and Vignette ads.
    - **Windows Media ASF** The URL of the audio or video file that will be displayed as a part of this ad. Used in the Windows Media Service ads.
16. Save the ad by clicking Save on the toolbar.
17. Preview the ad in the Preview area of the Ad Display section of the page.

Once the ad is saved, it is ready to be used on the site.

Creating a Direct Mail Campaign

Once the campaign is created, you can create a new direct mail campaign to inform your shoppers of this new discount or ad campaign. This can be useful in bringing shoppers back to your site to take advantage of the discount.

Note Before you can create a direct mail campaign, you must have created a list of users with e-mails using Business Analytics. The list can be viewed in the List Manager. More information on creating these user lists can be found in Chapter 5, "Business Analytics."

1. In the Campaign Manager, click the right-pointing arrow to the left of the campaign customer that you'll be creating this ad for. This expands the list of campaigns for this customer.
2. Select the campaign for which this ad will be created by single-clicking the campaign (see Figure 18-12).
3. Click the New Campaign Item toolbar button and select New Direct Mail from the list. This loads the Campaign Direct Mail page.
4. In the Direct Mail Properties section of the page (see Figure 18-17), you can define the contents of the e-mail that will be sent. You'll need to provide a name for the direct mail campaign.

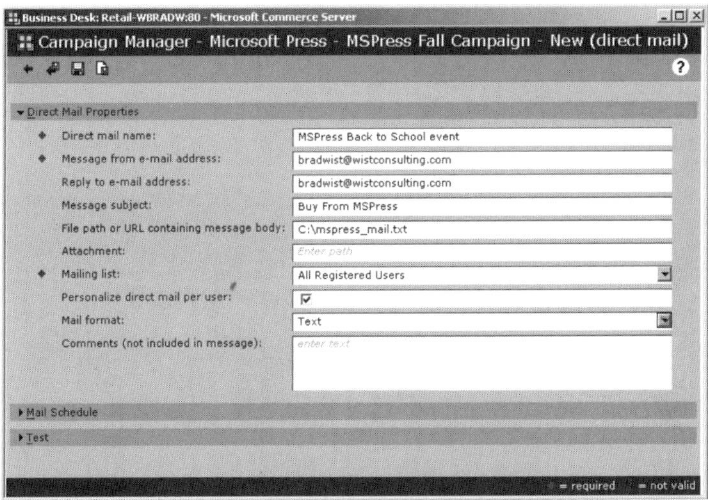

Figure 18-17. *The Direct Mail Properties section of the Direct Mail Campaign page is used to define the e-mails that will be sent as a part of the campaign.*

5. You'll also need to specify the Message From E-Mail Address. This is the address that will be used to send the e-mails.
6. You should provide a subject for the e-mail in the Message Subject text box.

7. You must provide a path to the file that has the message body. This can be either a text file, an HTML file, or an Active Server Page (ASP) file. You can provide code in the file that can be used to customize the e-mail for each recipient.
8. You can select the mailing list that will be used to define the recipients of the e-mail.
9. You can specify whether you want the e-mails to be personalized for each recipient using the Personalize Direct Mail Per User check box.
10. You can also define the format of the e-mails in the Mail Format text box, indicating whether they should be sent in either Text, MHTML, or MIME format.
11. In the Mail Schedule section of the page (see Figure 18-18), you can define when and how often the e-mail should be sent. You can specify the starting date and time for when the mail should be sent. You can schedule the e-mails for the appropriate day, and potentially for a time when the load on your network and servers will be lower.

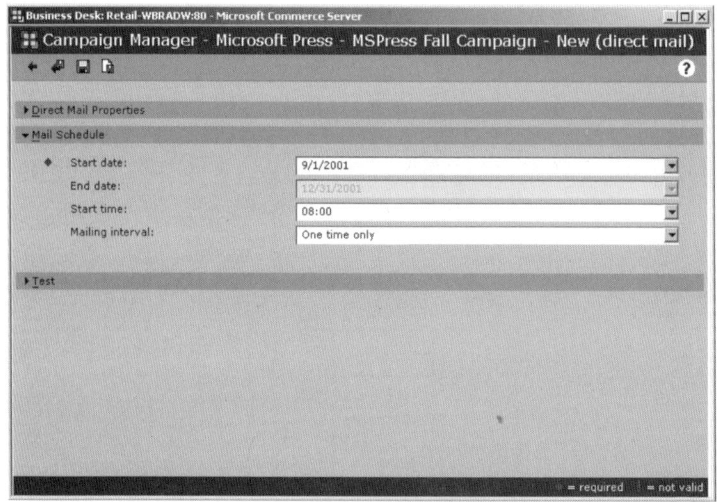

Figure 18-18. *The Mail Schedule section of the page is used to schedule when and how often the e-mails should be sent.*

12. You can also define whether the e-mails should be sent once or should be a recurring e-mail, sent every week, month, or on some other schedule. In the event that the e-mail is recurring, fields will be provided to establish the recurring schedule.
13. In the Test section of the page (see Figure 18-19), you can select a mailing list to use to test the transmission of the e-mails. When you click Send Test Mail, the e-mail is sent to the recipients in the list.

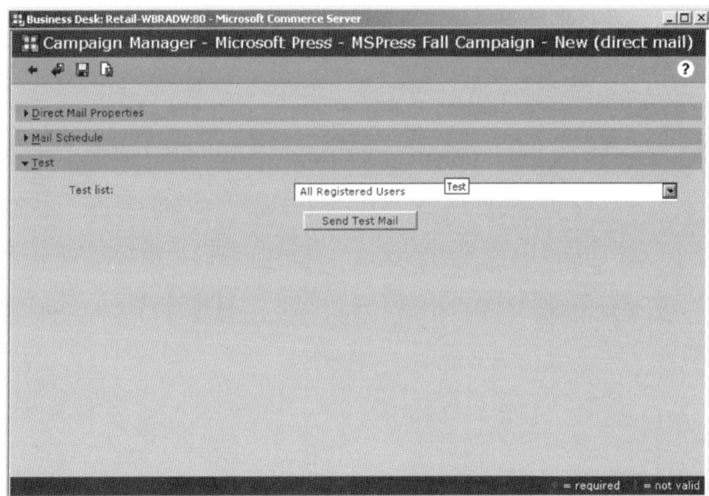

Figure 18-19. *The Test section of the page is used to prepare and perform a test of the e-mail being sent.*

14. Once you've completed the direct mail campaign, you should click Save on the toolbar.

Opting out of Direct Mail Campaigns

It's important to remember that if you're going to send out mass e-mails to your customers, you should provide a way for them to opt out of the e-mails so they can elect to be excluded from e-mails that you'll be sending. In most cases, you'll provide the ability to do this by providing a link in the e-mail to a page on your site. The link might look like the following:

```
<a href="http://www.mysite.com/
optout.asp?rcp_email=<emailaddress>

&campitem_id=<campaign item id>&campitem_name=<mailcampaign>">

Click here if you'd rather not receive more email updates</a>
```

This would provide the link to the page that would retrieve a list of users that have opted out of e-mails, using the ListManager object, as shown in the following code. It would then add the user to the list. This list is automatically used by the Direct Mail pipeline to exclude the listed users from the e-mails.

```
rcp_email = Request.Querystring("rcp_email")

campitem_id = Request.QueryString("campitem_id")

campitem_name = Request.QueryString("campitem_name")
```

(continued)

(continued)

```
sCampaigns = _
  Application("MSCSOptionsDictionary").s_CampaignsConnectionString

' open DB connection

set connCampaigns = CreateObject("ADODB.Connection")

connCampaigns.open sCampaigns

' create and initialize the ListManager

set listmanager = CreateObject("Commerce.ListManager")

listmanager.Initialize(sCampaigns)

' Get List ID

if campitem_id <> "" then

   sSQL = "SELECT g_dmitem_optout FROM dm_item WHERE " _
    & "i_campitem_id = " & campitem_id

   set rs = CreateObject("ADODB.Recordset")

   set rs.ActiveConnection = connCampaigns

   rs.Open sSQL

   list_id = rs(0)

   rs.Close

else

   On error resume next

   list_id = listmanager.GetListId("Opt Out")

   if Err.Number Then

      list_id = Null

      Err.Clear

   end if

end if

' If the list doesn't exist, create a new one

if isNull(list_id) then

   if (campitem_id <> "") then

      sListName = "Opt Out (" & campitem_id & ")"
```

(continued)

(continued)

```
      sListDescription = _
       "Direct mail opt-out list for campaign item: " _
       & campitem_id

   else

      sListName = "Opt Out"

      sListDescription = "Site-Wide Opt-Out list"

   end if

   lFlags = 0 + 4      'LM_FLAG_DEFAULT + LM_FLAG_OPTOUT

   list_id = listmanager.CreateEmpty(sListName, _
    sListDescription, lFlags, 0)

'  Set Opt out list

   if (campitem_id <> "") then

      sSQL = "UPDATE dm_item SET g_dmitem_optout = '" & list_id _
       & "' WHERE i_campitem_id = " & campitem_id

      connCampaigns.Execute sSQL

   end if

end if

' add user to the list

listmanager.AddUserToMailingList CStr(list_id), rcp_email
```

Creating a Discount Campaign

Once a campaign is created in the Campaign Manager page, you can create a discount for some or all of your products. The discounts might be buy one, get one at some percentage off; or buy two, get one free; or buy some products and get free shipping, just to name a few. To create a discount campaign, you can follow the directions provided in the following steps:

1. In the Campaign Manager, click the right-pointing arrow to the left of the campaign customer that you'll be creating this ad for. This expands the list of campaigns for this customer.
2. Select the campaign for which this ad will be created by single-clicking the campaign (see Figure 18-12).
3. Click the New Campaign Item toolbar button and select New Discount from the list. This loads the Campaign Discount page.
4. In the Discount Properties section (see Figure 18-20), you should provide the name for this discount.

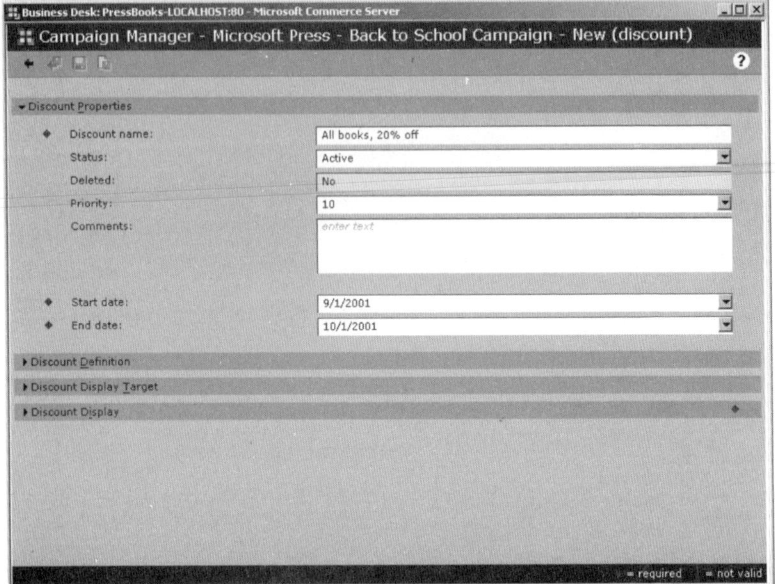

Figure 18-20. *The Discount Properties section of the Campaign Discount page is used to define the basic discount information, such as the name and when the discount is active.*

5. Set the Status to Active, or the discount will not be available for use.
6. Establish a Priority setting for the discount. The lower the number, the higher the priority, so a level 10 priority will be applied instead of a level 20 priority.
7. Set the start and end dates that define when the discount will be available in the Start Date and End Date text boxes.
8. In the Discount Definition section of the page (see Figure 18-21), you can define the actual discount that you're creating. First you'll define what products trigger the discount. If you select the Anything check box, the discount will be available when a customer buys any product. Otherwise, you'll select that the discount will be triggered when customers buy a given quantity or value of an identified product or products from a category. You can select the product using the drop-down list to specify where you'll get the product from. You can select the product from the Product Picker dialog box or build an expression to identify the products. You can also specify that any product will trigger this discount.

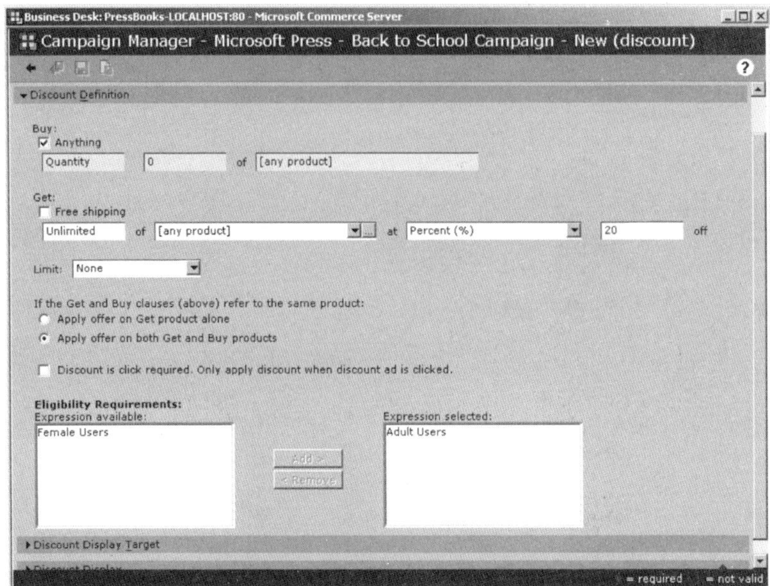

Figure 18-21. *The Discount Definition section of the Campaign Discount page is used to specify the discount that will be applied.*

9. Next, you'll specify the discount customers will receive, as well as what products the discount will apply toward. You can specify that shipping will be free by selecting the Free Shipping check box, or you can specify that particular products (or all products) will receive a discount of a percentage or particular amount off. You can also specify whether the discount will be unlimited or will apply to only a limited quantity of the identified products.
10. If the discount will apply only to new products, but not the products that triggered the discount, then you should select the Apply Offer On Get Product Alone option. To apply it to the product you chose that triggered the discount, select the Apply Offer On Both Get And Buy Products option.
11. If the shopper must click on the discount display to apply it, select the Discount Is Click Required check box.
12. Select the users who should be eligible for the discount by selecting from the Expression Available list box and clicking Add to move the expression to the Expression Selected list box.
13. In the Discount Display Target section of the page (see Figure 18-22), you define when the discount message will be displayed. You can select page groups and target groups that are used to define when the discount is displayed. You should define whether the targets you select will be used in addition to the targets of the discount, or instead of those targets.

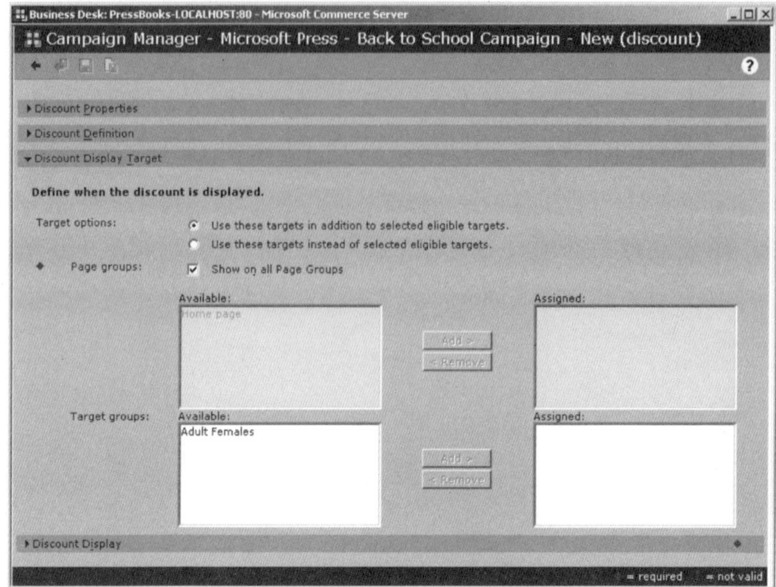

Figure 18-22. *The Discount Display Target section of the Campaign Discount page is used to define when the discount is displayed on the site.*

14. In the Discount Display section of the Campaign Discount page (see Figure 18-23), you can define how the discount is displayed on the site. You can start by defining an Exposure Limit, which limits the number of times a user sees the discount display during each session on the site.
15. You can then define the text to be shown in the basket when the discount has been applied in the Basket Display text box.
16. Finally, you can define the manner in which the discount is displayed on other pages. You'll do this by defining the Content Size and Content Type settings. The sizes and types available are the same as defined in the section "Creating an Ad Campaign," earlier in this chapter.
17. You can then fill in the appropriate properties to define the display of the discount display in the HTML text box, including defining the image or HTML code to be used.
18. Finally, once the discount is completely defined, save it by clicking Save on the toolbar.

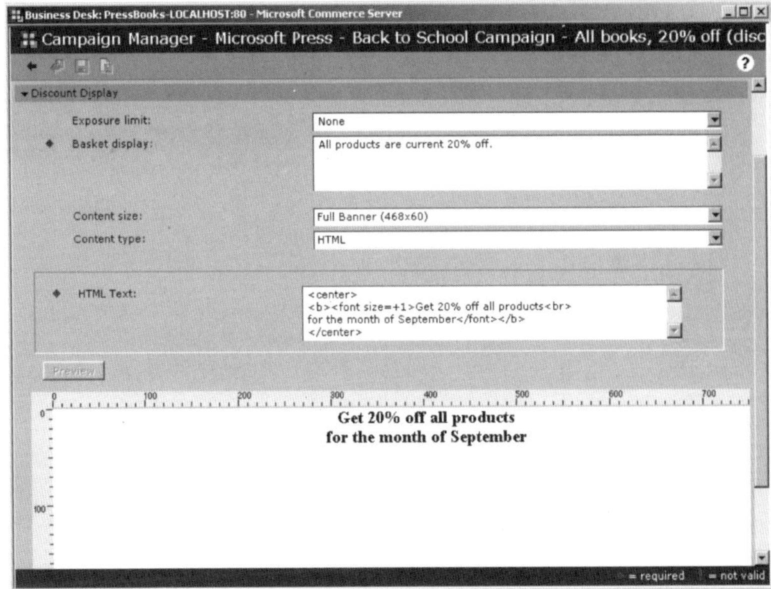

Figure 18-23. *The Discount Display section of the Campaign Discount page is used to define how the discount is shown on your Web site pages.*

Component Reference

The following sections summarize the content selection–related components. The tables provide a quick reference to the properties and methods of each of the components.

ListManager

The ListManager object can be used to manage lists of data, including mailing lists for use with direct mail campaigns. It can be created using the PROGID Commerce.ListManager. Its properties are listed in Table 18-1, and its methods are listed in Table 18-2.

Table 18-1. ListManager Properties

Property Name	Data Type	Description
ConnectionString	String	The connection string to the database that is used to store the lists
Status	Long	Current status of the object

Table 18-2. ListManager Methods

Method Name	Description
AddUserToMailingList	Adds a user to a mailing list.
CancelOperation	Halts the asynchronous operation that is currently running.
Copy	Creates a copy of a list.
CreateEmpty	Creates an empty list.
CreateFromDWCalc	Creates a list from an analysis report.
CreateFromFile	Creates a list from a file that contains comma-delimited records in the following format: <Mail-to address>, <User ID>,<Message format>,<Locale>, <Source URL> Only the <Mail-to address> is required.
CreateFromSegment	Creates a list from a data segment.
CreateFromSQL	Creates a list from a SQL query.
Delete	Deletes a list.
ExportToFile	Exports the specified list to the identified files.
ExportToSQL	Exports the specified list to a database table.
ExtractMailingList	Creates a mailing list based on another list that contains a field named *rcp_email*:.
GetListFlags	Returns the bitmask representing configuration settings about the list. The bit values are as follows: **0x0 – DEFAULT** It's a mailing list **0x1 – HIDDEN** List is hidden **0x2 – DYNAMIC** List is built dynamically **0x4 – USER** List contains an *rcp_guid* column **0x8 – GENERIC** It's a generic list **0x10 – MAILABLE** List contains an *rcp_email* column
GetListID	Returns the ID of the list.
GetListName	Returns the name of the list.
GetListProperty	Returns the value of a property of the list.
GetLists	Returns a recordset of all lists.
GetListUserFlags	Returns the UserFlags bitmask of the list, which is not used by Commerce Server 2000 but is available for use by external systems.
GetOperationInfo	Returns information concerning a list's operations.
GetOperations	Returns a recordset of all operations currently running on all lists.
Initialize	Initializes the ListManager object and connects it to the appropriate database.

(continued)

Table 18-2. *(continued)*

Method Name	Description
RemoveUserFromMailingList	Remove a user's e-mail address from the specified mailing list.
Rename	Renames a list.
SetDesc	Sets a description of the list.
SetListProperty	Sets the value of a property of a list.
Subtract	Removes the contents of one list from the contents of another list and puts the results in a new list.
Union	Combines the contents of two lists and puts the results in a new list.
WaitOnOperation	Causes the object to wait until an asynchronous operation is completed before it returns control to the calling application.

Chapter 19

Content Selection

After you've created campaigns, you will need to implement them on your pages so that you can display the proper advertisements or provide the intended discount for a given user. You also might want to target other content to particular users, based on a given set of criteria. For instance, you might want to display headlines, news items, or announcements that are of interest to each user. In each of these cases, you'll use the content selection framework (CSF) to identify and select the content to be displayed. In addition, you can use the Expression Evaluator component to determine if the current user and context meets criteria to display selected content.

At the end of the chapter is a section that summarizes the components of the content selection system and tables that provide a quick reference to the properties and methods of each of the components.

Selecting Content

The process of selecting content to be displayed on the site follows several basic steps. The steps are common, whether the content selected is advertisements, discounts, or other content that should be shown. These steps include the following:

1. **Filtering** Available content is filtered based on some defined selection criteria.
2. **Scoring** Scores are applied to available content, based on some criteria.
3. **Content selection** Content with the highest score is selected as that which should be displayed.

Content Selection Pipelines

Because these steps are common through the various types of content selection in Microsoft Commerce Server 2000, it's not surprising that they've been encapsulated with the content selection pipelines. These pipelines include a few additional steps to help round out this process, as shown in Figure 19-1.

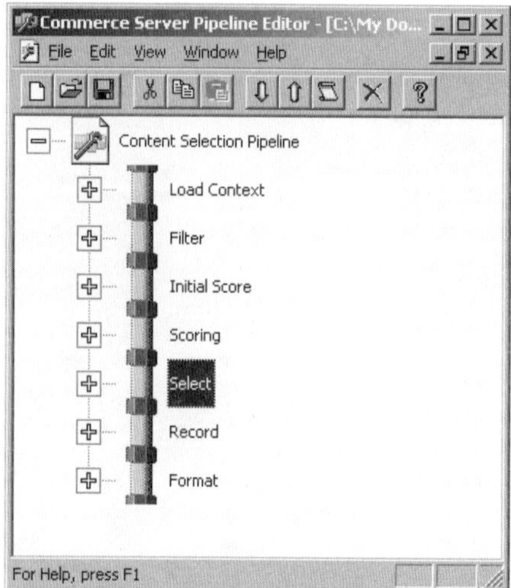

Figure 19-1. *The content selection pipelines include the basic steps that must be completed to select content for use on the site.*

Note Pipelines are covered in general in Chapter 16, "Pipelines." For more information on pipeline components, see Commerce Server 2000 Help or the Commerce Server 2000 SDK.

Initializing the Content Selection Components

Before you can begin making use of the Content Selection components, you'll need to initialize and configure the support components that the CSF components use. These include the appropriate Pipelines, Expression Evaluator, and Cache Manager objects.

Initializing the Pipeline Dictionary

You can initialize the Pipeline Dictionary, which will hold references to each of the pipeline files, as shown in this code sample:

```
Set dPipeline = Server.CreateObject("Commerce.Dictionary")

Const WEBSITE_ROOT_DIRECTORY = "\"
If appframework.VirtualDirectory = "" Then
   GetRootPath = Server.MapPath("\") & "\"
Else
' Commerce site is installed under a virtual directory.
```

(continued)

(continued)

```
    GetRootPath = Server.MapPath("\" _
     & MSCSAppFramework.VirtualDirectory) & c

End If

dPipeline.Folder = GetRootPath() & "pipeline\"

dPipeline.Advertising = dPipeline.Folder & "advertising.pcf"

dPipeline.Discounts = dPipeline.Folder & "discounts.pcf"

dPipeline.RecordEvent = dPipeline.Folder & "RecordEvent.pcf"
```

Initializing the Expression Evaluator

You can create and initialize the Expression Evaluator object, as shown here:

```
Set MSCSExpressionEvaluator = _
 Server.CreateObject("Commerce.ExpressionEvaluator")

MSCSExpressionEvaluator.Connect( _
 MSCSOptionsDictionary.s_BizDataStoreConnectionString)
```

Initializing the Cache Manager

Then, you can initialize the Cache Manager object with settings you'll need for content selection, as shown in this code sample:

```
'---------------------

' Get the Machine Name

'---------------------

Set oWshShell = Server.CreateObject("Wscript.Shell")

Set oEnv = oWshShell.Environment("Process")

sWebServerMachine = oEnv("COMPUTERNAME")


'---------------------

' Get the Port

'---------------------

Set mscsSiteCfg = CreateObject("Commerce.SiteConfig")

Call  mscsSiteCfg.Initialize(MSCSCommerceSiteName)

sWebServerBindings = _
 mscsSiteCfg(MSCSCommerceAppName).Value.Fields(  _
 "s_ServerBindings").Value

aWebServerBindings = _
 mscsSiteCfg.MakeArrayFromString(sWebServerBindings)

aServerBinding = Split(arrWebServerBindings(0),":")
```

(continued)

(continued)

```
For i = 0 To UBound(aServerBinding)
   If IsNumeric(aServerBinding(i)) Then
      iPort = CInt(aServerBinding(i))
   End If
Next
If iPort <> 80 Then
   sPort = ":" & CStr(iPort)
End If

'---------------------
' Build the Base URL for the site
'---------------------
sBaseURL = "http://" & sWebServerMachine & sPort
If MSCSAppFramework <> "" Then
   sBaseURL = sBaseURL & "/" & MSCSAppFramework.VirtualDirectory
End If

'---------------------
' Create CacheManager object
'---------------------
Set MSCSCacheManager = _
 Server.CreateObject("Commerce.CacheManager")
MSCSCacheManager.AppUrl = sMachineBaseUrl

'---------------------
' Create the LoaderConfig dictionaries
'---------------------
Set dCampaignConfig = Server.CreateObject("Commerce.Dictionary")
dCampaignConfig("ConnectionString") = _
 MSCSOptionsDictionary.s_CampaignsConnectionString
Set dCampaignConfig("Evaluator") = MSCSEvaluator
'---------------------
' Configure CacheManager for ads
'---------------------
```

(continued)

(continued)

```
MSCSCacheManager.RefreshInterval("advertising") = 5*60
MSCSCacheManager.RetryInterval("advertising") = 60
MSCSCacheManager.LoaderProgId("advertising") = _
 "Commerce.CSFLoadAdvertisements"
MSCSCacheManager.WriterProgId("advertising") = _
 "Commerce.CSFWriteEvents"
Set MSCSCacheManager.LoaderConfig("advertising") = _
 dCampaignConfig
Set MSCSCacheManager.WriterConfig("advertising") = _
 dCampaignConfig
'---------------------
' Configure CacheManager for discounts
'---------------------
MSCSCacheManager.RefreshInterval("discounts") = 0
MSCSCacheManager.RetryInterval("discounts") = 60
MSCSCacheManager.LoaderProgId("discounts") = _
 "Commerce.CSFLoadDiscounts"
MSCSCacheManager.WriterProgId("discounts") = _
 "Commerce.CSFWriteEvents"
Set MSCSCacheManager.LoaderConfig("discounts") = dCampaignConfig
Set MSCSCacheManager.WriterConfig("discounts") = dCampaignConfig
```

Initializing the Content Selection Framework

Finally, once you've initialized the supporting components, you can initialize the CSF. This involves creating the dictionary objects that will provide the context for each of the CSF pipelines, as shown in this code sample:

```
'---------------------
' The RedirectURL should be set to the full http path to redir.asp"
'---------------------
sBaseURL = "http://" & MSCSOptionsDictionary.s_NonSecureHostname
If MSCSAppFramework.VirtualDirectory <> "" Then
   sBaseURL = sBaseURL & "/" & MSCSAppFramework.VirtualDirectory
End If
sRedirectUrl = sBaseURL & "/redir.asp"
```

(continued)

(continued)

```
'--------------------
' Create Global Context for CSF Advertising
'--------------------
Set CSFAdvertisingContext = CreateObject("Commerce.Dictionary")
Set CSFAdvertisingContext("CacheManager") = MSCSCacheManager
CSFAdvertisingContext("CacheName") = "Advertising"
Set CSFAdvertisingContext("Evaluator") = MSCSExpressionEvaluator
CSFAdvertisingContext("RedirectUrl") = sRedirectUrl
Set oPipe = Server.CreateObject("Commerce.OrderPipeline")
oPipe.LoadPipe(MSCSPipelines.Advertising)
Set CSFAdvertisingContext("Pipeline") = oPipe
Set Application("CSFAdvertisingContext") = CSFAdvertisingContext

'--------------------
' Create Global Context for CSF Discounts
'--------------------
Set CSFDiscountContext = CreateObject("Commerce.Dictionary")
Set CSFDiscountContext("CacheManager") = MSCSCacheManager
CSFDiscountContext("CacheName") = "Discounts"
Set CSFDiscountContext("Evaluator") = MSCSExpressionEvaluator
CSFDiscountContext("RedirectUrl") = sRedirectUrl
Set oPipe = Server.CreateObject("Commerce.OrderPipeline")
oPipe.LoadPipe(MSCSPipelines.Discounts)
Set CSFDiscountContext("Pipeline") = oPipe
Set Application("CSFDiscountContext") = CSFDiscountContext

'--------------------
' Create an event processing pipeline which we call directly
   from redir.asp
'--------------------
Set oPipe = Server.CreateObject("Commerce.OrderPipeline")
oPipe.LoadPipe(MSCSPipelines.RecordEvent)
Set Application("CampaignsCSFEventPipe") = oPipe
```

Using the ContentSelector

The ContentSelector object is a special implementation of a Dictionary object that is used to execute the content selection pipeline. It provides the same functionality and capabilities of a Dictionary object. In addition, the GetContent method is used to execute the pipeline. It takes a Dictionary object as its single parameter. This dictionary requires a key named *pipeline* that will hold an OrderPipeline object for the content selection pipeline. This method returns a SimpleList that contains the content that has been selected.

Displaying Ads

The Retail site shows this in action on the banner.inc page, as the ContentSelector object is used to execute the pipeline, retrieve the list of ads that are available, and display them. In addition to the values passed in, you'll notice that you can define the number of ads or content items that you want to have returned by providing a value for a key on the ContentSelector named NumRequested. The current user's profile can also be sent to the pipeline using the key UserProfile, so that it can be used to help select the appropriate content, as shown here:

```
Set oCSO = Server.CreateObject("Commerce.ContentSelector")
oCSO.Border = 1
oCSO.TargetFrame = "_top"
oCSO.NumRequested = 1
Set oUserProfile = GetCurrentUserProfile()
If Not oUserProfile Is Nothing Then
   Set oCSO.UserProfile = oUserProfile
End If

Set Ads = oCSO.GetContent( Application("CSFAdvertisingContext") )

For Each Ad In Ads
   Response.Write(Ad)
Next
```

Tracking Ad Requests

When the content is selected using the content selection pipeline, the pipeline's Record stage is used to save the fact that the content has been requested for display. In this way, you can generate reports that identify how many times the content as been requested.

Tracking Ad Clicks

The content selection pipeline automatically records when an ad is selected for display. However, you still need to provide a means to track when an ad or discount is clicked. To do this, you can provide a redirector page. When users click an ad, they are sent to this page, which records the ad that has been clicked, and then redirects to the ad's target page. The click is recorded by running the RecordEvent content selection pipeline, shown in this code sample:

```
Set oPipe = Application("CampaignsCSFEventPipe")
sCacheName = Request.Querystring("CacheName")
If sCacheName <> "" Then
    Set dCache = _
     Application("MSCSCacheManager").GetCache(sCacheName)
    sEvt = Request.Querystring("evt")
    If sEvt = "" Then sEvt = "CLICK"

    ciid = CLng(Request.Querystring("ciid"))
    If ciid > 0 Then
       Set dictOrder = Server.CreateObject("Commerce.Dictionary")
       Set dictContext = _
        Server.CreateObject("Commerce.Dictionary")

       dictOrder("_winners") = ciid    'ID of the Content Item
       dictOrder("_event") = sEvt             'Name of the Event
       Set oFactory = dCache("Factory")
       Set oContentList = oFactory.CreateNewContentList
       Set dOrder("_content") = oContentList
       Set dOrder("_Performance") = dCache("_Performance")

       dContext("SiteName") = sCacheName
       If Request.QueryString("PageGroupId") <> "" Then
           dContext("PageGroupId") = _
            CLng(Request.QueryString("PageGroupId"))
       Else
          dContext("PageGroupId") = 0
       End If

       oPipe.orderExecute 1, dOrder, dContext, Errlvl
   End If
End If

Response.Redirect(Request.Querystring("url"))
```

Displaying Discounts

Similarly, you can display messages that define what discounts are available for a product or based on the user's basket. As before, you'll use the ContentSelector, setting appropriate keys, and executing the Discounts pipeline to retrieve a SimpleList of the discount content that will be shown, as shown here:

```
Set oCSO = Server.CreateObject("Commerce.ContentSelector")

' Set the basket and product affinity where supplied

If Not IsNull(slProductDetails) Then Set oCSO.Products = _
 slProductDetails

If Not IsNull(slBasketDetails) Then Set oCSO.Items = _
 slBasketDetails

oCSO.Border = 1

oCSO.TargetFrame = "_top"

oCSO.NumRequested = nDiscountsToShow

oCSO.Trace = False

Set mscsUserProfile = GetCurrentUserProfile()

If Not mscsUserProfile Is Nothing Then

   Set oCSO.UserProfile = mscsUserProfile

End If

Set Discounts = _
 oCSO.GetContent(Application("CSFDiscountContext"))

For Each Discount In Discounts

   Response.Write Discount

Next
```

Displaying Other Content

By creating and configuring a different content selection pipeline to provide for the selection of content, you can follow the same process described in the previous sections to select other custom content. The GetContent method of the ContentSelector object returns the content for you to display. For instance, the following code is adapted from the Commerce Server 2000 Software Development Kit (SDK) CSFHeadlines sample. It can be built into a Commerce Server pipeline as a component to adjust the score of headlines content and select the content to display based on the age of the headlines.

```
Const gLowestPriority As Long = 5
Const gMaxDaysToShowHeadlines As Long = 2

set oActiveRows = oContentList.ActiveRows
Do While Not oActiveRows.Eof
    DoEvents

    iRow = oActiveRows.RowNum
    Set flds = oContentList.Fields(iRow)

    iPriority = flds(1)
    dtHeadline = flds(2)

    dblMaxScore = gLowestPriority * gMaxDaysToShowHeadlines
    lDaysOld = DateDiff("d", Now, dtHeadline)

    dblScore = dblMaxScore - CDbl(iPriority * lDaysOld)
    if dblScore < 0.0 Then
       dblScore = 0.0
    end if

    oContentList.SetScore(iRow, dblScore, "", "")
    oContentList.MoveNext
Loop
```

Component Reference

The following sections summarize the CSF-related components that have been introduced in this chapter. The tables provide a quick reference to the properties and methods of each of the components.

ContentList

The ContentList object provides access to a list of content items. The object can be created through the ContentListFactory's CreateNewContentList method. The properties of the ContentList object are given in Table 19-1, and its methods are listed in Table 19-2.

Table 19-1. ContentList Properties

Property Name	Data Type	Description
ActiveRows	IRowCollection	Collection of content items that meet the Threshold and RowLimit properties and have not been filtered out
AllRows	IRowCollection	Collection of all content items
Count	Long	Number of content items in the object
Factory	IContentListFactory	Reference to the ContentListFactory that created this object
Fields	Fields	Fields collection for a row of content items
RowLimit	Long	Maximum number of content items that can exist in the ActiveRows collection
Sorted	Boolean	Flag that controls whether the content items in the ActiveRows collection are sorted by score
Threshold	Float	Score that content items must meet or exceed to be included in the ActiveRows collection
TraceMessages	ISimpleList	List of TraceMessage strings for a given content item
TraceMode	Boolean	Flag that indicates if score tracing is active (True) or inactive (False)

Table 19-2. ContentList Methods

Method Name	Description
AdjustScore	Adjusts the score of the content item by a multiplier
BuildIndex	Creates an index on the rows of content items based on the identified column
Filter	Filters the content items in the object based on the provided criteria
GetData	(C++ only) Retrieves the value of a particular field of a specified content item, based on the row and column
GetScore	Retrieves the score of a content item
Search	Returns a collection of content items that meet the given search criteria
SetData	(C++ only) Writes a value into a field of a content item, based on the row and column count
SetScore	Sets the score of a content item

ContentListFactory

The ContentListFactory component is used to maintain a list of content items that are available in the site. The object can be created using the PROGID Commerce.ContentListFactory. Its properties and methods are listed in Table 19-3 and Table 19-4, respectively.

Table 19-3. ContentListFactory Properties

Property Name	Data Type	Description
AllRows	IRowCollection	Collection of all content items
Count	Long	Number of content items
Fields	Fields	Collection of fields for a content item
Schema	IContentListSchema	Reference to the ContentListSchema that is used by this object

Table 19-4. ContentListFactory Methods

Method Name	Description
BuildIndex	Creates an index on the content items based on a given column
ConstructFromRecordset	Initializes the ContentListFactory from a recordset
CreateNewContentList	Creates a new content list with the schema defined by this object
GetData	(C++ only) Retrieves the value of a particular field of a specified content item, based on the row and column
Search	Collection of content items that meet the given search criteria
SetData	(C++ only) Writes a value into a field of a content item, based on the row and column count

ContentListSchema

The ContentListSchema object is used to manage the schema that the ContentListFactory uses. The object can be created with the PROGID Commerce.ContentListSchema. Table 19-5 lists its properties, and its methods are shown in Table 19-6.

Table 19-5. ContentListSchema Properties

Property Name	Data Type	Description
ColumnFlags	Long	Holds the value for the bitmap of column field settings
ColumnName	String	Name of the column
ColumnType	ColumnTypeEnum	Data type of the column
Count	Long	Number of columns
Locked	Boolean	Flag that identifies whether the schema can be modified

Table 19-6. ContentListSchema Methods

Method Name	Description
Add	Adds a new column
FindColumn	Returns the numeric position of a column, based on the column name
GetSchema	(C++ only) Returns the entire schema
SetSchema	(C++ only) Writes the entire schema

ContentSelector

The ContentSelector object is used to execute a content selection pipeline to select content for display. It can be created using the PROGID Commerce.ContentSelector. Its method is displayed in Table 19-7.

Table 19-7. ContentSelector Method

Method Name	Description
GetContent	Executes a content selection pipeline and returns a SimpleList of HTML or XML content items

ExpressionEval

The ExpressionEval object is used to evaluate expressions in a specific context or to evaluate expressions written in XML fragments. The expressions are maintained in the expression cache. The object can be created with the PROGID Commerce.ExpressionEval. The property of this object is listed in Table 19-8, and its methods are given in Table 19-9.

Table 19-8. ExpressionEval Property

Property Name	Data Type	Description
ExprCount	Long	Retrieves the number of expressions

Table 19-9. ExpressionEval Methods

Method Name	Description
Connect	Connects the object to the expression store
CreateEvalContext	Creates a new ExprEvalContext object
Eval	Evaluates an expression
EvalInContext	Evaluates an expression in a context that was previously loaded
EvalXML	Evaluates the provided XML fragment as an expression
FlushAll	Removes all expressions from the expression cache
FlushExpr	Removes a given expression from the expression cache
LoadAll	Loads all expressions from the expression store into the expression cache

(continued)

Table 19-9. *(continued)*

Method Name	Description
LoadExpr	Loads an expression from the expression store into the expression cache
ParseXML	Parses the given XML fragment to determine if it's a valid expression

ExpressionStore

The ExpressionStore object is used to access and maintain expressions in the database. The object can be created by the PROGID Commerce.ExpressionStore. Its methods are described in Table 19-10.

Table 19-10. ExpressionStore Methods

Method Name	Description
Connect	Stores the connection string to the expression store database
DeleteExpression	Deletes an expression
Disconnect	Disconnects from the expression store and clears the connection string
Export	Exports the expressions in a store to a file
GetAllExprs	Gets all expressions from the store
GetExpression	Gets an expression from the store
GetExprID	Retrieves the expression ID based on the given expression name
GetExprName	Retrieves the expression name based on the given expression ID
Import	Imports expression to the store from a file
NewExpression	Creates a new recordset that contains an empty expression
Query	Retrieves a recordset that contains expressions that meet the provided search criteria
RenameExpression	Changes the name of an existing expression
SaveExpression	Saves an expression to the store

ExprFltrQueryBldr

The ExprFltrQueryBldr object is used to convert an expression that has been written in an XML fragment to a SQL filter query string. The object can be created with the PROGID Commerce.ExprFltrQueryBldr. Its methods are listed in Table 19-11.

Table 19-11. ExprFltrQueryBldr Methods

Method Name	Description
ConvertExprToSQLFltStr	Converts an expression in XML to a SQL filter string
ConverExprUsingDict	Converts an expression in XML that references a Dictionary object to a SQL filter string

RowCollection

The RowCollection object is used to access the content items from the ContentList object. The object is created through the ContentList object. Table 19-12 lists its properties, and Table 19-13 gives its methods.

Table 19-12. RowCollection Properties

Property Name	Data Type	Description
_NewEnum	IUnknown	Allows iteration through each row in the row collection
Count	Long	Holds the number of rows in the row collection
EOF	Boolean	Identifies if the current row is beyond the number of rows in the collection
Fields	Fields	Contains the fields collection
RowNum	Long	Holds the ordinal position of the current row

Table 19-13. RowCollection Methods

Method Name	Description
MoveFirst	Sets the current row of the collection to the first row
MoveNext	Makes the current row of the collection the next row

Chapter 20

Predictor Service

One useful method for increasing sales and visibility of other products is to provide suggestions to users for products that might be of interest to them. For instance, if shoppers place the latest Tom Clancy novel in their basket, we might note that 63 percent of users who bought that book also bought the latest John Grisham novel. Based on that, we might provide a recommendation to the user for that product or perhaps for other products. Predictions can be generated based on an analysis of the shopper's buying habits at your site in the past, as well as the habits of other similar shoppers. The Predictor Service in Microsoft Commerce Server 2000 provides the basis for analyzing the data and making predictions about recommendations or other information.

At times, you might need to determine information about a user to select content or make choices about that user, even though he or she has not provided complete profile information for your site. You can use the Predictor Service to predict profile data, based on a user's site history and the data associated with shoppers who have similar histories. It does this by creating segments of users with similar profile data and organizing these groupings into a hierarchy of all users. The segments can be analyzed for patterns and used to predict information that might otherwise be missing from a shopper's profile.

The Predictor Service

The Predictor Service is a Microsoft Windows 2000 service that can be installed to provide predictive functionality on your Commerce Server 2000 sites. It is an optional installation that is not required unless you're planning to use prediction services on your site. You should install the Predictor Service when you install Commerce Server 2000 (see Chapter 1, "Installing and Configuring Commerce Server 2000").

Note Although a Commerce Server 2000 site can utilize multiple Predictor resources, you can only install one Predictor resource on a computer. Therefore, if you want to support multiple Predictor resources, you'll need multiple machines.

The Predictor Service makes heavy use of Microsoft SQL Server's Online Analytical Processing (OLAP) capabilities to build and analyze data models to generate predictions. The process of building these data models can be quite intensive and utilizes a great deal of memory. For this reason, it's recommended that you dedicate a server to building and maintaining the analysis models. Once a model is generated, you can then load it onto each of the Web servers in your farm by using the PredictorClient object's LoadModelFromDB method.

At the end of the chapter is a section that summarizes the components of the Predictor Service and tables that provide a quick reference to the properties and methods of each of the components.

Tip For performance reasons, you should provide a dedicated machine that will build the analysis models. This should be the same server that holds your Data Warehouse. This ensures that the performance of your Web servers does not suffer while the model is built. It also reduces network traffic while you build the model.

Analysis Models

The Predictor Service uses analysis models as the basis for generating predictions. These models are based on the SQL Server Data Warehouse and contain statistics about data on the site, such as user profile data, user purchase histories, and patterns of behavior. By performing statistical analysis using these models, the service is able to make a prediction and provide a measure of confidence in its accuracy.

Note Data concerning users and their behavior are gathered within the models, however, no data relating to an individual user is maintained.

Data about each model is maintained in the PredictorModels database table in the site's Data Warehouse database. The model itself is maintained in binary form within that table, in the Data field.

Commerce Server 2000 can build two types of analysis models: the prediction model and the segment model.

Prediction Models

Prediction models consist of a set of statistical information about the predictive relationships between users and transactions or other sets of data. The prediction model utilizes a *dependency network*, which includes a set of decision trees that show the statistical probability of one event predicting a second event. Prediction models are frequently used to make recommendations for a user based on the buying practices of other users. For instance, you might often see on a site a phrase that looks like this: "You have added *PRODUCT X* to your basket.

There are 12,567 users who purchased *PRODUCT X* who have also purchased *PRODUCT Y*."

Prediction Model View

You can view a prediction model that has been built using the Prediction Model Viewer through the Commerce Server Manager. To launch the viewer, perform the following steps:

1. Open Commerce Server Manager.
2. Open the Global Resources container.
3. Open the Predictor resource.
4. Open the Predictor container.
5. Click the Models container. The list of built models is displayed in the right pane.
6. Right-click the model you wish to view and select View Model from the shortcut menu.

This loads the predictor model, in the dependency network view (see Figure 20-1). Within the model, you'll see each of the products that are being examined in this model. You'll also see the dependencies and linkages between the various products, based on the statistics gathered from the Data Warehouse.

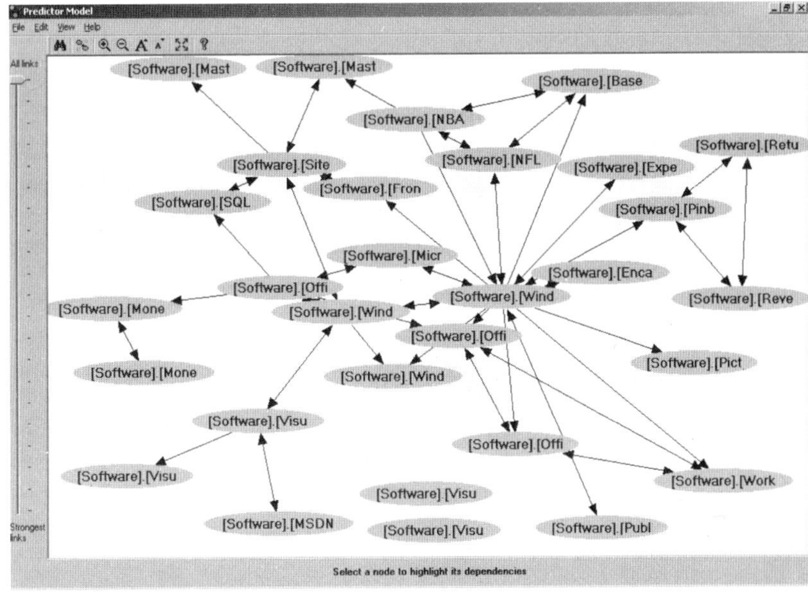

Figure 20-1. *The Predictor Model Viewer is used to examine the dependency network of the model.*

The dependency network view shows the various nodes in the network in a color-coded scheme (see Figure 20-2), as follows:

- **Green** This is the selected node.
- **Red** This node is predicted by the selected node.
- **Blue** This node predicts the selected node.
- **Purple** This node and the selected node predict each other.

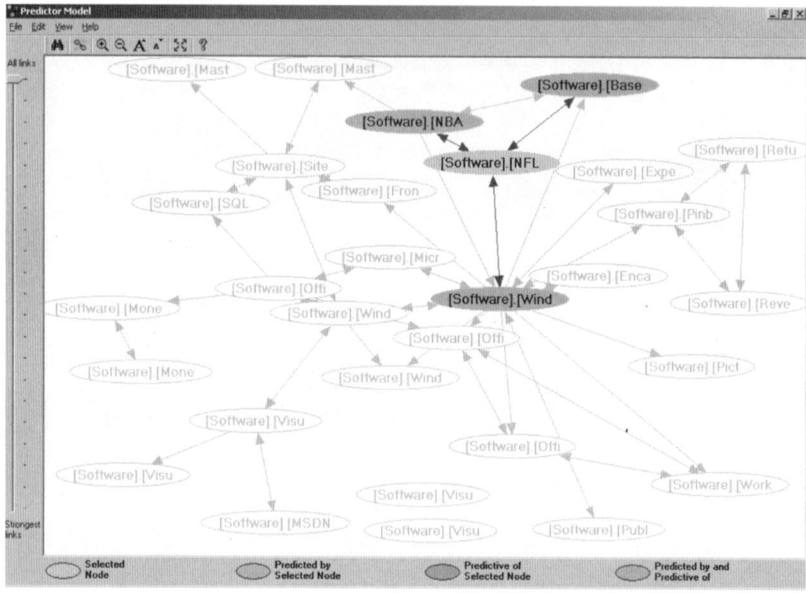

Figure 20-2. *The dependency network view color-codes the network nodes when you select a node.*

Decision Tree View

By double-clicking any node within the dependency network view, you'll load the decision tree view (see Figure 20-3). This view shows a more detailed statistical view of the relationships in the nodes and is read from left to right. It generally indicates that the presence of the first node causes the likelihood of the presence or lack of presence of the second node. For instance, in the example shown in Figure 20-3, the presence of the software product Microsoft NBA Inside Drive 2000 indicates the presence of Microsoft NFL Fever 2000 for 94 users, whereas 787 shoppers did not have the NFL software.

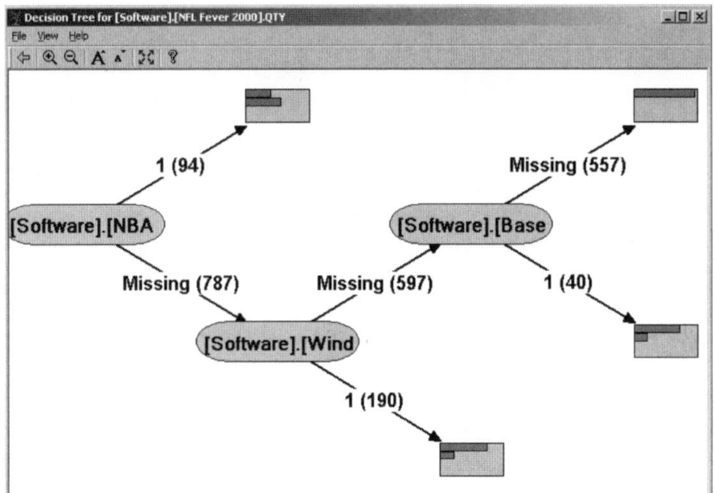

Figure 20-3. *The decision tree view is used to focus on the individual node and the nodes it predicts.*

By double-clicking one of the histogram leafs in the tree, you can view the probabilities that are calculated in greater detail. Continuing with the preceding example, if you double-click the histogram leading from the NBA Inside Drive 2000 title, you'll see Figure 20-4. This indicates that the presence of NBA Inside Drive 2000 with a quantity of 1 provides the following probabilities:

- .408 that NFL Fever 2000 is missing
- .571 that NFL Fever 2000 is present with a quantity of 1
- .0102 that NFL Fever 2000 is present with a quantity of 2
- .0102 that NFL Fever 2000 is present with a quantity of 3

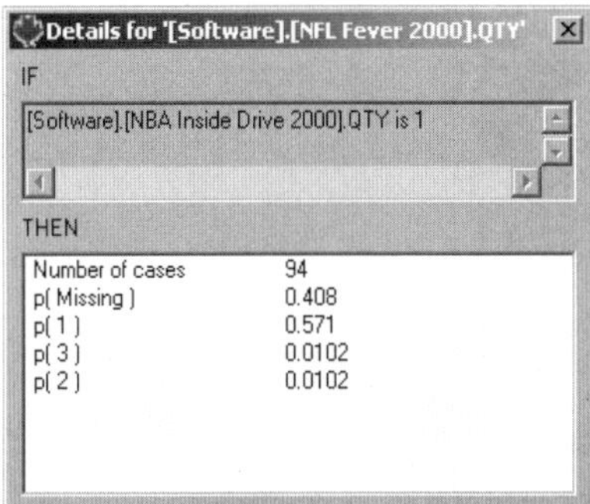

Figure 20-4. *The details of a node in the decision tree can be viewed by double-clicking that node.*

Segment Models

Segment models are used to organize and partition users into various groups based on their profile settings. Those segments can then be used to analyze and make predictions about other users based on their similarities to existing users. For instance, you might create a segment that divides users into male and female segments. You might further break those groups down into the home country of the user or the language of the user. Of course the segment model doesn't need to be used for analyzing user data. It can also be used to analyze transactions on your site and how products fit within those transactions.

Segment models are viewed from within the Business Desk, in the Analysis section, under the header Segment Viewer. When a segment is opened, the display (see Figure 20-5) shows the segments in the following three views:

- **Segment Hierarchy** Provides a hierarchy of segments, which shows how the segments are broken down
- **Segment Summary** Provides a summary of the properties and values that were used to create the current segment
- **Segment Comparison** Provides a comparison between the current and another selected segment, visually comparing those common properties and those that differ

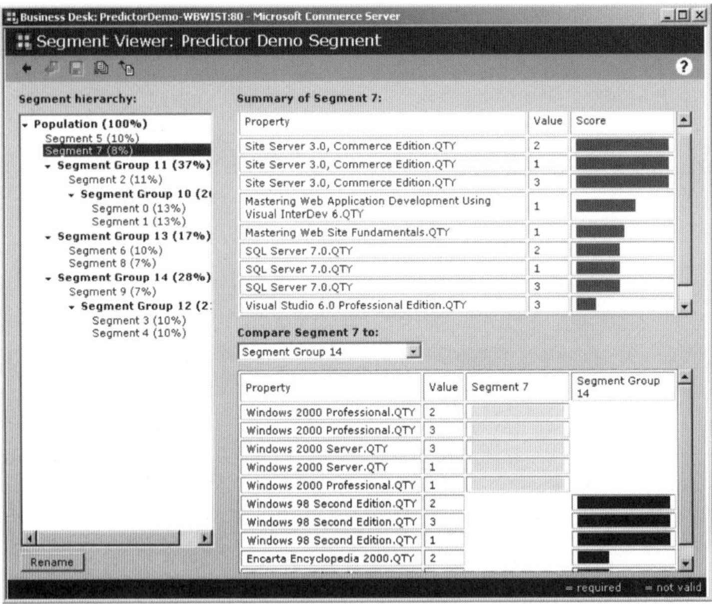

Figure 20-5. *The Segment Viewer can be found within the Business Desk for your site, and it can be used to examine the segments created based on the model used to build it.*

Model Configuration

Each Commerce Server 2000 site has a default analysis model configuration named Transactions. The model configurations are stored in the PredictorModelCfgs table in the Data Warehouse database.

The configuration is used to define which elements will be gathered and used in building the statistical analysis models. The configuration is used to map the data in the Data Warehouse to cases that are used in the models. Each case is a set of data, typically in name–value pairs, that are used to build the models. This data is stored in the PredictorDataTables table in the Data Warehouse database.

For instance, the Transactions model configuration defines that the CaseColumn is UserID, the PivotColumn is SKU, and the AggregateColumn is QTY. This indicates that for each user, the model retrieves the SKUs that have been purchased and adds the quantities to determine the total number of each SKU purchased. Furthermore, the source of this table is the TableName TransPredictor, which happens to be a view that is provided, which is defined by the following SQL script:

```
SELECT

   C.userid UserID,

   QUOTENAME(B.product_catalog) + N'.' + QUOTENAME
    (B.product_id) SKU,

   B.quantity QTY

FROM

   OrderGroup A,

   OrderFormLineItems B,

   RegisteredUser C

WHERE

   A.ordergroup_id = B.OrderGroup_id

AND

   C.RegisteredUserID = A.RegisteredUserID
```

If you need to provide additional models to generate different predictions, you can create your own model configuration on which to base the model. You'll need to define the source of the data, as a table or view, and the fields to use as the Case, Pivot, and Aggregate in the PredictorDataTables. You can then provide the entry in the PredictorModelCfgs table and make the model configuration available to build new models.

Model Effectiveness

When you generate a resource prediction, the Predictor resource provides scores that rate how effective the model was in calculating those predictions. The two scores that are calculated are the recommendation score and the data fit score. Both scores reflect only the performance of the models for the given case. When you're evaluating your score, you should ensure that your case is as broad as possible to cover the full spectrum of elements in the analysis model.

Recommendation Score

The recommendation score is calculated by taking the new prediction case data, such as the items a user has in his or her basket, and performing a search. Then, one item is removed from the list, and the search is performed again. In this instance, the item that was removed from the list should be one of the items that is recommended. If it is, the model is regarded as effective for the set of data you used in performing the search.

Data Fit Score

The data fit score is calculated by using two approaches to calculate the probability of an entry of missing data and then comparing them. It rates how well the model will perform in filling in missing data. The first approach considers the relationships and interdependencies between all of the properties. The second, known as the marginal analysis model, or straw-horse model, assumes that none of the properties are related and that they are all independent. Both predictions are made, and the first is divided by the second to provide a score.

Improving Accuracy

The accuracy of any model in making predictions is dependent on the number of data elements that make up the model. Generally speaking, the larger the sample size that is used to build the model, the more accurate the results will be. However, as you begin adding more and more cases, you begin to lose effectiveness, as performance degrades with little corresponding gain in accuracy. In general, you should plan on limiting the number of cases in your model to no more than 30,000 to 50,000.

The Commerce Server 2000 documentation provides some data to help you judge the amount of data to provide for your predictions. The scenario was created as listed in Table 20-1.

Table 20-1. Data Sizes in a Predictor Performance Scenario

Description	Average	Maximum
Number of products in the catalog	50,000	500,000
Number of cases to build model	30,000	No limit
Number of transactions per user	20	Total number of attributes
Size of computed model	100 KB	Limit by database
Max number of attributes predicted per call	10	Total number of attributes

With the scenario described in Table 20-1, tests were run on the Predictor resource. The tests were performed for the Predictor Service on a 400-MHz Pentium II with 512 MB of RAM, with client computers of 400-MHz Pentium II with 128 MB of RAM. The results are listed in Table 20-2.

Table 20-2. Results of Predictor Performance Testing

Test Criteria	Component	Minimum	Maximum	Average
Latency to make prediction	Client	0 ms	200 ms	100 ms
Throughput of prediction requests	Client	30 predictions per second per CPU	N/A	50 predictions per second per CPU
New model build time	Service	N/A	8 hours	1.5 hours
Load model from database	Client	N/A	30 seconds	10 seconds
Service start time	Service	N/A	45 seconds	10 seconds

As you can see, and as has been mentioned elsewhere, the Predictor resource can support a number of simultaneous users, averaging 50 predictions per second per CPU. In addition, the predictions are quick, with an average latency or delay of only 100 ms in retrieving the predictions. You can also see that the building of a model with this sizable amount of data can be a very time-consuming and resource-intensive process. For this reason, it is recommended that a server be dedicated for this functionality.

Managing Models

Predictor models are managed from within the Commerce Server Manager. You'll find them in the Predictor resource, in the Commerce Server 2000 Global Resources. The Model Configurations container lists the model configurations that are available to be used to build a model. The Models container lists all of the models that have been rebuilt.

Building Models

You'll build both the predictor and segment models from the Microsoft Management Console (MMC) snap-in using a very similar process.

Note Before you can build a model, you will need data in the Data Warehouse. See Chapter 5, "Business Analytics," for directions on using the Data Transformation Service (DTS) tasks to import data into the Data Warehouse.

Building a Predictor Model

To build a predictor model, you'll perform the following steps:

1. Open Commerce Server Manager.
2. Open the Global Resources container.
3. Open the Predictor resource.
4. Open the Predictor container.
5. Click the Model Configurations container to load the available configurations in the right pane.
6. Right-click the desired configuration and select Build from the shortcut menu.
7. In the first page of the Model Build Properties Wizard (see Figure 20-6), provide a name and priority.

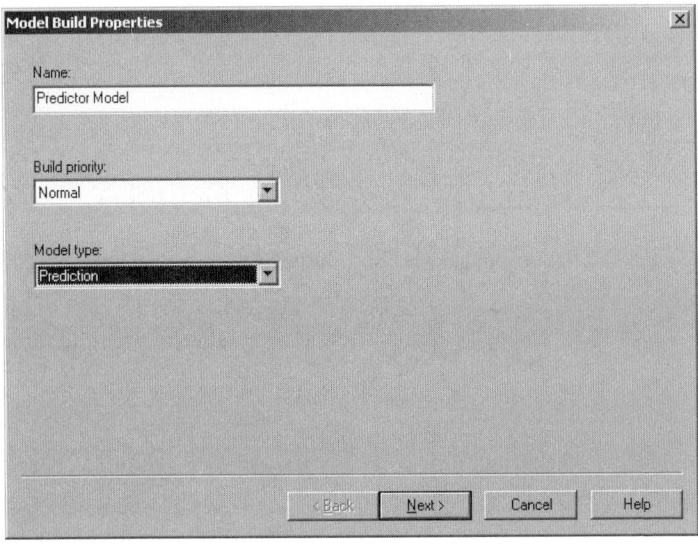

Figure 20-6. *The Model Build Properties Wizard is used to build a new predictor analysis model.*

8. Specify the Model Type as Prediction and click Next.
9. In the second page of the wizard (see Figure 20-7), define the properties that will identify how the prediction model is built. These properties include the following:
   - **Sample Size** Number of rows that should be used to build the model. The default value is –1, which indicates that all rows should be used.
   - **Measured Accuracy Sample Fraction** Fraction of the data used to score the accuracy of the model.

- **Measured Accuracy Maximum Predictions** Maximum number of predictions you want to present to the site.
- **Input Attribute Fraction** Fraction of properties to be used as input to the predictions. The default is –1, which indicates that all properties should be used.
- **Output Attribute Fraction** Fraction of properties to be used as output of the predictions. The default is –1, which indicates that all properties should be used.

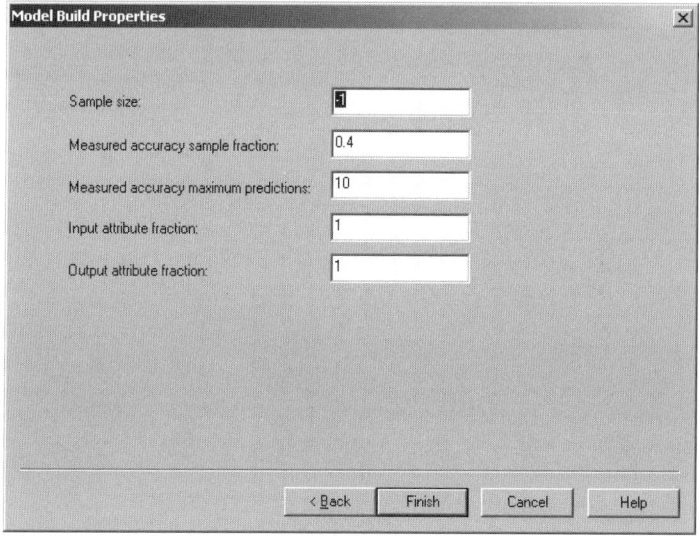

Figure 20-7. *The Model Build Properties Wizard is used to configure the model that is going to be built.*

Building a Segment Model

To build a segment model, you'll perform the following steps:

1. Open Commerce Server Manager.
2. Open the Global Resources container.
3. Open the Predictor resource.
4. Open the Predictor container.
5. Click the Model Configurations container to load the available configurations in the right pane.
6. Right-click the desired configuration and select Build from the shortcut menu.
7. In the first page of the wizard (see Figure 20-8), provide a name and priority.

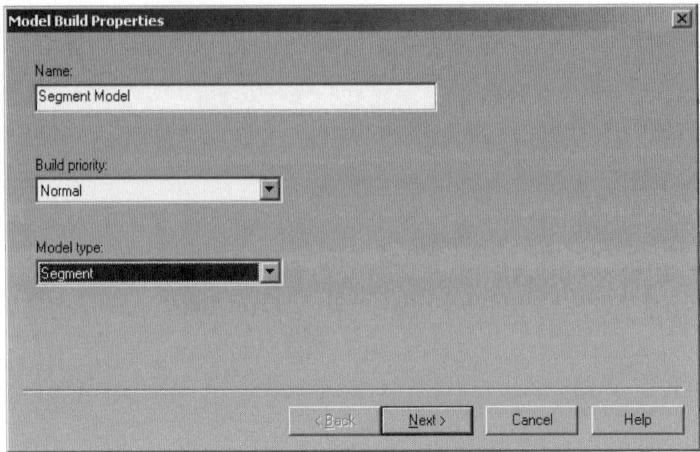

Figure 20-8. *The Model Build Properties Wizard is used to build a new segment analysis model.*

8. Specify the Model Type as Segment and click Next.
9. In the second page of the wizard (see Figure 20-9), define the properties that will identify how the segment model is built. These properties include the following:
   - **Sample Size** Number of rows that should be used to build the model. The default value is –1, which indicates that all rows should be used.
   - **Measured Accuracy Sample Fraction** Fraction of the data used to score the accuracy of the model.
   - **Measured Accuracy Maximum Predictions** Maximum number of predictions you want to present to the site.
   - **Input Attribute Fraction** Fraction of properties to be used as input to the predictions. The default is –1, which indicates that all properties should be used.
   - **Output Attribute Fraction** Fraction of properties to be used as output of the predictions. The default is –1, which indicates that all properties should be used.
   - **Number Of Segments** Number of segments that should be used to partition the user data.
   - **Buffer Size** (Bytes) Maximum amount of memory, in bytes, used by the clustering process.

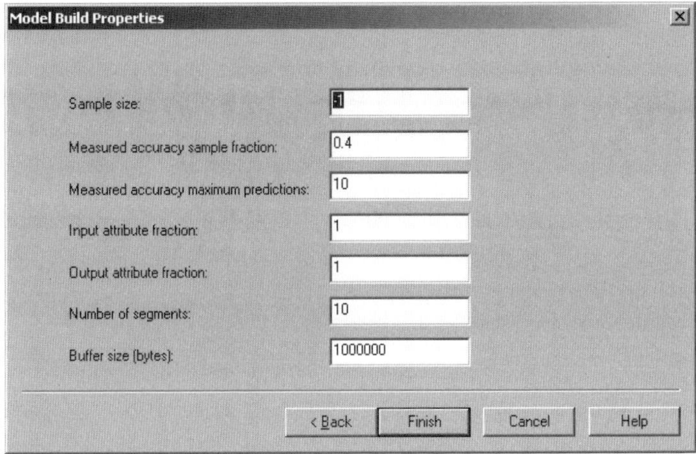

Figure 20-9. *The Model Build Properties Wizard is used to configure the segment model that is going to be built.*

Get Prediction

You can begin generating predictions once the models are built. To do this, you'll make use of the PredictorClient object on your site, as described in the following sections.

Initializing the PredictorClient Object

You can initialize the PredictorClient object in the GLOBAL.ASA file and store it in an application variable, making it accessible throughout your site, as shown here:

```
Const sModel = "Transactions"

set oConfig = Server.CreateObject("Commerce.SiteConfigReadOnly")

Call  oConfig.Initialize(MSCSCommerceSiteName)

connstr_db_dw = oConfig.Fields("Global Data Warehouse"). _
 Value.Fields("connstr_db_dw").Value

Set MSCSPredictor = _
 Server.CreateObject("Commerce.PredictorClient")

MSCSPredictor.LoadMModelFromDB sModel, connstr_db_dw

MSCSPredictor.fpPopularityPenalty = 0.8

MSCSPredictor.fpDefaultConfidence = 10

Set Application("MSCSPredictor") = MSCSPredictor
```

Making a Prediction

Once the object is initialized, you can use it on pages to make predictions. Typically, you'll do this on a user's basket page, when he or she has added some products to the basket. You can then suggest others in which the user might be interested.

The following code obtains the object and sets of the slPredict list of properties that you'll get predictions for. In this example, you'll get predictions of other SKUs based on the data being analyzed.

```
Set mscsPredictor = Application("MSCSPredictor")

Set dCase = Server.CreateObject("Commerce.Dictionary")

Set slPredict = Server.CreateObject("Commerce.SimpleList")


slPredict.Add "SKU"
```

Next, you'll build a dictionary that holds the products and quantities that the user has placed in the basket. The key of the dictionary entries will be built in the format used in defining the statistical queries in the analysis, as shown in the following sample code. For example, an entry might wind up looking like this: QTY([Software].[NFL Fever 2000]). The value for that dictionary entry will be the quantity place in the basket.

```
For Each sOrderFormName in mscsOrderGroup

    Set mscsOrderForm = _
     mscsOrderGroup.value.OrderForms.Value(sOrderFormName)

    For Each dItem in mscsOrderForm.Items

        sKey = "QTY([" _
         & dItem.product_catalog & "].[" _
         & dItem.product_id & "])"

        lQty = CLng(dItem.quantity)

        dCase(sKey) = lQty

    Next

Next
```

With that, you can generate the predictions by calling the Predict method of the PredictorClient object. This passes back two arrays that contain the predicted Properties and Values, respectively, as shown here:

```
lMaxPredictions = 2

mscsPredictor.Predict dCase, slPredict, _
 aPredictedProperties, aPredictedValues, lMaxPredictions
```

By looping through the returned arrays, you can retrieve each product that was predicted by the PredictorClient object. In this case, you only care about the predicted properties, as this array holds the information you need to derive the catalog and product. They'll be returned in the same format you provided as the key to the Case dictionary, as shown in the following code sample. For example, a returned entry might look like this: QTY([Software].[NBA Inside Moves 2000]).

```
If IsArry(aPredictedProperties) Then

   htmPrediction = "Others who have made similar purchases, " _
    & "have also bought...<BR>"

   Set regExpr = New RegExp

   For i = 0 to UBound(aPredictedProperties)

      regExpr.Pattern = "QTY" & "\(\[(.+)\]\.\[(.+)\]\)"

      sProperties = regExpr.Replace(aPredictedProperties(i), _
      "$1;$2")

      aProperties = Split(sProperties, ";")

      sCatalog = aProperties(0)

      sProduct = aProperties(1)

      htmPrediction = htmPrediction _
       & "<a href='product.asp?catalog=" & sCatalog _
       & "&product=" & sProduct & "'>" _
       & sProduct _
       & "</a><br>"

   Next

End If
```

Predictor Service Components Reference

The following sections summarize the components related to the Predictor Service that have been introduced in this chapter. The tables provide a quick reference to the properties and methods of each of the components.

PredictorClient

The PredictorClient object is used to load an analysis model and perform some predictions based on that model. The object can be created using the PROGID Commerce.PredictorClient. Its properties are displayed in Table 20-3, and its methods are shown in Table 20-4.

Table 20-3. PredictorClient Properties

Property Name	Data Type	Description
FpDataFitScore	Single	Returns data fit score, which signifies the effectiveness of the model to predict missing data.
fpDefaultConfidence	Single	Threshold for prediction confidence. If a prediction's confidence is below this, it is not shown.
bFailOnUnknownInputAttributes	Boolean	If this is set to True, prediction will halt when an unknown input attribute is encountered.
FpPopularityPenalty	Single	Penalty applied to the score of the most popular items so that they are not recommended as often.
fpRecommendScore	Single	Score of the recommendation that indicates the quality of list of recommendations generated.
SsiteName	String	Name of the site.

Table 20-4. PredictorClient Methods

Method Name	Description
Explain	Explains the prediction of a property by providing property/value/score triplets data that shows how the recommendation ranked
LoadModelFromDB	Loads a prediction model from the database
LoadModelFromFile	Loads a prediction model from a file
Predict	Makes product recommendations or predicts missing user profile data
PredictAllSegments	Calculates probabilities that a user belongs to each segment of the user population
PredictMostLikelySegment	Calculates the segment to which a user most likely belongs
SaveModelToFile	Saves a model to a file

PredictorServiceAdmin

The PredictorServiceAdmin retrieves information about the models that have been built and are available on your site. The object can be created using the PROGID Commerce.PredictorServiceAdmin. Table 20-5 lists the object's properties.

Table 20-5. PredictorServiceAdmin Properties

Property Name	Data Type	Description
DateLastStarted	Date	Returns the date the Predictor Service was last started
SlModelConfigs	SimpleList	Returns a SimpleList of available model configurations
SlModels	SimpleList	Returns a SimpleList of available models

PredictorServiceSiteAdmin

The PredictorServiceSiteAdmin object is used to manage the analysis models and their configurations. The object can be created using the PROGID Commerce.PredictorSiteAdmin. This object's properties are listed in Table 20-6, and its methods are listed in Table 20-7.

Table 20-6. PredictorServiceSiteAdmin Properties

Property Name	Data Type	Description
LcaseCount	Long	Number of cases used to build the model
DModelInfo	Dictionary	Dictionary that contains information on a particular model
SegmentLabels	Variant	Array that contains labels for segments

Table 20-7. PredictorServiceSiteAdmin Methods

Method Name	Description
DeleteModel	Deletes the specified model
DeleteModelConfig	Deletes the specified model configuration
GenerateSegmentList	Generates a list of members with the segment
Init	Initializes the Predictor object and connects to the Data Warehouse
RenameModel	Renames the model
RenameModelConfig	Renames the model configuration

PredModelBuilder

The PredModelBuilder object is used to build analysis models. The object can be created using the PROGID Commerce.PredictorModelBuilder. Table 20-8 lists this object's properties, and its methods are listed in Table 20-9.

Table 20-8. PredModelBuilder Properties

Property Name	Data Type	Description
dModelInfo	Dictionary	Dictionary that contains information on the current model
Priority	Enum	Identifies the priority for the build process. Values can be as follows: **PriLowest** –2 **PriBelowNormal** –1 **PriNormal** 0 **PriAboveNormal** 1 **PriHighest** 2
slRunningModels	SimpleList	Returns a list of running models
Status	Enum	Identifies the status of a build process. Values can be as follows: **PredBldRunning** 0: Running **PredBldPaused** 1: Paused **PredBldShuttingDown** 2: Stopping

Table 20-9. PredictorClient Methods

Method Name	Description
Pause	Pauses the building of a predictor model
Resume	Resumes the building of a predictor model that was paused
Start	Starts building a predictor model
Stop	Stops builing a predictor model
StopAllBuilds	Stops building all predictor models

Index

A

C

G

H

I

Q

R

S

X

About the Author

Brad is a Senior Applications Architect, a Microsoft Certified Solutions Developer, a Microsoft Certified Professional + Site Building, and a Microsoft Certified Trainer. He's been architecting and developing Windows and Web applications for nearly ten years using Microsoft technologies. He's written a number of articles for various publications over the past few years and has provided a number of conference and seminar presentations. When he's not working or writing, Brad spends time with his wife, son, family, and friends in the Virginia and Maryland region.

Send your comments to the author at *commerceserver@hotmail.com*.

The author prepared and submitted the manuscript for this book in electronic form using Microsoft Word 2000 for Windows. Pages were composed by nSight, Inc., in Burlington, MA, using Adobe PageMaker 6.5 for Windows, with text in Garamond Light and display type in ITC Franklin Gothic. Composed pages were delivered to the printer as electronic prepress files.

Cover Designer
Landor Associates

Cover Illustrator
Landor Associates

Layout Artist
Joanna Zito

Project Manager
Sarah Kimnach Hains

Tech Editor
Robert Dean

Copy Editor
Teresa Horton

Proofreader
Darla Bruno

Indexer
Jack Lewis

Editorial Assistant
Rebecca Merz

Proof of Purchase

Use this page as proof of purchase if participating in a promotion or rebate offer on this title. Proof of purchase must be used in conjunction with other proof(s) of payment such as your dated sales receipt—see offer details.

Microsoft® Commerce Server 2000 Pocket Consultant

0-7356-1416-4

CUSTOMER NAME

Microsoft Press, PO Box 97017, Redmond, WA 98073-9830